DVD
Studio Pro® 2
Solutions

Erica Sadun

SYBEX® San Francisco • London

Associate Publisher: DAN BRODNITZ
Acquisitions Editor: BONNIE BILLS
Developmental Editor: JIM COMPTON
Production Editor: LIZ BURKE
Technical Editor: TRAI FORRESTER
Copyeditor: PAT COLEMAN
Compositor: MAUREEN FORYS, HAPPENSTANCE TYPE-O-RAMA
Graphic Illustrator: TOM WEBSTER, LINEWORKS, INC.
CD Coordinator: DAN MUMMERT
CD Technician: KEVIN LY
Proofreaders: NANCY RIDDIOUGH, LAURIE O'CONNELL
Indexer: TED LAUX
Book Designer: FRANZ BAUMHACKL
Cover Designer: JOHN NEDWIDEK, EMDESIGN
Cover Illustrator/Photographer: JOHN NEDWIDEK, EMDESIGN

Library of Congress Card Number: 2003115545

ISBN: 0-7821-4234-6

Software License Agreement: Terms and Conditions

For Alberto, with all my love.

Acknowledgments

Books, particularly technical books, are never the work of a single person. The material between these covers is due in large part to the efforts and contributions of many others.

Let me start by thanking Aimee Mackey, formerly of Apple. Without Aimee, this book would not exist. She made herself available to answer technical questions with excellent knowledge and constant good cheer. Thanks as well to Brian Schmidt and Margaret Tinsley of Apple, who put up with my often-incoherent technical questions after Aimee's departure.

Next, let me thank the team at Sybex who turned this book into a reality. Thanks to Bonnie Bills, Jim Compton, Liz Burke, Dan Mummert, and Kevin Ly. Thank you as well to: Trai Forrester, my technical editor, who helped scour the book for errors and made many valuable suggestions; Pat Coleman, who patiently corrected my language and grammar; Maureen Forys of Happenstance Type-o-Rama for composition; and Ted Laux for creating the index.

Thanks also go to my wonderful agent, Neil Salkind of Studio B.

Let me also thank the people and companies who provided me with additional answers, review copies, and other materials and information that made this book as rich as it is. Thanks to Fred Johnson of Apple; Scott Wellwood of Adobe; Linda Sharps, The Omni Group; Jim Taylor of DVDDemystified.com; Yassit Yarocho of American Magnetic Media; Elizabeth Olson of Roxio; Allen Irby; Perry Paolantonio of NoFrillsDVD; Thorsten Lemke of LemkeSoft; Ross Cathriner, Benjamin Pracht of VideoLAN.org, and the Prelinger Archives.

Finally, let me thank my family, whose support, love, and tolerance makes it possible for me to write.

Foreword

At last, *you* are about to make history. Before there were recordable DVDs, even before the laser was invented, a small group of scientists at the 3M invented the ability to record television using optical discs. I am one of the old-timers privileged to have had hands-on involvement with that pioneering work. The "recorder" was the size of an SUV and took an SUV's power to record 30 minutes on a photographic film shaped like a 12″ floppy. For the past 30 years, I have worked for, or with, almost every company that has made a major contribution to recordable optical media. For me, DVDs have been long in coming.

Today, thanks to the breakthrough price and performance offered in Apple's DVD Studio Pro 2, you have *all* the tools you need to contribute to a revolution in communications. You can dramatically change education, entertainment, sales, or marketing. The potential for creativity is mind-boggling.

You have smartly chosen one of the best guides ever written on how to author DVDs. Erica Sadun has taken a complex program and what can be an overwhelming process to a level of clear understanding that matches the power of the tool itself. She puts every feature into context and then steps you through the process of building DVDs. Once you achieve mastery, you will be able to resolve communications problems with the most cost-efficient solutions in the history of optical disc recording.

Your new skills will help create the fusion of three technologies: computers, the Internet, and DVDs, which someday could displace books, magazines and television. Entirely new patterns of content distribution will be possible with low-cost DVD recording and duplication. New worldwide business models can be based on DVDs you create. You can become a profitable DVD creator who makes books like this all but obsolete.

Imagine, using only DVDs, the next publication from Erica could display live monitor views and keyboard/mouse actions on your screen with vocal directions, played from a set-top box as if she were in your living room. With a simple click you could interact with the author or publisher. You could learn to author how-to DVDs that hold their audience's attention until the last detail is understood and mastered.

So you see, this could be the last how-to book you will ever have to read. It's up to you. Boggle my mind, please.

—Lou Skriba

aka "Da Godfather" of Phase Changing erasable optical recording media such as DVD-RW/+RW/RAM

Contents

1950 NEWSREELS
Baby Compet
Rowing Soci
Fashion Sh
Jumping Pro

Chapter 9   Building and Using Slideshows   273

Chapter 10   Scripting DVDs   295

Chapter 11   Advanced Interaction Menus and Methods   325

Chapter 12   Building and Burning   353

Index   370

Introduction

Today, more and more people are becoming interested in DVDs as the distribution medium of choice. Universities, secondary, and elementary schools produce DVDs to supplement (or replace) traditional course work. Business enterprises use DVDs to create interactive catalogs and sales materials. Sporting clubs record their playoff games on DVDs and sell them as fund-raisers. Hospitals use DVDs to train their staff in new procedures and protocols. Churches offer DVDs as part of their mission and outreach programs. Ballet and karate studios provide recital and competition compilations on DVDs, and so forth.

In fact, the DVD format itself is more popular than ever. In November 2003, Disney released *Finding Nemo* for home viewing. According to MSNBC, more than 8 million units sold on its first day of release. Of those sold, roughly 80 percent were DVDs, reflecting a new level of consumer commitment to the DVD format. This wide acceptance makes DVDs, with their relatively inexpensive per-unit cost, a terrific way to distribute video.

Until recently, most Macintosh-based users were stuck using iDVD to create their DVD productions. Professional DVD authoring was priced out of the consumer and small-business market, but in August 2003, Apple dramatically dropped the price on DVD Studio Pro to less than $500. You don't have to settle for iDVD any more.

With its new, lower price and a totally rewritten interface that made it far easier to use, DVD Studio Pro came of age. The new version 2 release brings advanced DVD authoring to the rest of us. All the fussiness and limitations of iDVD have been swept away by the more comprehensive authoring features of DVD Studio Pro 2. You don't have to choose between 60- and 90-minute compilations—you set the length and the quality of the encoding. You don't have to settle for simple menus—DVD Studio Pro 2 provides advanced menu interactions, including invisible and automatically activating buttons. You're not limited by simple navigation—DVD Studio Pro 2 includes a scripting language that lets you provide intelligent and context-sensitive responses to the remote-control requests of your viewers.

DVD Studio Pro 2 offers all the tools you need to author slick, professional DVDs from your video footage. With it, you can create DVDs that include rich bonus features. DVD Studio Pro 2 can help you build DVDs with advanced interaction styles such as language selection, viewing angles, links to the Internet, "Easter eggs," and more. If you've seen a feature on a Hollywood DVD, chances are you can reproduce that feature in DVD Studio Pro 2 for your own use. This book will show you how.

How to Use This Book

DVD Studio Pro 2 Solutions is a complete hands-on introduction to authoring and burning DVDs with DVD Studio Pro 2. Each chapter introduces one piece of the DVD-authoring puzzle, providing both tutorial overviews and "solutions," step-by-step instructions that let you build real DVD projects using real data. Here are some tips for making the best use of this book.

Sit at your computer. You'll gain the most from this book when you work through each project as you read. This book provides a hands-on method of experiential learning. The philosophy behind this is that actual experience is the best way to absorb the techniques presented here. So sit down, launch your computer, open the book, and get ready to learn.

Find the supporting files and programs. The DVD icon in this book points you to supporting files on the companion DVD. Your DVD contains a wealth of material, including video, audio, text files, sample "builds," programs, and any other resources you'll need to complete each project. All supporting files were built using the NTSC standard, although instructions are found throughout the book for those of you using PAL.

Read and work through the steps. Each "solution" in this book is an exercise demonstrating a real-world authoring task you're likely to perform in building your own DVDs, presented as a series of easy-to-follow steps accompanied by one or more images. Read each step, and examine the images. Pictures showcase how your project will look as you work through the steps, providing visual as well as textual reinforcement.

Read the notes. Scattered through each chapter you'll find notes covering related or helpful topics. The notes point out shortcuts and advanced tricks, warn you about common mistakes and bugs, and point you to more great resources for your DVD authoring work.

The Companion DVD

The DVD that accompanies this book is a major component of this book's Solution projects. You'll find many videos, images, and software tools, all of which will help you better work your way through these projects.

Source files accompany each project: video, audio, stills, and so forth. This data lets you build the projects described in each Solution, to produce exactly the same results you see on each page. The project files appear courtesy of the Prelinger Archives (www.archive.org), which offers a huge collection of advertising, industrial, and educational films for public use.

Many of the projects, particularly those in the latter part of the book, contain item description files as well. Item descriptions rebuild portions of your projects so you can focus on the techniques covered in the chapters rather than spend your time involved in repetitious details.

In addition, the DVD includes the data files used to produce the examples used throughout the tutorial portion of each chapter. For example, you'll find extra overlay images in Chapter 3, subtitle files in Chapter 8, and so forth. Use these files to move beyond the Solutions and to experiment further with real-world data.

The DVD also contains a fair number of prebuilt DVD image files (.img) and build folders. You can play these back using Apple's DVD Player software, so you can explore many of the interactive elements discussed in the chapters.

Tools

Meet the tools you'll use throughout this book. These software packages provide everything you need to design and author your DVDs. You'll find several of these software titles on the accompanying DVD in a variety of forms. Adobe Photoshop is included as a 30-day demo. It's a time-limited program with full functionality, but it only works for the specified period of time unless you buy a license. GraphicConverter is shareware. It allows you to try the product before you buy. If you like the software, please send the requested fee to the developer.

DVD Studio Pro 2 www.apple.com/dvdstudiopro; $499 from Apple. DVD Studio Pro 2 is a superb DVD-authoring suite for consumers, prosumers, and DVD professionals.

QuickTime Pro www.apple.com/quicktime; $29.99 from Apple. For only $30, you can unlock your QuickTime player and enable the built-in Pro features. Go online to Apple's website and enter a credit card number. You'll receive a license and an unlock code, ready for immediate use.

Adobe Photoshop www.adobe.com/products/photoshop; $649 *You'll find a 30-day trial version of this software on the companion DVD.* Photoshop is the professional standard for image-editing software.

OmniGraffle www.omnigroup.com/applications/omnigraffle; $70. *You'll find a trial version of this software on the companion DVD.* OmniGraffle is a terrific diagramming program that allows you to lay out menus or plan and design your entire DVD project.

GraphicConverter www.lemkesoft.com; $30 shareware. *You'll a find trial version of this software on the companion DVD.* Graphic Converter is an image-processing program that lets you batch process large groups of images. Use it to resize your pictures to standard digital video size or convert between rectangular and square pixels.

bbDEMUX www.sourceforge.net/projects/macbbdemux; free. *On the companion DVD.* bbDEMUX has a drag-and-drop interface that lets you demultiplex MPEG files into their component streams.

MissingMpegTools/MoreMissingTools homepage.mac.com/rnc; free. *On the companion DVD.* The MissingMpegTools suite and its companion include a variety of helpful MPEG utilities.

VLC Media Player www.videolan.org; free. *On the companion DVD.* VLC Media Player is a cross-platform multimedia player that supports playback for nearly all varieties of MPEG.

DVD Calculator www.dvddemystified.com; free. *On the companion DVD.* Create your project bit budgets with this convenient Excel spreadsheet.

DVDSP Helpers http://homepage.mac.com/DVD_SP_Helper/; prices vary. *The companion DVD includes links to downloadable OS 9 and OS X versions of MPEGAppend.* The DVDSP Helpers include a variety of free and commercial software products that augment DVD Studio Pro 2's built-in encoding and MPEG processing.

Conventions Used in This Book

You'll see these small, helpful icons throughout the book:

Twirl key: ⌘ This symbol refers to the Command key on your keyboard.

Option key: ⌥ This symbol refers to the Option (Alt) key on your keyboard.

About the Author

When Erica Sadun was in fourth grade or so, she began writing School Desk User Manuals™, leaving them at the end of each year for the next desk occupant, carefully taped to the inside of her desk. In junior high and high school, these works metamorphosed into Locker User Manuals™. The tomes were short, humorous (at least to her), and decorated with her best efforts at illustration, and they were undoubtedly, in retrospect, thrown away by the janitorial staff long before the next school year began.

Nevertheless, a pattern had been set, and Sadun spent many of the years that followed gaining technical knowledge of obscure minutia and translating such knowledge into accessible documentation. While working on her doctorate, she began writing how-to texts professionally, for the first time earning money at what she loved. (Sadun earned her master's degree concentrating in digital imaging from the University of Pennsylvania and her doctorate concentrating in visual languages and interface design at Georgia Tech's renowned Graphics, Visualization & Usability Center.) She continues to write, focusing on bringing technical material to general audiences.

Sadun has written, co-written, or contributed to more than 20 books, which include several best-selling Sybex titles, including *iMovie 3 Solutions*, *Mac Digital Photography*, *Digital Photography Essentials*, and *Digital Video Essentials*. An unrepentant geek, Sadun has never met a gadget she didn't love.

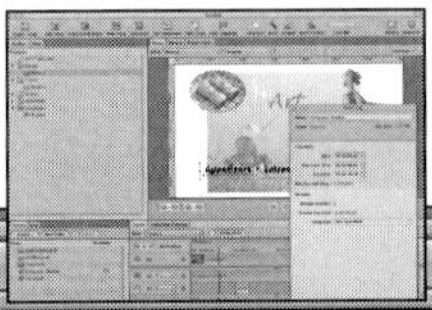

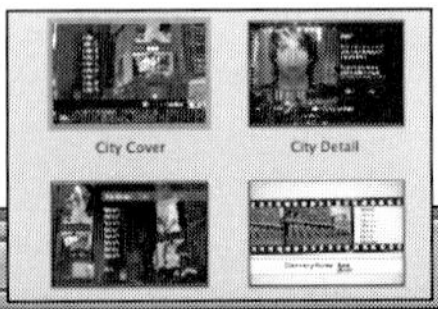

Settings
City Cover
City Detail
The
Art
of Food
Appetizers • Entrees • Sides • Deserts
Button 1
Slideshow 1
Button 3
Button 4
0
100
200
300
400
500
600

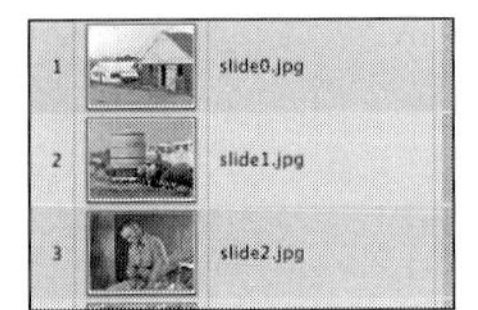
1 slide0.jpg
2 slide1.jpg
3 slide2.jpg

MODERN TRENDS
in Swine Production
THE UNITED STATES STEEL CORPORATION

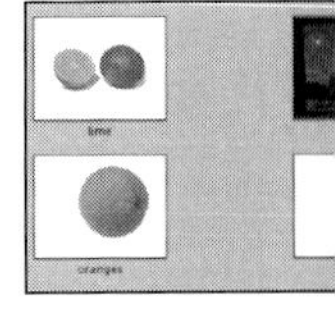
lime
oranges

Introducing DVD Studio Pro 2

DVD Studio Pro 2 is a new, powerful and flexible authoring tool for DVDs. DVD Studio Pro 2 helps you transform plain video into interactive media, complete with menus, subtitles, alternate tracks, and more. In fact, DVD Studio Pro 2 provides many of the professional features you'd normally find on Hollywood-produced DVDs. DVD Studio Pro 2 helps you coordinate these capabilities, putting them together to produce new ways of watching video.

Chapter Contents

DVD Studio Pro 2 means more than just movies. With DVD Studio Pro 2, you can create training materials, personal histories, interactive catalogs, event videos, and more. If you have video, audio, and graphics that you want to combine to present an interactive experience, DVD Studio Pro 2 will help you deliver that experience on the DVD platform.

In this chapter, you'll meet DVD Studio Pro 2. You'll explore the DVD Studio Pro 2 interface, learn how to customize your screen, and get started building your own DVD projects.

Configuring DVD Studio Pro 2

The best way to learn any program is to use it. To get started with DVD Studio Pro 2, you need to sit down at your computer and, in a metaphorical sense, get your hands dirty and your feet wet. If you have not done so already, install your copy of DVD Studio Pro 2. Navigate to your OS X Applications folder. Locate the DVD Studio Pro 2 icon and double-click it.

If this is your first time using DVD Studio Pro 2, you'll be greeted with the window that appears in Figure 1.1, which asks you to select a configuration.

Configurations tell DVD Studio Pro 2 how to select and arrange windows. Each configuration specifies which windows to display and where to display them. The introductory screen allows you to choose from Basic, Intermediate, and Advanced layouts.

Each layout provides a different look. The Basic layout offers a bare minimum of screens, to mimic the look of Apple's iDVD. Intermediate adds a timeline. The Advanced layout offers the greatest power and complexity. It contains all essential DVD Studio Pro 2 windows, with all the power that DVD Studio Pro 2 has to offer and is the configuration used throughout this book.

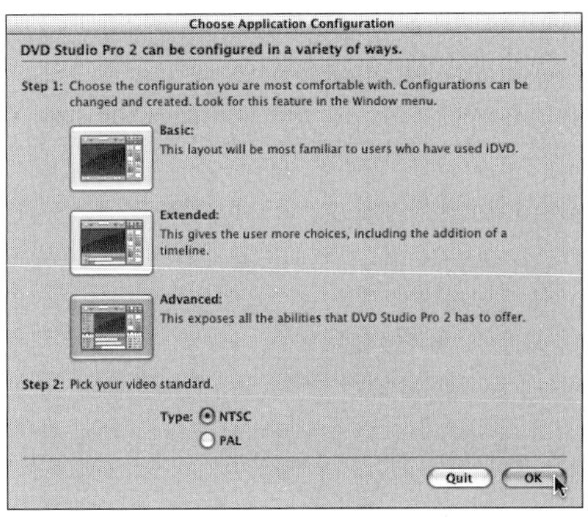

Figure 1.1 The first time you run DVD Studio Pro 2, the program asks you to choose an application configuration. Before clicking OK, select from the Basic, Intermediate, and Advanced configurations, and set your video standard (NTSC or PAL). Although DVD Studio Pro 2 offers easy ways to select configurations, you can revisit this dialog at will: quit DVD Studio Pro 2, remove the DVD Studio Pro 2 folder from ~/Library/Application Support, and relaunch.

NTSC (National Television Standards Committee) is the body that sets standards for television and video in North America, Japan, and parts of South America. PAL (Phase Alternating Line) is the video standard used in Europe (with the exception of France), the United Kingdom, Australia, and New Zealand.

Running DVD Studio Pro 2 for the First Time

Follow these steps to get started with DVD Studio Pro 2.

1. **Choose Advanced.** Click the small screenshot button to the left of the word *Advanced*. The Advanced configuration offers the most power and flexibility of all the configurations.

If you are familiar with iLife programs, do not be swayed by the Basic configuration's similarity to iDVD. DVD Studio Pro 2 is not iDVD. The similarity between the Basic configuration and iDVD is, at best, flimsy.

2. **Choose your video standard.** Select either NTSC or PAL, depending on your country of origin and the project you're about to build.

3. **Click OK.** DVD Studio Pro 2 accepts your settings and opens a new project using the Advanced configuration.

Choosing Configurations within the Program

After its first run, DVD Studio Pro 2 no longer displays the screen you saw in Figure 1.1. Instead, DVD Studio Pro 2 starts new projects using the last-selected configuration. To select a different configuration, follow these steps.

1. **Choose Window > Configurations.** DVD Studio Pro 2 opens a submenu that offers Basic, Intermediate, and Advanced configurations. Figure 1.2 shows this submenu.

2. **Choose an Advanced layout.** Select the Advanced option that matches the size of your screen.

   After selecting a configuration, DVD Studio Pro 2 resets the interface to the specified layout.

During a long and busy editing session, you may move and resize many DVD Studio Pro 2 windows, making changes you won't want to preserve. To quickly reset your windows to their original positions, choose Window > Configurations again, and choose the current configuration again.

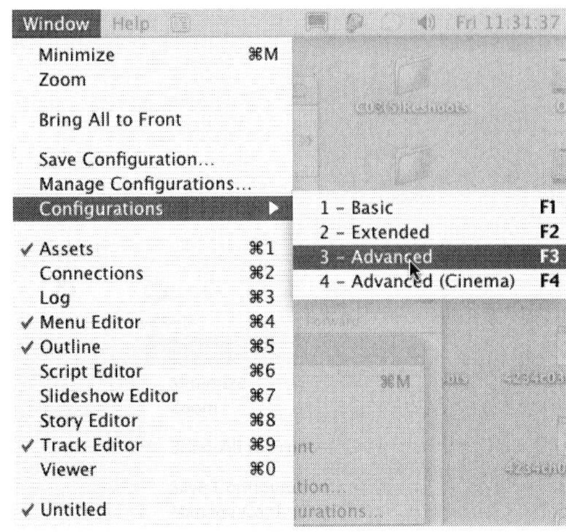

Figure 1.2 The Window > Configurations submenu allows you to select a configuration that matches your monitor. This figure shows the default list of built-in configurations. DVD Studio Pro 2 allows you to add to this list, introducing custom configurations to match your specific production needs. The configurations manager (choose Window > Manage Configurations) lets you add and remove configurations as needed.

Choosing a Video Standard within DVD Studio Pro 2

As with configurations, DVD Studio Pro 2 defaults to the last-used video standard. Follow these steps to set your video standard at any time.

1. **Choose DVD Studio Pro > Preferences (Command-,).** The Preferences window opens.

2. **Click Encoding.** The Encoding button appears on the top line, to the right of Destinations.

3. **Choose a video standard.** Select either NTSC or PAL to match your project to the country system in which it will be played.

4. **Click OK.** DVD Studio Pro 2 closes the window and updates your preferences.

Each DVD Studio Pro 2 project can use either the NTSC or PAL system, but not both at the same time. DVD Studio Pro 2 offers no standards conversion tools: you must convert material to the proper system before importing it. QuickTime Pro converts elementary video assets from one format to the other, with modest but usable results. Final Cut Pro, which uses the QuickTime engine, lets you export to both NTSC and PAL, regardless of the system used within your projects. By far the best conversion solution resides strictly on Windows: Canopus ProCoder offers the highest quality conversion tools. The sample material provided on the DVD Studio Pro 2 Solutions companion DVD uses the NTSC format.

Looking at the DVD Studio Pro 2 Interface

A careful look at the DVD Studio Pro 2 interface reveals how the program is structured on your screen. By default, Advanced configurations include a main window and two floating tool windows. Figure 1.3 shows a typical Advanced configuration. As you examine the layout, notice the following:

A tool bar appears at the top of the main window. This bar offers one-button access to many of the most common functions in DVD Studio Pro 2. The tool bar lets you bypass context-sensitive pop-up menus to get right to work.

The main window contains four subwindows. DVD Studio Pro 2 allows you to control the relative size of each subwindow, called a quadrant, so you can focus on the task at hand with the window real estate you need.

Each quadrant contains tabs. Tabs include Outline, Story, Connection, and Menu, among others. Each tab contains a different editor or information pane. Tabs allow you to organize your work, reduce clutter, and fit a lot more information on screen at one time.

Two floating windows appear above the main window. The Inspector and the Palette always appear as the frontmost windows of your interface. The Inspector provides context-specific controls for the program. For example, click a DVD menu, and the Menu Inspector allows you to set its name, its background image, and more. The Palette provides instant visual access to interface components such as buttons and menu layouts. The Palette also holds collections of audio, video, and still assets.

Manipulating the Interface

All DVD Studio Pro 2 windows are fully customizable. You can hide them from view, resize them, and more. DVD Studio Pro 2 offers you the power to configure the interface exactly how you'd like it to get your work done. To accomplish this, you need to master several interface manipulation techniques detailed here.

Working with Tabs

Tabs allow you to choose which editor or information pane to display in a quadrant. Common tasks include the following.

Selecting Tabs Click any tab to bring it to the front and display it.

Reordering Tabs To reorder within a line of tabs, drag the tab into its new position. DVD Studio Pro 2 makes space for the tab as it passes each of its quadrant mates.

Figure 1.3 The default look of the Advanced configuration includes an attached tool bar Ⓐ, within a paned main window Ⓑ, and two floating tools—the Inspector Ⓒ and the Palette Ⓓ.

Tearing off Tabs DVD Studio Pro 2 lets you to "tear off" tabs so they appear in new windows, as shown in Figure 1.4. These new windows do not "float." They can appear in front of or behind your main window, depending on window ordering. Use ⌘-` to cycle through your windows and display any hidden ones.

The Window menu places a check mark next to all selected tool tabs. When you find more than four checks in the menu, you know that you're working with extra open windows.

Moving Tabs between Quadrants DVD Studio Pro 2 allows you to move tabs from one quadrant to another and from one window to another. Place the cursor on any tab and drag that tab to any other tab line. This method is shown in Figure 1.5.

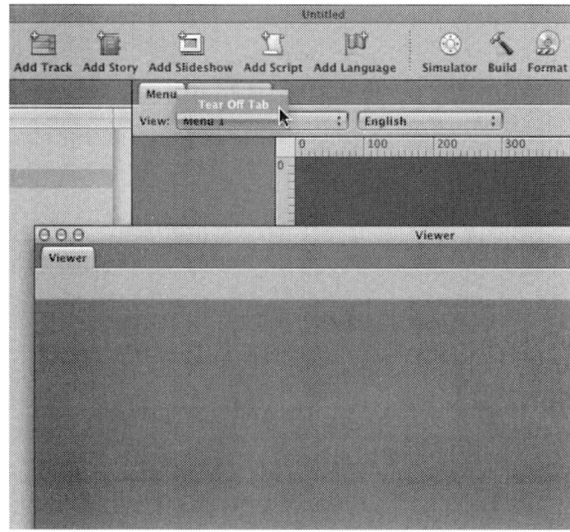

Figure 1.4 Tearing off tabs opens new DVD Studio Pro 2 windows. Control-click (right-click) any tab. Select Tear Off Tab from the contextual pop-up. Alternatively, drag the tab to some part of your screen other than the top tab lines of your windows.

Here are some key points to remember about tabs:

- When you close a tab window, the tab does not revert to your main work window. Use the Window menu (and its shortcuts) to reopen that tab. If, for example, you place the Outline tab in a new window and then close that window, you must choose Window > Outline (⌘-5) to see it again.

- When you drag the sole tab from a one-tab window into another tab bar, the window closes and the tab appears in that bar.

- Removing the last tab from a quadrant hides that quadrant. For example, you can see this if you move the Story and Outline tabs from the top-left quadrant. You must resize (discussed in the next section) to display the empty quadrant.

- To revert your display and restore your tabs, reload your configuration. Choose Window > Configurations and select any configuration.

Curious about the built-in shortcuts? Choose Help > Keyboard Shortcuts to view a complete list.

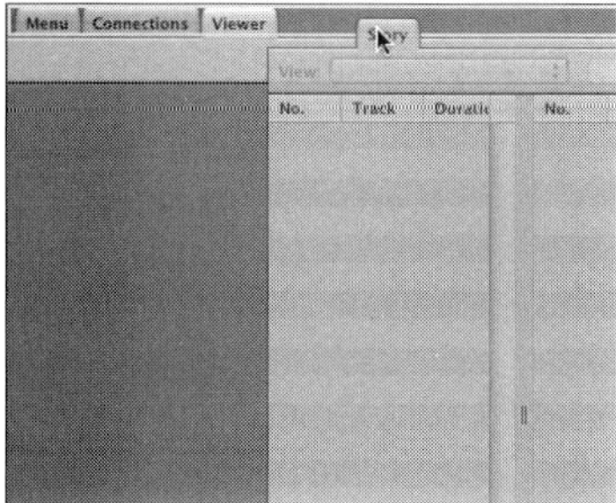

Figure 1.5 DVD Studio Pro 2 allows you to move tabs by dragging them to the top gray line of any quadrant. A blue outline surrounds this line when the cursor enters. To reorder tabs within a quadrant, drag the tab within the top line into its new position.

Adjusting Quadrants

DVD Studio Pro 2 allows you to resize the quadrants within your main window to give them as much or as little space as needed. Use the following techniques to customize your quadrant allocation.

- Move your mouse to any horizontal or vertical line between quadrants until you see the resizing cursor. The cursor appears as two parallel or horizontal lines with arrows on both sides. (When your horizontal and vertical lines meet, you'll see a plus-shaped cursor instead.) Unlike other resizing cursors used within the program, this cursor has a slight blue tint. To reapportion space, drag in any direction. If you drag entirely across, you may hide one or more quadrants.

When quadrants align, either vertically or horizontally, they resize together. Pressing ⌥ allows you to resize one quadrant independently of its mate.

- Hiding quadrants provides more screen space without opening new windows. To detect hidden quadrants, examine the sides of your main DVD Studio Pro 2 window. Studio Pro slightly thickened window edges indicate hidden quadrants. In addition, the resizing cursor appears over these thickened borders. To view a hidden quadrant (or quadrants), look for the resizing cursor to appear and then drag to display the quadrant.

  As with tabs, reselecting a configuration from the Window > Configurations submenu instantly reverts your quadrants to default positions.

Other Interface Elements

The DVD Studio Pro 2 Inspector, Palette and Toolbar all offer important functionality in addition to the main window and tabs. These interface elements extend the program, offering flexible tools that help you work on your projects.

Manipulating the Floating Windows

The Inspector and Palette, when visible, float over all other windows in your interface. (They have the highest window priority.) DVD Studio Pro 2 allows you to show, hide, and resize these floating tools as follows:

- To show either window, choose View > Show Palette or View > Show Inspector.
- Choose View > Hide Palette or View > Hide Inspector to close each window.

- Two keyboard shortcuts, ⌘-⌥-I (for Inspector) and ⌘-⌥-P (for Palette) toggle floating window visibility on and off. The Palette and Inspector buttons found at the very right of the toolbar also toggle window visibility.

- Move the Inspector or Palette by dragging the title bar at the top of either window.

- Resize the Palette by dragging the lower-right corner. You cannot resize the Inspector.

- To close a floating window, click the tiny close button (the X at the top-left corner of the window).

Revealing Basic's Hidden Quadrants

The Basic configuration hides a lot more than it shows. A little manipulation discloses the quadrants that you find in the Intermediate and Advanced configurations.

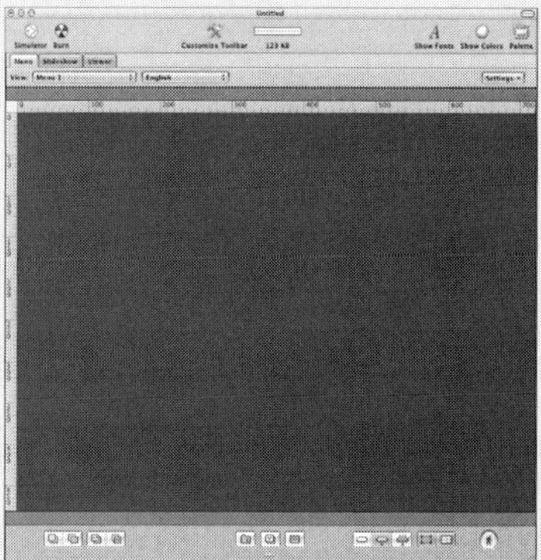

Dragging from the left reveals one new quadrant (below left). Dragging the bottom border exposes the remaining quadrants (below right).

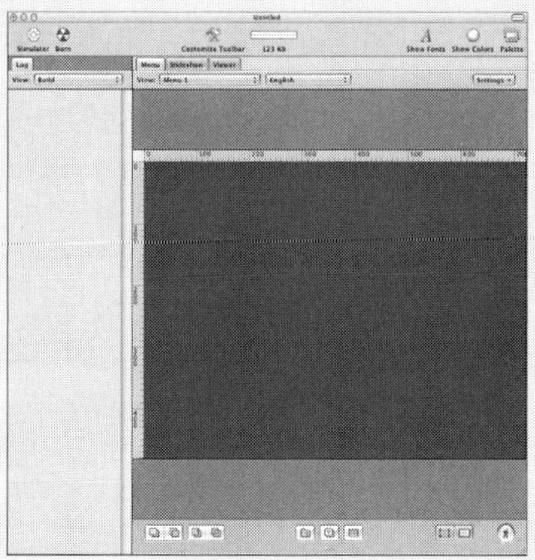

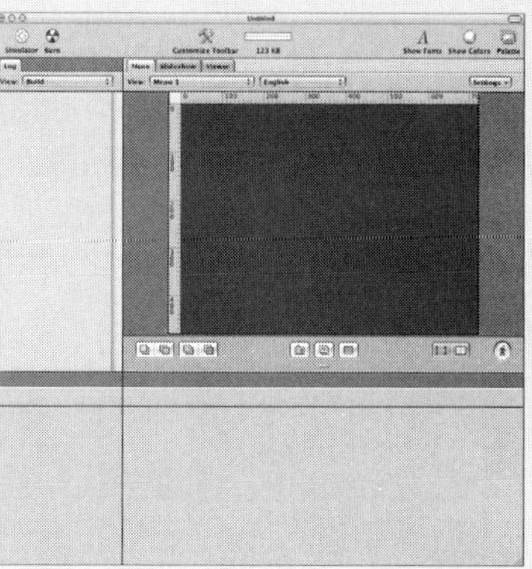

Customizing the Toolbar

As with many programs and tools in Mac OS X, DVD Studio Pro 2 provides full toolbar customization, offering one-button access to your most-used functions. Choose View > Customize Toolbar to open the interactive customization editor, as shown in Figure 1.6. In the editor, you can do the following:

Add Items Drag any icon up to the toolbar. The icons in the toolbar shift to make room for the new addition.

Remove Items DVD Studio Pro 2 provides a small "puff" animation when you drag an icon off the toolbar, letting you know it's been removed.

Reorder Items When unsatisfied with the toolbar order, just drag an item into a new position. As with adding, the icons in the toolbar shift to accommodate your repositioned icon.

Group Items Together Use separators to group icons by task. Add as many or as few separators to your toolbar as needed. The Space and Flexible Space icons offer alternative approaches for toolbar layout and grouping.

Use Defaults Click the default set icon toward the bottom of the window to restore default tool buttons.

Choose Icons, Text, or Both The Show pop-up menu at the bottom left of the customize window allows you to select from Icon & Text, Icon Only, and Text Only.

After making any changes to your toolbar, click Done to apply your changes and close the customization window.

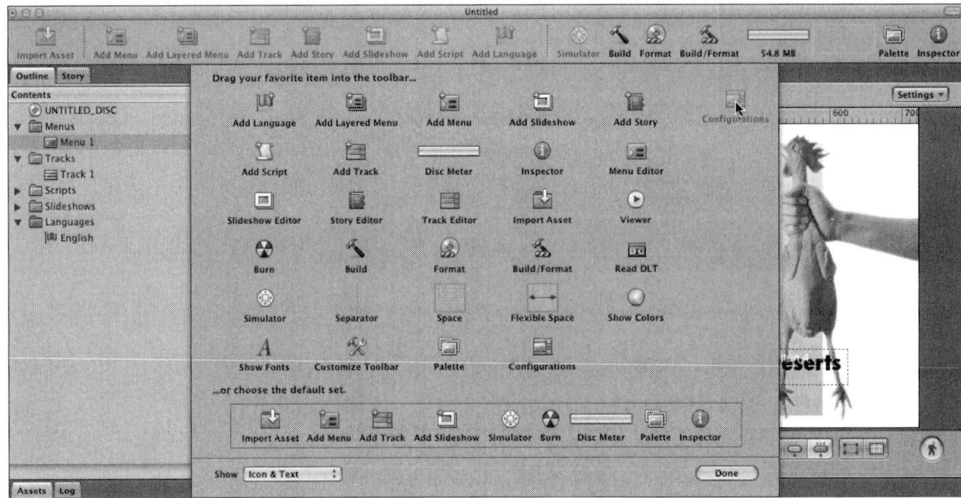

Figure 1.6 Customize your toolbar to include features you use the most. DVD Studio Pro 2 allows you to add, move, and group items as needed to create an effective set of one-click functionality.

Saving Configurations

Configurations define ways to display the various panes, panels, toolbars, and windows that make up the suite of tools. DVD Studio Pro 2 allows you create new configurations, in which it stores these positions and preferences. Here's how.

1. **Arrange your workspace.** Place your windows, quadrants, floating tools, and so forth exactly as you want them to appear the next time you load this configuration. Edit your toolbar as desired. Once you save, you cannot directly edit configurations in DVD Studio Pro 2, so be sure to place each window item thoughtfully.

Although you can't edit configurations directly, you can always make a change, save as a new configuration, and toss the old one.

2. **Choose Window > Manage Configuration.** This opens the small Configurations Manager window at the top of your workspace.

3. **Click +.** The plus-button instructs DVD Studio Pro 2 to create a new configuration based on your current layout.

4. **Scroll down.** Your new, untitled configuration appears at the bottom of the Configurations list below Default, as shown in Figure 1.7.

5. **Edit the name.** Double-click Untitled and rename as desired.

6. **Click OK.** This applies your changes and closes the Configuration Manager.

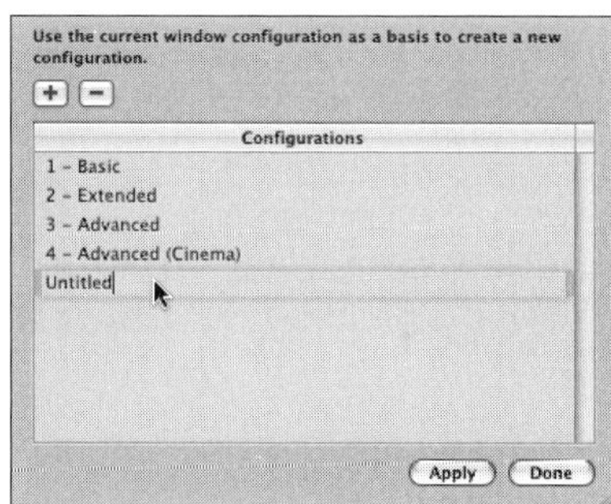

Figure 1.7 Creating a new configuration allows you to store the current window layout for later recall. Configurations store the location and ordering of toolbar buttons as well as your windows.

Newer versions of DVD Studio Pro 2 (2.0.1 and later) allow you to save configurations directly by choosing Window > Save Configuration.

Fast Facts about Configurations

- To restore DVD Studio Pro 2 to its factory defaults, locate the DVD Studio Pro 2 folder in your home ~/Library/Application Support folder. Quit DVD Studio Pro 2, drag this folder to the desktop or the trashcan, and launch the program again.

- Configuration files use .dspconfig extensions.

- Configuration files are based on XML (Extensible Markup Language). You can open .dspconfig files in TextEdit and read through them. For better readability, you might want to globally replace tabs with single spaces. (This does not affect performance or usability in any way.)

- When you use TextEdit to modify .dspconfig files, the changes do not appear until you launch the program again.

The Configuration Manager allows you to add, remove, and rename your configurations—including the DVD Studio Pro 2 defaults. Here are some of the ways you can use the Configuration Manger.

DVD Studio Pro 2 does not provide Undo support for these changes.

Removing Configurations Select any configuration and click – (the minus button) to remove it from the active set of configurations.

Renaming Configurations Double-click any configuration to open a text-edit field on its name.

Reordering Configurations DVD Studio Pro 2 uses alphabetic sorting (0–9, A–Z) in its Window > Configurations submenu. Name your configurations with this in mind. Unfortunately, this sorting does not apply to new items in the Configuration Manager window until you restart the program.

Viewing Configurations Click Apply after selecting a configuration to view it. Unfortunately, in early versions of DVD Studio Pro 2, this action closes the Configuration Manager. You must choose Window > Manage Configurations again to continue with your edits.

Understanding the Interface

DVD Studio Pro 2 with its cluttered interface may intimidate first-time users. Numerous windows—tabbed, paned, and floating—appear almost at random on your screen. Despite a superficially messy appearance, a logical structure underlies this visual confusion, and

DVD Studio Pro offers a solid structural workflow that allows you to build, test, and customize your DVD projects. Figure 1.8 shows a typical DVD Studio Pro 2 workspace with a project in progress.

Each DVD Studio Pro 2 window has a job to do. Some allow you to work with tracks; others help lay out your interface. Once you understand the role of each window, it becomes easier to see how they work together. It also helps that you can customize almost any DVD Studio Pro 2 interface through built-in and user-defined configurations.

Identifying Windows

A quick tour offers a great way to become acquainted with the main program windows. Visiting each window allows you to get an idea of their jobs and see what they look like.

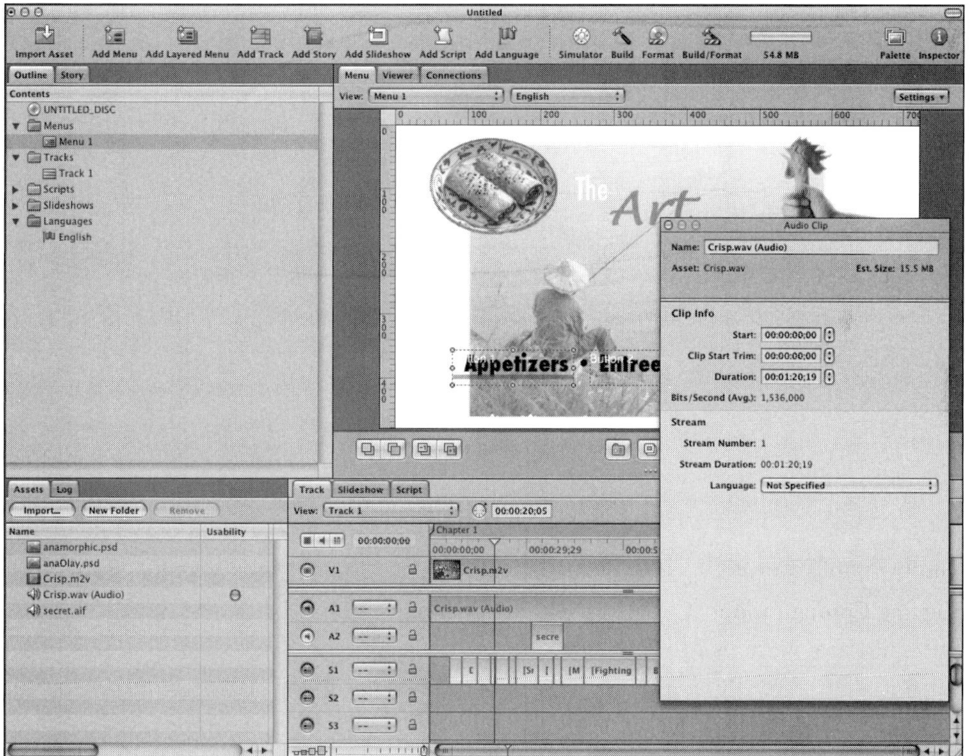

Figure 1.8 DVD Studio Pro 2 has a busy but flexible interface that allows you to build, test, and customize your DVD. This figure shows how your screen might look like while you are working on a project.

Assets

The Assets window (⌘-1) lets you organize and manage project assets. Here's where you store all the video, sounds, and graphic stills that you use to build your project. The Assets window conveniently displays information about these items, including their type, length, size, rate, and use.

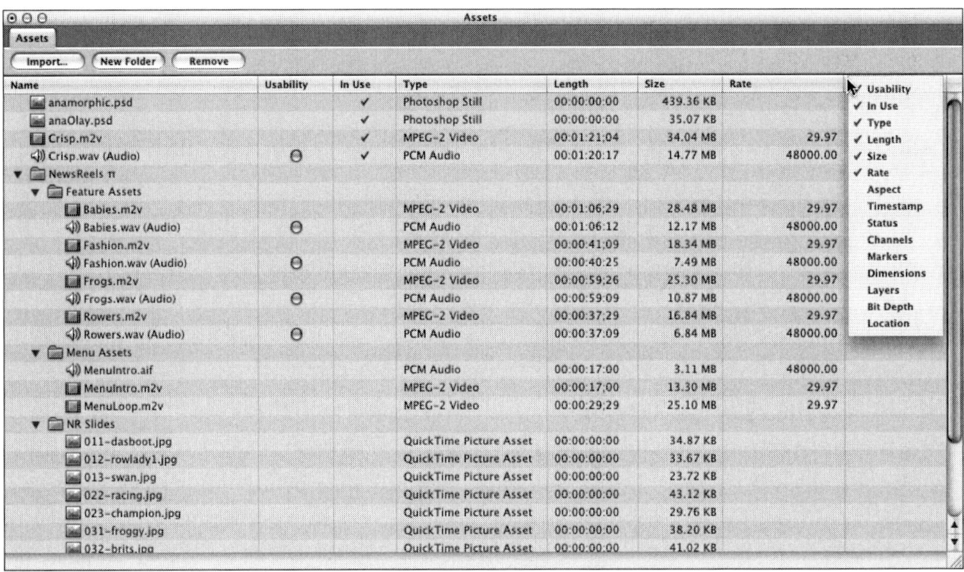

Connections

The Connections window (⌘-2) allows you to create disc navigation links between menus, markers, assets, and so forth. Connections specify the way your DVD flows over time: how items connect and how control moves from one item to the next.

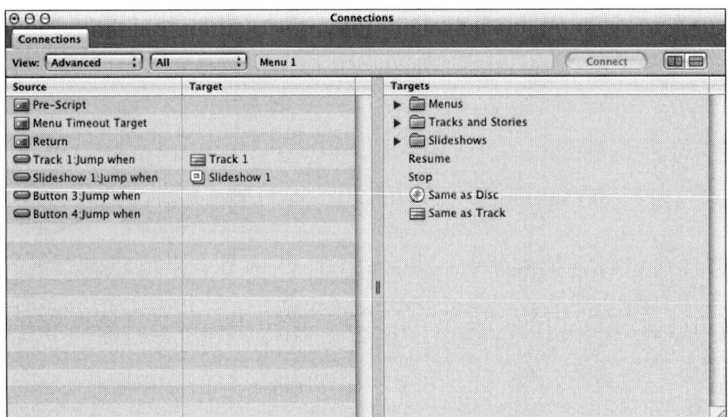

Log

The Log window (⌘-3) collects and displays a running description of the way you build, encode, and simulate your project. By providing a textual view of the progress of these operations, the Log allows you to supervise what's going on.

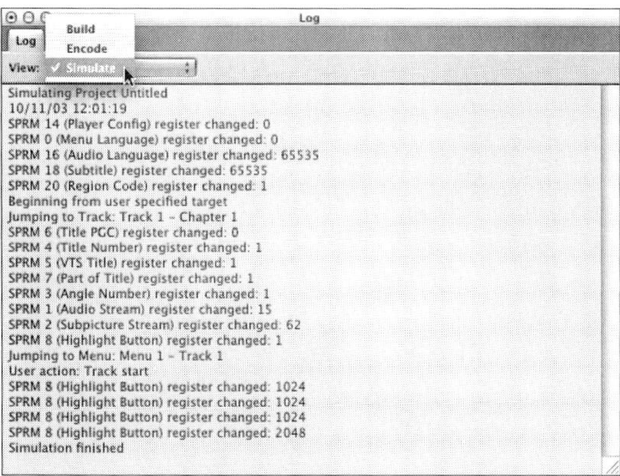

Menu Editor

The Menu window (⌘-4) provides interactive menu layout in which you can add buttons, define their navigation targets, add backgrounds, and more. You design project menus using this window.

Outline

The Outline window (⌘-5) provides an ordered list of the menus, tracks, scripts, slideshows, and languages that appear in your project. This window helps you manage these elements, allowing you to add, rename, or remove items as needed.

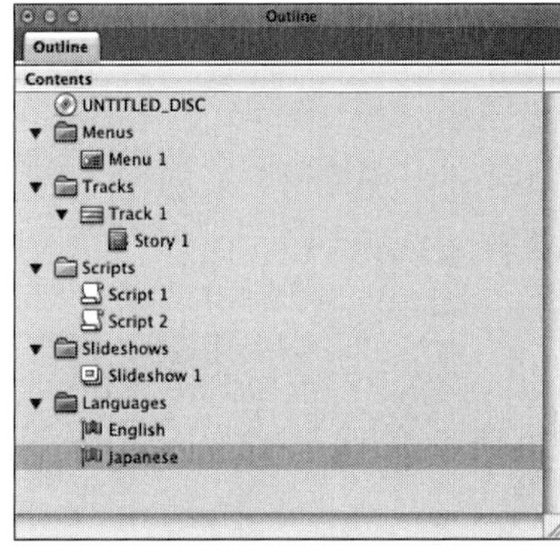

Script Editor

The Script Editor (⌘-6) allows you to add programmed functionality to your DVDs. DVD Studio Pro 2 offers a dialog-based approach to building scripts, so you need no programming experience, although such experience is a plus.

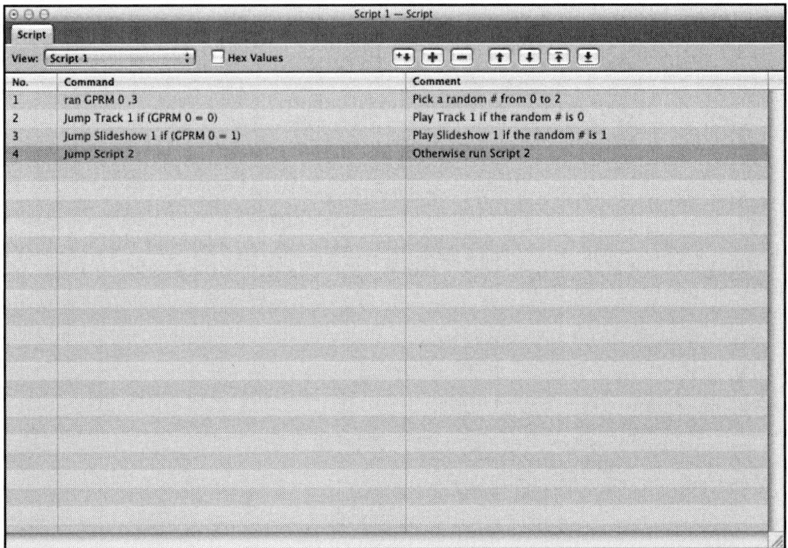

Slideshow Editor

When you want to combine a series of still images into a dynamic, interactive presentation, look no further than the Slideshow Editor (⌘-7). This editor allows you to import pictures, set their duration, add audio, and more.

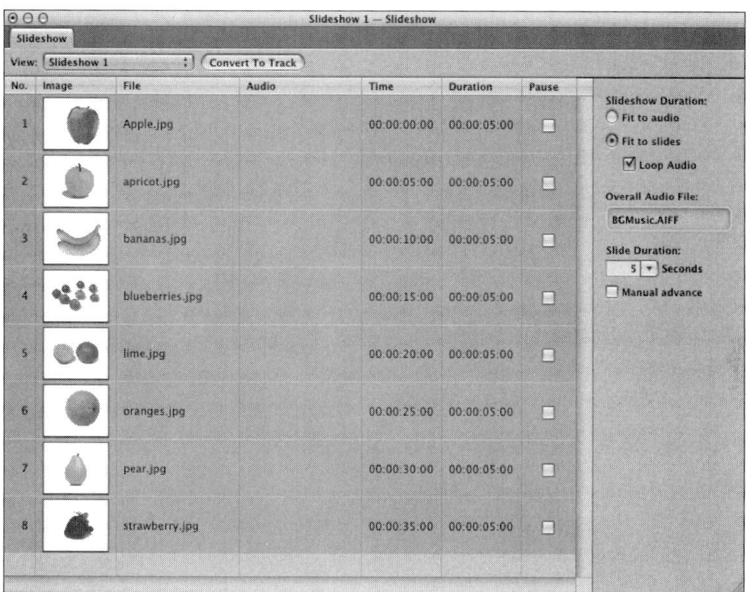

Story Editor

With the Story Editor (⌘-8), you can create a "story" that moves selectively through your tracks. Stories let you rearrange the way your movie plays back, to include (or omit) scenes or to mix up the playback.

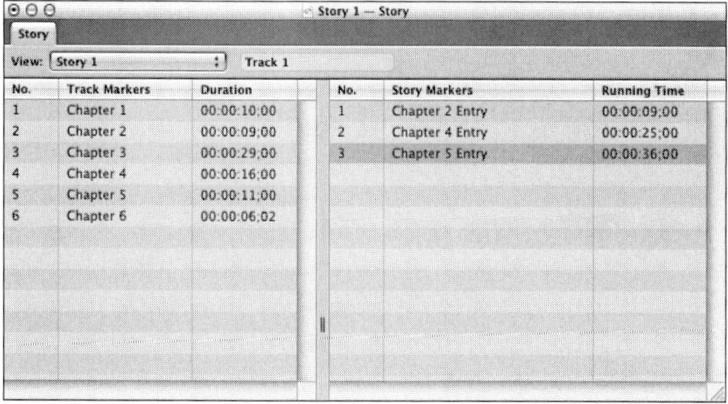

Track Editor

The Track Editor (⌘-9) allows you to build and edit your video, audio, and subtitle streams. Use this timeline to sequence your assets, add alternative languages, and more.

Viewer

As the name might suggest, the Viewer window (⌘-0) displays the contents of your audio and video tracks, providing playback that synchronizes with the playhead in your track editor. The Viewer window also helps you lay out your subtitles.

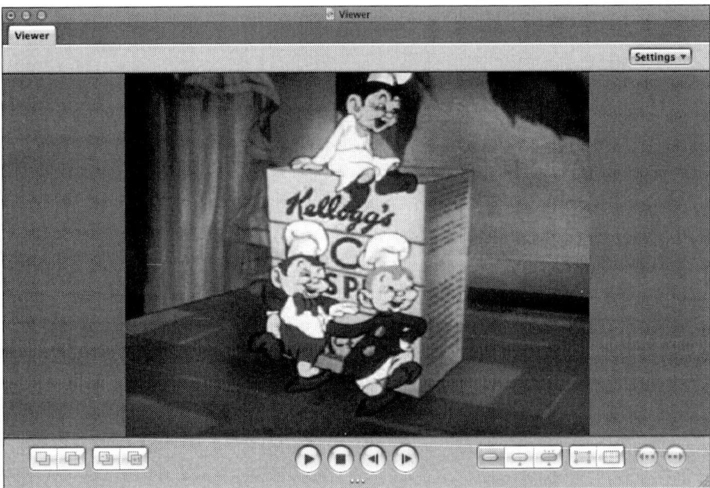

Palette

The floating Palette (press ⌘-⌥-P, or click the Palette button in the toolbar) offers quick access to built-in interface components, including templates, styles, and shapes. You can add to these components by building your own custom items. In addition, it offers media tabs that integrate with iPhoto and iTunes.

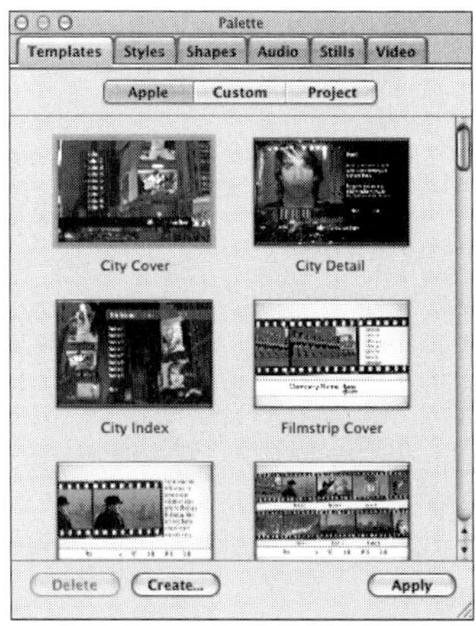

Inspector

Like the Palette, the Inspector (press ⌘-⌥-I, or click the Info button in the toolbar) floats over the other windows in your interface. It displays context-sensitive properties for selected items within DVD Studio Pro 2, allowing you to edit those properties using a series of tabbed sheets. (The name in the Inspector window's title bar always reflects the item being inspected.) Use the Inspector to specify the way your disc and its menus, tracks, scripts, slideshows, and languages behave.

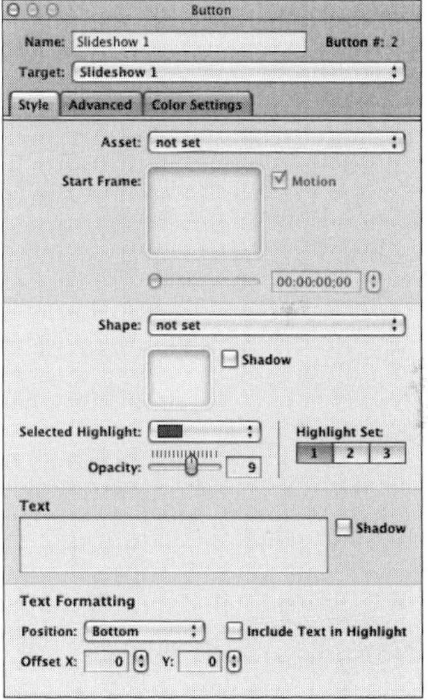

Simulator

The DVD Studio Pro 2 Simulator window (⌘-⌥-0) lets you preview, monitor, and interact with your DVD projects. It offers a virtual DVD player for you to test your work.

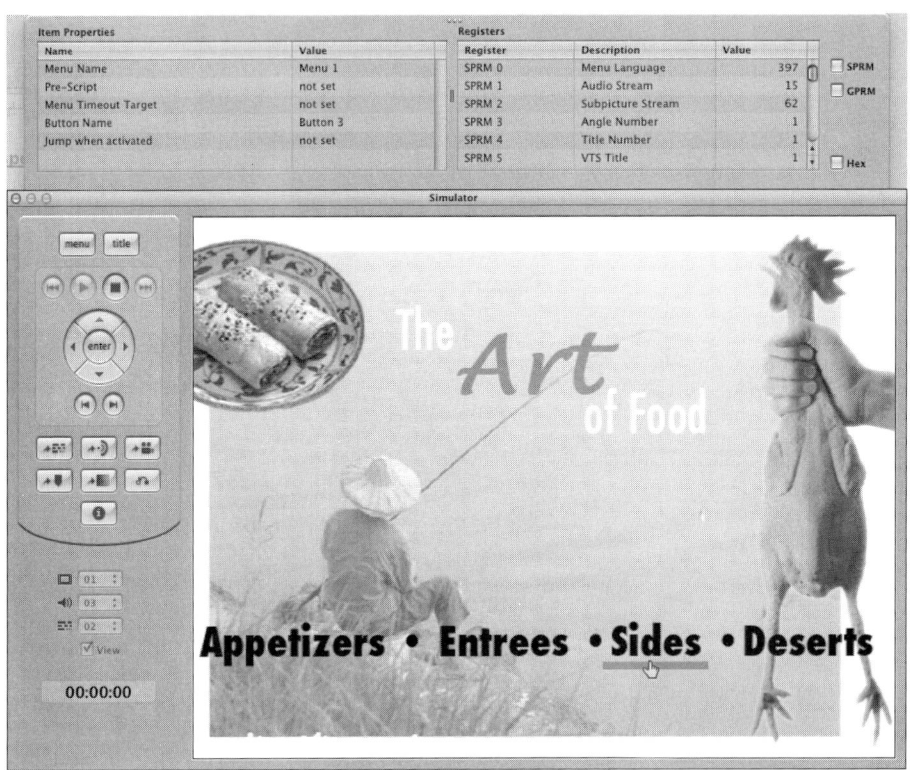

Using Projects

DVD Studio Pro project files store the way you define, lay out, and put together your DVD components, such as menus, tracks, scripts, slideshows, languages, and more. Project files remember all the work you've done so you can save and pick up editing exactly where you left off. Here are some tips about using DVD Studio Pro 2 projects:

Saving Projects To save your work, choose File > Save (Command-S). DVD Studio Pro 2 stores a record of your work up to the moment that you save it. Choose File > Save As (Command-Shift-S) to save to a new file name.

New Projects To begin a fresh new project, choose File > New (Command-N).

Reverting Projects Choose File > Revert To Save to discard changes to your project and revert to the last saved version.

Unlike iLife titles such as iMovie and iDVD, DVD Studio Pro does not "remember" current projects. DVD Studio Pro 2 begins a new project each time you launch the program from the Application icon. To load a recent project, choose File > Open Recent or double-click a project file icon.

DVD Studio Pro 2 project files are not actually files—they are OS X bundles. Each "file" contains both data files and folders. To see these components, select any DVD Studio Pro 2 project file and Ctrl-click (right-click) its icon. Choose Show Package Contents from the pop-up menu. Navigate to Contents/Resources. Here, you'll view the items that make up your project. Figure 1.9 shows the typical initial contents of this folder.

If you're curious, drag the ObjectDataB and ModuleDataB files into TextEdit to view their contents. Although they are not by any means text-based, they do use text labels that offer fascinating insight into the way DVD Studio Pro 2 stores projects.

Figure 1.9 Your DVD Studio Pro 2 project "file" is not a file at all. It's a bundle that contains data files and folders. The ObjectDataB file that appears in the Resources folder stores all the information about your project, including languages, tracks, colors, menus, formats, styles, streams, and more. The ModuleDataB file preserves the saved layout of your project. This ensures that your windows appear in the same positions that you left them.

Loading Assets

To build a house, you need bricks and wood. To build a DVD, you need properly encoded data files. DVD Studio Pro 2 project development begins by collecting sound, picture, and movie files called assets. Assets are the audio, still, and video files you use to build your tracks, menus, and slideshows.

DVD Studio Pro 2 offers two ways to organize and use assets in your projects: the Assets tab and the Palette. The Assets tab provides a list of folders and files that you can edit. The Palette offers easy-to-use integration with your iTunes and iPhoto libraries.

Using the Assets Tab

The Assets tab helps you import, organize, and understand your project assets. Figure 1.10 shows what a typical session might look like.

Folders and subfolders help organize your assets into logical groups. You can import entire folders (and their subfolders) at once, and DVD Studio Pro 2 will preserve the folder structure. The columns help identify and describe your assets, providing information about each item in a structured table.

DVD Studio Pro 2 Assets

DVD Studio Pro 2 places certain requirements on your assets. When your assets do not initially match these standards, DVD Studio Pro 2 will encode your files accordingly.

Video Standard DVD Studio Pro 2 supports both NTSC and PAL standards. All assets within any single project must use the same standard, either NTSC or PAL.

Video File Types DVD Studio Pro 2 accepts both MPEG-1 and MPEG-2 elementary streams at up to 1.856Mbps (MPEG-1) or 9.8Mbps (MPEG-2). All MPEG-2 video must use a 4:2:0 chroma format.

Dimension DVD Studio Pro 2 MPEG-2 movies and full-screen still images occupy 720×480 pixels (NTSC) or 720×576 pixels (PAL). MPEG-1 files use 352×240 pixels (NTSC) or 352×288 pixels (PAL). DVD Studio Pro 2 supports both 4:3 and 16:9 aspect ratios.

Frame Rate For NTSC projects, use 29.97 frames per second. For PAL projects, use 25 frames per second.

Audio Resolution DVD Studio Pro 2 accepts either 16-bit or 24-bit audio, using either 48 or 96kHz sampling.

Audio File Types DVD Studio Pro 2 supports Dolby Digital or AC-3 (64 to 448kbps), Stereo PCM (16b/48kHz/1536kpbs or 24b/96kHz/4608kbps) and MPEG-1 Layer 2 audio.

Name	Usability	In Use	Type	Length	Size
anamorphic.psd		✓	Photoshop Still	00:00:00:00	439.36 KB
anaOlay.psd		✓	Photoshop Still	00:00:00:00	35.07 KB
Apple.jpg		✓	QuickTime Picture Asset	00:00:00:00	12.02 KB
apricot.jpg		✓	QuickTime Picture Asset	00:00:00:00	9.93 KB
bananas.jpg		✓	QuickTime Picture Asset	00:00:00:00	10.98 KB
BGMusic.AIFF		✓	PCM Audio	00:01:54:00	20.90 MB
blueberries.jpg		✓	QuickTime Picture Asset	00:00:00:00	12.80 KB
Crisp.m2v		✓	MPEG-2 Video	00:01:21;04	34.04 MB
Crisp.wav (Audio)	⊖	✓	PCM Audio	00:01:20:17	14.77 MB
lime.jpg		✓	QuickTime Picture Asset	00:00:00:00	11.61 KB
▼ NewsReels π					
▼ Feature Assets					
Babies.m2v			MPEG-2 Video	00:01:06;29	28.48 MB
Babies.wav (Audio)	⊖		PCM Audio	00:01:06:12	12.17 MB
Fashion.m2v			MPEG-2 Video	00:00:41;09	18.34 MB
Fashion.wav (Audio)	⊖		PCM Audio	00:00:40:25	7.49 MB
Frogs.m2v			MPEG-2 Video	00:00:59;26	25.30 MB
Frogs.wav (Audio)	⊖		PCM Audio	00:00:59:09	10.87 MB
Rowers.m2v			MPEG-2 Video	00:00:37;29	16.84 MB
Rowers.wav (Audio)	⊖		PCM Audio	00:00:37:09	6.84 MB
▼ Menu Assets					
MenuIntro.aif			PCM Audio	00:00:17:00	3.11 MB

Figure 1.10 A typical session in the Assets tab. Notice the check marks for in-use items. The dots in the Usability column indicate encoding status for movies and audio that were not encoded prior to import. Here, Type, Length, Size, and Rate columns display important file status information that helps you manage your assets.

Here are some ways to manipulate the columns, to provide the most informative views of your assets.

Choosing Columns To choose which columns to display, move your cursor over any column header and Ctrl-click (right-click). Choose your columns from the pop-up list, as shown in Figure 1.11.

Repositioning Columns You can reposition columns by dragging. Move your cursor to any column header and drag the column to its new location.

Resizing Column Width Resize columns by moving your cursor into the horizontal row of column headers. A resize cursor appears at the boundary between each pair of columns. Drag the resize cursor to stretch or squeeze column width.

Sorting Assets When you select any column header (click its name), a small triangle appears to its right. This triangle indicates sorting. An upward triangle sorts assets in ascending order; a downward triangle indicates descending order. Click any selected column to toggle between the two sorting methods.

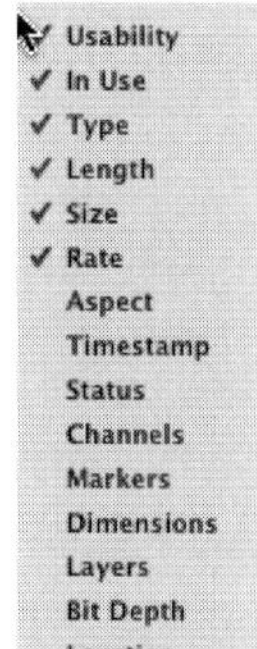

Figure 1.11 DVD Studio Pro 2 allows you to customize which columns to display. Choose from 15 available columns, as shown here. Ctrl-click (right-click) the name of any column to view this pop-up menu. Select any item to toggle its visibility between hidden and shown. Checked items indicate viewable columns. Unchecked items are hidden.

Importing Assets

Importing assets allows you to create a list of project building blocks with which you can construct your final DVD. Follow these steps to import assets into DVD Studio Pro 2.

1. **Open the Import Assets dialog.** The Import Assets dialog (shown in Figure 1.12) allows you to select files or folders to import into DVD Studio Pro 2. You can open this dialog in the following ways:

   - In the Assets window, click Import….

   - In the toolbar, click Import Asset.

   - Choose File > Import > Asset… (⌘-Shift-I).

   - Right-click (Ctrl-click) in the Assets window, and choose Import Asset… from the pop-up menu.

2. **Navigate to your assets.** Select the files and folders you want to include.

3. **Click Import.** DVD Studio Pro 2 adds the selected files and folders to the Assets window.

   Alternatively, if your screen dimensions allow, you can simply drag files and folders from the Finder and drop them onto the Assets window.

You can import AAC audio from the Apple Music Store into your DVD Studio Pro Assets window so long as you use the audio on an authorized computer. The DVD you produce will play in any computer or set-top player.

Examining Assets

DVD Studio Pro 2 offers several ways to look at your newly imported assets.

Columns Browse through the columns to view the attributes associated with an asset's data file. The information you can view depend on the columns shown.

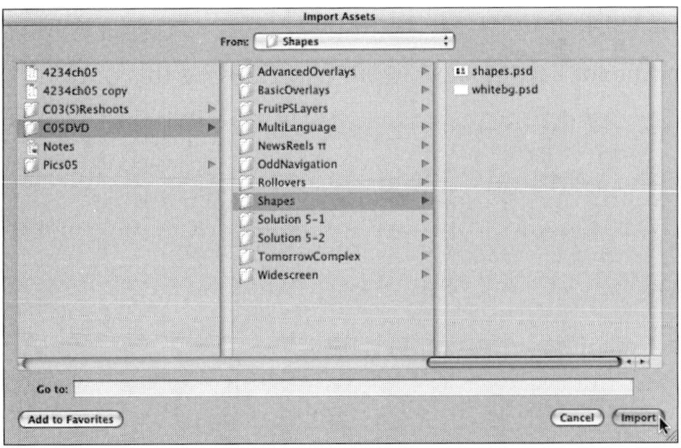

Figure 1.12 The Import Assets dialog allows you to import files, folders, or both. DVD Studio Pro 2 preserves the structure of nested subfolders when you import a structured collection of project assets.

Inspector The Inspector (⌘-⌥-I) allows you to examine and customize each of the files that appear in your Assets tab. Until an asset is used in a project, the Inspector shows only a general overview of that asset.

Viewer Double-click any asset (double-click its name) to preview it in the Viewer window. (Alternatively, Ctrl-click or right-click and choose Preview Asset….) If the Viewer window is hidden, DVD Studio Pro 2 will open the Viewer tab in a new floating window.

By default, when you import assets that have not previously been encoded, DVD Studio Pro 2 automatically encodes them in the background with Compressor. This lets you concentrate on authoring your disc rather than waiting for your computer to finish encoding and catch up to you.

Compressor, which ships with DVD Studio Pro 2, Final Cut Pro 4, Final Cut Express 1 and later, is explored further in Chapters 4 and 5.

Here are some key points to remember about background encoding:

Status The Usability column helps identify the encoding status of certain audio and video files. Yellow dots indicate that the files are, as yet, unencoded. Green dots reflect fully encoded assets. (Red dots let you know that DVD Studio Pro 2 is busy parsing the asset.)

When DVD Studio Pro 2 "parses" an encoded file, it scans the file to recover certain information such as the file's length, its type, and its overall integrity. When you import assets, DVD Studio Pro 2 creates small .par files in ~/Library/Caches/DVD Studio Pro Files. A typical parse file might be named Main-Menu.m2v.par, adding the .par extension to the original asset name.

Enabling Background Encoding In DVD Studio Pro 2, background encoding is enabled by default. To disable background encoding, Choose DVD Studio Pro > Preferences (⌘-,). Click Encoding, and choose Encode On Build. Click OK. Choosing this option delays encoding until you're ready to build your disc.

Viewing Encoding Preferences Use the Encoding preferences panel to set the bit rate, encoding method, and so forth for your background encoding. To view (and/or modify) the current settings, choose File > Encoder Settings (⌘-E) or Ctrl-click (right-click) in the Assets tab and choose Encoder Settings from the pop-up.

Finding MPEG Folders By default, Compressor stores your encoded files in a subfolder entitled MPEG. This subfolder appears in the same folder as and at the same level of your original asset, as described by Figure 1.13.

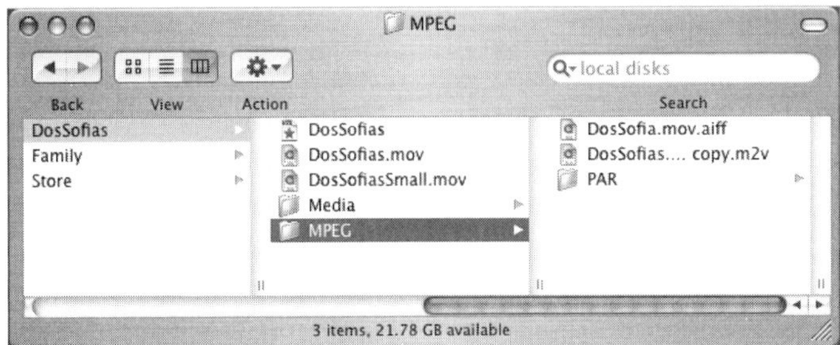

Figure 1.13 By default, the background encoder (Compressor) creates a new folder at the same level as your original asset. It names this folder MPEG and uses it to store the encoded files associated with the asset. Use the Preferences dialog (⌘-,) to select an alternate destination. Click Destinations and choose Encoding from the Show pop-up. Select from Same Folder as the Asset (Default), Project Bundle (saves to the project file, a la iDVD) or Specified Folder (click Choose to pick a folder). To set locations for your PAR folders, choose MPEG Parsing from the Show pop-up.

Managing Assets

Here are some key techniques you can use to manage the lists of assets in your Assets tab.

Removing Assets

To remove assets from your project, select an asset or assets and click Remove. Alternatively, select an asset and then choose Edit > Remove Asset or press Delete, or Ctrl-click (right-click) the asset and choose Remove from the pop-up menu. Here are some important points about removing assets:

- You can remove a single asset at a time or several assets at once. Your selection controls which items are removed. Select assets, folders, or both.

- Removing assets from your Assets tab display has no effect on the actual files on your computer. You remove the item or items only from the Asset tab.

- You cannot remove assets in use within your project. DVD Studio Pro 2 warns you when you try to do so.

Renaming Assets

DVD Studio Pro 2 allows you to rename assets to choose more meaningful names to use within your project. For example, you might rename f92x194j.m2v to main_movie.m2v. Here are some things to know about renaming:

- Changing an asset name does not affect the file on your computer. To view the original file, select the asset and choose File > Reveal In Finder. (Alternatively, Ctrl-click (right-click) and choose Reveal In Finder from the pop-up menu.)

- Changing an asset name does not override the built-in video- and audio-matching feature that loads same-named audio tracks when you add a video to the Track Editor. With the above example, if you added main_movie.m2v as a new video stream, DVD Studio Pro 2 would automatically add the matching audio file f92x194j.aif.

- Changing an asset name does not affect ordering. DVD Studio Pro 2 uses the *original* asset name to determine alphabetic ordering.

To enable audio matching, open the Preferences dialog (DVD Studio Pro > Preferences… or ⌘-,). Click Track, check Find Matching Audio When Dragging, and click OK.

Managing Folders

Asset folders work much as you'd expect, allowing you to group and organize your assets. Some folder management techniques include the following:

Adding Folders Click New Folder in the Toolbar to add a folder to your list of assets. Alternatively, Ctrl-click (right-click) within the Assets tab and choose New Folder from the Assets contextual pop-up menu, or choose Project > New Asset Folder (⌘-⌥-B). New folders appear at the same level as the currently selected item.

Renaming Folders Double-click a folder to rename it.

Reparenting Folders Drag items either into or out of folders to reparent them. Reparenting in the Assets tab does not affect the way items are stored on your computer.

Removing Folders Select a folder and click Remove to remove the folder and all items within it. You cannot remove items that are in use, nor can you remove their parent folders.

Relinking Assets

On occasion, DVD Studio Pro 2 won't be able to find an asset you've added to a project. You might have deleted it from your computer; you might have renamed it; or you might have moved it to a new folder.

When DVD Studio Pro 2 cannot find your files, it displays the asset name in bright red in the Asset tab. DVD Studio Pro 2 uses live links to your files, so this update happens in real time. (To see this at work, temporarily drag a file to a new folder and select that asset. Return the file to its original location to restore the link.) As Figure 1.14 shows, DVD Studio Pro 2 searches for, and occasionally detects, missing files whenever you load projects.

Relinking allows you to reconnect the project asset with an actual file on the computer. To do so, Ctrl-click (right-click) the asset name and choose Relink Asset. The Relink dialog appears. Navigate to your asset file and click Relink.

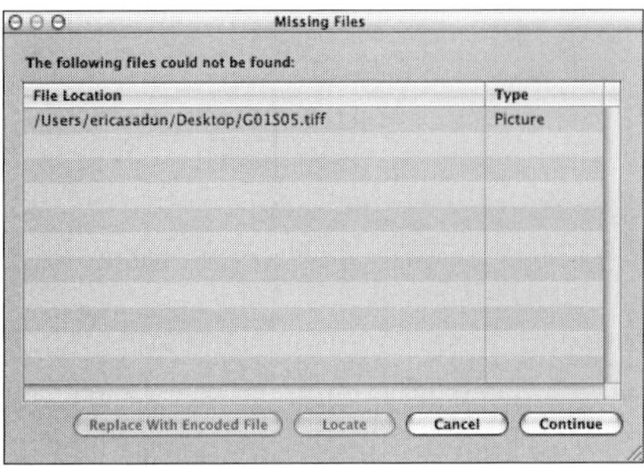

Figure 1.14 DVD Studio Pro 2 automatically scans for missing asset files whenever you load a project. When it finds them, it displays this alert. Click a filename to open the Relink dialog and search for that file.

Whenever you relink a file, DVD Studio Pro 2 automatically searches the folder you select to detect other missing files. When it finds them, it notifies you, saying "Other missing files were found. Should these also be relinked?" Click OK to automatically relink the detected files.

Using the Palette Media Tabs

The Palette (⌘-⌥-P) offers another way to access audio, video, and still images stored on your computer. Its three media tabs offer simple integration with the iLife applications that ship with Mac OS X.

The Audio Palette

The Audio palette provides direct access to your iTunes libraries as well as other collections of sound files. This palette provides a convenient way to iTunes audio in your DVD Studio Pro 2 projects.

Using the Audio palette, you can drag audio onto the Track Editor to create or add to audio streams. Or, you might add sounds to the Slideshow or Menu Editor to introduce a background track.

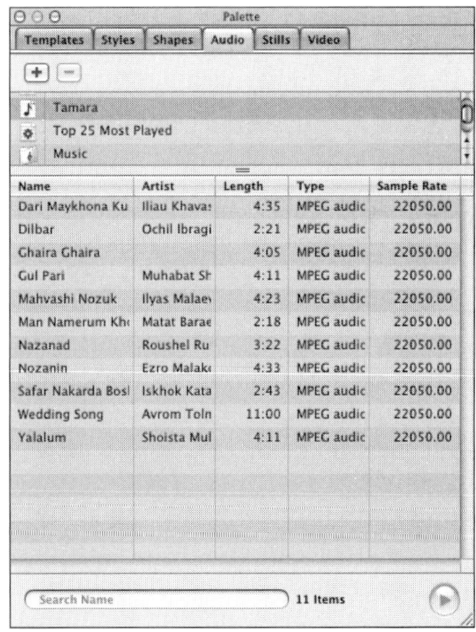

The Stills Palette

The Stills palette connects to your iPhoto library, allowing you to select images from your iPhoto albums. Use this palette to add images to your menus, slideshows, and tracks or store images in your Assets tab for later use.

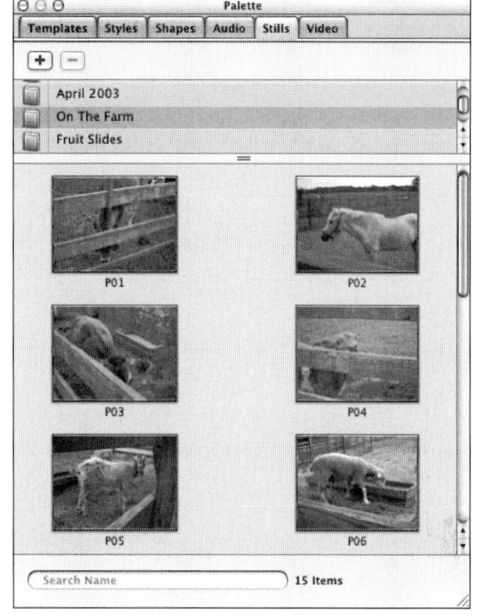

The Video Palette

The Video palette offers a collection of folders, from which you can choose individual movies. You can import any QuickTime-readable movie into DVD Studio Pro 2.

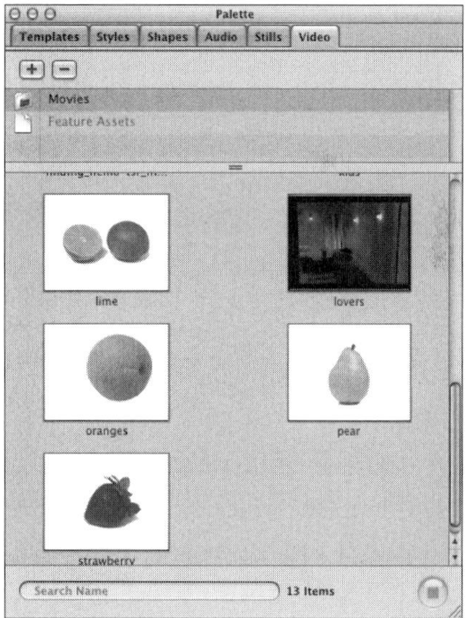

Using the Media Tabs

The following tips will help you make efficient use of the Palette media tabs (Audio, Stills, and Video):

Adding Folders Click the plus (+) button to add folders to the top pane of each media tab. You can add sound folders as new play lists, image folders as new albums, and video folders for viewing and use in your projects.

Your home Music folder (Audio), Pictures folder (Stills), and Movies folder (Video) appear by default in the top pane of the appropriate tab.

Removing Folders Click the minus (-) button to remove selected folders, albums, or play lists from the collection in the top pane. Removing items from the top pane won't affect sound and image libraries in iTunes or iPhoto.

Viewing Folder Contents Click any item in the top pane to view its contents in the bottom pane.

Resizing Panes The resize handle (it looks like a long equal sign) lets you apportion space between the top and bottom panes.

Searching Enter a search term in the space provided to search through your list. The term matches all files that include the string you enter, whether it occurs at the beginning, middle, or end of the filename. For example me matches both Mendelsohn.mp3 and Home.mp3.

Searching from the Palette does not look in or display subfolders.

Previewing Click the play button (right-pointing triangle button, Audio and Video tabs only) to preview sound clips before using them in your project.

To use media from the Palette, drag an item or items onto the DVD Studio Pro 2 menus, tracks, or slideshows you're editing. This lets you use media assets from the Palette just as you would use assets from the Assets tab.

Once you add an asset to any part of your project, the file appears automatically in the Assets tab with its In Use column checked. For example, if you drag an image to a menu and use it as a background, the image file shows up in the Assets tab.

When you want to store assets for later use, rather than using them immediately in the various editors, drag them directly from the Palette to the Assets tab. DVD Studio

Pro 2 adds them to the Assets list, parsing them and encoding them according to the way you set your preferences (choose File > Encoder Settings or press ⌘-E).

Solution: Build and Burn a Looping DVD

Whether you're building a display for your point-of-sale or for a trade show, a looping DVD presents your material without constant restarts and supervision, automatically continuing from the beginning each time the end is reached. In these steps, you'll build a simple looping DVD using the QuickTime movie of your choice.

You don't need to compress your movie or split it into audio and video components for this simple example. You'll use the built-in encoding of DVD Studio Pro 2 to process your QuickTime movie.

Add Your Movie

If you haven't done so already, start a fresh new project (choose File > New or press ⌘-N) before you begin.

1. **Select the Track tab.** In the typical Advanced layout, the Track tab appears in the lower-right quadrant.

2. **Locate the View pop-up menu.** It appears at the top left of your Track window. Track 1 should be selected. DVD Studio Pro automatically adds a track (Track 1) and a menu (Menu 1) to each new project.

3. **Locate V1, your primary video angle.** It appears near the top of your track editor slightly below the View pop-up menu.

4. **Drag a movie onto V1.** You'll find mainfeature.mov on the companion DVD. Watch your cursor. The small second arrow indicates a DVD Studio Pro 2–compatible movie. If you don't see this double-arrow while dragging your movie over V1, select a different movie.

5. **Drop your movie.** DVD Studio Pro 2 adds your movie and splits it into separate video and audio streams, typically V1 and A1. If you've enabled background encoding, DVD Studio Pro 2 begins encoding your movie and audio.

6. **Choose your language.** Locate the pop-up menu just to the right of A1. Choose English or the appropriate language.

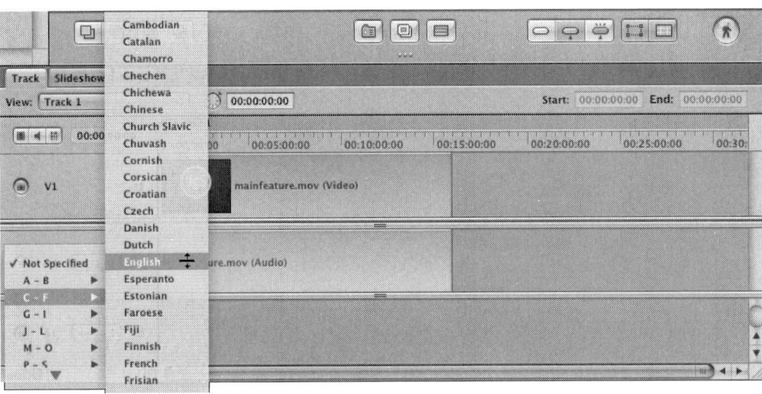

Set Up Your Disc

You'll need to open the Inspector (⌘-⌥-I) before you work through these steps.

7. **Select the Outline tab.** It appears in the top-left quadrant of your main window in default Advanced layouts.

8. **Select UNTITLED_DISC.** The Inspector (⌘-⌥-I) updates to show disc properties.

9. **Rename your disc in the Inspector.** Enter a disc name (for example, FIRSTLOOP) in the Name field of the inspector and press Return. You can use a maximum of 32 characters in the name.

10. **Set First Play.** Choose Tracks And Stories > Track 1 > [Track] from the Inspector's First Play pop-up menu (just below the Name line). First Play specifies what happens when a person inserts your DVD into a player. Here, you tell it to play Track 1.

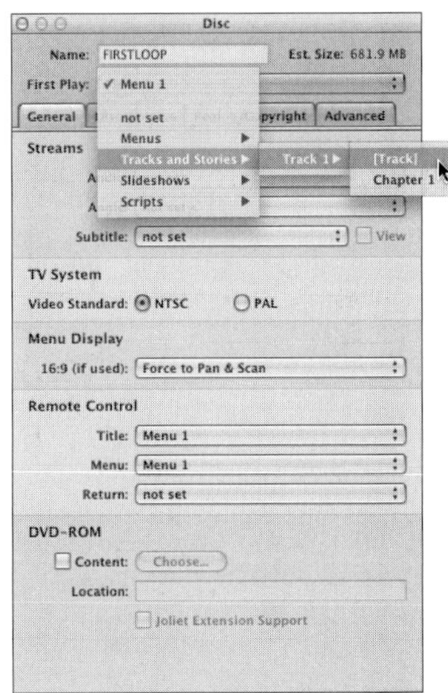

11. **In the Outline tab, choose Tracks > Track 1.** The Inspector updates again, showing your track properties.

12. **Set End Jump.** In the Inspector, choose Tracks And Stories > Track 1 > [Track] from the End Jump pop-up menu. This tells DVD Studio Pro to replay Track 1 after the track finishes playing, creating a loop.

Test and Then Burn Your Disc

Be sure to save your work before proceeding. Choose File > Save (⌘-S) and save to a new project, for example, MyFirstLoop.

13. **Click Simulator.** You'll find this button in your toolbar, toward the middle.

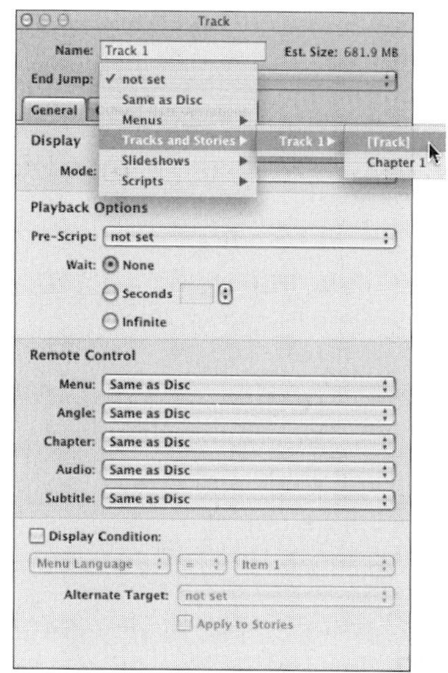

If you don't hear your audio track, be sure you've enabled background encoding and that DVD Studio Pro 2 has fully encoded the audio. The Simulator may not be available while your movie encodes.

14. **Watch the Simulator window.** Your movie should automatically begin to play in the Simulator window and then repeat after its finished. When you're satisfied that everything works as expected, click the Close button to close the Simulator window.

15. **Click Build.** This button appears in your toolbar, toward the right.

16. **Choose a build folder.** Navigate to where you want to build your disc. Select a folder and click Choose.

17. **Wait.** DVD Studio Pro 2 compiles your disc. The Log tab relates the progress of the compilation. Ignore the menu warnings. Your repeating loop disc doesn't use any menus. When the Compile Completed Successfully alert appears, click OK.

18. **Insert a recordable disc.** You might want to use a rewritable disc to keep your DVD costs down. When DVD Studio Pro 2 prompts for a blank disc, it sometimes rejects DVD-RW. To use DVD-RW, insert the disc before formatting and burning. When OS X asks what to do with your disc, click Ignore.

19. **Choose File > Burn (⌘-P).** DVD Studio Pro 2 burns your file to disc.

20. **Test your work.** Walk your disc over to a compatible set-top player and play it back to make sure that everything works as expected. You can also test your disc using Apple's DVD Player application.

Solution: Build and Burn a Looping Slideshow

Creating a slideshow loop is nearly as simple as creating a movie loop. In this project, you'll build a slideshow, add an audio track, and loop the results.

Build Your Slideshow

If you haven't done so already, start a fresh new project (choose File > New or press ⌘-N) before you begin.

1. A folder of slides, named FirstSlides appears on the companion DVD. Drag this folder onto the Slideshows folder in the Outline tab. DVD Studio Pro creates a new slideshow and adds these slides. You can add a maximum of 99 slides in any slideshow.

2. **Add audio.** Select an audio file and drag it into the Overall Audio File well.

3. **Select Fit To Audio.** This option scales slide duration to match the length of the audio track you just added.

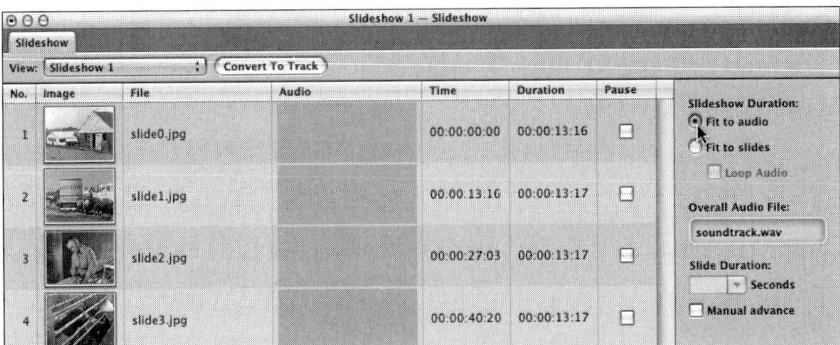

Set Up Your Disc

Be sure to open the Inspector (⌘-⌥-I) before you work through these steps.

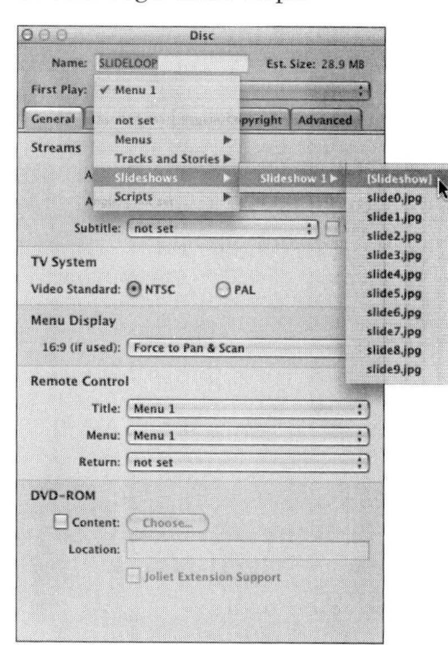

4. **Rename your disc.** Select the Outline tab and select UNTITLED_DISC. Edit the name in the Inspector to reflect your project (for example, SLIDELOOP).

5. **Set First Play.** Choose Slideshows > Slideshow 1 > [Slideshow] from the Inspector's First Play pop-up menu. As you saw with the previous project, First Play specifies what your DVD plays when it's inserted in the player.

6. **In the Outline tab, choose Slideshows > Slideshow 1.** The Inspector displays your slideshow properties.

7. **Set End Jump.** In the End Jump pop-up menu, choose Slideshows > Slideshow 1 > [Slideshow]. This creates a loop, returning to the start of Slideshow 1 after the show finishes.

8. **Delete Track 1.** Select Track 1 in the Outline tab and click Delete. Your project will not compile correctly if it contains a track with no video.

Finishing the DVD

Here, as with the previous project, all that's left is to save, test, and burn.

1. Save your work (choose File > Save or press ⌘-S) to a new project file.

2. Click Simulator to test your project.

3. Finish by writing your looping slideshow to disc (Build then Format, as you did in the previous solution).

In DVD Studio Pro 2, Build and Format are two distinct operations. Build creates structure, producing the folders (Video_TS, Audio_TS) and files (BUP, IFO, VOB, and so on) that make up your DVD. Format instructs DVD Studio Pro 2 to write those files to a blank DVD.

Expect the multiplexing ("muxing" the audio and video) of your project into the DVD-Video Specification file structure to take a few minutes depending on the speed of your computer.

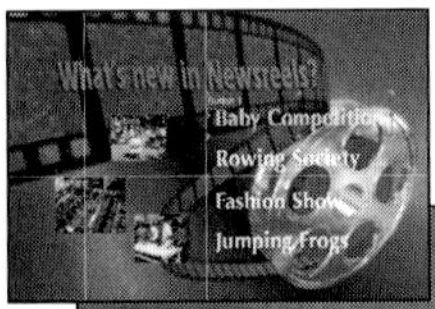

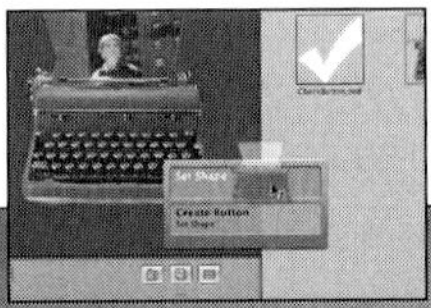

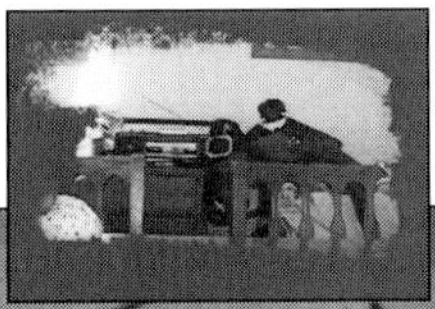

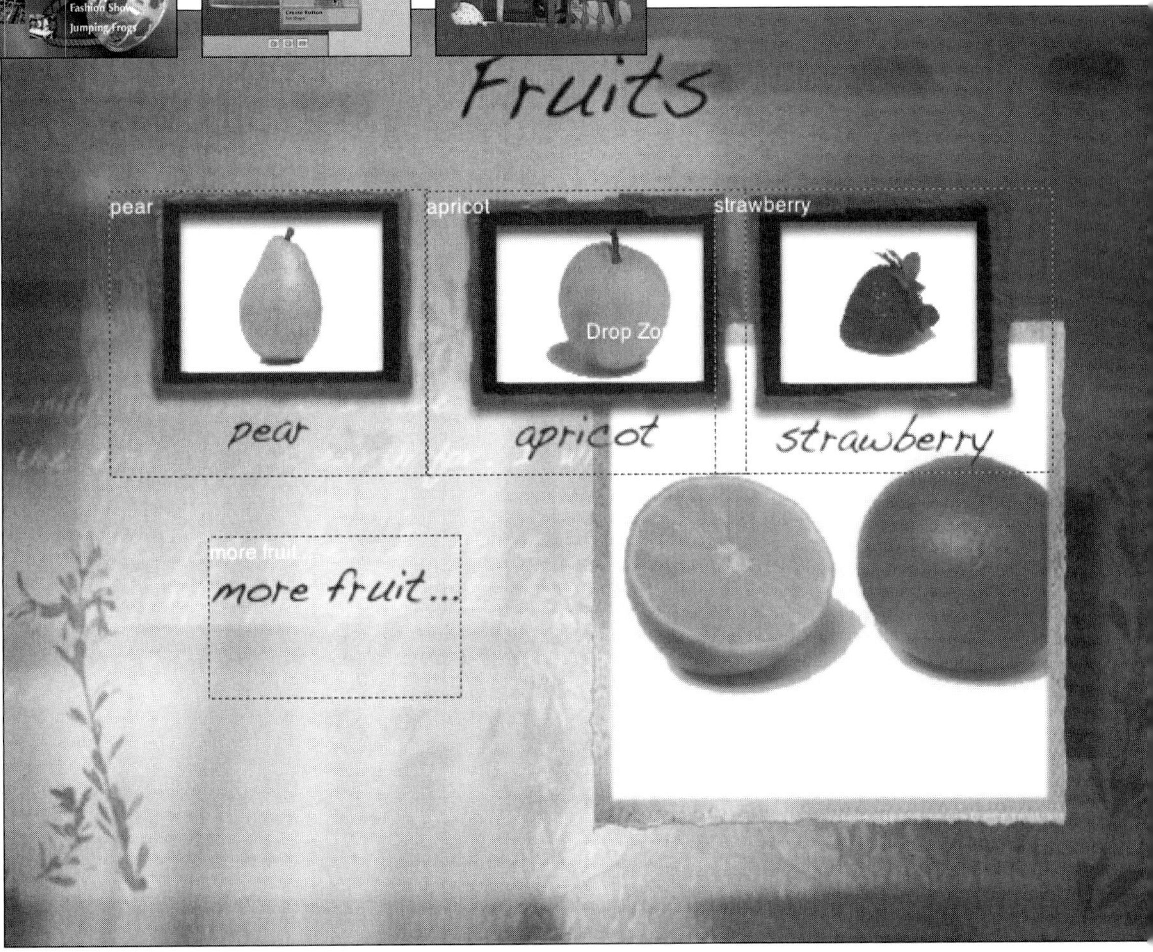

Fruits

pear

apricot

strawberry

Drop Zone

pear

apricot

strawberry

more fruit...

Building Basic Menus

DVD Studio Pro 2 menus add a layer of interaction to your DVD projects. At their simplest level, menus allow your audience to choose which video feature to watch or to select from a list of scenes. Advanced menus go further. They can offer different playback versions (such as a standard release and a director's cut), playback language choices, and more. In this chapter you'll discover the essential components of DVD Studio Pro 2 menus and learn how to build some basic project menus.

Chapter Contents

Types of DVD Studio Pro 2 Menus

You can build a DVD menu in more than one way. DVD Studio Pro 2 offers several techniques to create interactive DVD screens, each with its own strengths and weaknesses. Here are the kinds of menus you might build using DVD Studio Pro 2.

Standard Of all the DVD Studio Pro 2 menu styles, standard menus come closest to mimicking the iDVD menu design experience—although, surprisingly enough, they're the most complicated to build. Standard menus, the creation of which is discussed in this chapter, allow you to design your screens directly in DVD Studio Pro 2, adding buttons, sound, motion, text, and graphics to incrementally build your menu.

Overlay For the most part, overlay menus (which are properly a subset of standard menus) move menu design out of DVD Studio Pro 2 and into Photoshop or some other image layout program. The tools in Adobe Photoshop, OmniGraffle Professional, and so forth help lay out your buttons and design the way they highlight. Overlay menus come in varying degrees of complexity, including simple (using black-and-white overlays) and advanced (using grayscale or color overlays) highlight techniques.

Layered Also called Photoshop Layer Menus, these menus offer the greatest control over the way that buttons look and behave, providing full color and graphics for each stage of the button selection process. Layered menus let you break out of the "button box" and use the entire screen for feedback when you select items. Unfortunately, layered menus have several drawbacks: you can't use motion backgrounds or background audio, and interaction feedback is slowed down.

Mixed Mixed menus combine layered menus with overlay and standard menus to combine features from all presentation styles.

Widescreen (16:9) Widescreen menus, which can include any of the previous menu types, allow you to provide a menu presentation that fits both widescreen television sets and regular aspect (4:3) TVs.

Motion Motion menus refer to those menus, either standard or overlaid, that use moving video in their backgrounds. Motion menus are not a different class of menus, just a variation.

Identifying Menu Elements

Text, buttons, drop zones, and backgrounds each play a role in DVD Studio Pro 2 menus. As you can see in Figure 2.1, they create the overall look and feel of the menu, providing a visual theme for user interactions.

Text (A) Text adds descriptive but nonfunctioning labels to your menus. Use text to add explanatory titles or to lend an alphabetic flair to your menu art.

Figure 2.1 Elements of a DVD menu: Text Ⓐ, Buttons Ⓑ, Drop Zones Ⓒ, Background Ⓓ

Buttons (B) Buttons link to DVD assets, such as movies, slideshows, submenus, and more. They allow viewers to interact with the DVD, choosing what to see and what to do. Buttons come in a wide variety of shapes and looks—text, video, and graphics. Mix and match to build a distinctive look.

Buttons are the single element that most differentiate the *kinds* of menus available in DVD Studio Pro 2. The way you build buttons distinguishes standard menus, for example, from layered menus.

Drop Zones (C) Drop zones add art over your menu background, using still and moving elements. Like text, drop zones are nonfunctional. If you're familiar with iDVD, don't fall into the trap of thinking that drop zones are just for video. In DVD Studio Pro 2, drop zones add still images as well as moving images.

Backgrounds (D) Backgrounds provide a backdrop for all the features within your menus. Choose from full-screen video or stills and add optional looping audio to suit your taste.

Menu Creation Tools

You don't create menus solely within the confines of the Menu tab. Several other windows lend a hand in the menu-building process. Take a look through this list of tools, all of which directly assist with menu preparation:

The Menu Editor (⌘-4) The interactive Menu Editor (available from the Menu tab) helps you lay out menu items, such as buttons, drop zones, and text. Use the editor to build logical connections between menu elements and project assets.

The Outline Tab(⌘-5). The Outline tab provides direct access to the components that make up your project. Dragging items from the Outline tab to the Menu Editor provides an easy way to set connections for your menu and to populate buttons and drop zones with visual content.

The Assets Tab (⌘-1) You can drag items from the Assets tab to the Menu Editor to set menu backgrounds, assign sounds, build buttons and tracks, and more.

The Inspector (⌘-⌥-I) The Inspector helps you customize the way your menus and buttons look and behave. You'll use the Inspector a lot when working with menus.

The Connections Tab (⌘-2) You'll find a chart-based overview of all your menu connections in the Connections tab. Use this pane to review the material in your menu and make sure that each button leads to the asset you think it does.

The Simulator (⌘-⌥-0) There's no better way to test your menus than simulation. The Simulator window offers interactive previews, letting you check your menus before you build and burn your discs.

Project QuickStart: Moving from iDVD

As of version 2, DVD Studio Pro 2 lets you import iDVD projects. This feature does two important things: it lets you add DVD Studio Pro 2 finishing touches to your iDVD work before you burn; and it lets you use iDVD's intuitive menu editor to design your interface, taking advantage of iDVD's wealth of built-in themes.

To import an iDVD project, choose File > Open (⌘-0). Navigate to your iDVD project file (.dvdproj), select it, and click Open. Depending on the extent of the project, it may take a minute or two for DVD Studio Pro 2 to read in the entire file.

Don't attempt to modify your iDVD project "in place." Instead, choose File > Save As (⌘-Shift-S) to save your updated project out to a new DVD Studio Pro 2 project file (.dspproj).

Unfortunately, you cannot import third-party custom themes without a lot of extra work. DVD Studio Pro 2 stores its collection of iDVD theme material in /Library/Application Support/DVD Studio Pro 2/iDVD.

Looking at the Menu Editor

When you click the Menu tab and open the Menu Editor, you're greeted by a large central workspace and a number of buttons and menus. Among these, you'll find the following features to make the most out of your menu-editing tasks.

View Control (A) Click the View control to select the menu you wish to view from a list of all project menus. When you do so, the central viewing area updates to reflect the menu you're building.

Language Control (B) Click the Language control to choose the menu language you want to work on.

Settings Control (C) The Settings control helps specify how your Menu Editor looks and acts. Settings include safe zones, pixel shapes, and more. Although you may find it easier to use regular program menus or keyboard shortcuts, the Settings pop-up does join several menu-related settings into a centralized presentation.

Arrangement Controls (D) Use these buttons to reprioritize items within your DVD menu, specifying which items are in front and which are in back. In order from left to right, the controls are Move To Back (⌘-Shift-B), Move To Front (⌘-Shift-F), Move Backwards (⌘-]), and Move Forwards (⌘-[).

Figure 2.2 The Menu Editor. View control Ⓐ, Language control Ⓑ, Settings control Ⓒ, Arrangement controls Ⓓ, Add buttons Ⓔ, Button state controls Ⓕ, Outlines button Ⓖ, Guides button Ⓗ, Menu Motion button Ⓘ, Show/hide toolbar control Ⓙ

Add Buttons (E) From left-to-right, these buttons add linked DVD submenus (⌘-⌥-Y), new (and empty) slideshows (⌘-⌥-K), and new tracks (⌘-⌥-T).

Button State Controls (F) These buttons select how you'll view DVD buttons within your menu. Choose from (left-to-right) Normal, Selected, and Activated. (Press W to toggle between these three options.)

Outlines Button (G) Click this button to toggle DVD button outlines on and off. Button outlines offer a simple visual overview indicating where DVD buttons are placed. This comes in handy when you can't quite remember where you added a button, but at the same time it can clutter the Menu Editor workspace.

Guides Button (H) Like Photoshop, DVD Studio Pro 2 lets you drag layout guides from the rulers and use them to snap items into place. The button on the bottom right of the menu shows and hides ruler guides

Clicking the Guides Button doesn't affect the display of dynamic layout guides.

Menu Motion Button (I) Click this button (or press ⌘-J or the spacebar) to toggle DVD menu motion on and off. When this button is enabled, you'll preview the motion elements in your menu. When this button is disabled, you'll free a good deal of memory and allow your computer to run significantly faster.

Show/Hide Toolbar Control (J) Clicking this control shows or hides the Menu Editor's bottom toolbar. Click once to close. Click again to open. Hiding the toolbar provides a little more space for the display of your DVD menu.

Using the Outline Tab to Manage Menus

The Outline tab (⌘-5) contains an outline of your project and its component elements. It offers five folders, listing the DVD menus, tracks (and stories), scripts, slideshows, and languages being used. Among other features, you'll use this tab to create and manage your project DVD menus.

Here are some of the menu management tasks you can accomplish using the Outline tab:

Creating Menus. Choose one of the following options to add DVD menus to your project:

- Choose Project > Add To Project > Menu (⌘-Y) or Project > Add To Project > Layered Menu (⌘-Shift-Y).
- Click the Add Menu or Add Layered Menu button in the toolbar.
- Ctrl-click/right-click the background of the Outline tab and choose Add > Menu or Add > Layered Menu.

Naming Menus By naming DVD menus, you make it simpler to identify and use menu elements in your projects. For example, you might want to link to a submenu that contains several "making-of" featurettes. It's easier to recognize the name Casting Featurette than to recall that Menu 7 contains the items you need. DVD Studio Pro 2 allows you to edit DVD menu names in two ways: directly in the Outline tab or by using the Menu Inspector (⌘-⌥-I). In either case, select the DVD menu you want to rename in the Outline tab. Then click the menu name in the Outline tab, or select the Name field in the Inspector. Edit the menu name as desired and press Return to finish.

Reordering Menus Keep your Outline tab organized. Always list your menus in the order that makes the most sense for you and for your project. To reorder DVD menus, simply drag an item to its new position in the menu list. Figure 2.3 shows the Outline tab during a reordering operation.

Duplicating Menus You can always duplicate a DVD menu and then edit it. This allows you to test interface styles in parallel without making permanent changes to one menu or another. To duplicate a DVD menu, select it in the Outline tab. Choose Edit > Duplicate (⌘-D) or ⌘-click/right-click and choose Duplicate from the pop-up.

Deleting Menus Remove unused and unneeded DVD menus to keep your projects tight. To delete a menu, select its name in the Outline tab. Then choose Edit > Delete; or press the Delete key; or Ctrl-click/right-click and choose Delete from the Outline tab pop-up.

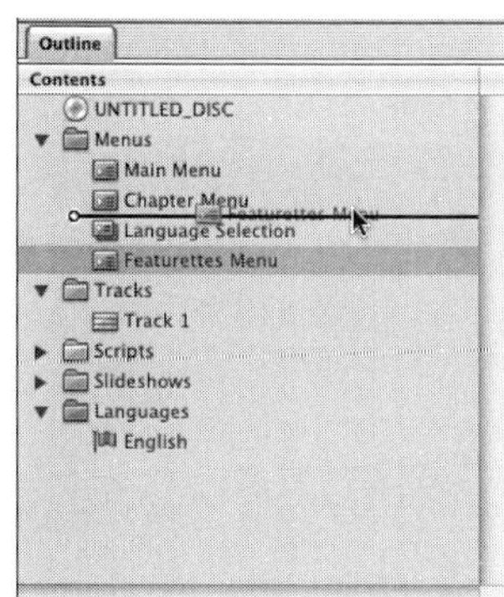

Figure 2.3 Reorder your DVD menus by dragging items into place in the Outline tab. Use whatever order most appeals to you and/or assists in organizing your project. The order has little or no effect on your final DVD.

Building Basic Menus

Once you've created a DVD menu element in the Outline tab, you can move your attention to the Menu Editor and begin to populate that menu with buttons, text, drop zones, and more. These steps describe the basic process you'll work through when building menus.

1.   **Organize your workspace.** Arrange the various windows and tabs so you'll have access to each of the menu creation tools described earlier in this chapter. Make

sure your Menu Editor is both visible (click the Menu tab) and very large. You'll concentrate most of your design effort within this window. Take a moment to enable those DVD Studio Pro 2 features, such as guides, rulers, and so forth, you use while building menus.

2.   **Choose a DVD menu to work on.** Follow the instructions from the last section to create, name, and order your menus. Select the name of the DVD menu you want to edit from the View pop-up at the top left of the Menu Editor window.

3.   **Add your menu items.** Add buttons, drop zones, text, and backgrounds to your DVD menu.

4.   **Organize your interface.** Resize, move, and otherwise customize the items in your DVD menu.

5.   **Prepare your buttons.** Connect your buttons to the assets they link to—movies, submenus, slideshows, and so forth—and then add some highlights to provide visual feedback in your DVD menus.

6.   **Test your disc.** Set the first-run property of your disc, and then simulate how the disc will play.

Enabling Design Features

Here are some design features you'll want to enable before you get down to work building menus:

Turn on Button Outline. Choose View > Show Button Outline And Name. Alternatively, click Button Outline on the bottom right of the Menu window. When active, this feature shows the location of all menu buttons, whether selected or not, and keeps you from "losing" buttons during the design process.

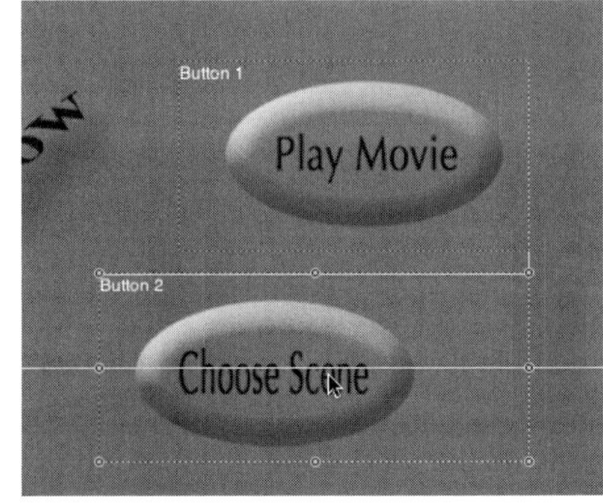

Enable Dynamic Guides. Dynamic guides help you align object centers and edges. Choose DVD Studio Pro 2 > Preferences (⌘-,) > Alignment. Check Show Dynamic Guides At Object Center and Show Dynamic Guides At Object Edges, and then click OK. When enabled, yellow guide lines appear as you drag items, helping you snap items into place.

Use ⌘-drag to bypass dynamic positioning guides and snapping. The Show/Hide Guides button at the bottom right of the Menu Editor does not affect dynamic guides.

Use layout aids. Handy layout options include the following:

- View > Show Guides (⌘-;)
- View > Show Rulers (⌘-R)
- View > Title Safe Area (⌘-Shift-E)
- View > Action Safe Area (⌘-⌥-E).

In DVD Studio Pro 2, guides and rulers work much the same as they do in Photoshop.

Using Drag and Drop to Build Menu Items

DVD Studio Pro 2 lets you drag items into the Menu Editor to create backgrounds, drop zones, and buttons. You can drag files from the Finder, drag assets from the Assets tab, or drag elements from the Outline tab to build up your menu one item at a time. By dragging and dropping you can add the following:

Video and Stills As Figures 2.4 and 2.5 show, you can drag video clips and still images onto the Menu Editor to create buttons, drop zones, backgrounds, and more. (To set menu backgrounds—only menu backgrounds—directly, you can drag clips and images to the menus listed in the Outline tab.)

Sounds Drag sounds into the Menu Editor to add background audio to your menus. Choose Set Audio from the drop palette. (As with menu backgrounds, you can drag sounds to the Outline tab menu names to set background audio.)

Tracks, Stories, and Slideshows Drag tracks, stories, or slideshows from the Outline tab to the Menu Editor to add buttons linked to those elements.

Unfortunately, early releases of DVD Studio Pro 2 tend to "hold on" to original versions of assets, even when you remove them and reload updated versions. (This particularly occurs after simulating.) If the Menu Editor does not seem to be responding properly to your changes, save your work and launch the program again.

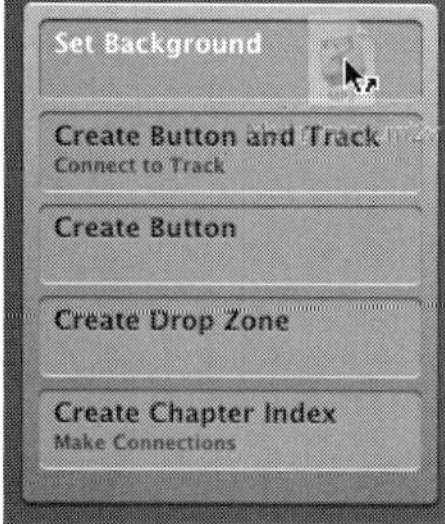

Figure 2.4 This drop palette appears when you drag a video asset onto your Menu Editor; you can drag videos from the Finder or from the Assets tab. Choose Set Background to assign that asset as the background of your motion menu. As you can see, you also have other options. Create Button And Track creates a new track from your asset and builds a graphical button that links to the track. Create Button builds a button that displays your video. Create Drop Zone places your asset as an additional background graphic. Create Chapter Index uses your video's chapter markers to build an entire scene-selection menu.

Figure 2.5 Choose from these options when dragging images onto the Menu Editor. Set Background assigns your image to the menu's background. Set Overlay builds menu highlight zones, using the "Photoshop layers" style of menu creation. Create Button creates a button that displays your image. Create Drop Zone adds a new background graphic. Create Submenu builds a new menu using your image as the menu background; a button appears in your original menu that links to the new menu.

Creating Buttons, Drop Zones, and Text

DVD Studio Pro 2 offers several drag-to-create variations that let you create buttons, drop zones, and text.

Create Buttons Drag on the Menu Editor background to create buttons.

Create Drop Zones ⌥-drag to create drop zones.

Create Text Double-click to add text.

 Adding the Shift key to a drag squares drop zones and constrains buttons to a 4:3 aspect.

Customizing Menu Items

After creating menu items, you can do the following:

Select Items Click any item to select it. Shift-click adds new items to your selection. ⌘-drag selects everything that intersects the drag.

Resize Items Select buttons or drop zones, and use the sizing handles to change item dimensions.

Rotate Items The Inspector lets you rotate drop zones and text via the rotation control at the bottom of the pane. Figure 2.6 shows how.

Name Items Select a button or a drop zone, and then use the Inspector to meaningfully rename it. Item names appear in the Menu Editor when you enable Show Button Outline.

Duplicate Items ⌥-drag selected items to duplicate them. Alternatively, choose Edit > Duplicate (⌘-D).

Delete Items Choose Edit > Delete or press the Delete key to remove selected items from your menu.

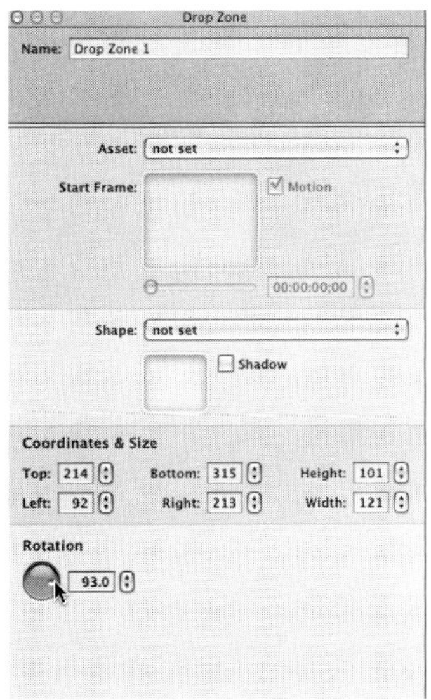

Figure 2.6 DVD Studio Pro 2 allows you to rotate drop zones and text. Select the item you want to rotate in the Menu Editor, and open the Inspector (⌘-⌥-I). Adjust the rotation control (found at the bottom left of the pane) as needed. Small angles (15 degrees, for example) work particularly well for many menu items. You can't rotate buttons. Unrotated rectangular buttons are the rule for DVDs.

Customizing Text

With text, you can add simple labels to your menus—and more. As Figure 2.7 shows, DVD Studio Pro 2 offers flexible control over menu text. Here are some tips for working with words and menus:

Figure 2.7 DVD Studio Pro 2 offers a high degree of text control directly within the program. Choose the font, size, alignment, orientation, rotation, and shadowing you need to produce the menu labels you design.

Add Text Double-click the menu background to create a new text field, and then type to add text. Alternatively, ⌘-⌥-drag adds a new text field, centered within the start and end of the drag.

Edit Text DVD Studio Pro 2 allows you to directly edit selected text. Alternatively, open the Inspector (⌘-⌥-I) and make your edits in the Text field.

Assign Fonts and Colors Open the Font and Color palettes (choose Format > Font > Show Fonts; choose Format > Font > Show Colors) to select typefaces and tints for your text. Select the text you want to modify, and then select new attributes from these floating windows. In addition, you can set font attributes by choosing from the following:

- **Bold**   Format > Font > Bold (⌘-B)
- **Italic**   Format > Font > Italic (⌘-I)
- **Underline**   Format > Font > Underline (⌘-U)

Align Text Select the text you want to align, and then choose Format > Text > Align Left (⌘-{ *or* ⌘-Shift-[), Format > Text > Align Center (⌘-| *or* ⌘-Shift-\), Format > Text > Align Right (⌘-} *or* ⌘-Shift-]), or Format > Text > Justify.

Add Drop Shadow The Drop Shadow check box appears in the Text Object Inspector just to the right of the Text Edit box. Check to add a drop shadow to your text.

Populating Drop Zones and Buttons

Drop zones add background video and images to your DVD menus. Use them to provide extra visual interest for more intricate menu presentations. A video drop zone might add a touch of movement to an otherwise still background. You might use an image drop zone to place a logo onto your menu or a small still from your feature. Whether you're adding moving images or stills, drop zones make it quick and convenient to produce compelling menu visuals.

Buttons are more active. They exist in the foreground rather than the background and allow viewers to make on-screen choices to watch movies, select viewing languages, and more. As you can with drop zones, you can spice up your buttons by adding pictures and video. In addition, buttons offer features not available to drop zones, such as labels and drop shadows.

Here are some tips that will help you make the most out of your drop zones and buttons:

Add assets. To fill a drop zone or a button, drag a movie or image asset onto it. Do not release the mouse. When the drop palette appears, choose Set Asset. You can only add proper assets, those videos or stills that appear in your Assets tab. Unlike iDVD,

DVD Studio Pro 2 won't let you add slideshows (or tracks, for that matter) to drop zones and buttons.

Select a start frame. Use the Drop Zone Inspector (shown in Figure 2.8) to choose a start frame for your video. The Button Inspector, which is similar, works in the same manner. To display only the selected frame, without movement, clear the Motion check box.

Figure 2.8 The Drop Zone Inspector helps you control the way your drop zones look and move. Use the Inspector to choose a start frame for your video or to set a shape for your drop zone. Other useful features include the Motion toggle check box, the Rotation control, and the Asset pop-up.

Adjust image placement. The shape of your drop zone or button limits the portion of your image or video that can be seen. To move your asset within the drop zone bounds, press ⌥-Shift and drag.

Select a shape. DVD Studio Pro 2 shapes let you frame button and drop zone assets in creative and surprising ways. Shapes add complex forms. Figure 2.9 shows how to add a shape to your menu items.

You can also set shapes by selecting from the Shape pop-up in the Inspector.

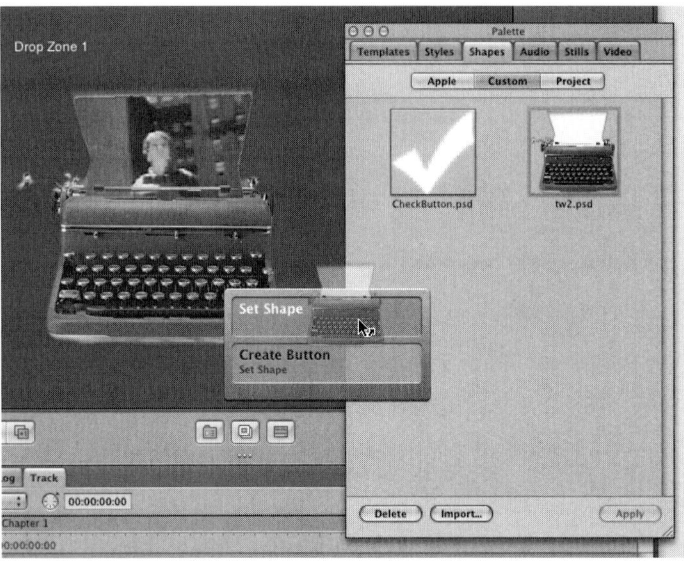

Figure 2.9 DVD Studio Pro 2 shapes transform drop zones and buttons. To apply a shape, open the Palette (⌘-⌥-P), click the Shapes tab, and drag a shape from the Palette onto the item in question. Choose Set Shape from the drop palette. DVD Studio Pro 2 overlays your asset with the shape you select, using masking, transparency and overall shape information to produce the final look. To adjust the placement of your asset within the shape, hold ⌥-Shift and drag the asset.

Working with Button Text

Unlike drop zones, buttons offer optional text in the form of labels. To add label text, select a button and open the Button Inspector (⌘-⌥-I). Enter your label in the Text field, which is toward the bottom of the Inspector, as shown in Figure 2.10.

Customize button labels the same way you customize the text you add directly to your menus. Click a button to select the item you want to work on. Then click the label to select the text. Choose Format > Fonts > Show Fonts (⌘-T) and Format > Fonts > Show Colors (⌘-Shift-T) to open the Font and Color palettes. Use these palettes to set the typeface, size, and color for your button labels.

Shapes do more than frames: they offer a way to create reusable custom highlights that don't require video or image assets. Shapes can provide small visual cues that work perfectly with text. Figure 2.11 shows what a text-based menu with shape highlights might look like.

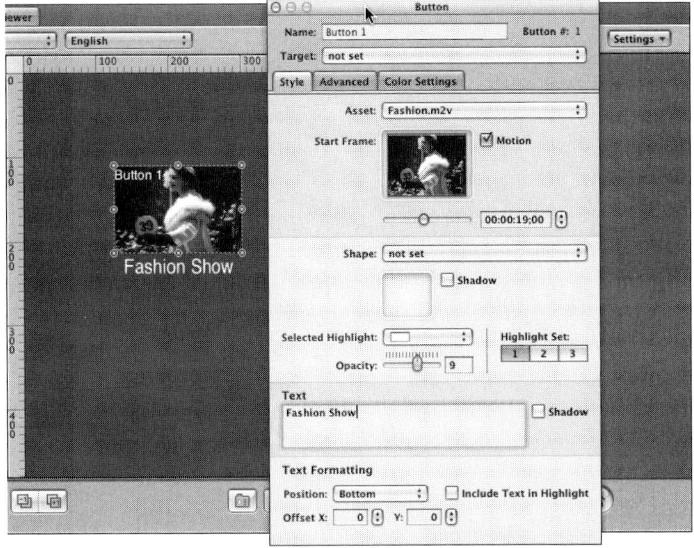

Figure 2.10 Add text labels to your button by editing the Text field found near the bottom of the Button Inspector. Check Shadow to add a drop shadow to your label. The Position pop-up specifies where to place the label with respect to the button shape. Choose from Bottom, Top, Right, Left, and Center. Choosing Center sets the label directly on the button shape. When you check Include Text In Highlight, DVD Studio Pro 2 adds a highlight to the label of your selected button, as well as to the button itself, during DVD playback.

Figure 2.11 Shapes allow you to build reusable custom highlights that don't require overlays to work. Use shapes to add simple emphasis to your text-based menus. DVD Studio Pro 2 makes it easy to build and import your own shapes for this purpose.

Follow these steps to create text and shape menus.

1.   **Choose a shape.** Open the Palette (⌘-⌥-P) and select the shape you want to use. Select a shape that provides simple highlighting. Instructions on building and importing your own shapes follow at the end of this chapter.

Two samples (CheckButton.psd and HandShape.psd) appear on the DVD that accompanies this book.

2. **Drag the shape to the menu editor.** Choose Create Button-Set Shape. A new button appears.

3. **Add placeholder text.** Open the Inspector (⌘-⌥-I) and enter some text (the actual text does not matter). Use the Font and Color palettes to customize the overall look of the text.

4. **Duplicate the button.** ⌥-drag the button to create as many copies of your original button as needed. Each button will share the same shape and the same text font and color.

5. **Edit the text.** Select each button in turn and add meaningful text.

Linking Buttons

In and of themselves, buttons don't actually *do* anything. Buttons come to life only when you link them to things, that is, when you add a *target*. Targets tell buttons what to do after they're pressed. Should the DVD start playing a movie? Should it link to a submenu? Start a slideshow? Play back just an edited portion (a "story") of your main feature? The way you link your buttons specifies how each button behaves.

Here, for your consideration, are three ways to set button targets in your project:

Use the contextual menu. Select a DVD menu button. Ctrl-click (right-click) and choose a target, as shown in Figure 2.12.

Use the drop palette. Drag a track, slideshow, menu, and so on from the Outline tab (⌘-5) onto your button, and choose Connect To from the drop palette.

Use the Inspector. Select your button, open the Button Inspector, and choose an item from the Target pop-up. As you can see in Figure 2.10 earlier in this chapter, the Target selection pop-up appears at the top of the pane, just below the button name. Not Set indicates that the button has no target as yet.

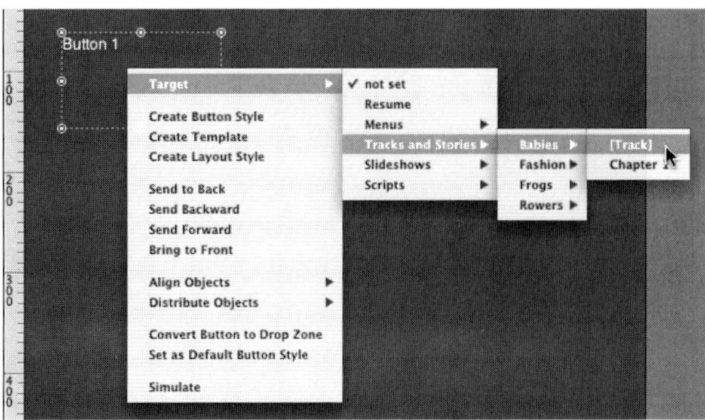

Figure 2.12 This contextual menu appears when you Ctrl-click (right-click) a selected button. Choose a target from the project elements listed. These elements correspond for the most part to those listed in your Outline tab.

Adding Button Highlights

DVD menus use highlights to indicate a selected button. When viewers use the remote control to move the selection from button to button, the highlight offers the visual feedback they need to make a proper choice. Without highlights, there's no suggestion as to which button has been selected and what will happen when your viewer clicks the Play button or presses the Return key.

Although it's possible to indicate button selection in more artistic ways, simple rectangular highlights play an important role in building working basic menus. Follow these steps to add rectangular highlights to your buttons.

1. **Select a button.** Select the button to which you want to add a highlight.

2. **Open the Inspector.** The Button Inspector offers three highlight sets, each with a default behavior.

3. **Click Highlight Set 3.** Set 3 defaults to a light purple-blue overcast that highlights your button rectangle.

4. **Optionally, include text in highlight.** If you've added a label to your button and want to extend the highlight to include it, check Include Text In Highlight. The option appears toward the bottom right of the Inspector

Creating aleady linked Buttons

The Menu Editor offers three special functions that create outline elements at the same time as they add buttons to your DVD menus. The editor buttons that control these functions are found at the bottom middle of your Menu tab. From left to right, these buttons add linked submenus (⌘-⌥-Y), new (and empty) slideshows (⌘-⌥-K), and new tracks (⌘-⌥-T). When clicked, they do three things: First, they create the element in question, adding it to the Outline tab. Second, they create a DVD button in the Menu Editor. Finally, they link that button's target to the element in question—and back. The element's end jump connects back to the menu and this button.

DVD Studio Pro 2 also offers two more options to add pre-linked buttons:

Create Buttons From Outline Items Drag items from your Outline tab to the Menu Editor and select Create Button from the Drop Palette. Use this method to add buttons that link to tracks, scripts, and more.

Create Buttons From Movies Drag movies from the Finder or from your Assets tab onto the Menu Editor. Choose Create Button And Track. DVD Studio Pro 2 builds a new track, adds your movie, and builds a pre-linked button that connects to it.

Setting the First Play

When you insert a DVD into a set-top player, the player looks for an item—a menu, a track, whatever—that it can start to play. It's up to you to decide which item this is. Follow these steps to prepare your disc to run properly upon insertion.

1. **Open the Outline tab** (⌘-5). The Outline tab contains the entire hierarchy of your disc and its elements.

2. **Select the disc.** It appears at the top of the window; the first item in the list.

3. **Name the disc.** Open the Disc Inspector (⌘-⌥-I) and edit the Name field that appears at the top of the pane. Setting a name specifies how your disc will be listed when inserted into a computer's DVD drive. It's good practice to add meaningful names to your discs.

4. **Set First Play.** Use the Inspector's pop-up to set the disc's First Play. Choose a track to add an introductory video or an FBI warning. Choose a menu to jump directly to an interactive screen. You can select from all the menus, tracks and stories, slideshows, and scripts you've built in your project. The item you select specifies what happens when the DVD begins to play.

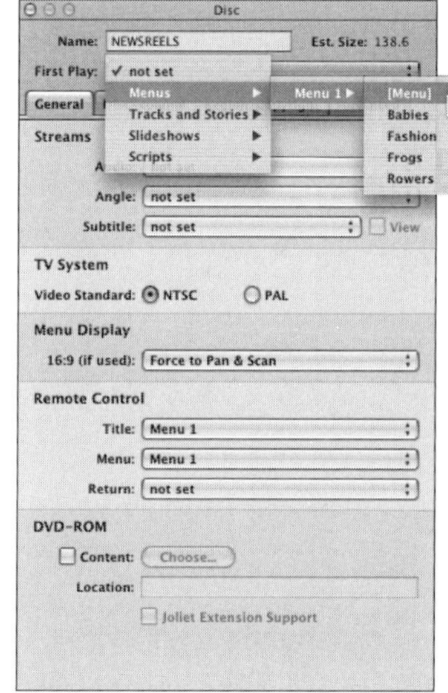

5. **Save.** Save your project changes to your hard disk.

Checking Your Menus

When you assemble your menus, you make a lot of assumptions. You assume that this button links to that asset because you vaguely remember setting its target. You assume that you set up your submenu correctly or you built your chapter list just right. Break through your assumptions by checking your facts—and by checking your menus. DVD Studio Pro 2 offers three main lines of defense against errors, which might include targeting errors, errors of omission, errors of design, and so forth. These defenses include the Inspector, the Connections tab, and the Simulator. Each plays a role helping you check your work.

- The Inspector offers an item-by-item approach to examining your project. Use the various panes and tabs within the Inspector window to spot-check connections and make sure you've set other item choices correctly.

- As Figure 2.13 shows, the Connections tab offers a broader overview. It shows how disc elements connect. Choose an item from the Outline tab—a menu, a story, a slideshow, and so on—and visually scan the links. Make sure that each item connects the way you expect.

- Go beyond simple fact-checking and use the Simulator to test your disc. The simulator does exactly what the name implies. It lets you test your disc using a simulated remote control to navigate through all the features in your project. If things don't work as expected, stop the simulation. Go back to the project and fix your mistakes. Then try again until you're satisfied with the way your project behaves.

Solution: Build a Custom Highlight Shape

You need not limit yourself to the default set of shapes in the Palette. DVD Studio Pro 2 makes it easy to design, build, and install your own shapes. Here's how you can create a highlight shape for the text menus discussed earlier in this chapter.

1. **Launch Adobe Photoshop.** Create a new RGB transparent image. Large works better than small; 200 × 200 is a good size. You can always resize your large shapes downward in DVD Studio Pro 2. Shapes that start too small can't be enlarged without compromising visual integrity.

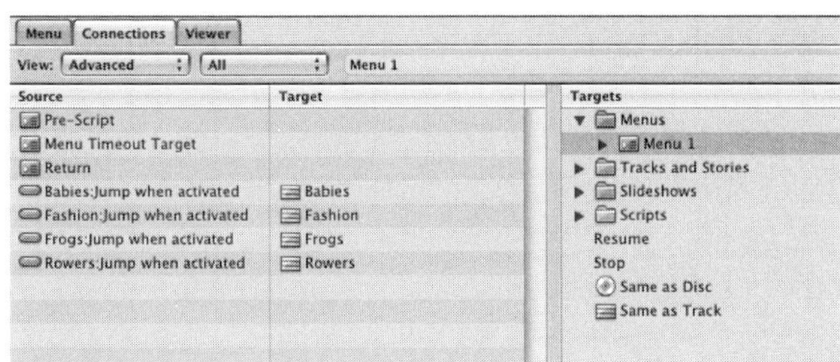

Figure 2.13 The Connections tab (⌘-2) lets you view connections in a single integrated window. Use the Outline tab to select the item whose connections you want to view. The connections appear in the pane on the left. Set connections by dragging items from the right pane onto the left or by using the pop-up (Ctrl-click/right-click the Target field in the left pane). The Connections tab is discussed further in Chapter 7.

2. **Reset your colors.** Press Shift-D. Click the invert-colors arrow at the bottom of the toolbar to reverse the colors, placing black in the background and white in the foreground.

3. **Draw a white shape.** This shape acts as your highlight. Pick a simple, identifiable shape that offers a clear visual highlight. Rasterize your shape (choose Layer > Rasterize > Shape) to convert it to a normal Photoshop layer.

4. **Duplicate your shape.** Select your shape layer in the Layers palette. Choose Layer > Duplicate Layer and click OK. Repeat to create a second copy. Name one layer Icon, a second Highlight, and a third Mask FG.

 DVD Studio Pro shapes must contain at least two layers, preferably the three or four described below. Single layer shapes are not supported.

5. **Create two new blank layers.** Fill the first layer with black. Leave the second layer blank. Name the blank layer Shape. Name the black layer Mask.

6. **Organize the layers.** Place the layers in this order: Icon, Highlight, Shape, Mask FG, and Mask.

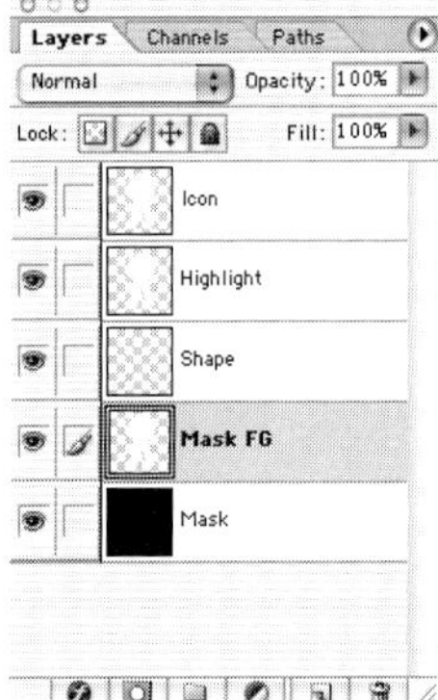

7. **Merge the mask.** Select the Mask FG layer. Choose Layer > Merge Down (⌘-E). Mask FG and Mask merge, creating a new layer called Mask. The black and white portions of the mask help DVD Studio Pro 2 know what to show (white) and what to hide (black) in your video.

8. **Save to disk.** Save your work to disk as MyFirstShape.psd and then return to DVD Studio Pro 2.

9. **Open the Palette.** Press ⌘-⌥-P. Open the Shapes tab, and choose Custom.

10. **Import your shape file.** Click Import. Navigate to your new shape, select it, and click Import. DVD Studio Pro 2 imports your new shape and adds it to the Custom Shapes palette. A copy of the imported PSD file appears in /Library/Application Support/DVD Studio Pro/Shapes.

11. **Test your shape.** Make sure your new shape works correctly by dragging it to the menu editor. Choose Create Button/Set Shape as shown here. A blank empty square appears.

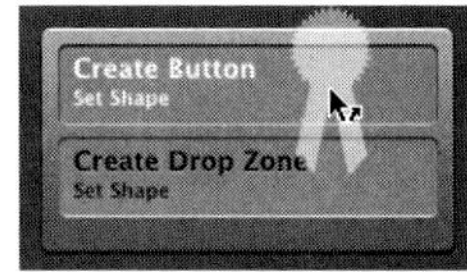

12. **Show the selected state.** Choose Edit > Select All (⌘-A) to locate your new "empty" button. Then choose View > Button State Selected. Your new button highlight appears.

Solution: Build a Custom Drop Zone Shape

Drop-zone shapes are similar to highlight shapes in structure, but the way you use each layer differs. Here, you'll create a simple framed shape.

1. **Launch Photoshop.** Create a new, well-sized (300 × 300, for example) RGB transparent image.

2. **Create your layers.** As with the highlight shape, create four new empty layers—Icon, Highlight, Shape, and Mask. The Highlight layer remains empty throughout these steps.

3. **Design your frame.** The frame should be a full-color graphic with a significant empty space in its middle. Add the artwork to the Shape layer.

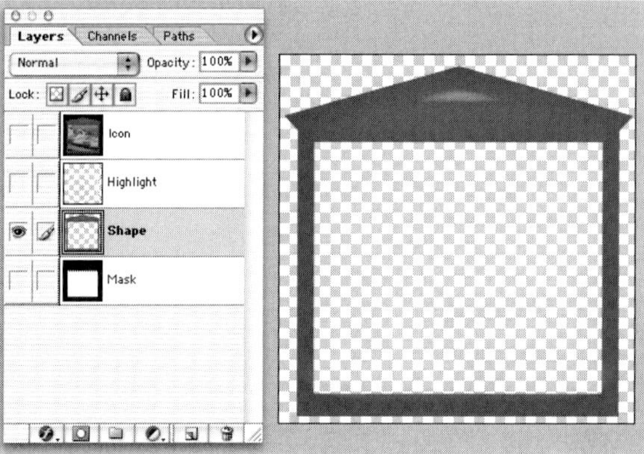

4. **Create a mask.** Select the inner, empty space of your frame. In the Mask layer, fill that selection with white. Invert the selection and fill with black. This black-and-white layer tells DVD Studio Pro 2 how to crop your video so it fits within the frame.

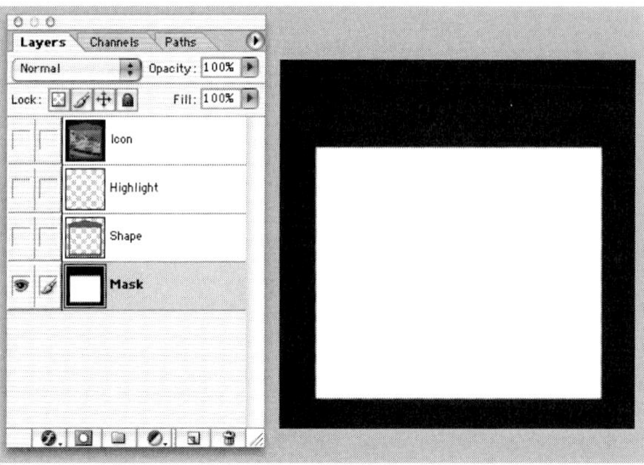

5. **Design an icon**. Create art that represents how your drop zone will look in use. Add it to the Icon layer.

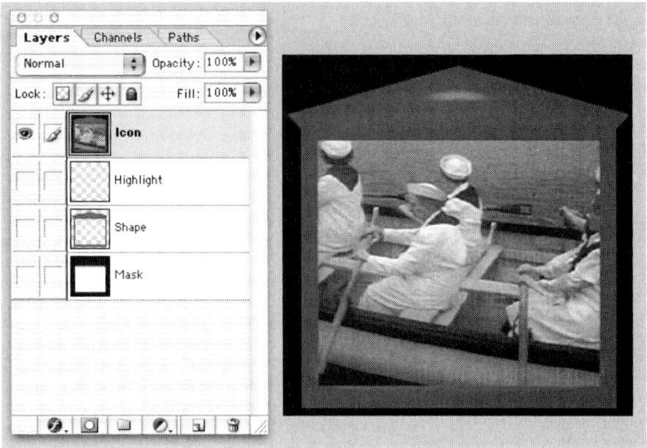

6. **Save**. Save your new shape to your hard disk. Return to DVD Studio Pro 2

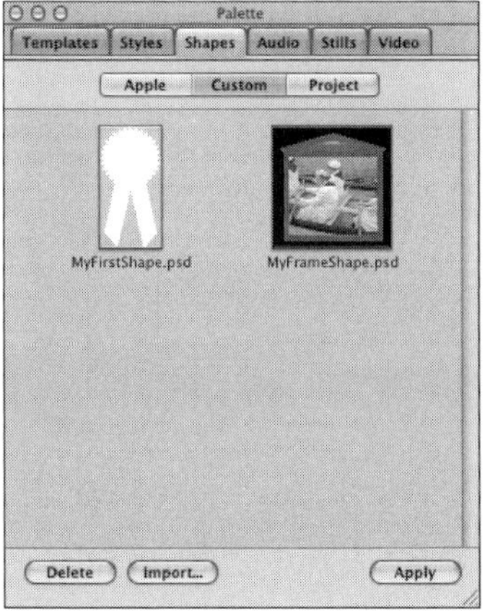

7. **Open the Palette**. Press ⌘-⌥-P. Open the Shapes tab. Choose Custom. Click Import, and import your new shape as you did for the highlight shape.

8. **Create a new drop zone**. Drag the new shape from the Menu Editor. Choose Create Drop Zone/Set Shape from the drop palette.

Once the drop zone is created, you're ready to insert contents. Assign an image or a video to the zone by dragging a file on top. Choose Set Asset.

Solution: Reuse iDVD Drop Zone Patches

Patches (POX files) provide one important feature that's missing from shapes. Patches let you use video to create motion in your backdrops. If you're familiar with iDVD, you've already seen this in action—the theater curtains that open and close over your drop zone video or the "brush strokes" that paint the drop zone video onto your menu background.

In these steps, you'll grab a copy of the Brush Strokes POX file and install it in DVD Studio Pro 2.

1. **Quit DVD Studio Pro 2.** Choose File > Quit (⌘-Q). You can't add patch files while the program is running.

2. **Expose iDVD 3.** Navigate to your applications folder and locate the iDVD 3 folder. Open it and select the iDVD program icon. Ctrl-click/right-click, and choose Show Package Contents from the pop-up. This option opens the Application bundle and displays the files contained within.

3. **Navigate to Contents/Resources.** Select 005_Brush_Strokes.theme. Again, Ctrl-click/right-click and choose Show Package Contents to display the hidden contents of the Brush Strokes theme.

4. **Navigate to the Brush Strokes' Contents/Resources.** Again open Contents, and then open Resources.

5. **Copy DropZone.pox.** ⌥-drag DropZone.pox to your Desktop. The file is just a little more than 36MB in size.

6. **Rename the POX file.** Change the name from DropZone.pox to **.BrushStrokes.pox**. Adding the small dot (⌥-8) in front of the name helps it stand out in the (unfortunately long) list of patch files.

7. **Add the POX file.** Navigate to /Library/ Application Support/DVD Studio Pro/ Patches. Drag BrushStrokes.pox into this folder.

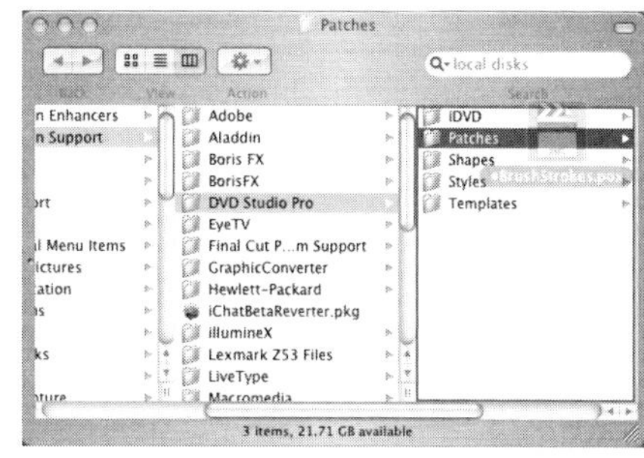

8. **Launch DVD Studio Pro 2.** When launched, DVD Studio Pro 2 loads all the materials (patch files, shapes, and so forth) found in the DVD SP Application Support library.

9. **Drag out a drop zone.** Open the Menu Editor. Press ⌥, and drag to create a new drop zone in your menu. Drop a video onto the drop zone, and add it as a new asset.

10. **Set the shape.** Open the Inspector and locate the Shape pop-up. Choose Shape > Patch Shapes > BrushStrokes.pox. (Your new patch item appears at the very bottom of the Patch Shapes list along with any other custom patches you've added to DVD Studio Pro 2.)

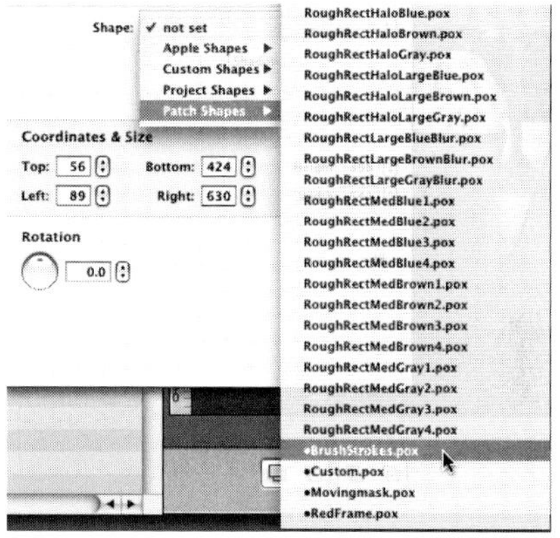

11. **Enable Motion.** Type ⌘-J (or click the Motion button at the bottom right of the Menu Editor) to enable motion and to preview the brush effects.

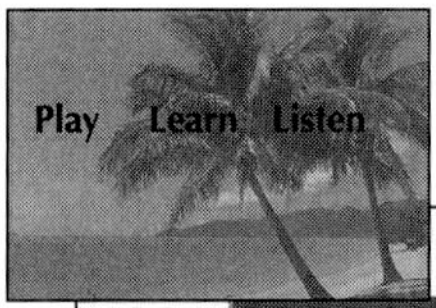

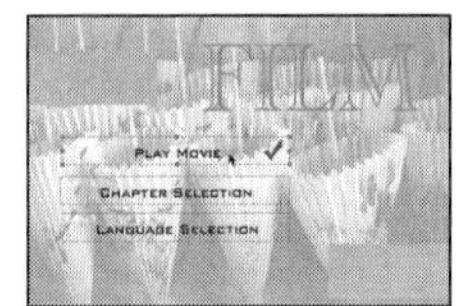
FILM
PLAY MOVIE
CHAPTER SELECTION
LANGUAGE SELECTION

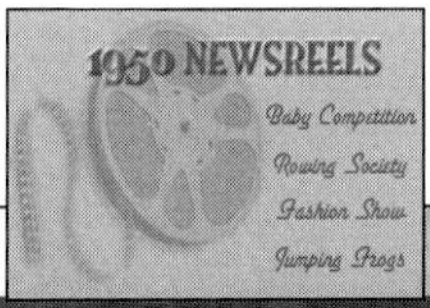

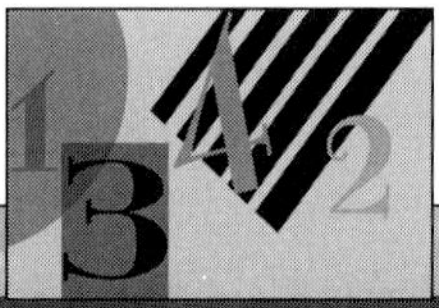

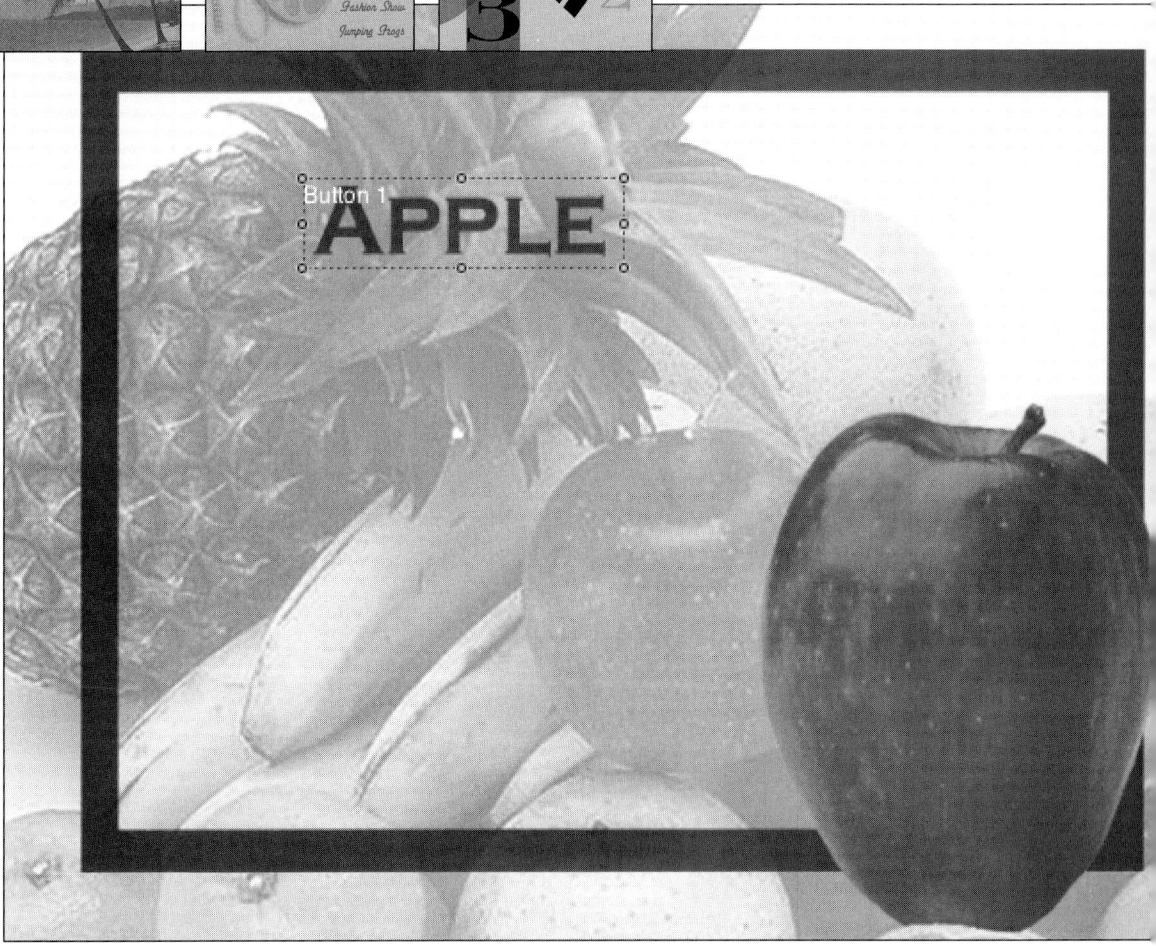

Scenes
Play...

3 Buttons:
one method
Pick S

Creating Overlay and Layered Menus

Photoshop plays an important role when working with overlay and layered menus. Although you can create basic menus entirely in DVD Studio Pro 2, it makes sense to use image-editing programs to build overlay and layered menu assets. Image editors allow you to build cohesive DVD interface design elements. Standard menus tend to reuse general-purpose menu items such as shapes and templates. Overlay- and layered-menu design creates one-of-a-kind, one-time-use assets built specifically for your DVD project at hand.

Chapter Contents

In this chapter, you'll discover how to create overlay and layered menus. You'll learn which resources you'll need to build, how to go about building them, and how to bring them into DVD Studio Pro 2 to create eye-catching DVD menus.

Creating Basic Overlay Menus

Of all DVD Studio Pro 2 menus, overlays can be the easiest to design and build. Overlays display button choice by adding highlights over the background art or video. You can approach highlights in many ways. You might add a check mark next to a button name or a pointing finger or an arrow. You might brighten the area within the button outlines or change its color. You might outline the edges of the button or add a line underneath. Possibilities are endless.

As a rule, overlay menus use two pieces of art, a background still (or video) and an overlay image. Use an image-processing program, such as Adobe Photoshop, to create still art. Import this artwork into DVD Studio Pro 2 and assign it to the background or the overlay of your menus.

When you use a motion-video authoring program, such as Adobe After Effects, Final Cut Pro, or QuickTime Pro, to build motion menu backgrounds, make sure to add the normal (unselected) button art directly to the video.

Create backgrounds that show the normal appearance of the menu before button selection. Use the overlay to define how buttons appear when selected. Figure 3.1 shows typical overlay art. It does not matter how many buttons you will use in your menu. A single overlay file provides all the artwork for all the buttons in your menu. You define the button areas using the Menu Editor.

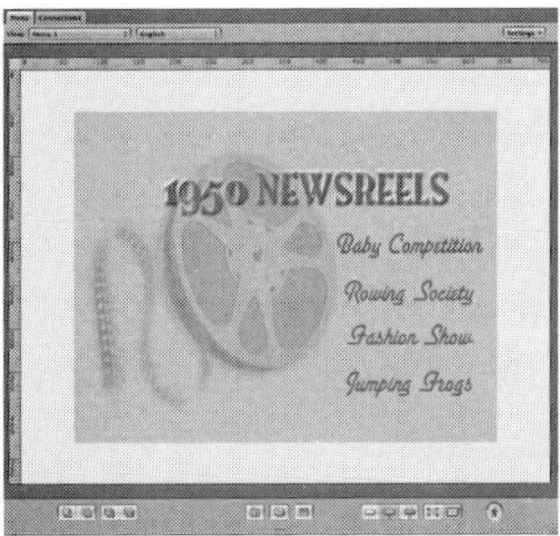
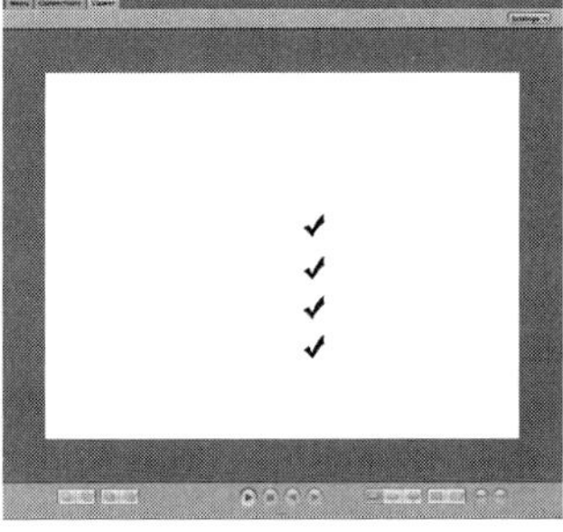

Figure 3.1 DVD Studio Pro 2 overlay menus use overlay files to define menu button highlights. Here you see original background art, an overlay graphic, and the results when a button is selected. Any black portion of the overlay that falls within button bounds appears as a highlight over the background art. The Button Inspector lets you set the color and intensity of the highlight.

Designing Black-and-White Overlays

In their basic form, using "simple color" settings, layered menu overlays use black highlights on a white background. As Figure 3.2 shows, the biggest enemy of simple overlays is the jaggies. It's up to you to design around this limitation—or you can step up to advanced overlays, which are described later in this chapter.

Figure 3.2 Jagged edges may form around the edges of your overlay highlight edges. Avoid complex highlight shapes when using simple black-and-white overlays.

In theory, nonblack pixels map to their closest values: white or black. In practice, middle-gray pixels can go either way and may produce odd results in your menus. Gain better control by preconverting your overlays. In Photoshop, choose Image > Mode > Grayscale and then choose Image > Mode > Bitmap. Select from any of the pattern methods such as threshholding, diffusion dithering, or pattern dithering, and click OK. What you see is what you'll get.

Consider these points when you design black-and-white overlays for use with your DVD Studio Pro 2 projects.

Rectilinear works best. When possible, use straight lines—vertical, horizontal, or diagonal.

Avoid small features. Keep your highlights simple. Fine details won't display well.

Be bold and thick. Use wide, solid highlight features. Avoid thin lines in particular.

Omit text. When possible, don't use text in black-and-white overlays. The human visual system is particularly sensitive to poor text display. Small defects, which might go unnoticed in simpler shapes, stand out in text highlights.

Button Roles

As the main interactive menu component, buttons play several roles (called "states") in overlay menus. These states change as the viewer interacts with their DVD remote control. When you bring your overlay and background into the Menu Editor, you define an onscreen look for each of these states.

Selected With a set-top DVD player, viewers typically navigate through a menu's buttons by using the arrow keys on the remote control. The focus shifts from one selected button to the next dictated by the remote. By defining the selection highlight, you tell DVD Studio Pro 2 how to bring a button into prominence.

Normal In the absence of user interaction, unselected buttons appear in their normal state. Define your normal highlights to indicate this unselected look.

Activated Activated highlights appear for a split second when viewers *activate* a selected button by pressing Enter. This feature works just like HTML "alinks," adding visual feedback that the player acknowledges the button choice.

Three small buttons toward the bottom-right of the Menu Editor (the ellipse, the ellipse with the arrow under it, the ellipse with the arrow and crown) visualize each button state—normal, selected, and activated. Alternatively, choose from the View > Button State submenu or type **W** to cycle through the three states.

Creating the Menu

Simple overlay menus are built out of a background, an overlay, and a certain number of buttons. In these steps, you'll discover how these pieces work together:

1. **Design a background.** Use your favorite image editor or graphic-design program, such as Adobe Photoshop or OmniGraffle Pro, to build a standard-sized menu backdrop, complete with button labels. Merge your layers and save them as a new, full-color 720 × 480 (720 × 576 PAL) image. (The first image in Figure 3.1 shows a typical still background.)

When using a motion video background, either add your button labels in your video editor or use the advanced overlay menu technique described later in this chapter.

2. **Create the overlay.** Remain in your image program and add button highlights (in black) to each of the button labels within your program. Once you've positioned the highlights exactly, hide your original art, and add a white background. Merge your layers and save a copy to disk as a new image. (The second image in Figure 3.1 shows a typical overlay.)

3. **Select a DVD menu.** Return to DVD Studio Pro 2. Open the Outline tab, and select the menu you want to work on.

To add new DVD menus, choose Project > Add to Project > Menu (⌘-Y) *or* click Add Menu in the toolbar *or* Ctrl-click (right-click) within the Outline tab and choose Add > Menu from the pop-up.

4. **Drag your background art onto the Menu Editor.** Locate your background material and drag it (from the Assets tab or from the Finder) onto the Menu Editor. Do not release the mouse. When the drop palette appears, choose Set Background.

5. **Drag your overlay art onto the menu.** Choose Set Overlay from the drop palette.

6. **Choose View > Button State > Selected.** Alternatively, click the Selected button on the bottom right of your menu window. This choice lets you view highlights within your buttons as you create them, helping you position your button outlines more effectively.

7. **Create your buttons.** Drag out your buttons on the main Menu Editor canvas. By default, any drag that starts on the menu background creates a button. Use the sizing handles at the button's corners and edges to ensure that the button reveals the entire label and highlight. Figure 3.3 demonstrates how a button reveals highlights in the Menu Editor.

Hold the option key while dragging to resize symmetrically around the center.

8. **Open the Button Inspector.** Select any button. Choose View > Show Inspector (⌘-⌥-I) or click the Inspector button at the far right of the toolbar.

It's wise to extend buttons over text labels, even when highlights are located outside the labels. This allows computer-based viewers to select a button by placing their mouse on the associated label.

Figure 3.3 Buttons reveal all highlights within their bounds. Here, an overly large button discloses several highlights.

9. **Choose a highlight color.** In the Inspector, choose any of the 16 selected highlight colors, which include red, white, yellow, blue, and so on. Choose a color that coordinates with your background yet provides an easily identified, pleasing (and not too contrasting) visual accent.

When you change a button's highlight settings, you change the settings for the entire menu. It doesn't matter which button you choose. All buttons in set 1 use the same highlight color and opacity. Ditto for sets 2 and 3.

10. **Set the highlight opacity.** Adjust the intensity between 0 (completely transparent) to 15 (completely opaque). Lower numbers add a light see-through effect to your highlights. Higher numbers provide more solid-looking elements. Figure 3.4 shows the portion of the Inspector that controls highlight settings for simple overlays.

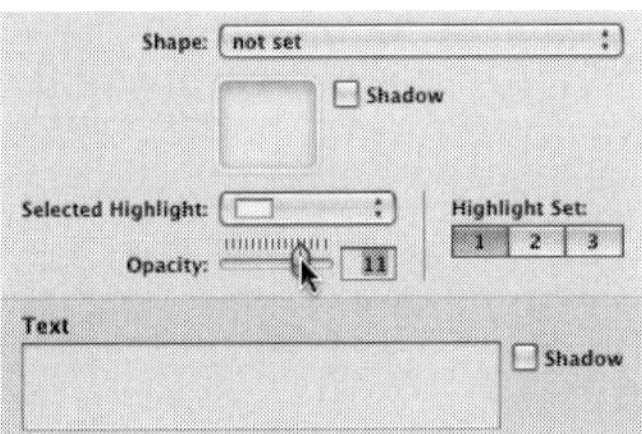

Figure 3.4 The Button Inspector lets you set your highlight color and opacity. Select a color that works well with your background art, and adjust the opacity to blend or contrast as needed. As a rule, choose Highlight Set 1 for simple (black-and-white) overlay menus.

Understanding the Mystery of the Highlight Sets

You can assign each button in your menu to any one of three highlight sets in the Button Inspector. The set you select defines the highlight color and levels assigned to that button. You can customize each set as needed. The default behaviors for simple overlays (overlays using just black and white) are as follows. You can modify each set from these defaults.

- **Set 1**   Highlight areas appear yellow. When activated, buttons return to the standard look, hiding the highlight. Set 1 works particularly well for basic black-and-white overlays.

- **Set 2**   The selected button's background gets a light pink/purple tint; the highlight is yellow. Upon activation, the button changes to a more saturated pink.

- **Set 3**   Highlight areas appear in brown. The rest of the selected button receives a blue overcast. When activated, the button flashes bright aqua-green. With its light-bluish button cast, set 3 works well for basic video motion buttons.

11. **Add your links.** Bring your menu to life by linking each button to a track, story, slideshow, or menu. Select from the Outline view and drag items to their buttons. For basic overlay menus, choose Connect To for each option, for example, Connect To Track, Connect To Story, Connect To Slideshow, and Connect To Menu, as shown in Figure 3.5.

Figure 3.5 When working with simple overlay menus, always select the Connect To option from the drop palette.

Moving on to Advanced Overlay Menus

Unlike simple overlay menus, advanced overlays use as many as three highlight colors in each menu. These additional colors let you produce interfaces with more complexity and greater visual appeal. Use these extra highlights to expand the range of colors in your menus, or, more typically, use shades of the same color to produce anti-aliased effects for smoother, better-looking graphics.

Setting up advanced overlays takes a bit more time, thought, and effort than setting up simple overlays, but the results are usually worth it. Figure 3.6 contrasts results using the same overlay graphic with simple color mapping and advanced color mapping.

Grayscale and Chroma

Grayscale and chroma refer to two overlay schemes (or mapping types) that produce virtually identical results. Although simple overlay menus use white backgrounds and black foregrounds to define highlight areas, advanced overlay menus add two extra colors to set extra highlights. The Color Settings tab in the Button Inspector allows you to use these advanced schemes to set highlights for your buttons.

Figure 3.6 Using advanced color sets allows you to produce smoother, better-looking highlights in your overlay menus. Contrast these screen shots. The left image uses a simple black and white overlay and displays many jagged artifacts. The right image uses two additional gray levels to produce basic anti-aliasing.

Simple overlays, using black and white, require just 1 bit of information per pixel. Complex overlays use 2 bits per pixel, adding two additional colors for a total of four.

Grayscale mapping adds two colors of gray, at 33% and 67% intensity. Chroma mapping adds pure red and pure blue. Other than the colors used, the two mapping types are indistinguishable. This book uses grayscale mapping exclusively because it's far easier to deal with and it lends itself to anti-aliasing tasks in a way that chroma mapping is unable to match.

The main contrast between developing simple overlays and advanced overlays lies in the extra bookkeeping. More detail is involved. With simple overlays, you drag out a button, set the selected and activated highlights—and you're pretty much done. For advanced overlays, you must set the normal, selected, and activated highlights for each of the 4 available colors—that's a total of 12 colors and 12 sliders for each button set.

Follow these steps to design and use advanced overlays.

1. **Design your overlay.** Use Photoshop (or any other favorite image editor) to lay out your highlights in a standard-sized RGB image (720 × 480 NTSC, 720 × 576 PAL). Limit color choices to black, 33% gray, 67% gray, and white. Match your overlay to the background art you'll use. Be sure to save to an RGB file. Grayscale files won't load properly in DVD Studio Pro 2.

To convert grayscale art to these 4 color levels in Photoshop, choose Image > Adjustments > Posterize. Enter 4 for the number of levels and click OK.

2. **Add the overlay to your menu.** Return to DVD Studio Pro 2, and drag the overlay onto the Menu Editor. Before releasing the mouse, choose Set Overlay from the drop palette.

3. **Drag out your buttons.** Drag on the Menu Editor background to create new DVD menu buttons. With any button selected, open the Button Inspector (⌘-⌥-I). The settings you'll adjust apply to all buttons in your menu.

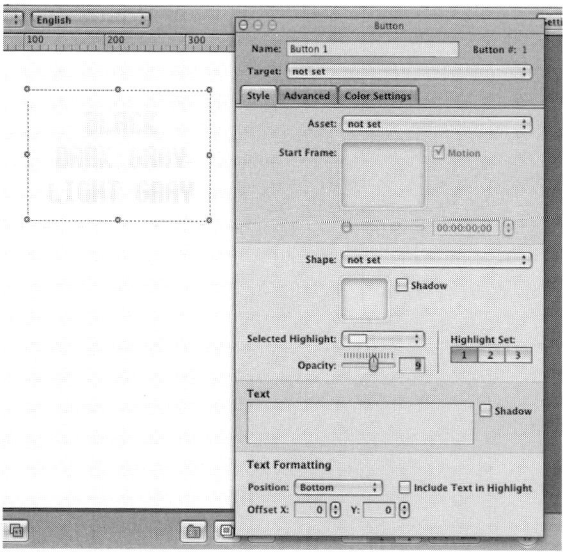

Menu Design Secrets

Here are a couple of tips for working with highlight menus.

- **Reveal highlights.**   Use ⌘-drag, which is properly a selection feature and not a viewing feature, to take a kind of X-ray eyes approach to viewing your menus. When you hold down ⌘ and drag the mouse, you reveal the "selected" highlights of all buttons that intersect the drag. Items within the drag remain selected after you release the mouse.

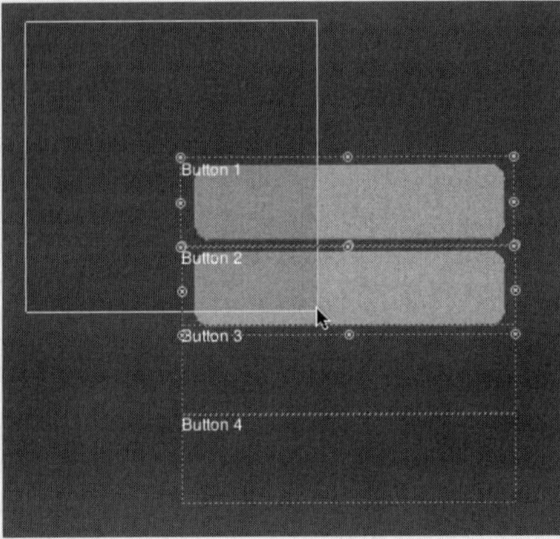

- **Use keyboard shortcuts for advanced viewing.**   Press P to toggle between square and rectangular pixels. Pressing Q alternates between background, overlay, and composite (combined background and overlay) views. Pressing W toggles between normal, selected, and activated button states.

4.   **Open Color Settings.** In the Button Inspector, click the Color Settings tab. By default, Overlay Colors is set to Simple.

Simple color settings let you set the normal, selected, and activated colors and transparencies for black-and-white overlays. Choose a button set to work on by clicking 1, 2, or 3.

5. **Click Advanced, and then click Grayscale.** The Button Inspector updates to adjust advanced grayscale color mapping. Take note of several features in this panel. First, look at the four key colors: black, dark gray, light gray, and white. (For chroma, key colors are black, red, blue, and white.) Each key has a color pop-up and opacity sliders. These control the corresponding highlight in your overlay. Next, notice the Select States (normal, selected, and activated). When working with advanced overlays, you can set key highlights for each of these three states. Finally, notice the Set indicator. As with all DVD Studio Pro 2 menus, buttons belong to any one of three button sets. Each set defines its highlights independently of the others.

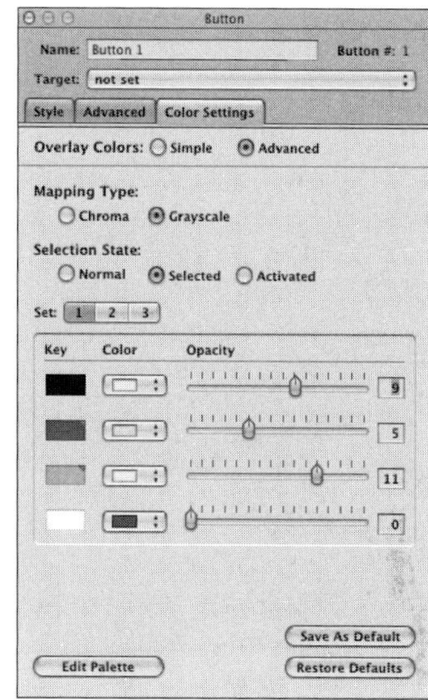

6. **Choose a button set.** Click the number of the button set you want to work on. Unless you're working with multiple button sets, it's convenient to leave this set to 1.

Buttons are created with a default of Set 1. To change the set for any button, select it, open the Button Inspector Style tab, and choose another set.

7. **Click Normal.** Normal is the state for all unselected buttons. Adjust the colors and opacities for all four of your normal highlight colors.

8. **Repeat for Selected and then for Activated.** Click Selected and adjust the four highlights. Then click Activated, and adjust those four highlights.

You have now set up to 12 highlight values. When chosen properly, these settings allow you to go beyond simple overlays to create anti-aliased text or pushbutton effects (as you'll see in the solutions that follow in this chapter). Here are a few key points to keep in mind when choosing the highlights:

Select Normal for Always See highlights. Enable Normal highlights when you want to see them all the time in all nonselected buttons. Although legitimate design reasons exist to use Normal highlights, it's usually easier to design always-see elements into background art. Adding buttons over stock motion video is one common use of normal highlights.

Don't overplan Activated highlights. Activated highlights usually appear as a brief flash. Select a strong enough contrasting color to give your viewer sufficient feedback that the button press has done something but don't sweat the details. A simple color change usually does the job.

Selected highlights must stand out on their own. A passerby glancing at a television playing your DVD should notice the selected menu button immediately. When viewers have to press the arrow buttons to determine which button is selected, you've failed as a menu designer. Figure 3.7 demonstrates a too-subtle overlay strategy.

Use one tone to anti-alias. Whether you're anti-aliasing text or shapes, a single color makes your highlights work in tandem. Choose the same highlight tint for each of your four keys. Then set your black key opacity to 15, set dark gray to 10, set light gray to 5, and set white to 0. With these settings, the highlight color you select shades to match your overlay.

For other maximum opacities, scale accordingly. For example, set the black key to 9, set dark gray to 6, set light gray to 3, and set white to 0. This progression of 100%, 67%, 33%, and 0% matches the natural shades in four-color anti-aliased art.

When using multiple highlight colors, use rectangular art. Rectilinear shapes avoid edges with anti-aliased detail, ensuring that you don't mix highlight colors. Use this effect sparingly and with forethought. Too many colors on a menu can irritate viewers. (The file 3tones.psd on the companion DVD provides an example of multicolor highlight art. The eyes, pupils, and mouths each use one color.)

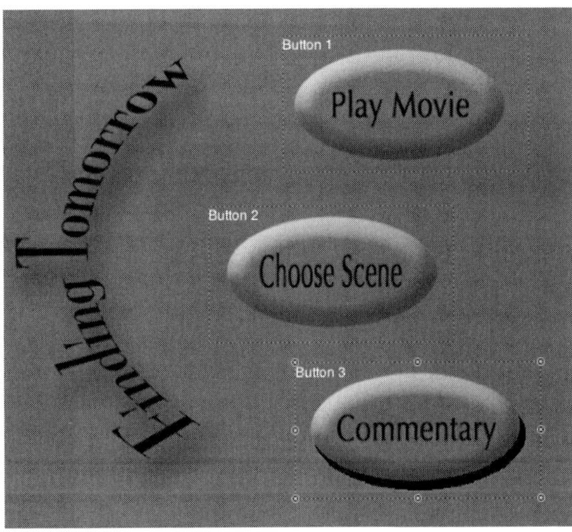

Figure 3.7 Be bold when designing DVD highlights. Here, a small button drop-shadow proves insufficient to grab immediate viewer attention. Viewers should notice button selections without having to experiment with the remote control.

Adding Layered Menus

Layered menus, also known as Photoshop menus, allow you to create full-color menus with full-color highlights that break out of the button highlight mindset. As Figure 3.8 shows, layered menus let you add custom graphic touches over the entire space of your screen. Unfortunately, this high level of visual control comes at a price. Layered menus have the following in common:

They don't work fast. In fact, on some set-top DVD players, viewers can become frustrated by the slow response time for layered menus.

They don't include motion. You can design tremendous varieties of full-color feedback, but motion isn't one of the facets you can use.

They don't include audio. Layered menus don't allow background music or other audio elements. Each time the viewer uses the remote to change from one button to another, the DVD player must play a different internal sequence, ruling out the possibility of sound accompaniment.

They don't support several DVD Studio Pro 2 features. You can't use shapes, text, templates, or styles with layered menus.

In theory, you can add standard menu overlays to your layered menus to create what's called mixed or hybrid menus. Why you'd want to do this is another matter entirely.

Figure 3.8 Layered menus use the entire screen to provide menu feedback. Contrast this to overlay menus, which only provide feedback within button boundaries. In this example, the selected fruit appears at the bottom-right of the screen while the button text changes color to lime green, apple red, blueberry blue, or orange. Layered menus offer the greatest visual control of all menu types.

Designing the Layered Menu

Photoshop menus certainly live up to their name, as the entire design process takes place in Photoshop. (Or, if you'd like to save a bit of money, Photoshop Elements. In fact, you can use any image-editing program that produces layered PSD files.) Once you import a properly created PSD file into DVD Studio Pro 2, it takes just a few moments to transform it into a working layered menu. In the following steps, you'll create a layered menu file.

The instructions here build 4:3 menus. 16:9 menus are discussed later in this chapter.

1. **Create a large 4:3 RGB image.** In Photoshop, open a new RGB image using a 4 to 3 width to height ratio. Start with 720×540 (NTSC) or 768×576 (PAL).

2. **Design a background.** Add background art to your image, and merge it into a single layer. Name this layer Background.

3. **Create three layers for each button.** Add art for each button's Normal, Selected, and Activated state. Name each layer accordingly, in a way you can easily understand and recognize later in DVD Studio Pro 2 when you assign art to your button states. Here, the layers are named (for example) Apple-Normal, Apple-Selected, Apple-Activated, Orange-Normal, Orange-Selected, Orange-Activated, and so on. Group the buttons logically in the Layers palette (see Figure 3.9).

4. **Prepare each layer for broadcast.** (NTSC only) Select each layer (including the background) in turn, and choose Filter > Video > NTSC Colors.

5. **Resize the menu to DV sizes.** Choose Image > Image Size. Clear the Constrain Proportions check box. Set your NTSC menu to 720 × 480 or your PAL menu to 720 × 576.

6. **Save.** Save your work to disk.

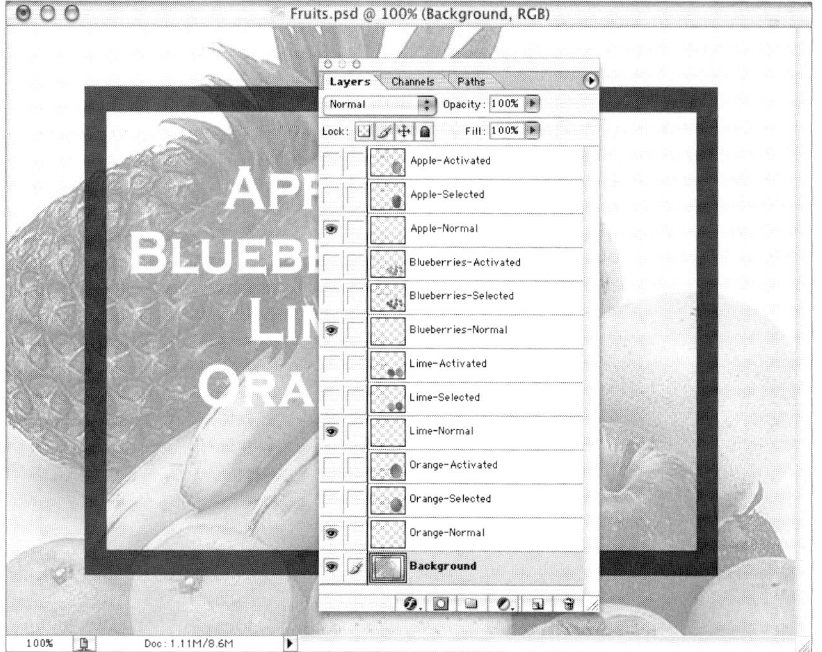

Figure 3.9 Overlay menu graphics can quickly become cluttered. You must add three layers (or more!) for each DVD menu button plus a layer for background art. A sensible naming strategy and layer ordering will best help you design and manage the menu complexities.

You now have a Photoshop PSD file with 1 + 3*N layers, in which N is the number of buttons in your menu.

Creating the Layered Menu in DVD Studio Pro 2

In this section, you'll learn how to use the PSD menu file you just created to build layered menus in DVD Studio Pro 2. Follow these steps to import and use your file.

1. **Create a new layered menu.** Layered menus are not the same as standard menus. Choose Project > Add To Project > Layered Menu (⌘-Shift-Y) *or* Ctrl-Click(right-click) in the Outline tab and choose Add > Layered Menu *or* click Add Layered Menu in the toolbar. DVD Studio Pro 2 creates a menu icon in the Outline tab that looks much, but not quite, like a normal menu icon. Select the new menu.

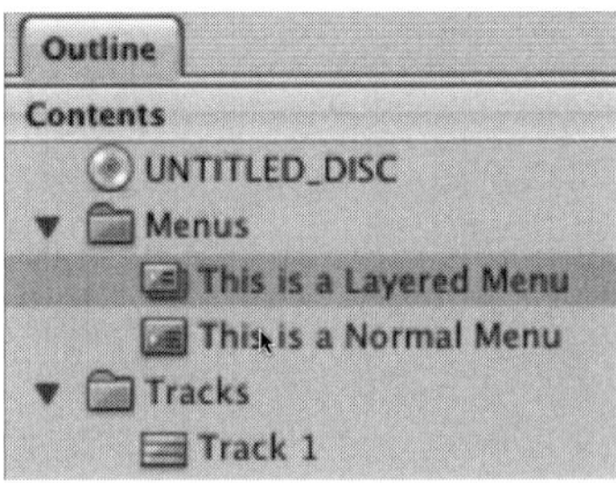

The curious (or eagle eyed) will notice that the layered menu icon contains two lines rather than three and a small drop shadow.

2. **Add a button and turn off highlights**. Drag out a button on the background of your new menu. Open the Button Inspector (⌘-⌥-I). Choose Color Settings > Advanced > Grayscale > Set 1. Click Normal, and set all four opacities to 0. Click Selected, and set all four opacities to 0. Click Activated, and set all four opacities to 0.

3. **Add your art.** Drag your PSD file from the Finder or from the Assets tab to the background of your menu. Choose Set Background (No Layers Visible).

4. **Define your background art.** Click on the background of your menu. In the Menu Inspector, choose the General tab. Locate the background layer list, a scrolling list with the headings Show and Layer Name. Scroll down to your background layer. Check Show. The background art appears in your menu.

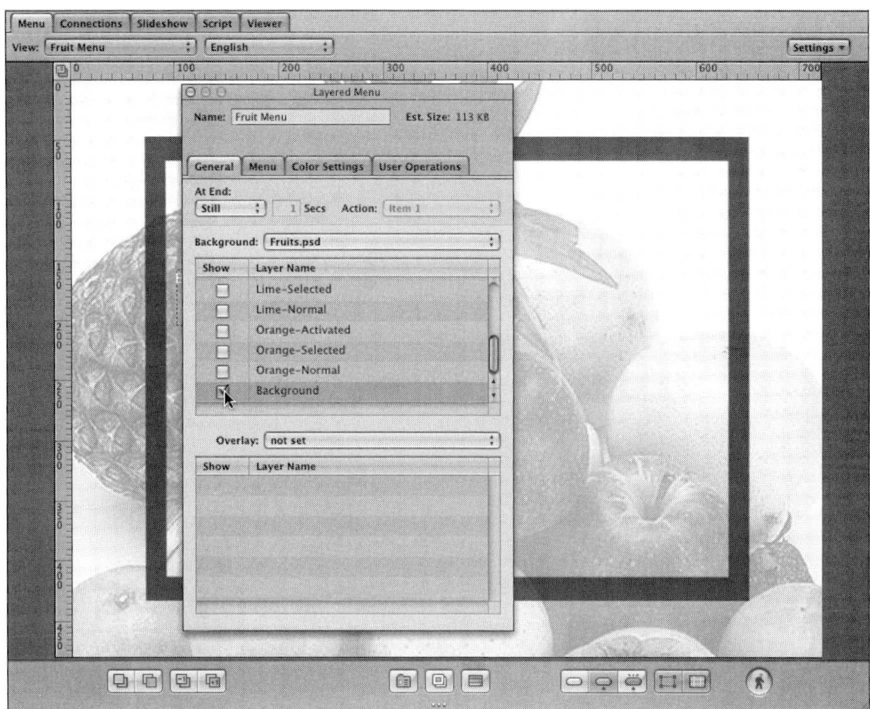

5. **Select the button.** Choose Edit > Select All (⌘-A) or turn on button highlights to locate it. In the Button Inspector, open the Layers tab. (This tab does not appear for buttons in normal menus.)

6. **Choose the button art.** Three columns of check boxes allow you to select layers for the Normal (leftmost), Selected (middle), and Activated (rightmost) states of your button. Select one set of layers (for example, apple_normal, apple_ selected, and apple_activated) and assign them to your button. Use the three

Show State buttons at the bottom right of the Menu Editor to preview the look for each state.

7. **Position your button.** Move it into place and resize as needed. The button outline sets the dimensions where computer-based viewers can use a mouse to select and activate the button.

8. **Repeat.** Create another button, assign its art, and resize. Repeat until you've added all the buttons for your menu.

9. **Test**. To test your menu, assign it as your disc's first play, and then simulate.

Never assign a layer to more than one button or button state. The project may simulate correctly, but it will not work properly once built. 

Controlling Button Order

Out-of-order buttons can add a touch of whimsy to your DVD menus. Figure 3.10 depicts how a wacky random-looking interface might appear.

Figure 3.10 Careful button navigation settings allow you to create whimsical out-of-order presentations that behave predictably when viewers use the arrow keys on their remote controls. Use the Advanced tab in the Button Inspector to set button navigation by hand. Choose Auto Assign Buttons Now from the Settings pop-up to revert to default geometric button navigation.

Despite this nonlinear layout, the menu buttons should respond in numeric order to the up, down, left, and right arrows on the viewer's remote. This table shows how you might want the DVD menu to react:

Selected Button	Left and Up Arrows	Down and Right Arrows
Button 1	Button 4	Button 2
Button 2	Button 1	Button 3
Button 3	Button 2	Button 4
Button 4	Button 3	Button 1

In these steps, you'll instruct DVD Studio Pro 2 how to respond to viewer navigation.

1. **Add your buttons.** Add your buttons to your menu and name them meaningfully.

2. **Create a navigation list.** Build a table like the previous one to help you plan how your menu should react to each button press.

3. **Inspect a button.** Select one of your DVD menu buttons. Open the Button Inspector (⌘-⌥-I), and click the Advanced tab.

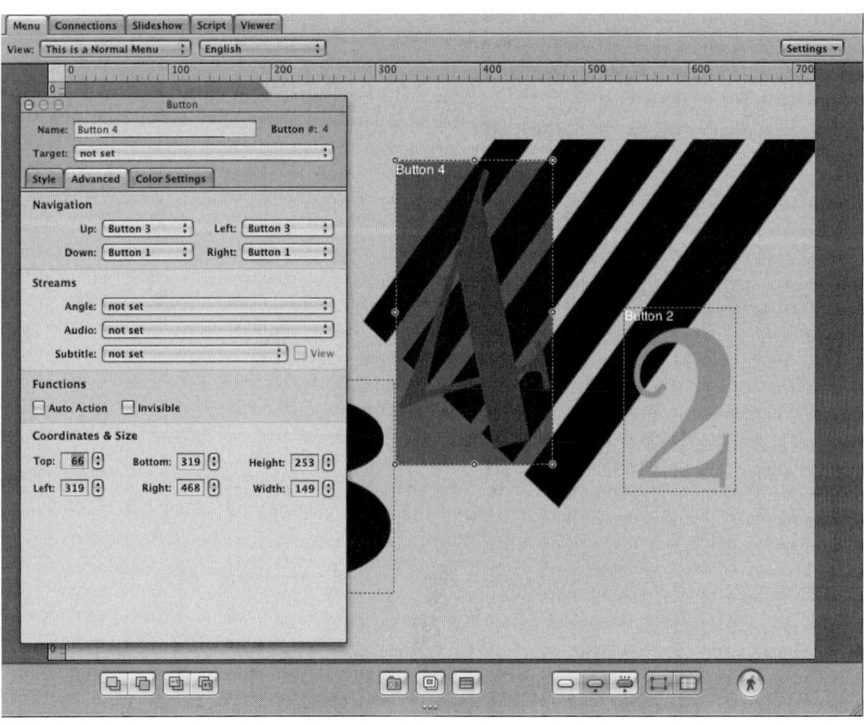

4. **Specify the navigation.** Use the up, down, left, and right pop-ups to specify which button to select for these viewer remote arrow presses. Match them to the values in the navigation table you created.

5. **Repeat.** Repeat for each button in your menu, setting the navigation per your table.

6. **Test.** Set your disc's first play to this menu. Click Simulate to test the results.

Capturing Styles and Templates for Reuse

DVD Studio Pro 2 allows you to recycle styles associated with text, buttons, or entire menus by storing reusable descriptions on your palette. Use and reuse these styles within your projects or make them self-contained, saving them for future creative endeavors.

To build a style, select the item you want to save: a text field, a button, or a menu. Open the Palette and choose (for text) Styles > Custom > Text, (for buttons) Styles > Custom > Buttons *or* (for menus) Templates > Custom. Click Create. Name the style and check either Project or Self-Contained. Click Save. DVD Studio Pro 2 stores a copy of your style on disk (either in your project file or in /Library/ Application Support/DVD Studio Pro) and adds it to the Project or Custom pane.

Templates store the entire look of your menu, including background text and art. (In contrast, menu styles store only button locations and fonts. When in doubt, use menu templates rather than menu styles).

You can do the following:

- **Stylize text and buttons.**   Add text styles to either text objects or buttons; button styles apply only to buttons. Drag the style of choice onto a menu item, and then choose either Apply To Text Object or Apply To Button.

- **Add new text objects and buttons.**   When you drag text and button styles to the background of your menu, DVD Studio Pro 2 allows you to create new items using these styles. Choose either Create Text Object or Create Button.

- **Assign defaults to the menu.**   Choose Set Default Button Style or Set Default Text Style from the drop palette to change the menu's defaults. Items created by direct manipulation (dragging out buttons, double-clicking to add text) will use these default settings.

- **Apply a menu template.**   Drag a template from the Palette onto your menu background, and choose Apply To Menu from the drop palette.

Creating Language-Specific Versions of Your Menus

When you prepare for a variety of viewing languages, you expand the audience that can watch and enjoy your DVD. Follow these steps to create an alternate menu language.

You can add as many as 16 languages per menu. DVD player language settings specify which version plays back. When there's no specified language (or the player can't find a matching language), the DVD plays the first available language.

1. **Add a new language.** Open the Outline tab. Choose Project > Add To Project > Language (⌘-/) *or* click the Add Language button in the toolbar *or* Ctrl-click (right-click) the Outline tab background and choose Add > Language from the pop-up. DVD Studio Pro 2 creates a new language, typically similar to the first, such as English-2.

2. **Set the new language.** Select the new language element, and open the Language Inspector (⌘-⌥-I). It has only one pane and one control—the Language Code. Use the pop-up to select the correct language.

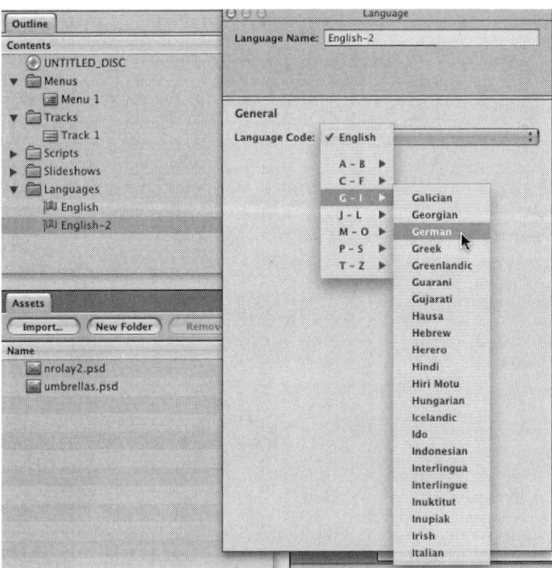

3. **Create a menu.** Build a menu using your primary language. In the Menu Editor, make sure that the language is set correctly by looking at the language pop-up. It appears in the line just below the tab and above the main workspace. Make sure

to leave your button outlines enabled (choose View > Show Button Outline
And Name).

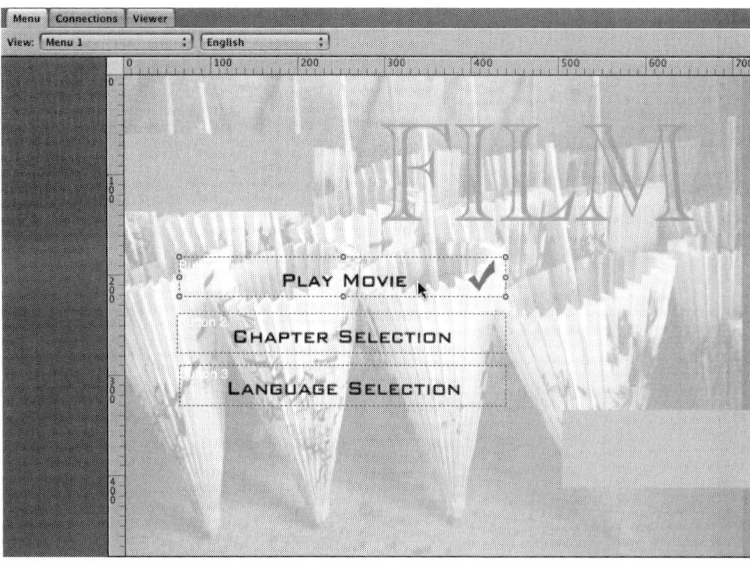

4. **Select the alternate language**. After you finish laying out your primary language
menu, choose your alternate language from the language pop-up. All menu elements, except for your buttons and their connections, disappear. You can set a
completely different look for each language.

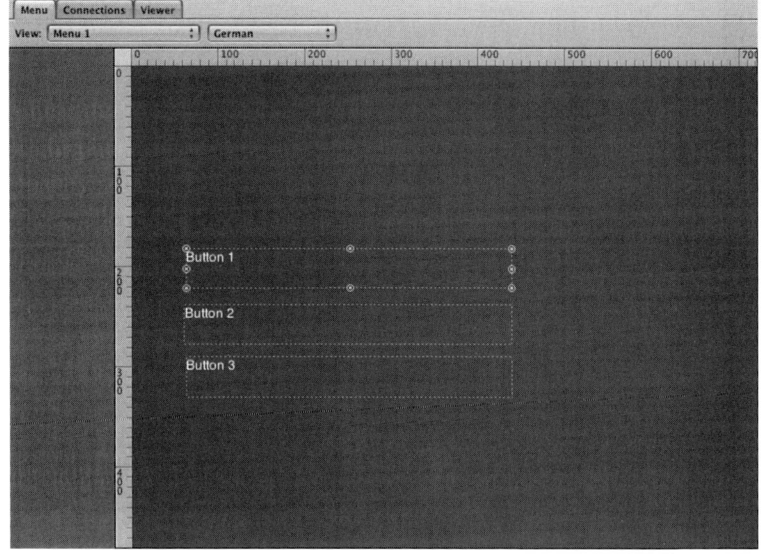

5. **Optionally, copy your style.** Copying and applying a style can save time when you want to keep the same look for all your languages. Reselect the primary language. Choose Project > Create In Menu > Template *or* Ctrl-click(right-click) the menu background and choose Create Template. DVD Studio Pro 2 prompts you to name your new template. Enter a name, check Self-Contained, and click Save.

6. **Optionally, apply your style.** Choose the alternate language. Open the Palette (⌘-⌥-P), and choose Templates > Custom. Drag the style back to the Menu Editor, and choose Apply To Menu from the drop palette. The menu updates, looking similar to the original language.

7. **Edit the menu.** Customize all the written and cultural elements to match your chosen language. Use your knowledge of the destination language and culture to make your edits.

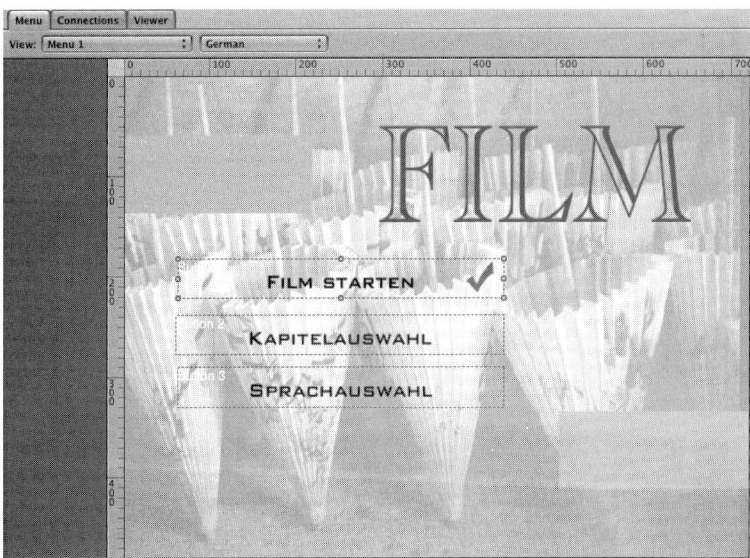

8. **Repeat.** You can repeat the previous steps to add as many as 16 languages to your menu.

Testing Your Multilanguage Menu in DVD Studio Pro 2

DVDs use three kinds of language settings: for menus, for audio streams, and for subtitles. Each can be set separately and does not directly affect the other. The DVD player specifies which language is used for your menu. To choose a menu playback language, follow these steps.

1. **Open the Preferences dialog.** Choose DVD Studio Pro > Preferences (⌘-,).

2. **Choose Simulator.** Click the Simulator icon on the top line of the Preferences pane.

3. **Select a language.** Choose a language from the DVD menu pop-up. Be warned. The Preferences pane doesn't use the handy A-B/C-F/and so on shortcuts found elsewhere in DVD Studio Pro 2. You may need to let the pop-up scroll up or down in order to select the language you need.

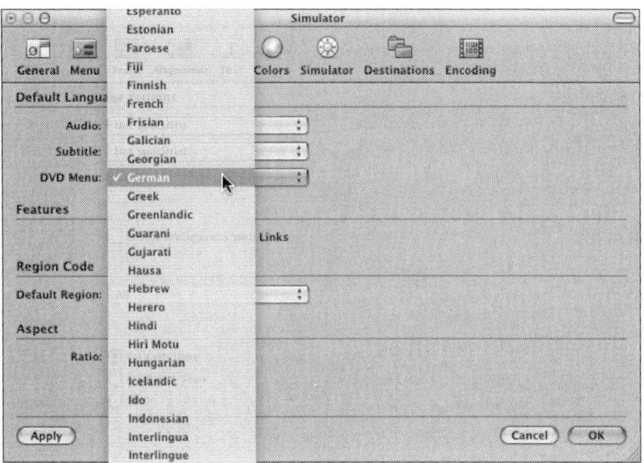

4. **Test.** Set the first play of your disc to the menu you want to test, and then click Simulate (in the toolbar). The menu that plays back should match the language you selected.

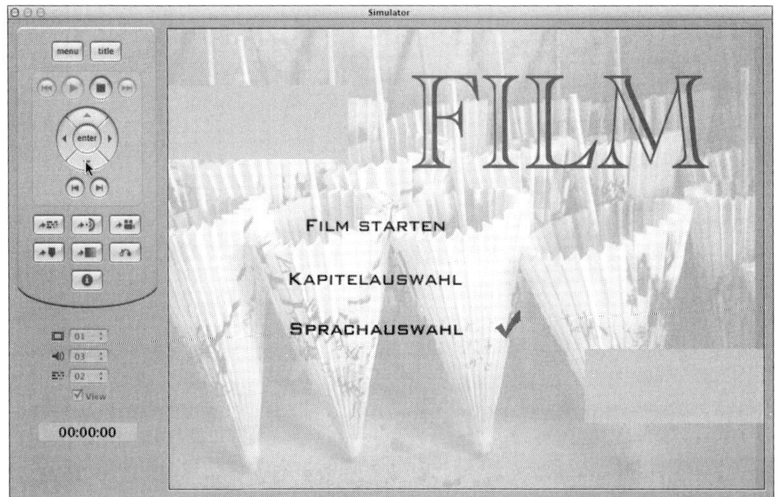

Testing Menus with Apple DVD Player

At times, you need to go beyond the Simulator and test your menus in real DVD players. If all you've built is a menu, keep in mind that DVD Studio Pro 2 won't let you build discs without tracks. You can add a dummy "track" by dragging any image file onto the Tracks folder in the Outline tab. (Drop the image on the word *Tracks*.) Set your disc First Play to your menu, and you're ready to build the Video_TS and Audio_TS folders. Click Build in the toolbar. Once you've built your project to disk, you can do the following:

- **Test in Apple DVD Player.** Launch the player and choose File > Open Video_TS Folder (⌘-O). Navigate to the Video_TS folder you just built, select it, and click Choose. Click the Play button to play your menu.

- **Test in a DVD set-top player.** Insert a freshly erased DVD-RW disc, and tell OS X to ignore it. In DVD Studio Pro 2, click Format and burn your project to disc. Walk the disc to a compatible DVD player and test it.

Testing Your Multilanguage Menu in Apple DVD Player

Apple DVD Player lets you change your DVD menu language by updating Preferences. Follow these steps to select a language.

1. **Open Preferences.** Choose DVD Player > Preferences.

2. **Locate the language settings.** Click the Disc tab. The default language pop-ups allow you to choose language settings for your audio, subtitles, and menu.

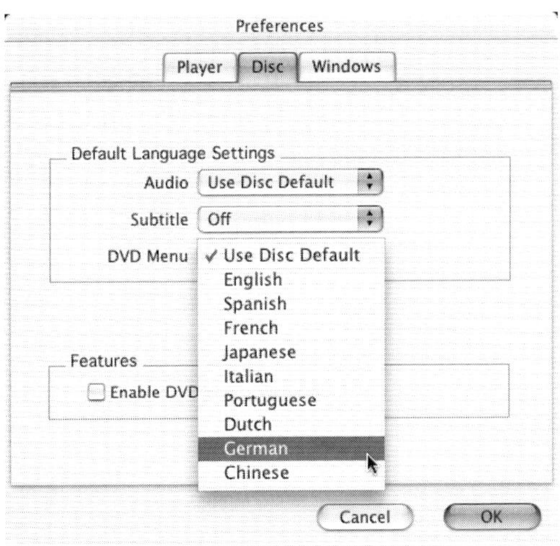

3. **Choose a menu language.** Select a language from the DVD menu pop-up or choose Use Disc Default.

4. **Click OK.** This closes the Preferences dialog and accepts your new settings.

Building Widescreen Menus

All DVD Studio Pro image assets use the same dimensions—720 × 480 NTSC, 720 × 576 PAL. When you want to include widescreen assets in your project, you must compress them horizontally to fit these fixed sizes. This produces a squeezed result known as an "anamorphic" image. During widescreen playback, the DVD set-top player restores the image's original dimensions, enabling your viewers to see the menu art as originally designed.

In these steps, you'll design, import, and express widescreen DVD menus.

1. **Create 16:9 art.** Use Photoshop (or other image-editing software) to build new RGB 853 × 480 (NTSC) or 1024 × 576 (PAL) images for your background, overlay, or layered art.

2. **Compress the dimensions.** In Photoshop, choose Image > Image Size. Clear the Constrain Proportions check box, and set the new width to 720 pixels. Save copies of your anamorphic art to disk.

3. **Add a menu.** Import your image assets into DVD Studio Pro 2. Add a new menu to your project, and open the Menu Inspector. Click the Menu tab, and select 16:9 Aspect Ratio. The Menu Editor workspace resizes, using the 16:9 aspect.

4.   **Build your menu.** Add to your menu just as you normally would. You can use shapes, overlays, or layered resources.

5.   **Select a display method for 4:3 screens.** Select the disc in the Outline tab. Open the Disc Inspector, and click the General tab. For Menu Display, choose either Force To Letterbox or Force To Pan & Scan. If you choose Force To Pan & Scan, expect the TV to clip parts of the left and right portions off your menu.

Here are a few points to keep in mind about using widescreen menus:

- Limit the buttons. Unlike normal menus, which allow you to add as many as 36 buttons per menu, you can add at most 18 buttons to 16:9 menus. DVD Studio Pro 2 creates two overlays for each 16:9 menu—one for 4:3 display, and one for 16:9 display. This cuts the number of available buttons in half.

- Use separate tracks. When you include both 16:9 and 4:3 menus in your project, DVD Studio Pro 2 expects you to use at least two tracks, one widescreen and one normal. Don't attempt to mix and match menu types with only one track.

- DVD @ccess works on one menu type per project. When you use DVD @ccess, the Apple extension that adds web linking to your DVDs, you can add it to 16:9 menus *or* 4:3 menus but not both. If you want to use DVD @ccess with 16:9 menus, you cannot have any 4:3 menus in your project. When 4:3 menus are present in your project, DVD @ccess works only on those menus.

Solution: Add Anti-Aliased Text Highlights

The literate human brain is amazingly sensitive to subtleties in text. Jagged text edges stick out strikingly. Well-chosen aliased text highlights add pleasing and nondistracting visual elements to your menus. In these steps, you'll use advanced overlays to add an anti-aliased touch to text highlights.

Copies of the background and overlay used in this Solution are found on the companion DVD as LetOverlayBG.psd and LetOverlay.psd.

1. **Design your menu background.** In Photoshop, design a full-sized RGB background image. Add well-defined button art using light-colored text labels. Choose Edit > Copy Merged (⌘-Shift-C), and then choose Edit >Paste (⌘-V) to add a fully merged topmost layer to your art. Save to disk.

2. **Design your overlay.** Without closing your original image, discard all layers except your text. Change all text color to black and add a white background. Flatten your image (choose Layer > Flatten Image), and posterize to four colors

(choose Image >Adjustments > Posterize). Save a copy of this altered file to disk as your new overlay.

3. **Create a new menu.** In DVD Studio Pro 2, start a new project and select Menu 1 from the Outline tab.

4. **Add your background and overlay.** Drag your menu background to the Menu Editor, and choose Set Background from the drop palette. Repeat with the overlay, choosing Set Overlay from the drop palette.

5. **Add your buttons.** Drag within the Menu Editor to add a menu button for each item you designed into the background. Surround the entire background button art to accommodate computer-based viewers who can select items with their mouse.

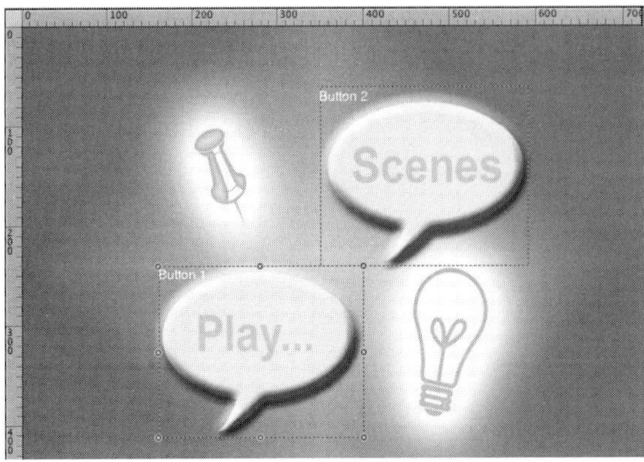

6. **Open Color Settings.** Select one of your buttons. Open the Button Inspector (⌘-⌥-I), and click the Color Settings tab. Choose Advanced, and then choose Grayscale. Ensure that Button Set 1 is selected.

7. **Set all Normal values to zero.** Click Normal, and move the Opacity sliders for all four key colors to 0. The colors for these items are irrelevant. Zero opacity ensures these highlights won't be seen.

8. **Set each Selected key to one color.** Click Selected. Use the color pop-ups, and set the same highlight color for all four keys, in this case black. This exercise approximates anti-aliasing by using different shadings of the same color.

9. **Adjust the Opacity sliders to 33%, 67%, and 100%.** Use the black key slider (the top one of the four) to set the overall opacity level for your highlight. Here, a value of 12 provides a slight translucency. Set the dark gray key opacity to two-thirds of that value (here, 8) and the light gray to one-third (here, 4). Set the white key to 0. These levels allow the text in the selected button to appear smooth without noticeable jagged edges.

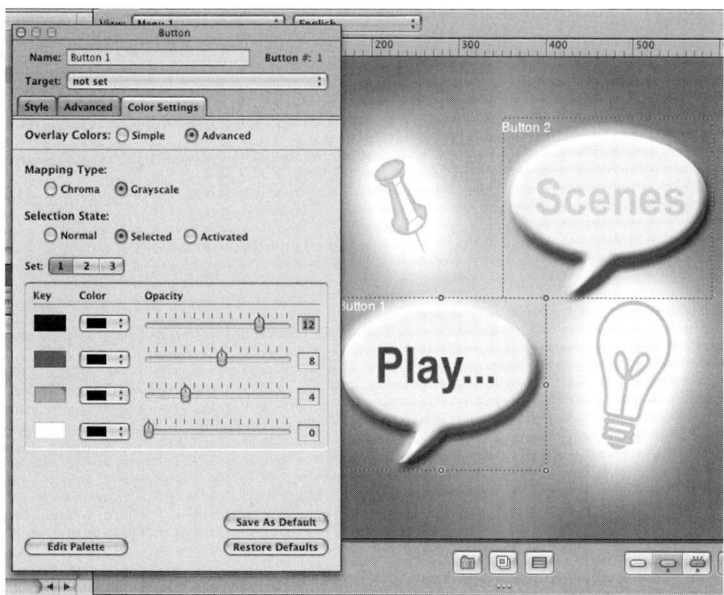

10. **Adjust the Activated colors.** Click Activated. Select an activated color, such as bright pink, and set the same highlight color for all four keys. Use the same Opacity settings that you chose for Selected.

11. **Simulate.** Click Simulator in the toolbar, and test your new interface. If all is well, save your project to disk.

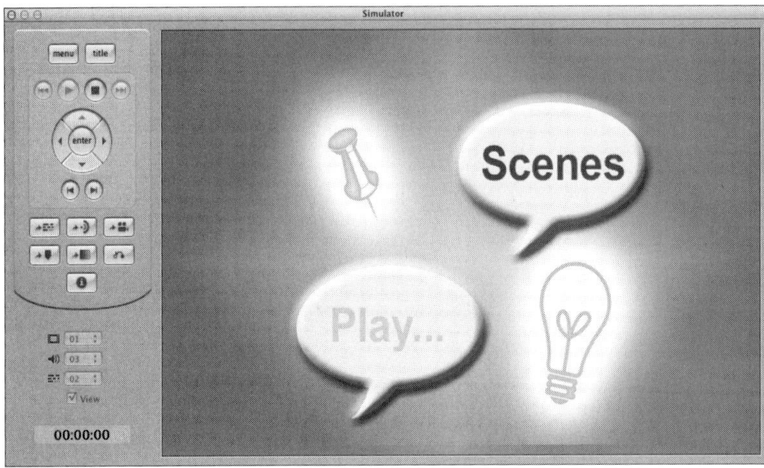

Solution: Add a Pop-Out Button with Advanced Overlays

For years, computer designers have created simple, three-dimensional buttons by using three colors of gray. DVD Studio Pro 2 overlays let you achieve the same effect with advanced overlays. In these steps, you'll add popping buttons to your DVD menus.

1. **Create a menu background.** In Photoshop, design a full-sized RGB background image, leaving space for buttons but without any buttons actually in-place. Merge and save to disk. (You'll find 3ButtonsBG.psd on the companion DVD.)

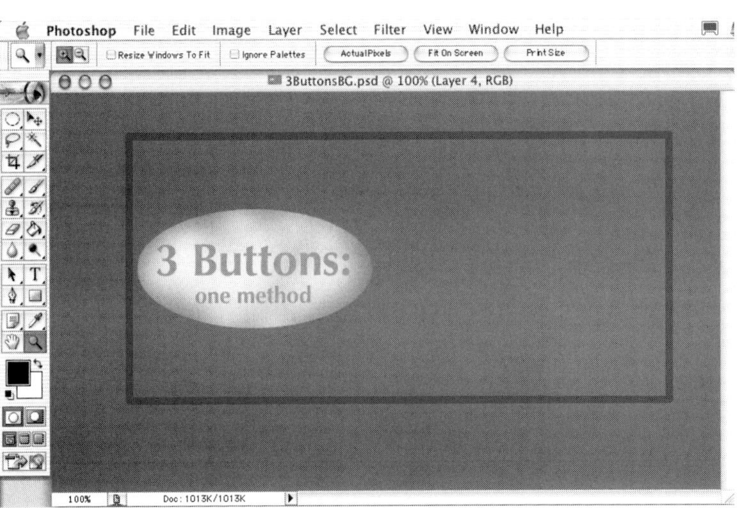

2. **Build your 3-D buttons.** Remaining in Photoshop, create a new full-sized RGB overlay of your 3-D buttons. Use dark gray (67%) rectangles for the centers of your buttons. Add light-gray (33%) highlight lines to the top and left of your rectangles and black (0%) lines to the bottom and right. Use thick lines, at least 4 pixels wide. Add a white background, merge your art, and save to disk as your overlay art. (See 3Buttons.psd on the companion DVD.)

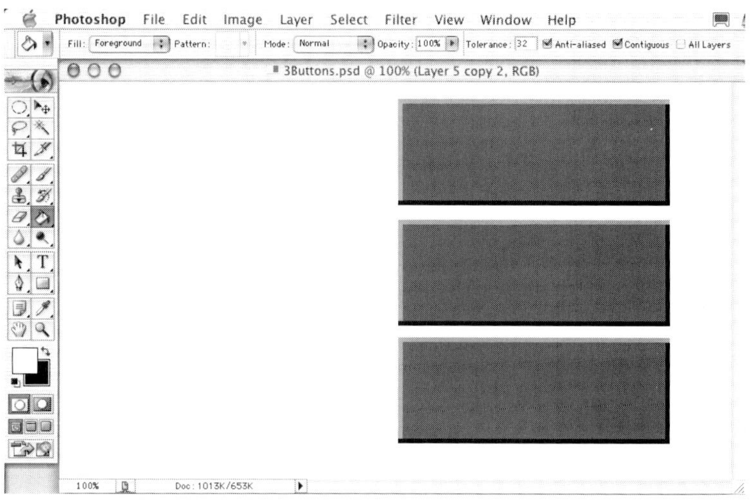

3. **Start a new menu.** In DVD Studio Pro 2, open a new project and select Menu 1 from the Outline tab. In turn, drag your background and overlay art to the menu. Use the drop palette to set them as your menu's background and overlay.

4. **Drag out your buttons.** Drag on the Menu Editor background to add each of your buttons. Since you haven't indicated any buttons in the background art, only add the buttons you actually need.

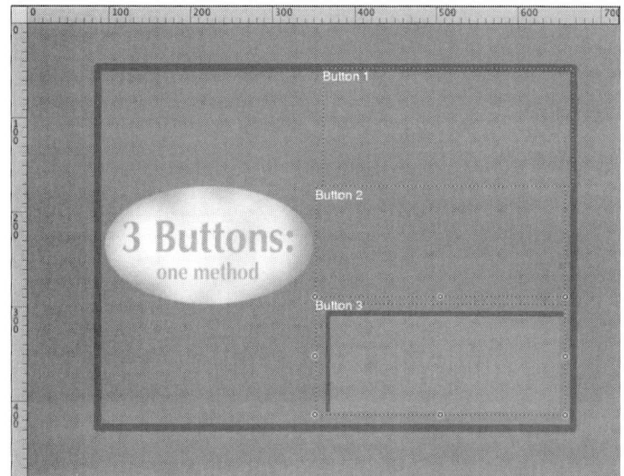

5. **Set the Normal levels.** Select any button. Open the Button Inspector (⌘-⌥-I). Click the Color Settings tab, and then click Advanced. Click Grayscale, and then click Normal. Choose one color for all four keys (olive green in this example). Set the black, dark gray, and light gray opacities to 10. Set the white opacity to 0. Each button you created should now appear in the Menu Editor.

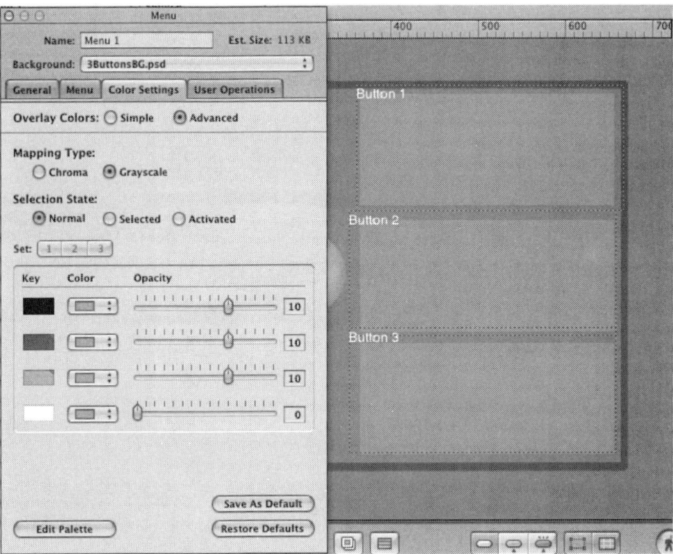

6. **Set the Selected levels.** The Selected highlights introduce the 3-D button effect. Click Selected in the Button Inspector. Set all four keys to the same color used for Normal levels. Set the black key to Opacity level 5, the dark gray to 10, and the light gray to 15.

7. **Set the Activated levels.** Click Activated. Choose a brighter version of the color you used for the normal and selected levels, and set all four keys to that color. Set the black, dark gray, and light gray opacities to 15. This creates a bright buttonwide flash when activated.

8. **Label a button.** Select a button, and click the Style tab in the Inspector. Enter some text. Set the label position to Center, and check Include Text

In Highlight. Select the text, and use the Font and Color palettes to customize the look. (The sample shown here uses 36-point Marker Felt and a
dark-brown color.)

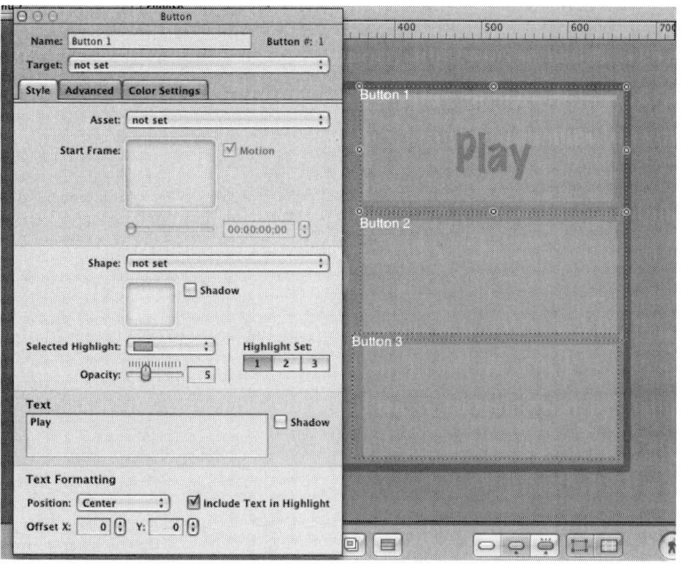

9. **Copy the style.** Select the button you just labeled. Ctrl-click(right-click) and
   choose Create Button Style. Name your new style Pop-Button Style, and save it
   as a new Self-Contained style.

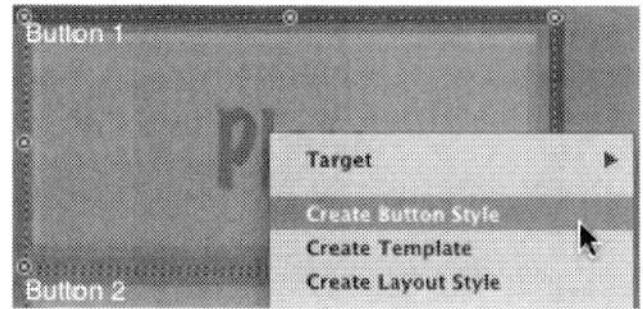
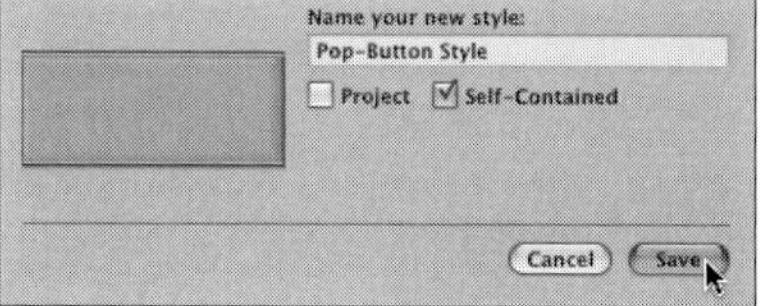

10. **Apply the style to your remaining buttons.** Drag your new style from the
    Palette onto each button. Choose Apply To Button from the drop palette.

11. **Edit the button titles.** Select the text for each button in turn and edit
    as needed.

12. **Simulate.** Click the Simulator button (on the main toolbar) and test your new interface. Unselected buttons will appear flat and dim. Selected buttons will pop out of the interface with brighter text and a three-dimensional look.

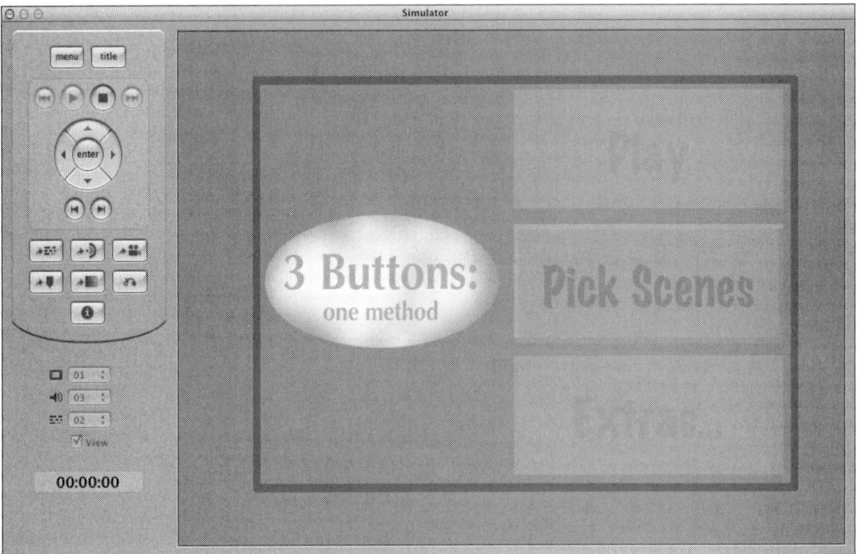

Solution: Create a Rollover Menu

Rollover buttons (also called "drop-down menu buttons") allow you to provide your viewers with the kind of interaction they might normally see on web pages and other computer-based applications. They consist of a series of titles, which when selected reveal more selectable buttons. This creates an effect similar to a program menu bar, where when selected the File, Edit, and Help titles reveal selectable menu items.

Once you understand how layered menus work, drop-down menu buttons are surprisingly easy to design although a little tedious to build. They consist of two kinds of buttons—main buttons which, when chosen, reveal a group of selectable drop-down buttons, and the drop-down buttons, which link to targets in your DVD project.

Follow these steps to build your menu assets in Photoshop and author them in DVD Studio Pro 2.

1. **Create a new file in Photoshop.** Open a new, transparent RGB image using a 4:3 aspect ratio. Start with 720×540 (NTSC) or 768×576 (PAL).

2. **Add background art and text.** Build the menu background, including the text for the main menu items. Merge these into a single background layer.

3. **Add normal art for each main button.** Recall that the background contains the text for each main button. Add a tinted selection for each button in your background. Keep the tint light. This art will merge with the selection art for each of your submenus. Place each normal selection item in a separate layer.

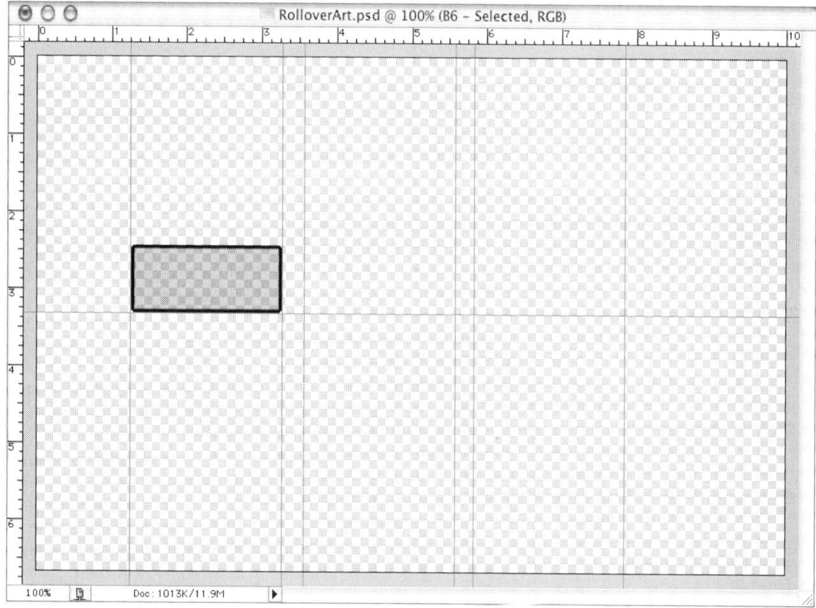

CHAPTER 3: CREATING OVERLAY AND LAYERED MENUS

4. **Add activated art for each main button.** Keep it simple. Main buttons have no function other than accessing their drop-down button groups. A copy of the normal art with a darker tint should do the trick.

5. **Add selected art for each main button.** When your viewer selects a main button, its associated drop-down buttons are revealed. Use a dark tint for the button itself and unselected shades for the items in the associated drop-down button group. Add any text for the drop-down buttons.

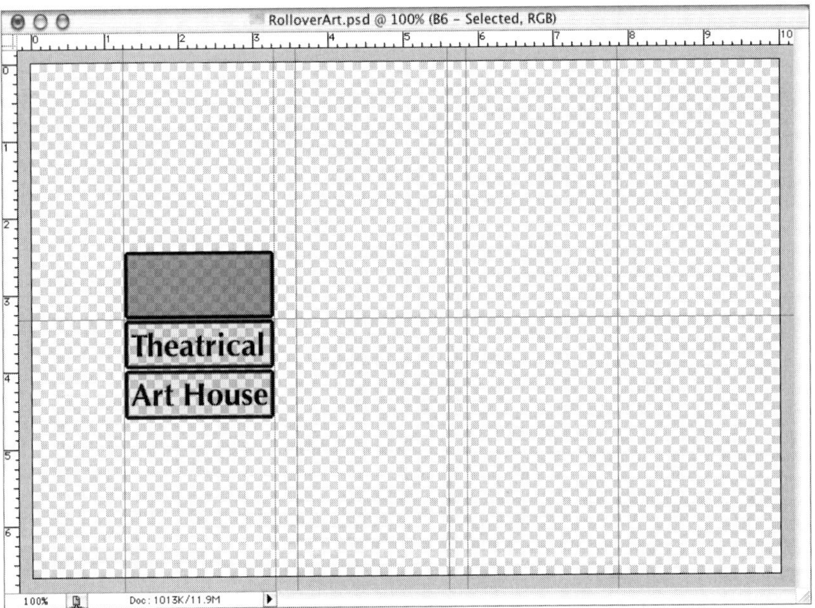

At this point, you have created normal, activated, and selected art for each of the main buttons in your project. Next, you'll develop the layers for the drop-down items.

6. **Add an empty layer for each drop-down button.** These buttons are not seen when their "parent" button isn't selected. Add a layer without content.

7. **Create the selected drop-down button art.** Adapt the selected art from the parent button to highlight each selected item. Tint the main button more lightly, and leave any unselected buttons in the revealed set in their original state.

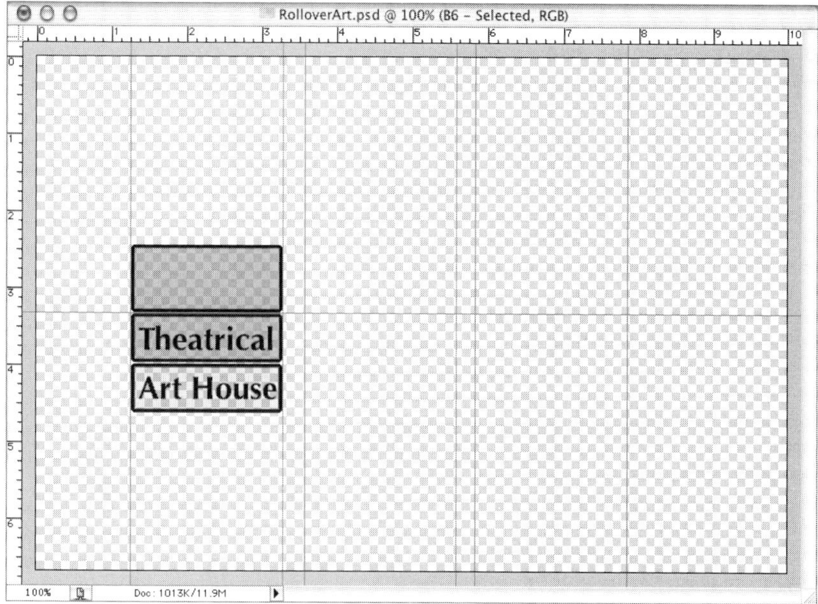

8. **Create the activated drop-down button art.** Copy each selected art layer, and add a visual flair to the selected button to create an activated version.

9. **Review your art.** You will have created a huge number of layers for this project. The 3-item main menu with 2-item button groups shown here contains 28 layers.

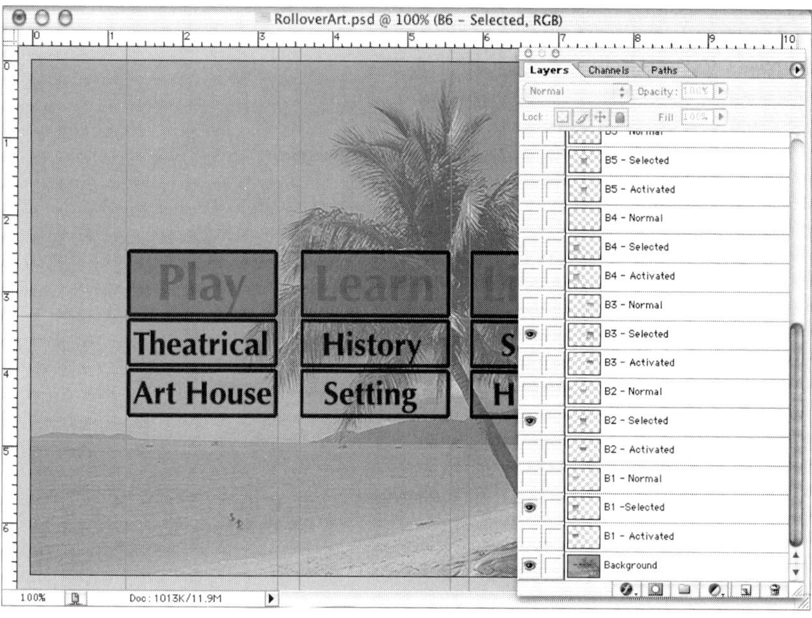

10. **Resize the menu to DV sizes.** Choose Image > Image Size. Clear the Constrain Proportions check box. Set your NTSC menu to 720×480 or your PAL menu to 720×576.

11. **Save.** Save your work to disk.

    You have now created a complex-layered PSD file similar to RolloverArt.psd, which can be found on the companion DVD. Return to DVD Studio Pro 2 to build your rollover menu.

12. **Create a new layered menu.** Click Add Layered Menu in the toolbar. Double-click the new menu to open it in the Menu Editor.

13. **Add your background art.** Drag your menu art onto the Menu Editor. (For this project, use RolloverArt.psd.) Choose Set Background/No Layers Visible from the drop palette.

14. **Make the background visible.** Open the Menu Inspector, and click the General tab. Scroll through the layers of your art until you find the background layer, and check it. The background art appears.

15. **Drag out your first button hot spot.** Select the button, and open the Button Inspector. Assign the art for each button state. Recall that the first column corresponds to Normal, the second to Selected, and the third to Activated. If you've named your layers well, this should proceed easily. Move and resize your button as needed to fit the art.

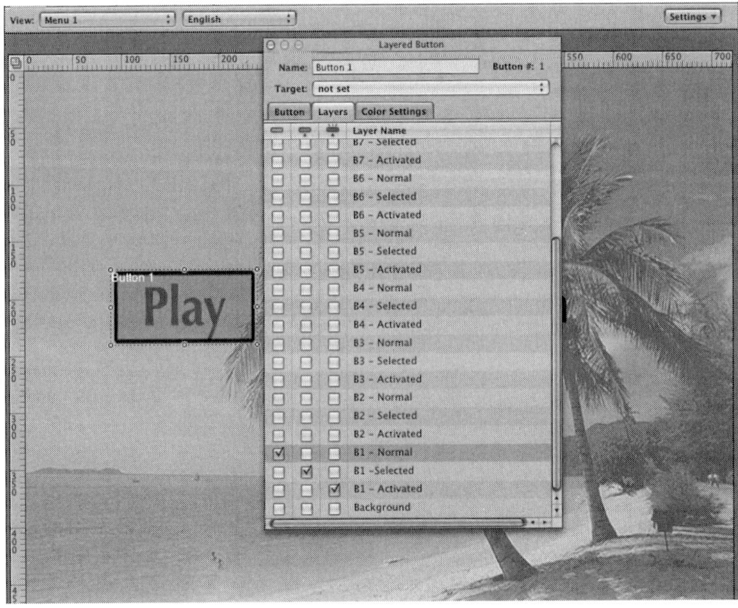

16. **Add the remaining buttons.** Repeat the previous step to add the rest of the buttons for your menu: drag out each button, set the button state art, and resize into position.

17. **Define button navigation for your menu.** Decide how you want your buttons to react to arrow-key presses from the remote control. Left and right requests can move between the drop-down button groups. Up and down requests should stay within button groups. The following list shows a navigation grid for this project. To make this grid work, select each button in turn, open the Button Inspector (⌘-⌥-I) and set the Up, Down, Left, and Right pop-ups in the Button tab.

Button	Up	Down	Left	Right
Button 1	1	4	1	2
Button 2	2	5	1	3
Button 3	3	6	2	3
Button 4	1	7	4	2
Button 5	2	8	1	3
Button 6	3	9	2	6
Button 7	4	7	7	2
Button 8	5	8	1	3
Button 9	6	9	2	9

18. **Simulate.** Save your work to your hard disk. Ctrl-click (right-click) the Menu Editor background, and choose Simulate from the pop-up. The DVD Studio Pro 2 Simulator window opens. Use the simulated remote and/or your mouse to scroll through the new drop-down menu buttons.

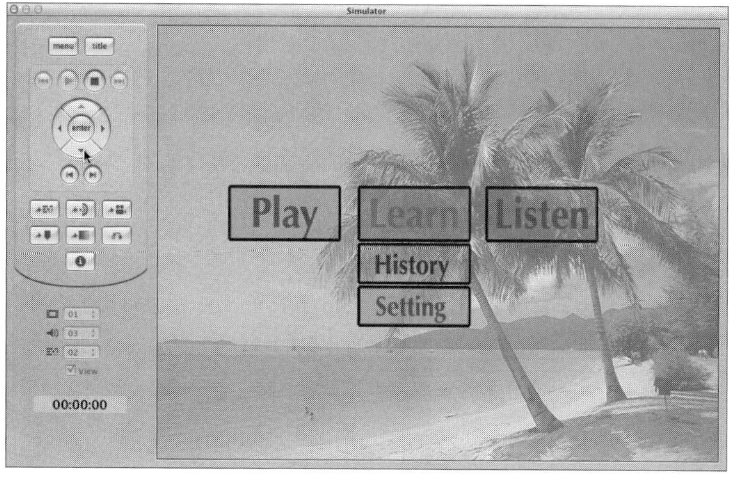

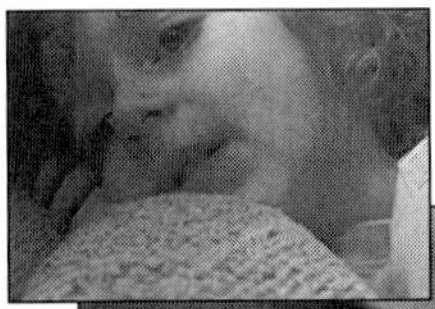

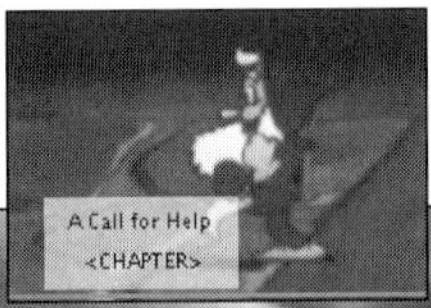
A Call for Help
<CHAPTER>

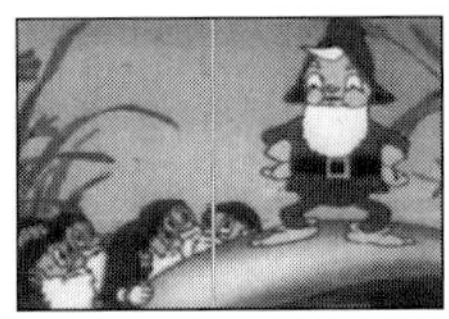

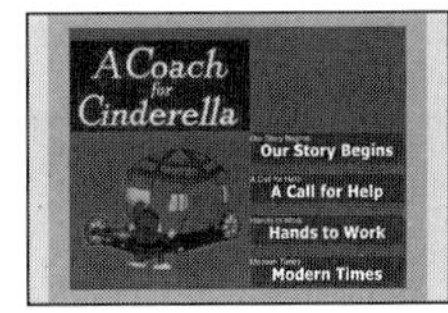

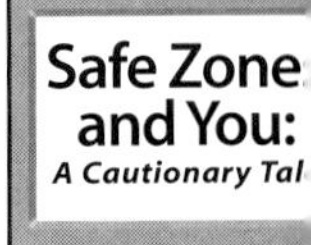

Prelinger
Archives

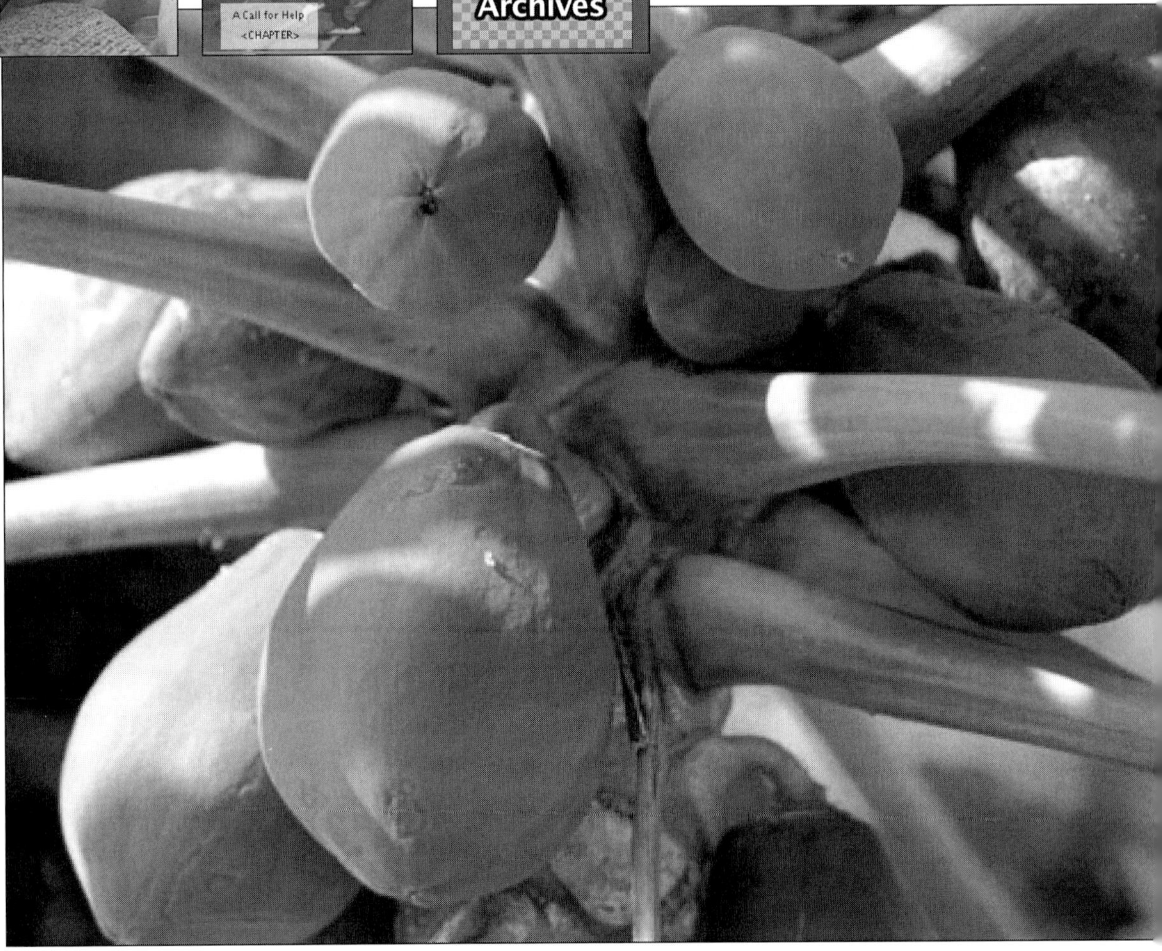

A Coach for Cinderella
Our Story Begins
A Call for Help
Hands to Work
Modern Times

Safe Zone
and You:
A Cautionary Tal

Preparing Video Assets

In the first three chapters, you explored the interface of DVD Studio Pro 2—its tool windows, its organization, and so forth—and you learned how to create some fairly sophisticated menus. In this chapter, you'll turn your attention to data—how to prepare video and audio sources for DVD Studio Pro 2 projects. As you'll discover, it sometimes takes a bit of planning and thought get your assets ready for DVD Studio Pro 2. In this chapter you'll learn how to collect, assemble, and modify your assets to bring out their best and produce the best visuals and audio for your DVD viewers.

Chapter Contents

Preparing Safe Colors

Television sets, particularly those using the NTSC system, have certain physical display limitations. Oversaturated colors and overscanning are two display problems that crop up over and over again. If you prepare "safe" video, your viewers can watch your DVDs with the best viewing quality and can avoid having to deal with cropped video and bleeding colors.

DVD Studio Pro 2 makes no accommodation for safe video. The video (and stills) you supply are the video (and stills) the program uses. You must implement any video safety measures before importing data into DVD Studio Pro 2. Plan and prepare your video accordingly. In this section, you'll learn why safe colors are important and how to implement this feature in Final Cut Pro, iMovie, and Photoshop before you move your video assets into DVD Studio Pro 2. You'll then learn how to keep your content within safe zones.

Avoiding Saturated Colors

Most television sets built for the American markert aren't built to display bright, saturated color. Strong colors, particularly reds, can bleed across the screen, extending beyond their natural boundaries and producing unpleasant viewing artifacts. Vivid colors may look great on your computer monitor and awful on your TV. Properly prepared DVD footage should not bleed. Avoid this problem by preprocessing your video assets to limit color amplitude into a safe range.

NTSC (National Television Standards Committee) brightness-limiting filters, which are available for most Macintosh video and image-editing software, can help. These filters cut off the top (and sometimes the bottom) extremes of illumination levels, producing a narrower dynamic range. Typical filters use a 5% cutoff, limiting the brightest and darkest colors to a middle 90% window.

The exact approach depends on the color model used. Luminance reduction affects brightness without changing chrominance (color). Saturation reduction subdues individual color channels, adjusting each color as needed.

The safe color effect can be subtle, producing slightly subdued colors that have been barely desaturated.

PAL (Phase Alternating Line) video uses a different color model than NTSC and produces fewer saturated color problems.

Safe Colors with Final Cut Pro and Final Cut Express

Both versions of Final Cut allow you to inspect your clips to determine when luminance (brightness) or chrominance (color) values exceed normal broadcast levels. Figure 4.1 shows range-checking feedback in Final Cut Pro 4, indicating areas of concern. Detecting these problems allows you to fix them on a frame-by-frame basis or by applying a filter across an entire clip or sequence.

Many of the methods in this chapter (including range checking, setting safe colors, and so on) apply to both Final Cut Pro and Final Cut Express. If you're using Final Cut Express, you should be able to follow the steps without changes.

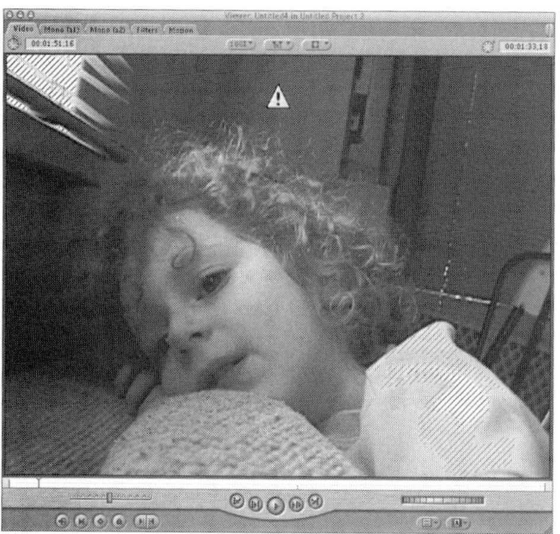

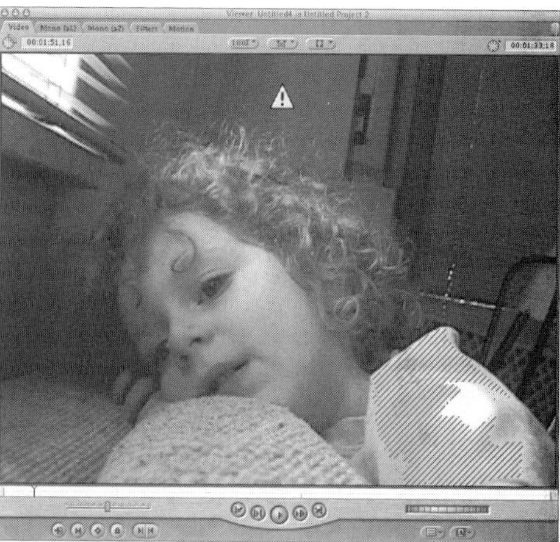

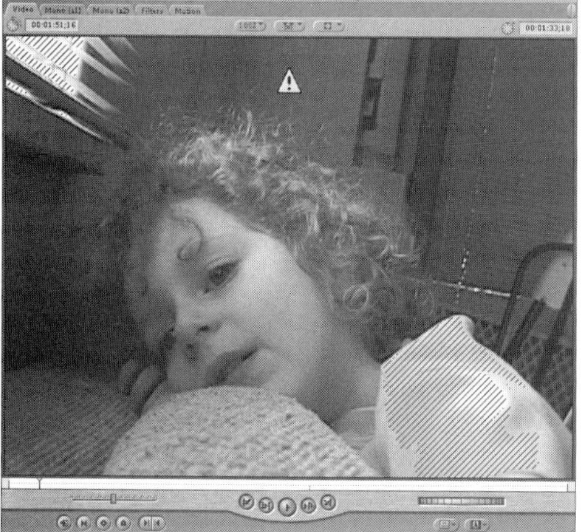

Figure 4.1 Range Checking in Final Cut Pro 4: Excess luma (top left), excess chroma (top right), combined excess luma and chroma (bottom left). Final Cut Pro provides broadcast-level range-checking feedback in two ways. The "warning sign" exclamation point indicates the existence of luma (top left) or chroma (top right) values that are out of gamut for broadcast standards. Individual zebra striped portions indicate those areas affected by illegal levels. Here, the top left image depicts excess luminance in both the window and on the brightest areas of the subject's shoulder. The top right image shows excess chrominance on the subject's shoulder, but not in the window. The bottom left image shows the combined warning areas.

Final Cut's range-checking methods include the following:

Scanning for Brightness Levels To visualize those portions of your video that exceed broadcast brightness levels, choose View > Range Check > Excess Luma. Red zebra stripes indicate luminance above 100%. Green stripes indicate luminance between 90% and 100%. A green check mark displays when all luminance values are legal. A yellow warning sign indicates out-of-gamut luminance.

Scanning for Color Levels Choose View > Range Check > Excess Chroma to detect overly saturated colors. All illegal chrominance levels appear with red zebra stripes. As with brightness levels, the green check mark indicates that all chroma within the displayed frame is legal. The yellow warning sign cautions about out-of-gamut chroma.

Scanning for Both Color and Brightness Choose View > Range Check > Both to detect all out-of-gamut pixels. The green check mark and yellow warning sign work as they do with the other two options. Choose View > Range Check > Off to turn off range checking.

Final Cut offers several color-correction filters to adjust out-of-broadcast-range pixels and bring them into broadcast legal limits. Of these, the one most useful to the DVD Studio Pro 2 user is Broadcast Safe. With a single command, Broadcast Safe transforms clips with illegal luma and chroma values and brings them into broadcast compliance. To use Broadcase Safe, follow these steps:

1. **Select a clip.** Choose any clip that has illegal luma or chroma values.

2. **Apply Broadcast Safe.** Choose Effects > Video Filters > Color Correction > Broadcast Safe. This filter scans your clip for out-of-gamut pixels and adjusts them to broadcast levels.

Final Cut Pro offers many other professional color-calibration features as part of its program suite, helping you capture and produce accurate color for all your digital video projects.

Safe Colors with iMovie

Unlike Final Cut Pro, iMovie offers neither out-of-gamut detection nor a built-in brightness and color limiter. Fortunately, it's simple to program iMovie plug-ins. You'll find a copy of the Sadun NTSC Safe Colors plug-in (Sadun NTSC 0.1) on the DVD that accompanies this book. This plug-in helps you bring your video into NTSC broadcast compliance. Follow these steps to use the plug-in:

1. **Quit iMovie.** iMovie must not be running when you install plug-ins.

2. **Install the color safe plug-in.** Drag a copy of the Sadun NTSC plug-in from the companion DVD to your ~/Library/iMovie/Plug-ins folder.

3. **Launch iMovie.** iMovie loads the new plug-in as it launches.

4. **Select your clip or clips.** Select your clips from the Timeline or from the Clips Viewer.

5. **Open the Effects palette.** The Effects palette lists all installed iMovie plug-ins.

6. **Choose * NTSC Safe Colors.** The asterisk at the start of the plug-in name ensures that the plug-in appears at or near the start of the list of effects. Figure 4.2 shows the Effects palette with the correct filter selected.

7. **Click Apply.** iMovie applies the filter to your selected clips, limiting their dynamic range and ensuring they comply with NTSC broadcast-safe colors.

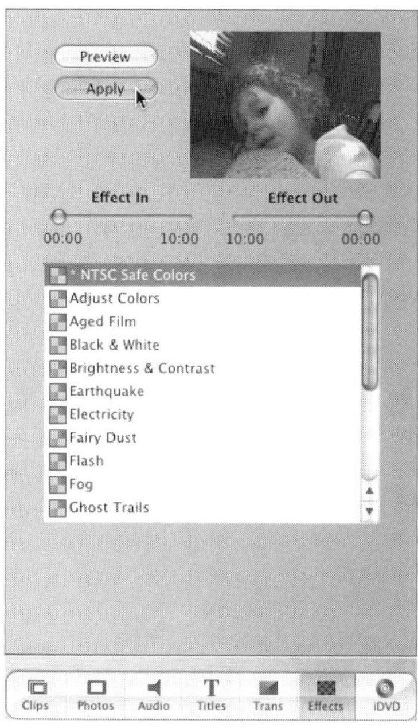

Figure 4.2 The Sadun NTSC Safe Colors filter appears toward the top of the list of installed effects—the asterisk that precedes its name helps sort it toward the beginning. When applied to the selected clips, it limits the clip's dynamic range of colors to comply with NTSC broadcast standards. Unlike the Final Cut Pro filter that uses a luminance and chrominance model, the iMovie filter uses an RGB color model, limiting each color channel individually into a safe range. It uses the Adobe- and Apple-recommended range of tones, allowing only levels between 15 and 235 out of a possible 256 tones (0–255).

Safe Colors and Adobe Photoshop

Still images play an important role in DVD Studio Pro 2. You can use stills in slideshows and in menus or directly in videos. Like video clips, still images are subject to legal and illegal colors. Adobe Photoshop helps you prepare your stills for DVD Studio Pro 2 with its built-in limiting filter. Follow these steps:

1. **Open your image in Photoshop.** Select the image you want to use in your DVD Studio Pro 2 project and open it in a new Photoshop window.

2. **Select All.** Choose Edit > Select All (⌘-A) to choose all the pixels in your image.

3. **Apply the NTSC filter.** Choose Filters > Video > NTSC Colors.

4. **Save your image.** Once filtered, your image is ready to be saved and used in your DVD Studio Pro 2 project.

💿 If you need to process more than one image at a time, you can use batch processing in Photoshop. A Color Safe droplet appears on the DVD that accompanies this book.

Using Safe Zones

Picture tubes in most consumer television sets in the United States *overscan* to compensate for component aging over time. (This problem does not affect LCD televisions.) Overscanning hides display flaws at the edges of your picture tube by producing a bigger picture than your TV actually shows. The extra areas are hidden behind a faceplate. Since only part of the image appears on-screen, broadcasters use two rules-of-thumb, called "action safe" and "title safe" to position images and text so they'll display reliably on all television sets. Figure 4.3 shows how overscanning can produce an image that counters your expectations. Items that stray from the safe zones may not display correctly.

Safe Colors: Text and Borders

Sometimes an ounce of prevention really is worth a pound of cure. Two video color problems, chroma crawl and moiré effects, are best dealt with by designing the content of your video to prevent their occurrence instead of relying on filters to correct them afterward.

Chroma crawl, a form of video distortion, appears when high-contrast colors appear directly next to each other, such as red next to blue or green, typically when displaying text and shape borders. The distortion appears as small flickering edge noise where one color meets another.

This problem is particularly noticeable with still menus, which display for extended periods of time. You should be able to see this effect in action by building the "Cinderella" project at the end of this chapter—it uses high-contrast colors in the main menu.

When you design text for your DVD, choose more subdued colors over highly saturated ones to avoid chroma crawl. Pastels and grays work particularly well in these contexts. Don't be afraid to use softer colors. They'll look terrific on your TV screen.

Text presents a particular problem because many letters contain thin high-contrast lines. Always use large fonts with thick features. Avoid thin fonts and those with serifs. Anti-aliasing your text can help avoid boundary problems.

Thin, high-contrast lines in your video can also cause display problems. When displayed horizontally, single-pixel-wide lines may flicker, creating an irritating visual buzz. When displayed in grids, thin lines may produce artificial rainbow or moiré patterns on your viewer's TV. As a rule, avoid thin, high-contrast lines. If you can't, be sure to thicken lines and blur them slightly to avoid high-contrast artifacts.

Broadcasters use two kinds of safe zones when developing video content. Each zone plays a specific role.

Action Safe Limiting action to the action safe zone ensures that critical visual elements remain on-screen at all times, even if they are slightly clipped. A viewer can follow the drama of a passed football when the arm begins just off screen and moves into view throughout the shot. A football pass that starts off-screen and remains off-screen is unacceptable. The action safe zone helps you position your action throughout your clip. Action safe generally corresponds to the inner 90% of your screen, clipping 5% on the top, bottom, left, and right of the display.

Title Safe When an item must be fully visible throughout an entire shot, you must limit it within the title safe zone. The title safe zone is more restrictive than action safe and is chosen such that every pixel within it should remain on-screen at all times. The human brain proves more sensitive to clipped text than you might think. Any overscanning

Figure 4.3 Of all display elements, titles are the most "fragile." Viewers notice immediately when even a small part of a title gets clipped. The first image shown here depicts a standard NTSC-sized 720 × 480 title still. You might expect it to appear on-screen as designed, with the white space and visibility intact. The second image shows how most people expect the still to display. Unfortunately, the third image with its partial letters and missing white space better predicts the results you'll encounter. Use safe zones, as shown in the final image, to help design images that display reliably and accurately on all television screens.

defects in on-screen text, such as titles, are particularly noticeable. Cut off just a bit of a title, and the problem jumps out of the TV into the awareness of your viewers. Title safe uses 10% clipping, preserving the middle 80% of your picture's height and width.

Safe Zone Dimensions

The dimensions of the action safe and title safe zones are as follows.

System	Normal	Action Safe	Title Safe
NTSC	720 × 480 pixels	648 × 432 pixels	576 × 384 pixels
Pixels	(0,0) to (720,480)	(36,24) to (684,456)	(72,48) to (648,432)
PAL	720 × 576 pixels	648 × 518 pixels	576 × 460 pixels
Pixels	(0,0) to (720,576)	(36,30) to (684,548)	(72,58) to (648,518)

Staying within Safe Zones

To ensure that your footage, stills, and titles remain in the safe zone, use one or more of the following methods:

Shoot for the Zone Plan and shoot your footage with the action safe zone in mind. As the simplest solution, a little planning goes a long way. Action-safe footage will display correctly, always, on all televisions.

Shift and Resize It's occasionally necessary to use third-party plug-in "filters" (video image processing) to shift your footage and recompose your shots. This approach is slow and tedious and degrades your video. When possible, shoot your footage right the first time.

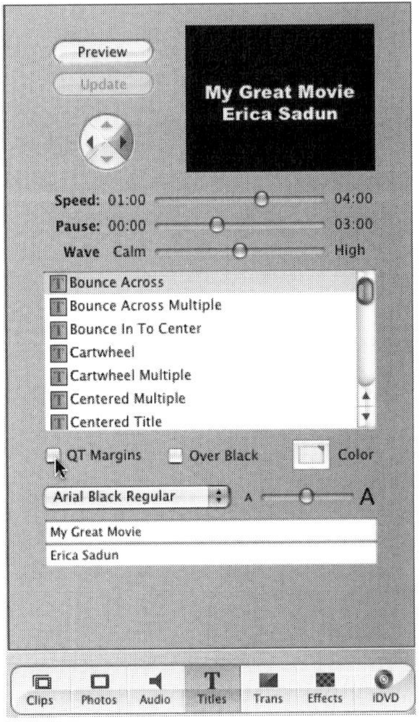

Figure 4.4 iMovie's QuickTime Margins feature turns the notion of title safe on its head. Instead of constraining titles to the inner 80% of your frame, QT Margins lets you break out of the default title-safe "box" and extend your text from one end of the frame to the other. QT Margins assumes that you'll display your video only on computers and are thus immune from overscanning limitations.

Disable QT Margins (iMovie) iMovie helps you limit titles to the title safe zone of your footage. Locate the QT Margins check box in the Titles palette. In iMovie, disabling QT Margins turns on title-safe tilting. QT Margins, which stands for QuickTime Margins, allows your titles to extend fully from one side of your image to the other. Figure 4.4 shows this iMovie option.

Use Zone Overlays (Final Cut Pro) Final Cut offers Broadcast Safe Zone overlays that you can use when adding visual details to your projects. Choose View > Show Overlays to enable overlays (Ctrl-⌥-W), and then choose View > Show Title Safe to display both action-safe and title-safe outlines, as shown in Figure 4.5. These overlays do not affect your footage in any way and can be used as reference during editing.

Design Stills for the Zone Still images meant for video use safe zones too. Photoshop has no built-in overlays, but you can easily construct a safe-zone grid. To use it, add it to your stills as a new layer. Lay out the visual components as needed, and hide the layer with the grid. Figure 4.6 shows a typical, reusable grid.

Figure 4.5 Final Cut Pro's Title Safe overlay provides a visual grid to help size and place your titles. Be sure to enable overlays (choose View > Show Overlays or press Ctrl-⌥-W) and show the broadcast safe zones (choose View > Show Title Safe) to visualize the title-safe overlays in your windows. Dragging the Video tab out to its own window and displaying the Controls tab allows you to design text overlays and see them in the context of title safe at the same time.

Figure 4.6 A Photoshop Safe Zone layer helps you lay out your stills for DVD Studio Pro 2. When finished, discard or hide the layer before saving. Safe zone templates appear on the DVD that accompanies this book.

Resize and Embed Both Photoshop and Graphic Converter (www.lemkesoft.com) allow you to batch process still images to resize and pad them into compliance with action safe or title safe. Graphic Converter has the edge in offering fast, convenient results.

Understanding Pixel Shape

Computer monitors and television sets use slightly different pixel shapes. Computers use square pixels—the distance from each pixel to its nearest horizontal or vertical neighbor is equal. Video pixels are rectangular—horizontal and vertical distance between pixels are unequal. This difference occurs for compelling reasons.

Both NTSC and PAL standard video use 4:3 aspect ratios. Because DV (the digital video standard) uses 720 pixels per line, TVs would need to display 540 vertical lines to maintain a strict 4:3 aspect (1.333) with square pixels. NTSC offers 480 visible lines, and PAL offers 576. To fill the 720 ×540 space, NTSC pixels must stretch a little vertically and PAL pixels must squeeze.

This means that what you see isn't necessarily what you get. To predict what the picture on your computer will look like on a television set, you must resize it to match the output aspect ratio. You must also design with scaling in mind so that your images appear undistorted in your final DVD.

Understanding pixel size and scaling your images fare necessary before you resize pictures for safe zones.

Safe Zones in DVD Studio Pro 2

DVD Studio Pro 2 allows you to overlay your Menu Editor and Viewer with safe zone templates for controlled layout. Choose any of the following methods to use these overlays:

- In the Menu Editor or Viewer, open the Settings pop-up in the upper-right corner. Choose Title Safe Area or Action Safe Area to toggle the overlays on and off.

- Choose View > Title Safe Area (⌘-Shift-E) to toggle the title safe overlay.

- Choose View > Action Safe Area (⌘-⌥-E) to toggle the action safe overlay.

Once you can see the overlays, here's a trick to help you use them:

1. Open the Menu Editor and resize the Menu tab quadrant to its largest size, hiding the other quadrants as needed.

2. Choose View > Show Guides (⌘-;).

3. Choose View > Show Ruler (⌘-R).

4. Drag guides from the ruler to the edges of the safe zone overlay you want to use. Watch the context pop-ups to position the guides exactly.

With the guides in place, you can use built-in positioning to place items within and precisely on the borders of your safe zone.

- **Occupy the zone.** Use the Distribute feature (choose Arrange > Distribute Objects) to make the most of your safe zone space.

- **Align your buttons.** You might want to arrange buttons along the right side of the zone. Snapping makes this happen. (Choose Arrange > Align Objects > Right. Select the aligned objects, and snap them to the guide.)

- **Go to opposite extremes.** To set items at catercorner, just snap them to opposite corners. Or add two copies of a temporary object to space your items out farther from the corners themselves. Snap the spacers to the corners. Snap your items to the spacers. Discard the spacers.

Follow these steps to prepare your stills.

1. **Design for the target aspect ratio.** Begin with an image that uses the targeted display aspect ratio (4:3 for normal video, 16:9 for widescreen), and design your graphics for that aspect. Use the following chart to help choose your dimensions.

Aspect	Design Image Sizes
4:3 (1.333)	720 × 534 for NTSC, 768 × 576 for PAL
16:9 (1.78)	854 × 480 for NTSC, 1024 × 576 for PAL

2. **Scale to DV sizes.** Use Photoshop or Graphic Converter to rescale your image to proper DV dimensions after you're finished with the menu or still graphic design. Your image will squeeze slightly after you scale, but don't worry. On a TV, the pixels reshape to display properly.

System	DV Dimensions
NTSC (4:3, 16:9)	720 × 480
PAL (4:3, 16:9)	720 × 576

3. **Import into DVD Studio Pro 2.** Bring your images into DVD Studio Pro 2 as new assets.

4. **View an image.** Click the Viewer tab and select one of your image assets.

5. **Choose a pixel shape.** Select pixel shapes from the Viewer's Settings menu. (The Settings menu in the Menu Editor offers the same choices.) Choose Settings > Square Pixels to match the view you'd see in Photoshop. Choose Settings > Rectangular Pixels to preview how your asset will look when displayed on a television set.

In DVD Studio Pro 2, "shapes" help create menus without overlays. When imported, shape graphics automatically scale to maintain their aspect ratio. An imported square shape appears square in the Menu Editor and Viewer (when displayed with rectangular pixels) but when viewed in the Inspector (⌘-⌥-I), the scaled dimensions are revealed. A 100 × 100 square shape imports as 100 × 90 (NTSC) or 100 × 94 (PAL).

Preparing Stills with Graphic Converter

For those people frustrated with Photoshop's slow and awkward batch processing features, Lemke Software GraphicConverter provides a useful alternative. This shareware product allows you to batch convert entire folders of still images before importing them into DVD Studio Pro 2. This process is important because DVD Studio Pro 2 offers no safe-zone scaling. All processing for title safe and action safe must occur before import into the program.

Preparing GraphicConverter for Batch Operations

GraphicConverter allows you to add "batch operations" to its batch processor. These operations act as filters and are applied to each picture that passes through the converter. In the following steps, you'll remove any existing batch operations, to make sure that no unwanted operations take place on your images.

1. **Open the batch converter.** Launch GraphicConverter if needed. Choose File > Convert (Ctrl-⌘-M) to open the Batch window.

2. **Remove all existing batch operations.** Click Batch, select any existing items from the Batch Table, and click Delete. Repeat until no batch items exist.

Batch Scaling

Always design images using their target aspect ratios and then scale for import. Follow these steps to scale 4:3 and 16:9 stills to proper DV sizes so you can use them in your DVD Studio Pro 2 projects.

1. **Add a new Scale batch item.** In the Batch window, select Scale, and then click Add. Click the Size radio button. Set Width to 720. In the NTSC system, set Height to 480. In the PAL system, set Height to 576. Uncheck Proportional, check High Quality Scaling, and then click OK.

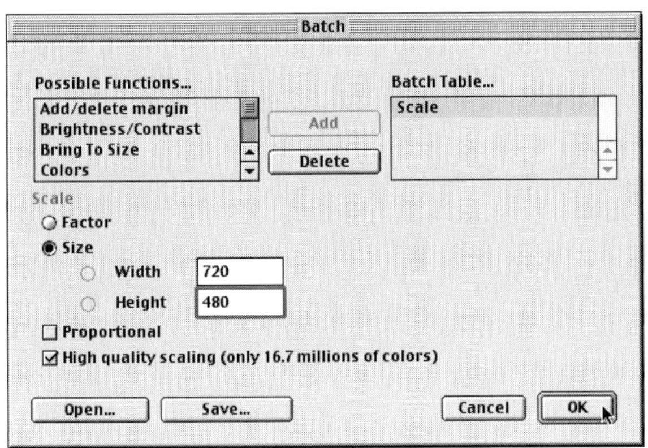

2. **Select the files to convert.** In the left column, navigate to your images. Select the files you want to convert. In the right column, navigate to a destination folder.

3. **Click Convert.** GraphicConverter resizes your 4:3 and 16:9 stills to DV sizes.

4. **Remove the Scale batch operation.** Click Batch, select Scale from the Batch Table, and click Delete. This restores the Batch window to its previous clean state.

Scaling Odd-Sized Images

At times you'll want to include nonstandard-sized images in your DV projects. The steps in the next section, "Batch Preparation for Safe Zones," embed odd-sized images in proper DV-sized, safe-zone compliant stills. In these steps, you'll adjust the pixel shapes in your odd-sized images to ensure that they'll display properly on TV sets.

Use this guide to determine the proper vertical scaling for your image.

Target Aspect Ratio	NTSC DV 720 × 480 (1.5)	PAL DV 720 × 576 (1.25)
4:3 (1.33)	1.13	0.94
16:9 (1.78)	0.84	0.70

1. **Add a new Scale batch item.** In the Batch window, select Scale, click Add, and then click the Factor radio button. Set X to 1.0. Use the above guidelines to select a vertical scaling number. Enter that value in Y. Uncheck Proportional, check High Quality Scaling, and then click OK to accept these settings and dismiss the Batch window.

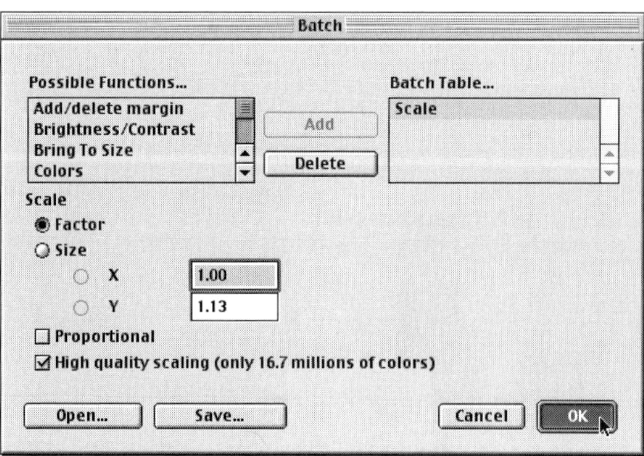

Scaling to a factor changes the size of your image proportionally. For example, a factor of 1.5 stretches your image by 50%, no matter the original size. Scaling to a size changes your image proportions to a set number, such as 720 × 480 pixels.

2. **Select the files to convert.** In the left column, navigate to your images, and select the files you want to convert. In the right column, navigate to your first destination folder.

3. **Click Convert.** GraphicConverter adjusts pixel dimensions to match your target system.

4. **Remove the Scale batch operation.** Click Batch, select Scale from the Batch Table, and click Delete.

Batch Preparation for Safe Zones

Follow these steps to add a matte around your still images. This process converts your images twice. In the first pass, it squeezes them down so they'll fit in either the action or title safe zone of your project. In the second pass, it pads them back up to full DV frame sizes (720 × 480 NTSC, 720 × 576 PAL).

1. **Add a new Max Size batch item.** In the Batch window, select Scale, and then click Add. For action safe, set Max Width to 648, and set Max Height to 432. (In the PAL system, use 518 for height.) For title safe, set Max Width to 576, and set Max Height to 384. (In the PAL system, use 460 for height.) Uncheck the Invert Dimensions For Vertical Images check box, check the Proportional check box, clear the Fit To Value(s) check box, and then click OK to accept these settings and dismiss the Batch window.

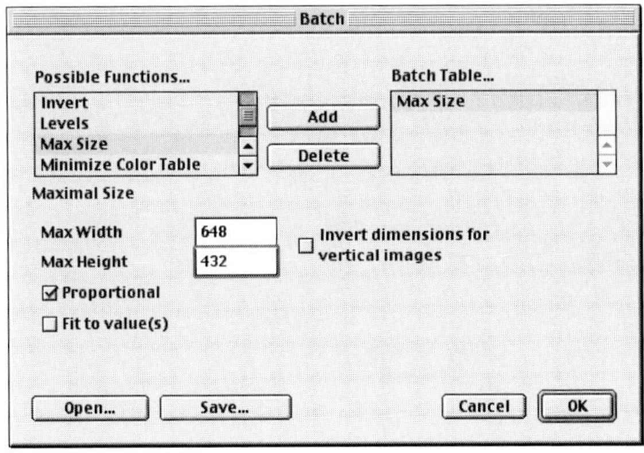

2. **Select the files to convert.** In the left column navigate to your images, and select the files you want to convert. In the right column, navigate to your first destination folder.

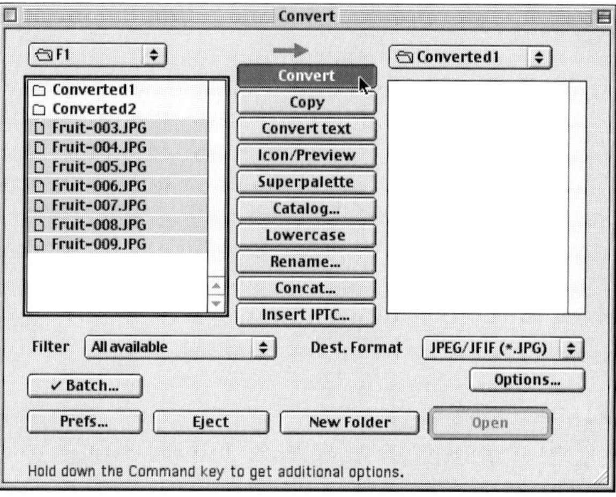

3. **Click Convert.** GraphicConverter squeezes your images into the safe zone sizes you specified in the Max Size batch item. Wait for the program to finish converting your selections.

4. **Remove the Max Size batch operation.** Click Batch, select Max Size from the Batch Table, and click Delete.

5. **Add a new Bring To Size batch item.** Remain in the Batch window. Select Bring To Size, and click Add. For the NTSC system, set the width to 720 and set the height 480. For the PAL system, set the width 720 and set the height to 576. In the Width section, click the Center radio button. In the Height section, click the Center radio button. Keep black as your padding color. Click OK to accept these settings and dismiss the Batch window.

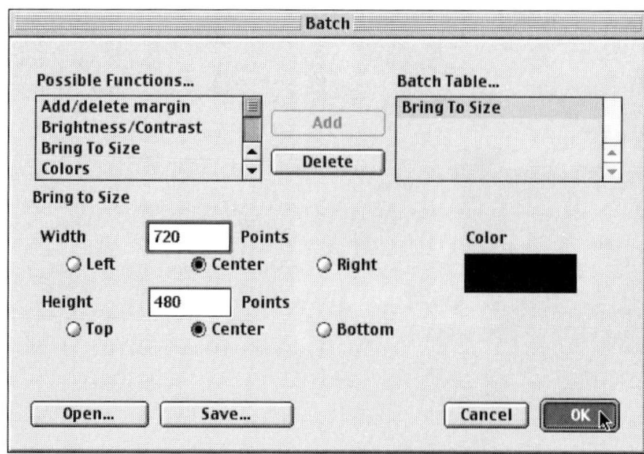

6. **Select the files to convert.** In the left column, navigate to the images you converted in step 5, and select the affected files. In the right column, navigate to your second destination folder.

Now your images are resized and buffered and will import perfectly into DVD Studio Pro 2 with proper safe-zone sizing. Compare the before and after shots in Figure 4.7.

Chapter and Compression Markers

In Final Cut, iMovie, QuickTime, and Compressor, markers point to important frames in your movies. Markers act like a kind of video "comment" track (in the programming sense, not the director's commentary sense), adding reference points within your clips. For those authoring DVDs, two kinds of markers play a special role: chapter markers and compression markers.

Chapter markers, which are discussed further in Chapter 7, divide video into discrete blocks that you can navigate with your DVD remote control. Next Chapter and Previous Chapter buttons let you skip from one portion of your video to another. Both the QuickTime MPEG Encoder and the standalone Compressor applications read and use chapter markers, producing encoded MPEG files with intact chapter references. Further, DVD Studio Pro 2 lets you use these to create chapter menus.

Original: 521 × 754

Converted: 298 × 432 image within 720 × 480 background

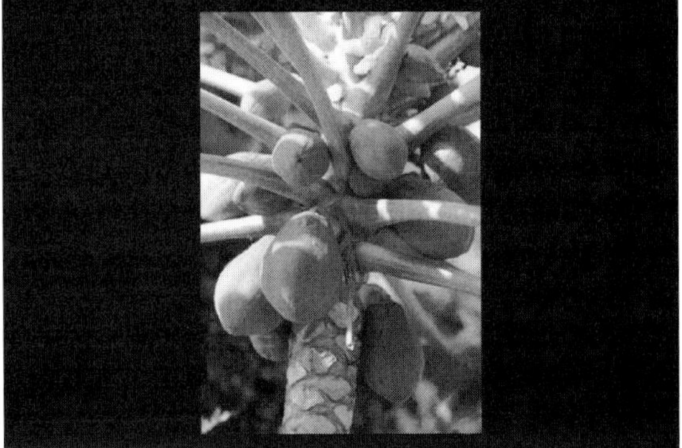

Figure 4.7 The Lemke Software GraphicConverter offers convenient batch-processing tools to help prepare still images for DVD Studio Pro 2. Here, you see before and after images for one item when following the steps detailed in this section. Notice how this procedure inlays the image into a proper DVD Studio Pro 2 shape while using the broadcast safe zone.

122

Compression markers play a different role. They show points where your video content changes abruptly, such as a cut from a dim interior shot to a brightly lit exterior. These markers hint at places where Compressor should add keyframes (I-frames).

Working with Markers in Final Cut Pro and Express

Both Final Cut Pro and Final Cut Express automatically add compression markers at each edit point within your project. Figure 4.8 shows how you can instruct Compressor to ignore compression markers to produce better MPEG-2 encoding.

Adding Chapter Markers in Final Cut

Follow these steps to add chapter markers to your clips or sequences in Final Cut.

1. **Set the playhead.** In the Timeline, drag the playhead to any point where you want to add a marker.

2. **Press the M key.** Alternatively, press the backquote key (`) or choose Mark > Markers > Add or click the Add Marker button in the canvas (it's just to the right of the Mark In and Mark Out buttons in Final Cut Pro 4). Depending on whether you've selected from a clip or a sequence, a new marker appears in the video viewer or the sequence timeline.

3. **Press M again.** The Edit Marker window opens, as shown in Figure 4.9.

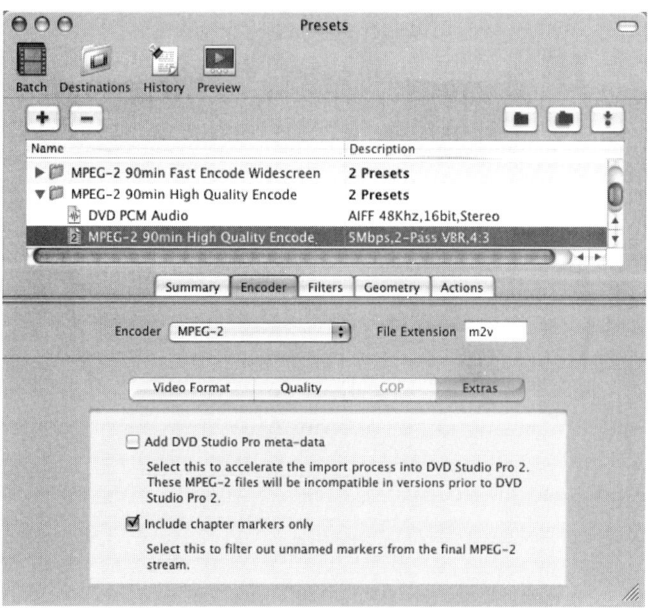

Figure 4.8 The Extras pane in Compressor allows you to exclude compression markers. Open the Presets window (click Presets in the Batch window). Select any MPEG-2 encoding. Click the Encoder tab and click Extras in the horizontal button list. Select Include Chapter Markers Only.

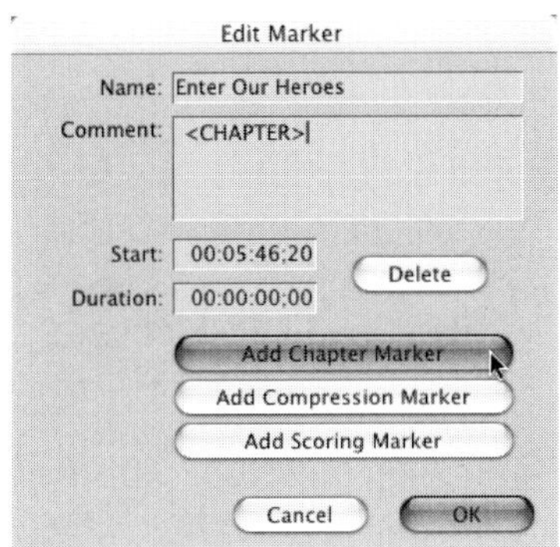

Figure 4.9 Adding meaningful chapter names in Final Cut Pro 4 makes it simple to build chapter menus in DVD Studio Pro 2. DVD Studio Pro 2 uses these names to create button labels.

4. **Enter a name.** Default marker names are typically set to Marker 1, Marker 2, and so forth. Click in the Name field and update the marker name to something more memorable and meaningful. DVD Studio Pro 2 uses the text you enter to produce button labels for chapter menus.

5. **Click Add Chapter Marker.** This notifies Final Cut Pro that you want to treat this marker as a chapter. Final Cut Pro adds a <CHAPTER> comment to your marker.

6. **Click OK.** Final Cut Pro closes the Edit Marker window and updates the marker information per your changes.

Adding Compression Markers

In Final Cut Pro, adding compression markers works just like adding chapter markers. Follow the steps in the previous section, but click Add Compression Marker rather than Add Chapter Marker. Feel free to skip step 4. Names are not important when working with compression markers—they will not appear in DVD Studio Pro 2.

In addition to the compression markers you set, Final Cut Pro automatically adds a compression marker at each of your project's edit points. Unlike Compressor, which gives you the option to use the compression markers to place I-frames at the scene changes, the QuickTime MPEG Encoder ignores these automatic compression markers but includes all the markers you add by hand.

Removing Markers

You can easily remove markers from your clips and sequences. Select any marker (Figure 4.10 shows a nice trick for accomplishing this) and press M to open the Edit Marker window. Click Delete. Final Cut Pro removes the marker from your project. To remove all the markers from the selected asset, choose Mark > Markers > Delete All.

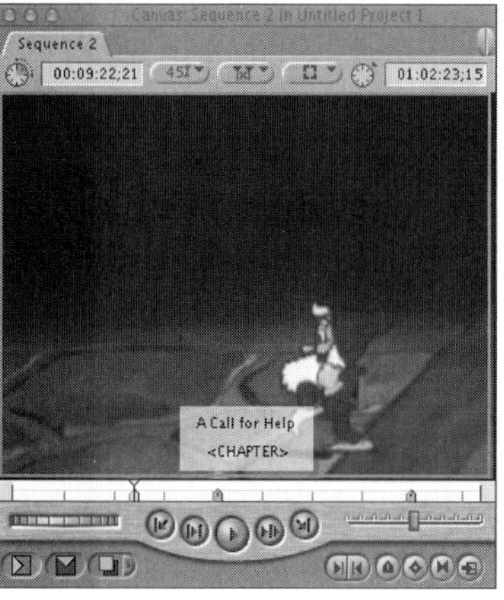

Figure 4.10 Final Cut Pro provides many helpful visual cues. When your playhead rests on a marker, an overlay appears in the canvas. To enable overlays, choose View > Show Overlays (Ctrl-□-W). To navigate between markers, choose Mark > Next > Marker (Shift+Up arrow) and Mark > Previous > Marker (Shift+Down arrow) Name your marker by selecting it, pressing M, entering a new name, and clicking OK.

Important Marker Facts

Here are some key points to remember about markers when working with Final Cut Pro:

Don't add more than 99 chapter markers. DVD Studio Pro 2 allows you to add at most 99 chapter markers per MPEG-2 video stream that will make up the video in a track. Remember this when working in Final Cut Pro.

Compression markers force I-frames. DVD Studio Pro 2 does not use compression markers. They're only important during the compression process, in which they force keyframes (I-frames) to occur. Use compression markers sparingly.

Leave space between markers. Markers should not appear within one second of each other or within one second of the start or end of each clip.

Multi-angle streams require identical markers. When you are working with multi-angle tracks, MPEG structures must match exactly. Place your markers precisely by time code in the same positions for each sequence you plan on encoding to MPEG-2.

DVD Studio Pro 2 lets you add chapter markers in the Track tab. This feature can help when you import sources already encoded to MPEG-2, which may not contain chapters, into DVD Studio Pro 2.

Creating Chapter Markers in iMovie

The recent release of iMovie 3 allows you to add chapter markers to your movies. These chapter markers work the same way as those you create in Final Cut Pro and are compatible with DVD Studio Pro 2, iDVD, and QuickTime Player. Follow these steps to add chapter markers to your iMovie project.

1. **Edit your movie.** Finish building your movie before you proceed to adding chapters.

2. **Position the playhead.** Move the playhead to the position where you want the new chapter to appear.

3. **Open the iDVD palette.** Click the iDVD button (it appears just to the right of Effects) to display the palette.

4. **Click Add Chapter.** iMovie adds a new chapter to your project. If you're viewing the timeline, you'll notice that a small yellow diamond appears at the top of your timeline at the location of the chapter.

5. **Edit the name.** Double-click the default chapter title, enter a meaningful chapter name, and press Return. Keep the name succinct. The screen space for chapter menus on a TV is limited. Figure 4.11 shows the iDVD palette with three chapter markers.

6. **Save your work.** iMovie automatically adds the new chapter markers to the reference movie that appears at the top level of your iMovie project folder.

Keep the following in mind when working with iMovie and markers:

iMovie markers are limited in number. Although iDVD allows 99 markers per track, iMovie 3 supports only 36 markers per project. A warning dialog appears when you try to add the thirty-seventh, reminding you about iMovie's 36-marker limit.

Space out your markers. Don't place markers within one second of each other or within one second of the start or end of your movie. This provides adequate space for a compressor to adjust the GOP (Groups of Pictures) structures to accommodate your chapters. iMovie will not let you add markers that are too close. It displays a warning when you try.

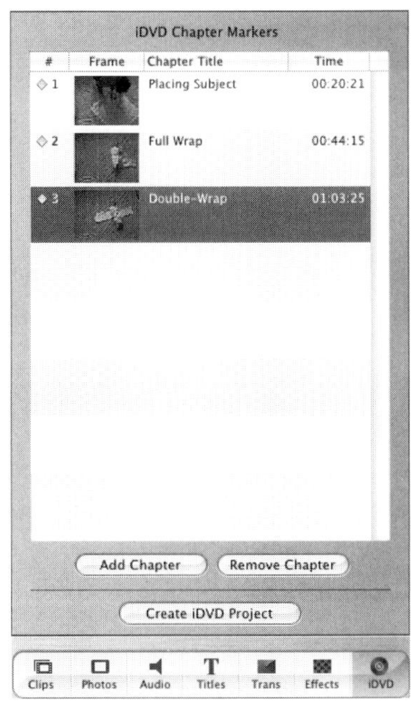

Figure 4.11 iMovie's iDVD palette allows you to add, remove, and name your chapter markers. To add a marker, set the playhead and click Add Chapter. (You can move the playhead to the beginning of a clip by selecting the clip in the Clip Viewer. This allows you to add a marker to the first frame of that clip.) To remove a chapter, select it and click Remove Chapter. To rename a chapter, double-click its name, edit the name, and press Return.

Groups of Pictures, better known as GOPs, are the smallest component of MPEG encoding. They consist of a sequence of frames, including one keyframe followed by a pattern of compressed frames. Typical GOPs last for 15 frames or less.

Markers appear in time order. iMovie sorts your markers by time. If you insert a marker between two other markers in the timeline, it appears in the iDVD palette between those two.

You can't move markers. If you need to adjust a marker, remove it, set the playhead as needed, and add a new marker.

Adding Chapter Markers in QuickTime Pro

At times, its convenient to skip video-editing programs when you want to add chapter markers directly to already-edited video. QuickTime Pro ($29, www.apple.com/quick-time) simplifies the process. Follow these steps.

1. **Review your movie.** Open your movie in QuickTime Pro and watch the footage. Click the Pause button each time you reach a point where a new chapter should begin. Adjust the playhead to the precise frame desired, and choose Window > Show Movie Info (⌘-I). On paper, make a list of each marker's precise time (see the Current Time in the Movie Info window) and chapter name.

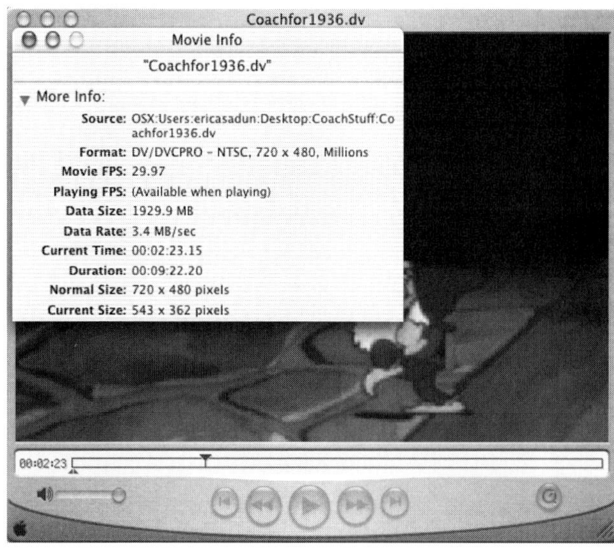

2. **Create a new text file and list your chapters.** You'll need to store your chapter list in a form that QuickTime Pro can read. Launch TextEdit and create a new file (choose File > New or press ⌘-N). Choose Format > Make Plain Text (⌘-Shift-T)—QuickTime can't read rich text format. Type the names of your chapters, one title per line. Save the file to disk (choose File > Save or press ⌘-S).

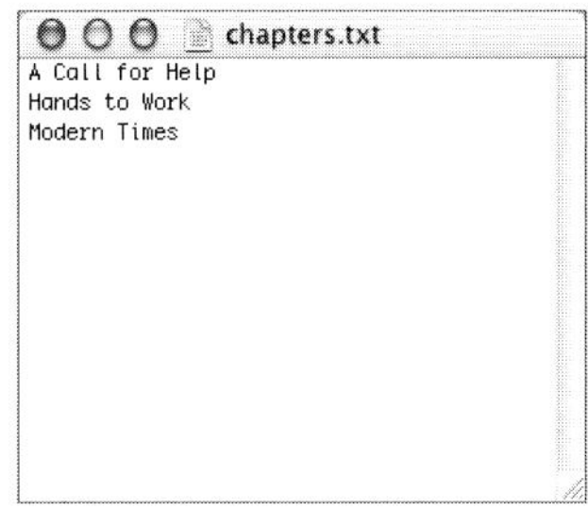

3. **Import your chapter titles into QuickTime Pro.** Return to QuickTime Pro. Choose File > Import. Navigate to your text file, select it, and click Open. QuickTime imports the list of chapters and creates a new text-only movie.

4. **Convert your titles.** Choose File > Export (⌘-E). A Save Exported File As dialog appears. Select Text To Text from the Export pop-up, and enter a filename. Don't overwrite the file from step 3. Navigate as needed to where you want to save your file, and click Save. QuickTime Pro converts your chapter titles to a standard form, complete with time codes, font information, and so forth.

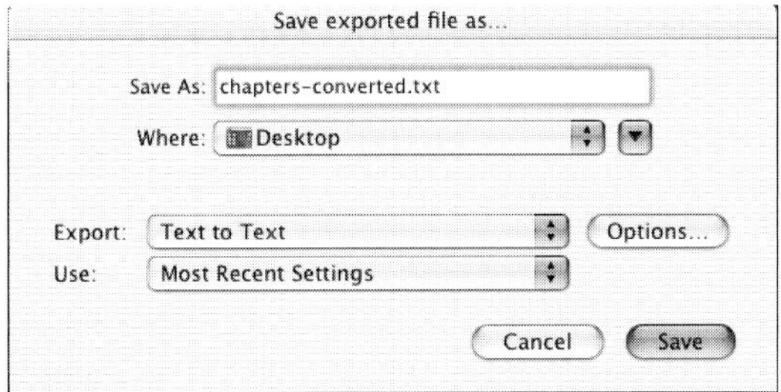

5. **Edit your converted titles.** Return to TextEdit and open the converted text file. Notice how the start times for each chapter default to 2-second increments.

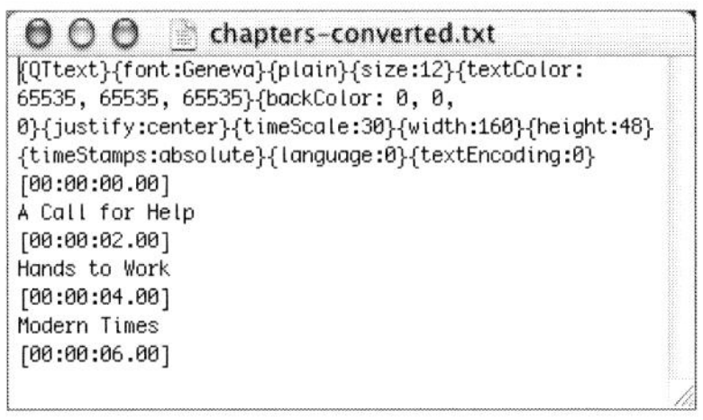

6. **Modify the start times.** Update the start times to match those you noted in step 1 for each chapter. Save your changes to disk.

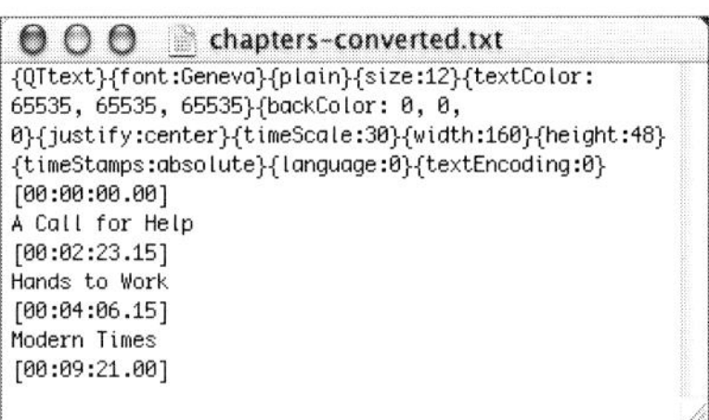

7. **Import your updated titles.** Return to QuickTime Pro. Choose File > Import. A file open dialog appears. Navigate to the text file you just edited, select it, and click Open. QuickTime Pro opens the text in a new window that contains a single text track.

8. **Copy the title track to memory.** Choose Edit > Select All (⌘-A), choose Edit > Copy (⌘-C), and then close the titles window (choose File > Close or press ⌘-W).

9. **Paste the title track onto your video.** Bring your original video window to the front. Choose Edit > Select All (⌘-A) and scale the text track over the video: choose Edit > Add Scaled (⌘-Shift-⌥-V).

10. **Use the text track for chapters.** Choose Movie > Get Movie Properties (⌘-J). The Movie Properties dialog opens. Select Text Track from the left pull-down menu and Make Chapter from the right. Click Set Chapter Owner Track, choose Video Track, and click OK. A chapter menu appears in the lower-right corner of your QuickTime Player window.

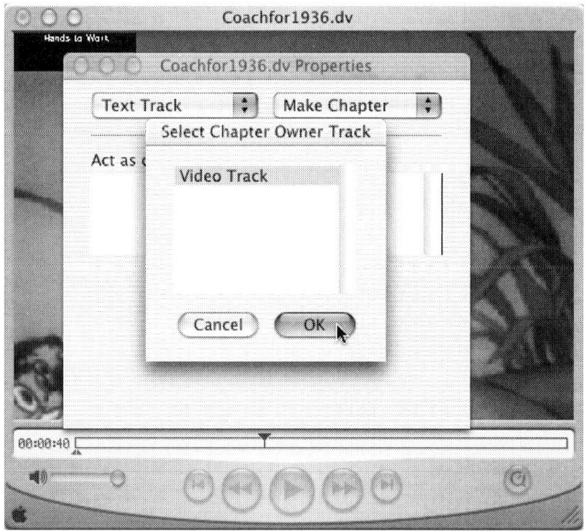

11. **Hide the text.** Choose Edit > Enable Tracks to open the Enable Tracks dialog. Click the On button to the left of Text Track. The On button switches to Off, and QuickTime hides the track from view without affecting the chapters. Click OK to close the Enable Tracks dialog.

12. **Save your file.** Choose File > Save and save your work to disk. If your video is in DV format, save it as a new QuickTime movie file. You need not make the movie self-contained.

Adding Chapter Markers in Compressor

Apple's Compressor ships with both DVD Studio Pro 2 and Final Cut Pro 4. Compressor is a stand-alone program that helps you submit video and audio files for batch compression. Using it couldn't be simpler—just add files, choose presets, and submit your job—but Compressor does a lot more than you might expect. Hidden within Compressor's simple interface are some powerful tools. In this section, you'll learn how to add chapter markers to your video from within Compressor.

1. **Launch Compressor.** You'll find a copy of Compressor in the Applications folder of your OS X disk. Navigate to its icon and double-click to open Compressor's Batch window.

You may be prompted for a serial number the first time you run Compressor.

2. **Add a video file.** Drag the video file you want to compress into the Batch window, as shown in Figure 4.12.

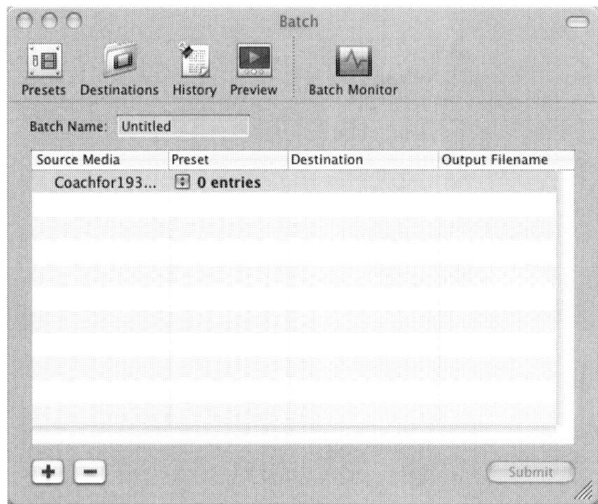

Figure 4.12 When added to Compressor's Batch window, a new video file has no presets, no destination, and no output filename. You can set each of these features by selecting a preset from the pop-up. Consider naming your batch by editing the Batch Name text field. A well-chosen batch name helps you monitor the progress of your batch by instantly identifying it in Compressor's Batch Monitor program.

3. **Select a preset.** Choose a preset. For example choose MPEG-2 120min Fast Encode > All from the Preset pop-up. Double-click the second entry, MPEG-2, to open the preview window shown in Figure 4.13.

Zoom Pop-Up Set the size of the preview window. Choose 50%, 75%, or 100%, or resize the window by dragging the sizing handle in the window's lower-right corner.

In and Out Points Set your video's In and Out points by editing the text boxes or by dragging the in and out handles.

Scrubber Bar Adjust the playhead within the Scrubber bar to scan through your movie.

Split Handle Apportion space between the source (left) and destination (right) portions of the preview. This helps you compare the quality of the original and compressed images.

QuickTime Playback Controls The large Play/Pause button appears in the middle flanked by Fast Forward and Fast Reverse buttons. The two outside buttons move to the Next and Previous markers.

Add/Remove Marker Button Place new markers with this button or remove existing markers at the playhead.

Name Marker Button Use this button to assign a name to your marker.

Dimension buttons These two buttons toggle the display between the source and the preset aspect ratios.

Figure 4.13 Compressor's preview window helps you interactively adjust your compression settings: Ⓐ Zoom pop-up, Ⓑ In and Out points, Ⓒ Scrubber bar, Ⓓ Split handle, Ⓔ QuickTime playback controls, Ⓕ Add/Remove Marker button, Ⓖ Name Marker button, Ⓗ Source and Preset dimension buttons.

4. **Set the playhead.** Set the playhead to point at the frame that starts your new chapter.

5. **Click the Add Marker button.** Compressor adds a new marker at the playhead.

To remove markers, use the Next and Previous Marker buttons to move the playhead to a marker, and then click the Add/Remove Marker button.

6. **Click the Name Marker button.** Compressor prompts you to enter a name. Type a name and click OK. Keep the name short and meaningful, with proper upper- and lowercase. DVD Studio Pro 2 uses the name exactly as typed.

7. **Repeat.** Repeat steps 4 through 6 until you've finished adding chapters to your video.

8. **Submit.** As you submit your job, Compressor uses your chapter markers to compress your video.

Choosing an Audio Format

The DVD specification supports several native audio formats. DVD Studio Pro 2 allows you to use these formats in your projects without further encoding. These formats include the following:

MPEG-1 Layer 2 Audio You're probably a lot more familiar with MPEG-1 Layer 3 audio than you are with Layer 2. That's because MPEG-1 Layer 3 audio is better known as MP3, the compression scheme of choice for portable audio. Like MP3, MP2 offers highly compressed, high-quality digital audio. The number ordering is significant. MP2 debuted earlier than MP3 and thus is at a lower "layer": each standard layer encompasses all the layers introduced before it and expands upon them. MP2 can produce near CD-quality sound at about 192kbps. MPEG-1 Layer 2 audio is classified as an *optional* audio format for National Television Standards Committee DVD and as a *mandatory* audio format for PAL/SECAM.

DVD Studio Pro 2 supports both optional and mandatory audio formats in accordance with the official DVD specification. The specification states that DVDs must provide at least one mandatory audio track per disc. In theory, if you want to use optional formats, you must first add a mandatory format. In reality, not all players support optional audio formats. MP2, which is a mandatory format for PAL but not for NTSC, may not be compatible with many commercial NTSC players. Dolby offers a discussion of the matter at http://dolby.com/digital.

Dolby Digital AC-3 Audio Dolby Audio provides highly compatible, robust multi-channel audio with 5.1 surround sound. The name derives from its speaker support. With 5.1, you can play audio on as many as five separate speaker channels (left, center, right, left-surround, and right-surround) and one subwoofer channel. Subwoofers produce those low-frequency effects that you feel more than you hear. Apple provides an AC-3 encoder with DVD Studio Pro 2 that allows you to set your audio channels to produce the precise playback configuration you need. Dolby Audio support is universal on National Television Standards Committee DVD players and nearly universal on recent PAL units. Dolby Digital AC-3 is a *mandatory* format for both NTSC and PAL/SECAM.

Dolby Digital AC-3 is the compressed option of choice for nearly all professional authors of Phase Alternating Line DVD, particularly over MP2. Although PAL system DVD players allow you to play MP2 audio (it's a mandatory format for PAL), it's rarely used. One Australian DVD manufacturer mentions that after years of DVD authoring and producing hundreds of DVDs, his company never once used MPEG Audio, favoring AC-3 instead.

Pulse Coded Modulation (PCM) DVD Studio Pro 2 supports three kinds of PCM audio: raw, WAVE (Waveform Audio File Format), and AIFF (Audio Interchange File Format). The three differ slightly in their naming and header information. The PCM audio format is more or less uncompressed, producing very high fidelity. Unfortunately, as is always the case with the tradeoff between compression and quality, PCM files are very large and take up more bandwidth on playback. As a *mandatory* audio format for both NTSC and PAL/SECAM, PCM audio is completely compatible with all DVD players worldwide.

In addition to its high quality, PCM offers a particular bonus for simple stereo soundtracks. Those in your DVD audience that lack equipment with multichannel capabilities can enjoy the soundtrack in its full original quality. With AC-3, an audience that has non-multichannel equipment must listen to a degraded Dolby Digital downmix.

You can use more than one audio format in your DVD Studio Pro 2 projects, but you can't mix and match for menus, slideshows, and streams:

Menus DVDs store all menus in the same logical section of the disc, in what's known as the video title set menu domain. Because they're stored in the same place, you must keep your audio consistent throughout. If you use AC3 audio in one menu, use it in all menus.

Slideshows You can use different audio formats for different slideshows, but you can't use multiple audio formats within a single slideshow. Each slideshow must use one audio format for all its slides.

Audio Streams Each track in a DVD Studio Pro 2 project can have a maximum of eight audio streams, and each audio stream can use a different format—AC-3 or PCM. (Unfortunately, DVD Studio Pro 2 doesn't support DTS (Digital Theatre Sound) audio streams in this release.)

Wherever possible, keep to one audio type throughout your project or assign different kinds of audio consistently. (For example, you might assign Dolby Digital to all your A1 audio streams and PCM to all your A2 audio streams, etc.) Set-top DVD players use different decoders (software that allows the player to produce sounds from the data files that make up the DVD's audio) for each audio format.

Each time your DVD audio encoding changes, the player switches to a new decoder. This process takes anywhere from a half-second to two seconds. This can cause playback delays and can end up muting the first second or so of your audio until the decoder catches up with the playback. If you do offer multiple audio streams on your DVD, use the scripting capability of DVD Studio Pro 2 to keep the same format/track stream number audio playing.

As a rule of thumb, consider adding as much as two seconds of digital silence at the beginning of your Dolby Digital (AC-3) audio streams. Your video clips will need lengthening to match the added audio padding. The Dolby Digital Professional Encoding Guidelines (http://dolby.com/tech/L.mn.0002.DDPEG1.pdf) recommend that you "always have at least two seconds of digital black silence at the beginning of the bitstream. This gives the large amount of digital circuitry in playback systems time to lock and start decoding before the real material starts playing. It is not necessary to leave digital black at the end of the file." More Dolby-specific recommendations follow in the section on encoding AC-3 sound with A.Pack.

Preparing Sound with QuickTime Pro

QuickTime Pro allows you to convert many audio formats into DVD Studio Pro 2–compatible (and sometimes more important, A.Pack-compatible) AIFF files.

A.Pack is an audio file compression utility, which is bundled with DVD Studio Pro.

Follow these steps to convert your audio.

1. **Launch QuickTime Pro.** Don't confuse QuickTime Pro with QuickTime Player. They both use the "same" program, but QuickTime Pro offers a collection of advanced editing and export features. Purchase your license from Apple's website and unlock QuickTime Pro's full suite of power tools.

2. **Open your file.** Choose File > Open Movie In New Player (⌘-O). An open file dialog appears. Navigate to your audio file (or movie file with audio track), select it, and click Open.

3. **Begin your export.** Choose File > Export (⌘-E) to open the Export dialog. Navigate to where you want to save your audio and enter a name in the Save As line. Do *not* click Save.

4. **Choose Sound To AIFF.** Locate the Export pop-up at the bottom of the Export dialog, as shown in Figure 4.14. Choosing Sound To AIFF allows you to export using the AIFF PCM format.

5. **Click Options.** The button appears to the right of the Export pop-up. Choosing Options opens the Sound Settings dialog, in which you can specify how you want QuickTime to create your AIFF file.

6. **Adjust your sound settings.** Set Compressor to None, and set Rate to 48.000 by using the pop-up. In the Size section, click the 16 bit button, and in the Use section, click the Stereo button. (See Figure 4.15.) These settings create an uncompressed PCM AIFF file that you can use with DVD Studio Pro 2.

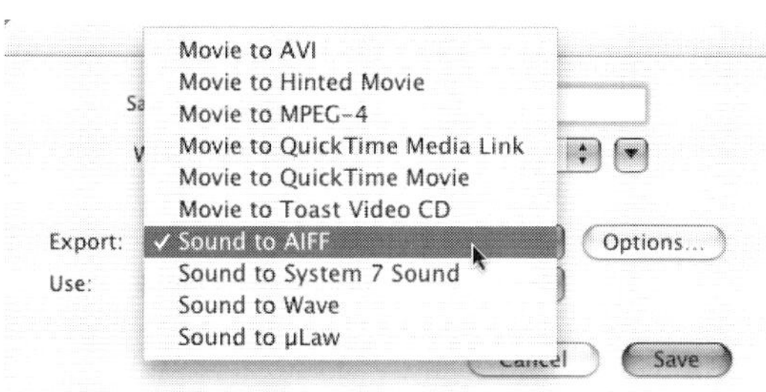

Figure 4.14 QuickTime's Save Exported File As dialog allows you to convert from one audio format to another. More options appear when you export from a movie than from an audio-only file. The options shown here appear when exporting audio from a movie.

DVD Studio Pro 2 accepts raw, AIFF, or WAV PCM files at 16 and 24 bits, using mono or stereo sound with 48kHz or 96kHz sampling

7. Click OK. This applies your changes and closes the Sound Settings dialog.

8. Click Save. QuickTime Pro converts your audio and saves it to the file you specified in step 3.

You now have a fresh, new 16-bit, 48kHz, stereo PCM AIFF file.

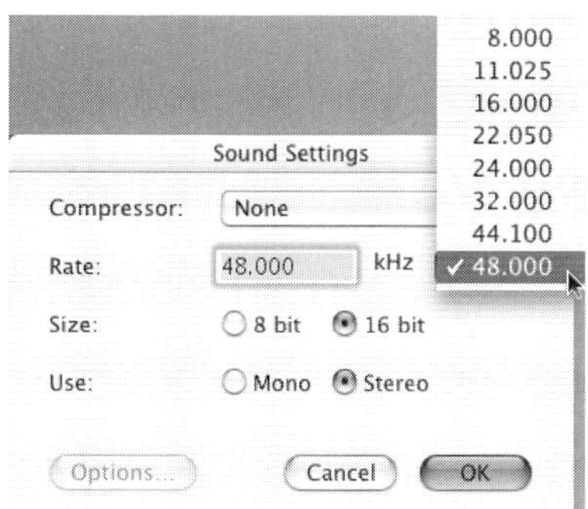

Figure 4.15 Many QuickTime export settings allow you to further customize your output. When you export sound to AIFF, clicking Options opens the Sound Settings dialog. Here, you can set the compressor, data rate, sample size, and number of channels. The Options button, in the lower left of the dialog, is grayed out when producing uncompressed AIFF files.

Converting MPEG Audio

Some DVD authors use set-top DVD recording units to compress their video in real time. They copy the compressed files back to the Macintosh and use utilities such as bbDemux (free, http://sourceforge.net/projects/macbbdemux) to separate the video object set files (VOBs) back into their component video and audio streams.

Unfortunately, MPEG audio extracted by these utilities often proves incompatible with DVD Studio Pro 2. MoreMissingTools (free, http://homepage.mac.com/rnc/) helps you work around this problem.

Follow these steps to convert MPEG –2 audio to WAV files:

1. **Launch MoreMissingTools**. The More Missing Tools window, shown in Figure 4.16, opens. This window provides a variety of MPEG conversion and processing options.

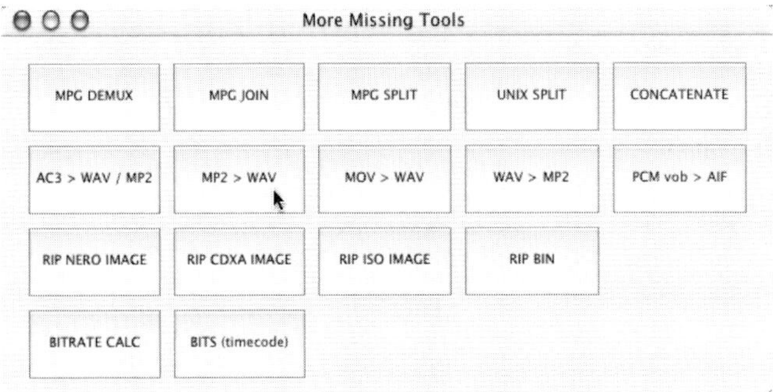

Figure 4.16 MoreMissingTools allows you to perform a variety of convenient MPEG operations, including demuxing (demultiplexing), joining, and converting audio. The program offers GUI (graphical user interface) front-end to command-line based operations that run in Terminal shells.

2. **Choose your file.** Click MP2 > WAV to open the Choose File dialog. Navigate to your MPEG Audio file, select it, and click Choose. A sample rate dialog appears.

3. **Select the sample rate.** More MissingTools prompts you to select an output sample rate. Choose 48000 and click OK.

4. **Wait.** More MissingMPEGTools launches OS X's Terminal application and begins to process your audio. When the program completes its task, you'll see "Decoding of *[your filename]* finished." The converted file appears in the same folder as the original. You can use your converted WAV file directly in DVD Studio Pro 2 or use A.Pack to compress it down to AC-3.

Solution: Build a Custom, Reusable Template

In theory, DVD Studio Pro 2 templates add prebuilt styles to a menu. In practice, they let you build styled chapter menus from tracks. In these steps, you'll create a self-contained reusable template that you can use again and again.

The file cinderella.jpg appears on the companion DVD for your use in this project.

1. **Start a new project.** Launch DVD Studio Pro 2 and create a fresh new project (choose File > New or press ⌘-N).

2. **Select the default menu.** It appears in the Outline tab and is labeled Menu 1. New projects in DVD Studio Pro 2 always contain one default menu and one default track.

3. **Drag an image onto the menu.** Drag a custom background image from the Finder onto the Menu Editor. As the image enters the Menu Editor, the drop palette appears. Choose Set Background and release the mouse.

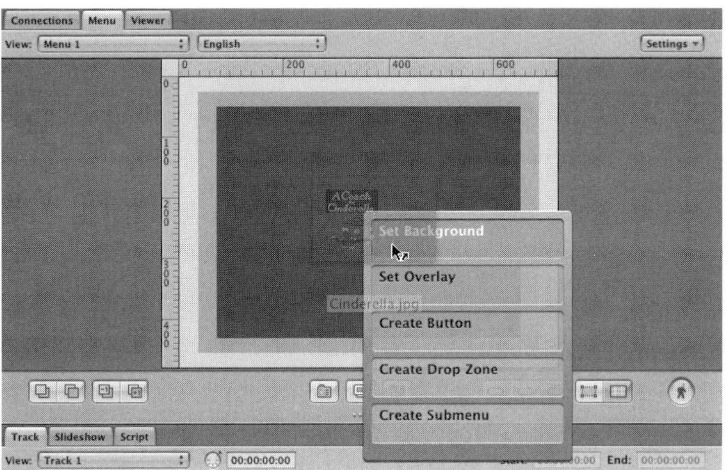

4. **Add a button.** Move the cursor onto the menu workspace and drag out a new button. If you can't see the button after dragging, toggle Show/Hide Button Outlines (in the lower right of the Menu Editor), or choose View > Show Button Outline And Name.

5. **Customize your new button.** Open the Inspector (⌘-⌥-I) and select your button. Add text—any dummy text will do—and style the button to your taste. The text adds placeholders for chapter names when you use this template for a chapter menu. For this project, use the following options:

   - Select Square Burgandy 90p from the Shape pop-up. This burgundy color helps highlight the issue of high-contrast boundaries and visual noise discussed earlier in this chapter.

   - Check the Shadow check box for the shape.

   - In the Highlight Set section, click 3 then choose a bright yellow color from the Selected Highlight pop-up.

   - Type the word Button into the Text field, and check the Shadow check box.

   - In the Text Formatting section, select Center from the Position pop-up, and check Include Text In Highlight.

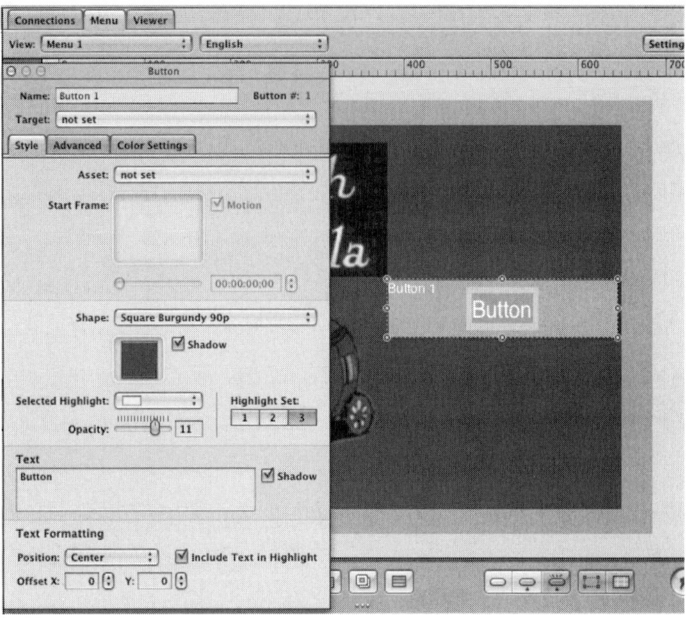

6. **Select a button label font.** Choose Format > Font > Show Fonts. The Fonts window opens. Select your button text. (Double-click the label on your button in the Menu Editor.) Set the font for your labels. For this project, select Verdana Bold 24. Your selected text updates as you choose each option.

7. **Resize your button.** Adjust your button boundaries to match the size of your new font. Size the button so you can add several copies to your window.

8. **Duplicate your button.** ⌥-drag your button. DVD Studio Pro 2 creates an exact copy. Hold down Shift to ensure that you drag in a straight line. Repeat until you've added several buttons. The number of buttons you add determines the number of chapters your menu can display. For this project, add at least four buttons.

9. **Align and distribute your buttons.** Select all your buttons. (Click the first button, and then Shift-click each remaining button. Alternatively, select the menu and choose Edit > Select All or press ⌘-A.) Use the Arrange menu to create perfect alignment and distribution. For this project, choose Arrange > Align Objects > Left and Arrange > Distribute Objects > Vertically.

10. **Set the first play.** In the Outline tab, select UNTITLED_DISC. Ctrl-click (right-click) and choose First Play > Menus > Menu 1 > [Menu]. First Play specifies the item that your disc plays when it's inserted. Always set First Play before you test your new interface.

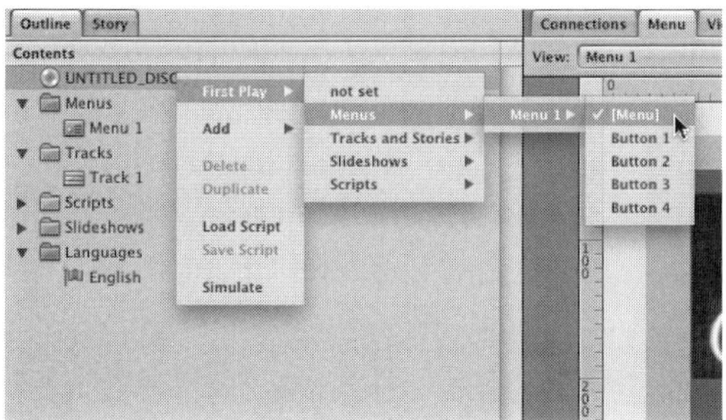

Alert readers will note that your disc's first play is set to Menu 1 by default. Regardless, it's good practice to confirm First Play settings before simulating.

11. **Simulate.** Click Simulator (its in the toolbar at the top of your main window) and test your interface. Make sure the highlights and colors work as desired. Close the Simulator (click the tiny x button in the upper-left corner) when finished.

12. **Open the Palette.** Choose View > Show Palette (⌘-⌥-P). Click the Templates tab and choose Custom.

13. **Create your new template.** At the bottom of the Custom pane, click the Create… button to open a small new dialog over the Palette. Enter a name for your template (here, use Cinderella) and check the Self-Contained check box. Click Save.

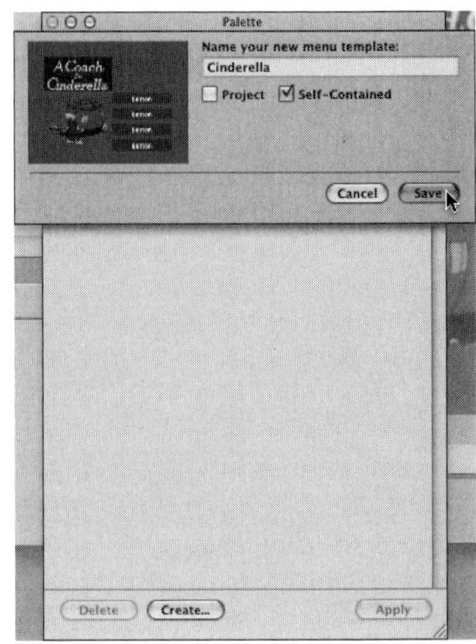

DVD Studio Pro 2 creates a new file called (in this case) Cinderella.dsptemplate and stores it in /Library/Application Support/DVD Studio Pro/ Templates. As the extension suggests, this file stores your entire menu structure—background, buttons, and styles—for quick recovery and reuse.

Solution: Create a simple Chapter Menu

DVD Studio Pro 2 offers many chapter-friendly features. Among them is Studio Pro the convenient ability to add a track's chapters to a menu. In the following steps, you'll choose a template to configure a chapter menu.

This solution project follows up on the previous one and uses the Cinderella template you built.

1. **Start a new project.** Launch DVD Studio Pro 2 and create a fresh new project (choose File > New or press ⌘-N). If you're continuing from the previous solution, you don't have to save your work to disk as a new project. You've already saved the template you'll use here.

2. **Name your project.** In the Outline tab, select UNTITLED_DISC. Open the Inspector (⌘-⌥-I) and set the disc name to CINDERELLA.

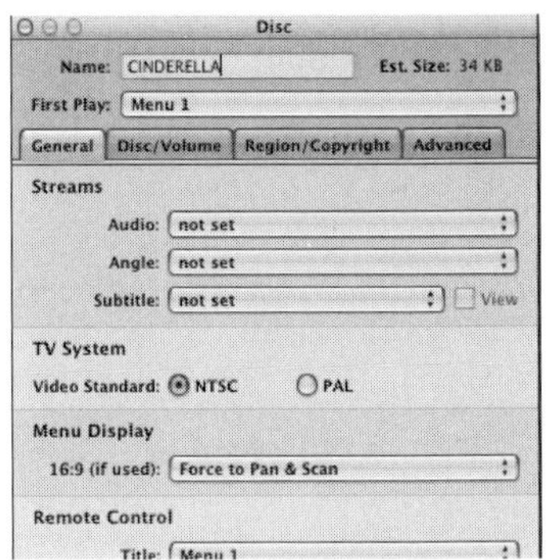

Please make a note of the following points:

• Your disc's First Play is set to Menu 1 by default.

• Your new project already contains one menu (Menu 1) and one track (Track 1).

3.  **Import audio and video.** In the Assets tab, drag your assets from the Finder into the Assets window. For this project, add Cinderella.AC3 and Cinderella.m2v from the companion DVD.

4. **Add your assets to Track 1.** Select Track 1 in the Outline Tab, and then open the Track tab. Drag your video file (Cinderella.m2v) from the Assets tab to V1 in the Track tab, and drop it. DVD Studio Pro 2 automatically includes the matching audio in A1 (Cinderella.AC3). DVD Studio Pro 2 loads any video chapter markers and adds them to the track.

This step assumes that you've set Find Matching Audio When Dragging in your preferences. Choose DVD Studio Pro > Preferences to open the Preferences window, and click the Track check box.

5. **Correct the first marker.** Select the first marker, Chapter 1. DVD Studio Pro 2 automatically adds an extra marker at the start of your track. Open the Inspector (⌘-⌥-I) and rename the marker to Our Story Begins.

6. **Set your language.** Choose English (en) from the pop-up next to A1. (It's in the C-F submenu).

7. **Set your end jump.** Return to the Outline tab, and select Track 1. Open the Inspector (⌘-⌥-I) and click the End Jump drop-down, and choose Menus > Menu1 > [Menu]. This tells DVD Studio Pro 2 to return to your main menu after playing your track.

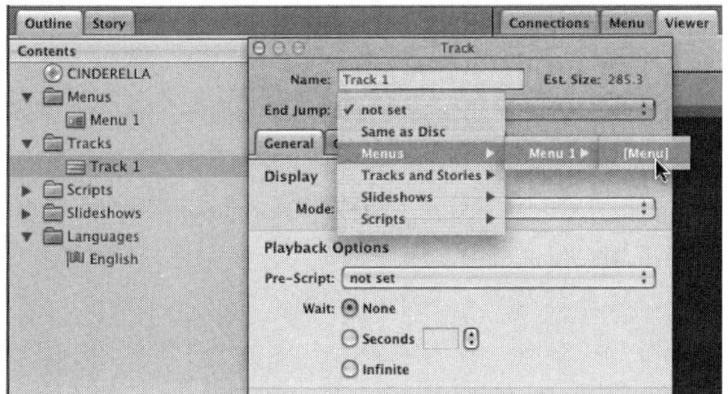

8. **Open the Menu Editor.** Select the Menu tab to make the window visible.

9. **Drag your track.** Select Track 1 from the Outline tab and drag it onto your menu. Continue to hold down the mouse button. A drop palette appears. Select Create Chapter Index and release the mouse. DVD Studio Pro 2 opens the Choose Template or Layout Style Window and prompts you to select a template or a layout style.

10. **Choose your style.** For this project, click the Templates tab, choose Custom > Cinderella, and click OK.

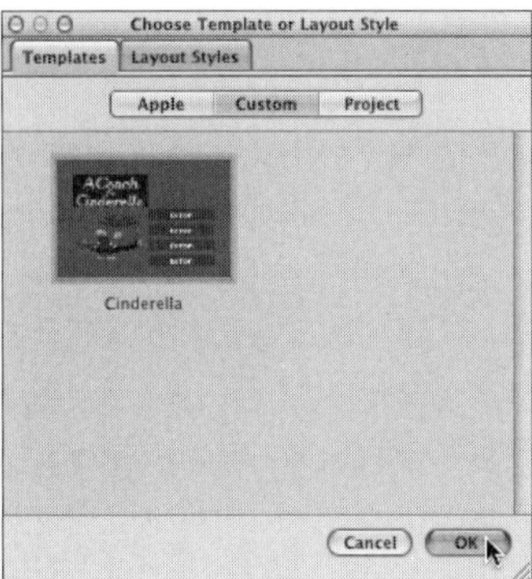

11. **Inspect your menu.** After you select Cinderella, DVD Studio Pro 2 loads the template you created in the previous solution and uses the chapter titles from your video to create the buttons.

The second "title" that appears on each button is actually the button name. Click the Show/Hide Button Outline button to toggle the name display on and off.

You now have a complete, working project. You can save your project to disk (choose File > Save or press ⌘-S), test it (click Simulator), and burn it (click Build/Format).

When burning to DVD-RW, always insert the disc before attempting to burn with DVD Studio Pro 2. Tell OS X to "ignore" it. Then proceed with your normal format. This bypasses the tendency of DVD Studio Pro 2 to balk when given a DVD-RW rather than a DVD-R disc. Toast Titanium (www.roxio.com) offers excellent DVD-RW "quick erase" functionality. Choose Recorder > Erase (⌘-B).

Ivory Soap
Sunbeam 
Cheerios 
Classic Commercials 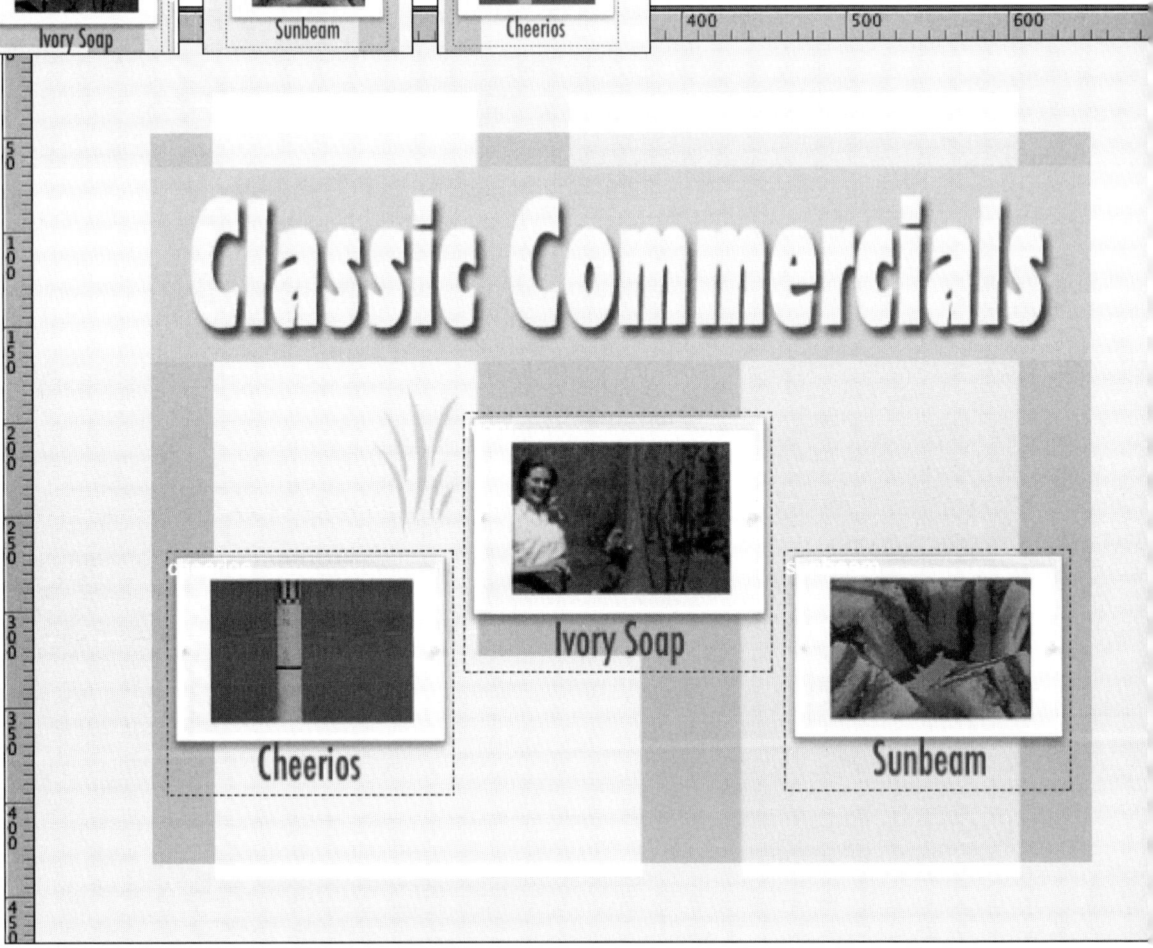
Ivory Soap
Cheerios
Sunbeam

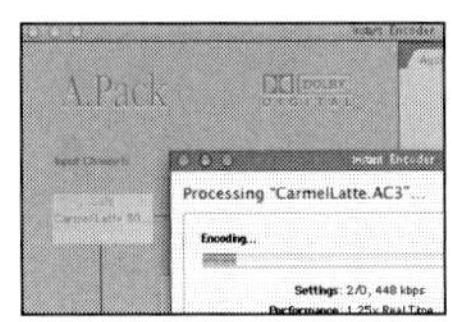
A.Pack
DOLBY
Processing "CarmelLatte.AC3"...
Encoding...
Settings: 2/0, 448 kbps

Set Background
Set Overlay
Create Button
Create Drop Zone
Create Submenu

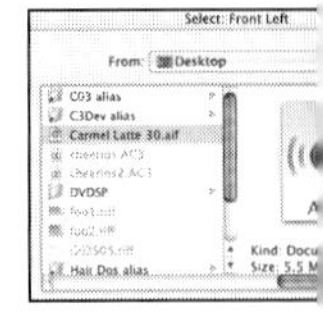
Select: Front Left
From: Desktop
CD3 alias
C3Dev alias
Carmel Latte 30.aif
Cheerios.AC3
Cheerios2.AC3
DVDSP
TestList
Test HR
Hair Dos alias

Compressing Video and Audio

Compressing video and audio is both a science and an art. If you search around the Internet, you can find professional compressionists—people who work with color, sound, and human perception to create top-quality data for Hollywood DVDs. Experienced compressionists balance technical details such as disc capacity and bandwidth with a practiced "eye" (and "ear") that can detect and fix tiny presentation flaws.

Chapter Contents

DVD Studio Pro 2 and its companion software Compressor and A.Pack help you create projects that your audience can watch and listen to without needing such professional assistance. With easy-to-use presets and simple drag-and-drop operations, these tools make it simple to compress your video and audio for DVD Studio Pro 2 projects. Your compressed data won't match the perfection of the professional compressionist, but they'll be accessible to a wide audience.

Bit Rates, Compression, and Playback

Whenever you compress an audio or a video file, you make decisions about bit rate (also called data rate), the rate at which data plays back over time. The bit rate you choose affects three things: the amount of data you can store on a given disc, the quality of that stored data, and the disc's ability to be played back in real time.

Recordable discs can store a predefined amount of data and no more. (That amount is called either disc space or disc capacity.) The more you compress your data, the more data you can store on a disc. Unfortunately, the more you compress your data, the more quality suffers, producing compression artifacts that include the infamous MPEG-2 "blockiness" that pop up in high-motion sequences. Higher compression, with its lower bit rates, does allow you to create longer discs, albeit with lower-quality video and sound. (Hollywood movies get around the quality/disc-space problem by using higher-capacity discs.)

Disk Capacities

Many Hollywood movies use pressed DVD-9 discs. The DVD-9 format uses dual layers—two layers on a single side—to store up to 8.5GB per disc. The larger size allows DVDs to store entire two-hour movies on a single-sided disc at high quality. DVD set-top players read each layer by focusing their lasers to different depths.

A 4.7GB disc actually stores about 4.38GB of data. The higher 4.7 number represents the number of bytes available on a DVD in base 10, assuming 1,000,000,000 bytes per gigabyte. Computers use binary (base 2), not base 10. On your computer, each gigabyte represents 1,073,741,824 bytes. So it takes approximately 4.377197 of these binary gigabytes to store the 4,699,979,766 bytes available on a typical consumer-grade recordable DVD blank.

When discussing bit rates, DVD developers use decimal (base 10) notation, not binary. The notation 192Kbps refers to 192,000 bits per second, and not to 196,608. (This latter number uses the binary 1024 kilobits rather than 1000 kilobits).

Most playback systems can only process, decompress, and output data at certain rates. When given too much data, the unit may hesitate or otherwise interrupt the smooth flow of audio and video. Choosing a lower bit rate than your player can handle ensures that your audience experiences your production without interruption. Software DVD players, particularly those on laptops, are notorious for slow, jerky playback.

Table 5.1 summarizes the issues of bit rate, compression, and playback.

▶ **Table 5.1** How Bit Rates Affect Disk Space, Quality, and Playback

	Lower Bit Rates	Higher Bit Rates
Disc Space	Items compressed at lower bit rates occupy less space on disc, permitting longer projects. At 2Mbps, you might store 4 hours of video on a standard 4.7GB DVD-R disc.	High bit rates mandate shorter projects— you can fit only so much data on a disc. iDVD uses 8Mbps video encoding for one hour of video per 4.7GB DVD-R disc.
Quality	Lower bit rates compromise quality, producing compression artifacts.	Higher bit rates ensure that audio and video play back with the best fidelity.
Playback	As bit rates decrease, the amount of time and effort it takes to decompress and display also decrease. Low bit rate projects generally play back without hesitations or other player-related interruptions, particularly on computers with software DVD players.	Depending on the player, high bit rates can tax the playback unit causing hesitations or other playback concerns. This problem manifests itself particularly on computers using software DVD players.

Choosing Bit Rates

The realities of DVD playback have to take certain limits into account. At each moment, a DVD player can produce some combination of audio, video, and subtitles. Each of these components has to be read from disc and displayed, and each uses a certain bit rate. The sum total of these bit rates—video plus audio plus subtitles—cannot exceed 10.08Mbps (the maximum "instantaneous" bit rate) at any time. DVD Studio Pro 2 and Apple's Compressor take these issues into account by offering you safe preset data rates that stay within maximum guidelines.

Compressor's preset rates include 60 minutes at 7Mbps, 90 minutes at 5Mbps, and 120 minutes at 3.5Mbps. Choosing one of these presets ensures that you'll have plenty of room on your disc for a single video track plus audio plus a subtitle track or four. If you want to skip presets, both Compressor and QuickTime MPEG-2 Encoder allow you to manually choose video compression levels between 2Mbps and 9Mbps.

Bit Budgets

Some of you will need to approach bit rate choice more mathematically. A bit-budget calculator—one is included on the companion DVD—helps you work through the details. (Jim Taylor's DVDCalc.XLS can be found with the chapter materials on the disc that accompanies this book. Jim is the author of *DVD Demystified* (www.dvdde-mystified.com), the absolute classic reference book about the DVD standard. Jim is also the author of the Internet DVD FAQ.) This section introduces the math behind the calculator, working through several examples that describe the bit-budgeting process.

Creating a Bit Budget to Select a Bit Rate

The following steps help you determine the bit rate at which to encode your main movie feature. Please keep in mind that the figures here are in decimal, not binary format.

1. **Determine the size of your disc.** General recordable DVD-R discs offer 4.7GB of data.

2. **Convert from bytes to bits.** 4.7 gigabytes corresponds to 37.6 gigabits, or 37,600 megabits. For bit budgets, it's easier to work with megabits than gigabits since most streams are rated in megabits per second. Each byte has 8 bits.

   capacity-in-bytes × 8 = capacity-in-bits

   4.7 gigagytes (GB) × 8 = 3.76 gigabits (Gb)

3. **Add a cushion for overhead.** Jim Taylor suggests a 4% overhead. 96% of 37,600 megabits leaves 36,096 megabits to work with.

   capacity × (1 – overhead) = adjusted disc capacity

   37,600Mb × (1 – 0.4) = 36,096Mb

4. **Calculate the size of each stream.** To determine the space each stream (audio, video, or subtitle) occupies, you multiply its duration in seconds by its rate. For example, a 90-minute 448Kbps (0.448 Mbps) audio track occupies just over 2419MB. As a rule of thumb, assume that each subtitle track uses a bit rate of 0.010Mbps.

   duration-in-seconds × rate-in-Mbits/second = size-in-Mbits

   90 minutes × 60 seconds/minute × 0.448 megabits/second = 2,419 megabits

5. **Calculate the available space on your disc.** Sum the sizes of each nonfeature stream (such as menus, video transitions, and introductory videos) to determine the total space used. Subtract this number from your adjusted disc capacity. This (nonnegative!) number tells you how much space is left for your main feature movie or movies.

   adjusted disc capacity – total space used = remaining space

6. **Calculate the total audio and subtitle data rate.** Sum the bit rates for your feature's audio and subtitle streams to determine the total data rate used.

stream 1 bit rate + stream 2 bit rate + … = total audio/subtitle data rate

7. **Calculate the maximum possible bit rate for your main movie(s).** The maximum bit rate allowed at any instant is 10.08Mbps. To determine the maximum bit rate available for your feature or features, subtract the total audio and subtitle data rate from 10.08.

10.08 – total audio/subtitle data rate = maximum movie bit rate

8. **Calculate the length of your movies.** When using more than one feature, determine the total length of your movie material in seconds. Take all video tracks and alternate angles into account as well.

feature length 1 + feature length 2 + … = total movie length (in seconds)

9. **Calculate the maximum average bit rate for your main movie(s).** After setting aside disc space and bandwidth audio, subtitles (subpictures), motion menus, introduction videos, transition videos, and so forth, use whatever is left for your main features. Divide the space available (in megabits) by the duration of your movies (in seconds) to determine the remaining bandwidth (in megabits per second). You can compress at this rate or below.

remaining space/total movie length = highest possible average bit rate
A few examples will show these calculations in action.

Example 1

This simple DVD Studio Pro 2 project contains a 90-minute main feature with bilingual audio and subtitles and two 30-second motion menus.

V1	Feature
A1	English Soundtrack
A2	French Soundtrack
S1	English Subtitles
S2	French Subtitles

Motion Menu 1

Motion Menu 2

Track	Duration	Bit Rate	Size
English audio track (Stereo 2.0)	90 minutes × 60 seconds/minute = 5400 seconds	0.224Mbps	5400 seconds × 0.224Mbps = 1209.6Mbits
French audio track (Stereo 2.0)	5400 seconds	0.224Mbps	1209.6Mbits
English subtitles	5400 seconds	0.010Mbps	5400 seconds × 0.010Mbps = 54Mbits
French subtitles	5400 seconds	0.010Mbps	54Mbits
Total audio/subtitle data rate		**0.468Mbps**	
Motion menu 1	30 seconds	5.0Mbps	30 seconds × 5.0Mbps = 150Mbits
Motion menu 2	30 seconds	5.0Mbps	150Mbits
Total space			2827.2Mbits
Remaining space			36,096 − 2827.2 = **33,268.8Mbits**

- The **maximum bit rate** for this movie is 10.08Mbps − 0.468Mbps = 9.612Mbps.
- The highest possible **average bit rate** is 33268.8Mbits/5400 seconds = 6.16Mbps.

Compressor's 90-minute 5Mbps preset closely matches this calculation. Working with Compressor, you might go with the 90-minute preset or adjust the quality up to 6Mbps for better video fidelity. Figure 5.1 shows how you might adjust your settings for this example.

Example 2

This example presents a more complicated structure. It contains two movie features—one 20 minutes in length, and the other 35. In addition, the second feature uses a mixed-angle track with 15 minutes of alternate video angles (perhaps to hide violent

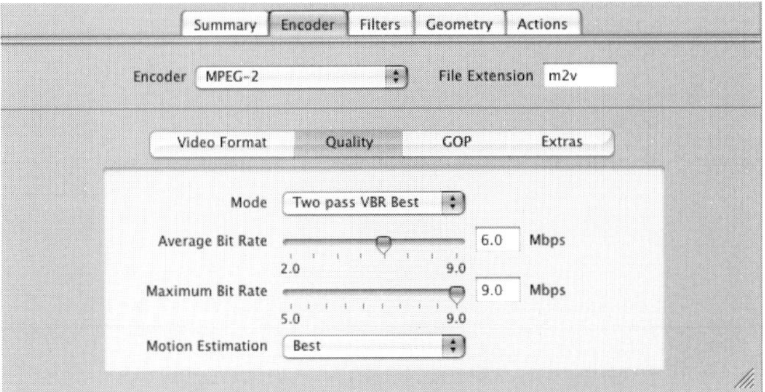

Figure 5.1 You might want to create a custom encoding for the project described in Example 1. Here, you see Compressor's Encoder tab. From this tab you can choose the compression mode (Constant Bit Rate, Variable Bit Rate, or 2-Pass Variable Bit Rate) and the average and maximum bit rates. Motion estimation allows you to optimize for high-motion video. Choose from Good, Better, and Best.

scenes from innocent eyes or some such reason). This project also uses a 30-second introductory video, a 5-second transition video, and a 20-second motion menu.

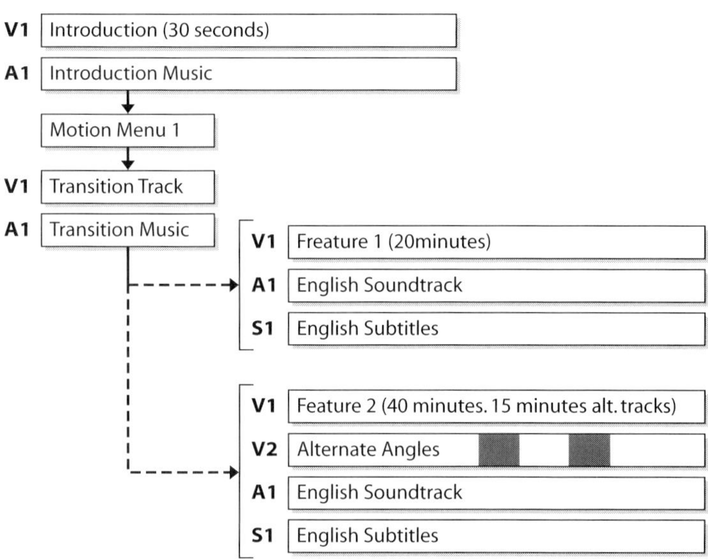

	Duration	**Bit Rate**	**Size**
English audio track (Dolby 5.1)	20 minutes + 40 minutes = 60 minutes × 60 seconds/minute = 3600 seconds	0.448Mbps	3600 seconds × 0.448Mbps = 1612.8Mbits
English subtitles	3600 seconds	0.010Mbps	3600 seconds × 0.010Mbps = 36Mbits
Total audio/subtitle data rate		0.458Mbps	
Motion menu	20 seconds	8.0Mbps	20 seconds × 8.0Mbps = 160Mbits
Introduction video	30 seconds	8.0Mbps	30 seconds × 8.0Mbps = 240Mbits
Introduction audio (Dolby 5.1)	30 seconds	0.448Mbps	30 seconds × 0.448Mbps = 13.44Mbits
Transition video	5 seconds	8.0Mbps	5 seconds × 8.0Mbps = 40Mbits
Transition audio (Dolby 5.1)	5 seconds	0.448Mbps	5 seconds × 0.448Mbps = 2.24Mbits
Total space			2104.48Mbits
Remaining space			36,096 − 2104.48 = 33991.5Mbits

- The **maximum bit rate** for this movie is 10.08Mbps − 0.458Mbps = 9.622Mbps.

- The movies on this disc occupy 75 minutes (20 for the first feature + 40 for the second + 15 for the extra video angles), or 4500 seconds. The highest possible **average bit rate** is 33991.5Mbits/4500 seconds = 7.55Mbps.

This movie's run-time is 60 minutes. Even with the mixed angles that bring the video duration to 75 minutes, these calculations show that the project matches well to Compressor's 60-minute 7.0Mbps preset.

Compressing Video with QuickTime MPEG-2 Encoder

QuickTime's MPEG-2 Encoder is a simple-to-use tool. It doesn't provide the convenience of Compressor (encoding in the background) or the presets ("I'll take '2 Hour MPEG-2' encoding please"), but it does provide a way to export directly to MPEG from many applications, including iMovie and QuickTime Pro. When you install the MPEG-2 export codec on your system (it should install with DVD Studio Pro 2), the MPEG-2 export option appears in all applications that support QuickTime export.

Exporting Final Cut Pro Video to MPEG-2

Follow these steps to export video from Final Cut Pro and retain DVD Studio Pro 2 markers:

1. **Select the item you want to export.** Select a clip or a sequence in your browser or timeline.

2. **Choose File > Export > QuickTime Movie….** Final Cut Pro displays a Save dialog.

3. **Choose DVD Studio Pro Markers.** This option appears in the Markers pop-up, as shown in Figure 5.2.

4. **Save as usual.** Navigate to where you want to save your movie and enter a name. Check your other settings, and then click Save.

If desired, you can open your exported video in QuickTime Pro and export it using the QuickTime Pro MPEG-2 Encoder.

Figure 5.2 Final Cut Pro prompts you to choose which markers to include before you save. Choices include None, DVD Studio Pro Markers (chapter + compression), Compression Markers, Chapter Markers, Auto Scoring Markers, and All Markers. Use the Settings pop-up to select your output file format. In the Include pop-up, specify whether to save audio and video, audio only, or video only. Additional check boxes allow you to choose whether to recompress your frames and whether to create a self-contained movie.

Exporting to MPEG-2 from QuickTime and iMovie

Follow these steps to export to MPEG-2 from iMovie or QuickTime Pro:

1. **Export your movie.** Choose File > Export (iMovie: ⌘-Shift-E; QuickTime Pro: ⌘-E).

2. **(iMovie Only) Choose Expert Settings.** From the Export pop-up, select To QuickTime, from the Formats, select Expert Settings, and then click Export.

3. **Select Movie To MPEG-2.** It appears in the Export pop-up.

4. **Navigate.** Specify where to save your file and how to name it. By default, the MPEG-2 Encoder creates a multiplexed M2V file.

5. **Click Options.** The QuickTime MPEG-2 Exporter window opens. It contains two tabs, Video and Quality.

6. **Choose the Video tab.** Set your video options:

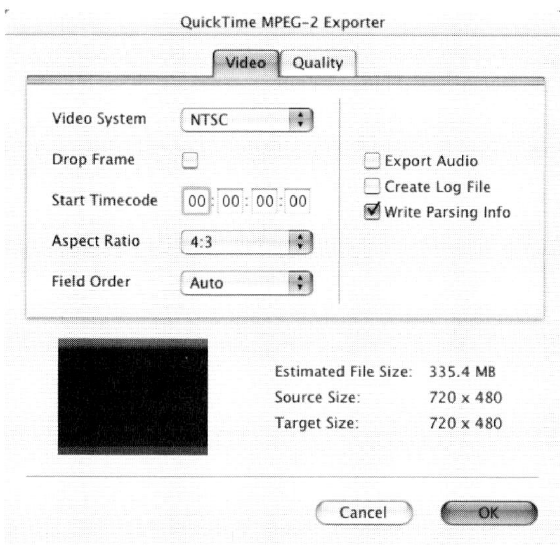

Video System   Select PAL or NTSC to match your source video.

Drop Frame   This setting tells QuickTime to compensate for the difference between 29.97 fps and 30 fps video (NTSC only)—it comes to about 4 seconds per hour. In past versions of DVD Studio Pro, selecting Drop Frame produced subtitle problems, and selecting non–Drop Frame produced problems with audio sync. DVD Studio Pro 2 is still too new to predict what bugs will crop up and where.

Start Timecode   You can use a nonzero start time to mimic a video clip cut from an MPEG stream.

Aspect Ratio   If you shot your footage in 16:9 (widescreen), be sure to select the corresponding option from the Apsect Ratio pop-up.

Field Order   Choose Auto unless you need a specific field ordering (top or bottom). As a rule, digital video files use bottom field dominance.

Export Audio   Check to include audio in your export, or leave unchecked to compress video only, which has advantages. It produces unmultiplexed MPEG. You can compress your audio separately with A.Pack.

Create Log File   Select to create a text-based log of the encoding process.

Write Parsing Info   Creates the parsing information such as the file length, type, and integrity.

7.   **Click the Quality tab.** Choose your quality options:

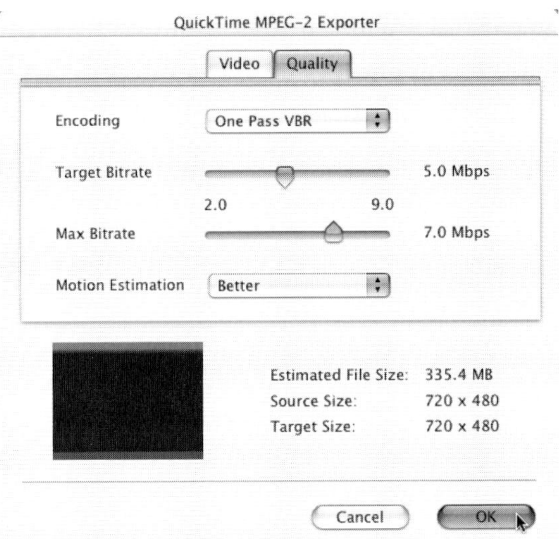

Encoding   Select from One Pass, One Pass VBR, and Two Pass VBR. Variable bit rate (VBR) encoding produces better-quality results but takes more time than constant bit rate encoding (CBR). Two-pass encoding raises the quality bar even further, but at a cost of encoding time.

Target Bit Rate   Set the overall bit rate level for your project. As a rule, 4Mbps creates a 2-hour DVD (on 4.7 general DVDs). A level of 5Mbps produces 90-minute DVDs, and 8Mbps produces high-quality one-hour DVDs.

Max Bit Rate   By setting the maximum allowable bit rate, you limit how much data is produced over any period of time. Some DVD players cannot handle high bit rates, even if the data proves to be compressible.

Motion Estimation   As with any video compression, motion must trade off with video quality. Choose Good for low-action videos, such as talking heads or business reports. Choose Best for sports and other high-action video. Better provides a middle ground, where low- and high-action mix.

8.   **Click OK.** QuickTime accepts your settings and closes the QuickTime MPEG-2 Exporter dialog.

9.   **Click Save.** Wait as QuickTime exports your movie to MPEG.

Unfortunately, this export process monopolizes QuickTime (or iMovie, if you exported from iMovie). You must wait for encoding to complete before moving on to other tasks.

Encoding with Compressor

Apple's new Compressor program ships with both DVD Studio Pro 2 and Final Cut Pro 4. Compressor is a stand-alone program that helps you submit your files for batch compression. All you need to do is add your source files, choose your presets, and submit the batch. Compressor runs fully automated in the background of your computer, freeing you to proceed with other tasks.

Compressor can convert files to many kinds of output formats, including MPEG-2, the video format for DVD. Compressor is simple and easy to use, providing a quick way for you to get your compression jobs done.

Don't let Compressor's outward simplicity deceive you though. Compressor provides a flexible and powerful encoding solution that goes well beyond simple MPEG-2 compression.

To export your work directly from Final Cut to Compressor, without saving to an intermediate QuickTime file, choose File > Export > Using Compressor. Compressor launches, adding your file (a "job") to its current to-do list (a "batch"). Choose your compression options and submit the batch job list for processing.

You'll find a copy of Compressor in the Applications folder of your OS X disk. Navigate to the Compressor icon and double-click to launch. The first time you run Compressor, it may ask you to enter a serial number, depending on whether you installed from Final Cut or DVD Studio Pro 2.

Using Compressor involves four simple steps.

1.   **Add source files.** Choose File > Import (⌘-I). Navigate to your files, select them, and click Import. Alternatively, drag your files to the Compressor window or export from Final Cut.

2.   **Select presets.** Choose a preset from the pop-up list to the right of the filename in the Source Media column. To encode both audio and video, choose All from

the preset submenu. Choose DVD PCM Audio or MPEG-2 to encode either audio or video individually

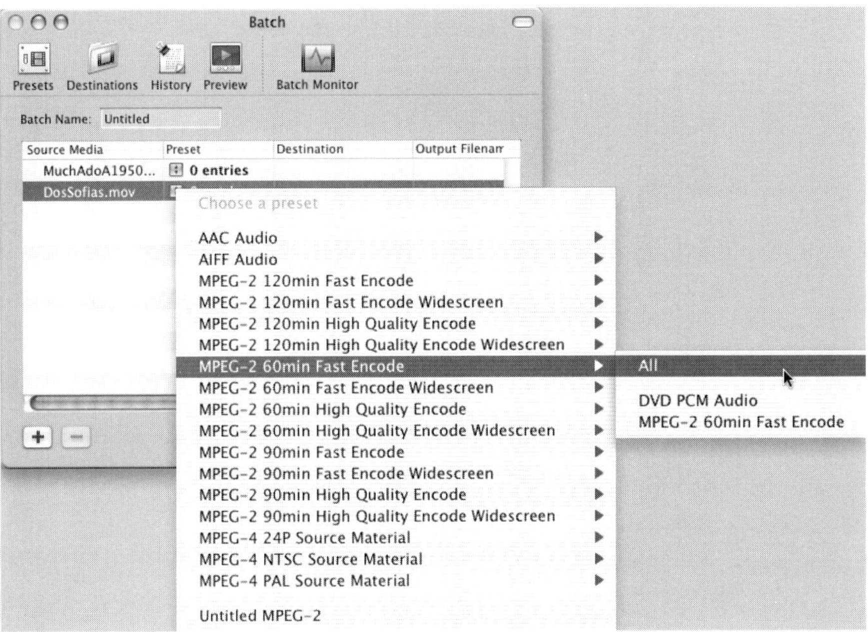

Converting between Video Standards

Unfortunately, converting between video standards is one of the tasks a DVD author must occasionally confront. You might be asked to take a project created in one video standard and save it to a different format for distribution in another country.

Converting between standards is a pre-authoring task, done before you start work in DVD Studio Pro 2. Prepare your video by first converting it and then compressing.

In theory, you can use Compressor to compress, for example, an NTSC video to PAL MPEG-2. (Choose Presets > Encoder > Video Format.) The results won't be ideal.

Final Cut can convert your files better, although not perfectly. Create a new sequence and update its settings to match the new standard. Add your original digital video clips to the new sequence, and let Final Cut handle the conversion. You may need to matte your image to compensate for the different number of lines between the two systems.

You'll obtain best results by using a tool dedicated to standards conversion such as Canopus ProCoder, a Windows-only product.

3. **Choose a destination.** Use the Destination pop-up to select where Compressor saves your encoded files. Choose Source to save in the same folder as the original material. Choosing Desktop saves to the desktop, and choosing User's Movies Folder saves to ~/Movies. Choose Other to select a custom destination.

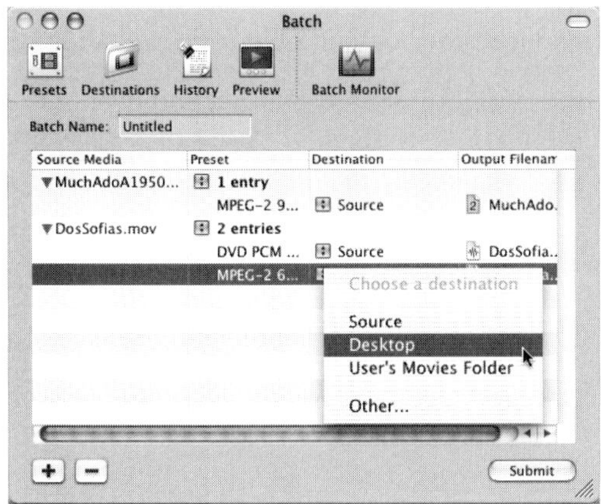

Compressor uses the source filename as the root for the output filename.

4. **Click Submit.** Compressor accepts your job and begins to process it.

5. **Monitor your progress.** Batch Monitor, which appears in the Utilities subfolder of your OS X Applications folder, allows you to monitor Compressor's progress. To view, click Batch Monitor on the Compressor toolbar.

Batch Monitor allows you to stop, resume, delete, and view job information. Select any item, and click the appropriate button on the Monitor toolbar.

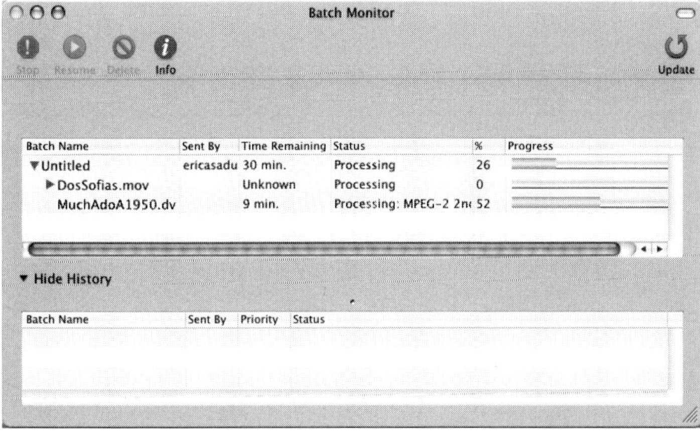

Creating Custom Presets

You can build your own presets to create custom MPEG-2 Compressor settings. The following steps demonstrate how. Unsurprisingly, Compressor uses many of the same settings as QuickTime Pro to encode your video files to MPEG-2. Refer to "Compressing Video with QuickTime MPEG-2 Encoder" to read more about these settings.

1. **Click Presets.** The Presets button is in the toolbar at the top of Compressor's Batch window. Clicking Presets opens the Presets window.

2. **Click + and choose MPEG-2.** Find the + button at the top left of the Presets window, just under the toolbar. Click it to open the pop-up, and then select MPEG-2 from the list. Compressor creates a new item called Untitled MPEG-2 and adds it to the bottom of the Presets list. A small "film" icon with the number 2 precedes the name.

Compressor handles more than MPEG-2 and AIFF compression. Other options include QuickTime, TIFF, and MPEG-4.

3. **Name your preset.** Double-click Untitled MPEG-2 and enter a new name. Try to choose a name that describes what the preset will do. For example, you might create a preset that builds a 60-minute MPEG-2 file with an inset watermark and name it 60-Min MPEG-2 Watermark. Make up for any deficits in naming by filling out the Description field. Double-click No Description and add a description. Once you name (and possibly describe) your preset, Compressor's Preset menu updates to reflect the new name.

4. **View your preset.** Select your new preset from the list and click the Summary tab. MPEG-2 presets default to uncropped 720 × 480 frames using a 4:3 aspect ratio with auto field dominance. Average data rate is set to 5Mbps (about 90 minutes), and the maximum date rate is set to 8Mbps. The default encoder uses

a one-pass variable bit rate with high quality and best motion estimation and closed 15-length GOPs using an IBBP structure.

IBBP refers to the sequence of frames used to build your GOPs. GOPs are groups of pictures, a structured set of frames that make up the basic component of MPEG-2 files. GOPs are built from three kinds of frames: I-frames are keyframes (properly "Intraframes") and use the least compression. B-frames are "Bidirectional" and use information from both the frame before and the frame after to achieve the highest levels of compression. P-frames are "Predictive" look forward to the following frame, and provide medium compression. A typical GOP sequence might be IBBPBBPBBPBBPBP.

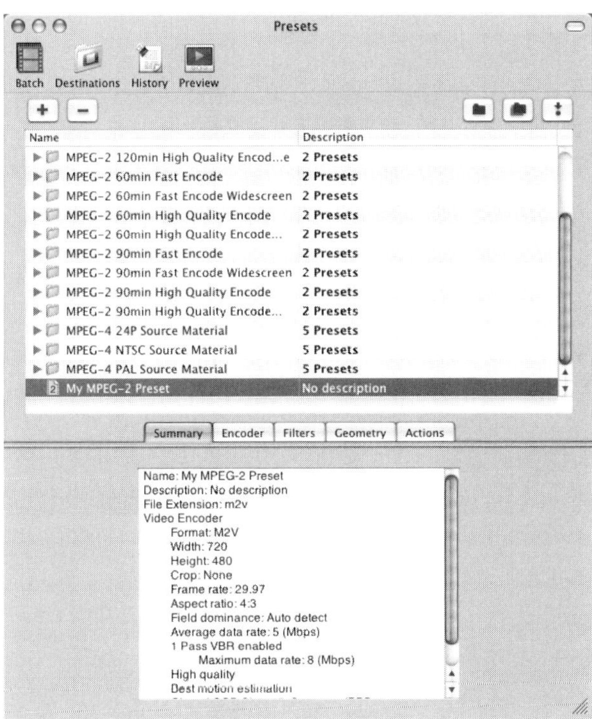

5. **Set your video options**. Choose Encoder > Video Format. This panel helps you set video system and field choices. To use, select your format (NTSC or PAL), your aspect ratio (4:3 or 16:9), and field dominance (Automatic, Top First, or Bottom First). Make sure that your aspect ratio matches the source material you intend to feed the compressor—use anamorphic (squeezed, as most digital video cameras produce widescreen) or full widescreen footage (with a true 16:9 ratio)

for 16:9 compression. Optionally, set a starting timecode and choose whether to use drop frame.

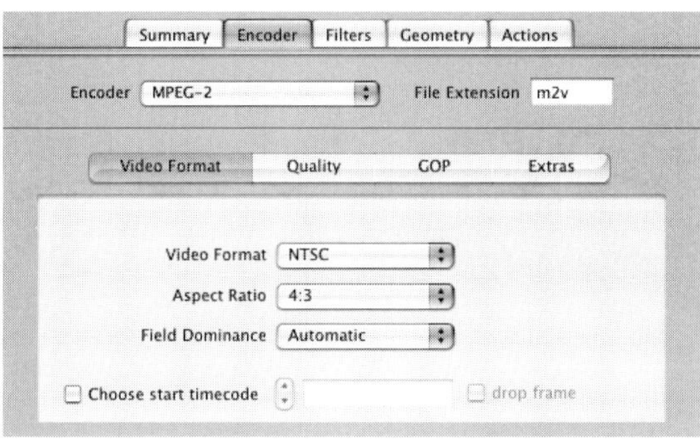

6.   **Set your quality.** Choose Encoder > Quality to view the Quality panel. Choose your encoding quality by selecting from five options: One Pass CBR, One Pass VBR, One Pass VBR Best Quality, Two Pass VBR, and Two Pass VBR Best Quality. These settings produce increasingly better video compression at a cost of longer compression times. Adjust the sliders to set your average and maximum bit rate, per the discussion earlier in this chapter. (You can also enter a number directly in the boxes to the right of the sliders.) Choose a motion estimation from Good (low motion: talking heads), Better (moderate motion: mixed action), or Best (high motion: sports and other rapidly changing scenes).

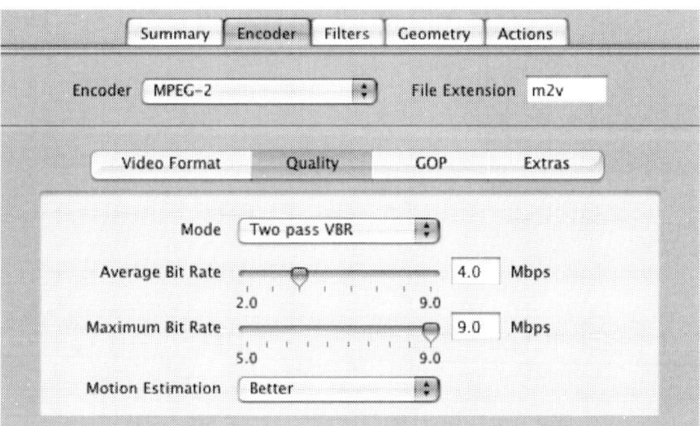

7.   **Optionally set your GOP structure.** If desired, choose Encoder > GOP to open the GOP settings panel. Do not change these settings unless you're familiar with and comfortable with GOP structure. Decide which GOP structure to use, select Open or Closed, select a GOP size, and confirm by examining the Pattern line. Shorter GOP patterns with shorter GOP lengths work best for high-motion video.

Open GOPs use data from the previous and following GOPs, providing more efficient compression. Closed GOPs do not—they're self contained. Always choose closed GOPs when working with mixed-angle DVDs and when your product will be distributed on any of the DVD recordable formats.

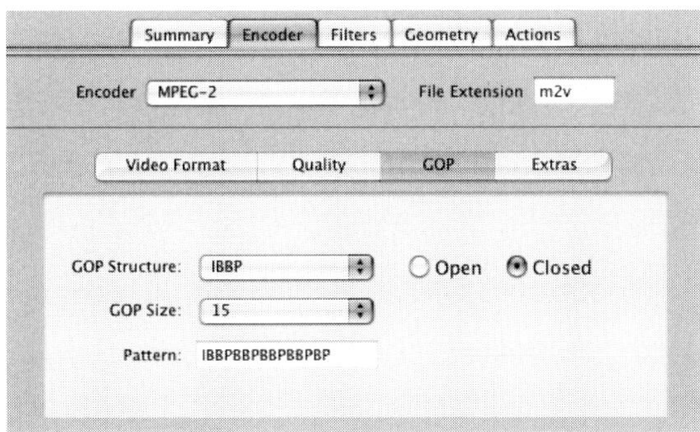

8. **Prepare for DVD Studio Pro 2.** Choose Encoder > Extras to view a panel with two important settings. Check Add DVD Studio Pro Meta-Data to add parsing information to your compressed MPEG-2 file. If you want to bypass compression markers, check Include Chapter Markers Only. Left unchecked, this setting forces I-frames at all compression markers in your source video. For Final Cut video, this includes both the markers you added and all edit points, ensuring keyframes at video transition points.

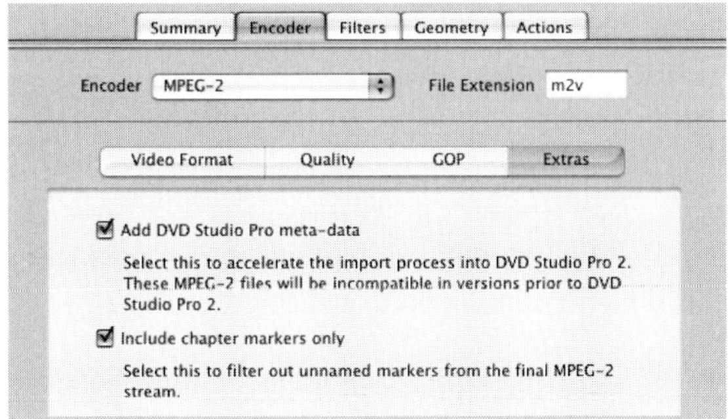

9. **Optionally select filters.** Compressor allows you to add filters before you encode. Click the Filters tab to see the available choices. Plan carefully before adding filters to your batch. You can't "remove" filters from your compressed video except by re-encoding from scratch. As a rule, avoid filters unless you absolutely need to use them: watermarks and text overlays may prove useful to

many DVD Studio Pro 2 authors. To add a filter, check the box next to its name. Options appear to the right. Customize these as needed.

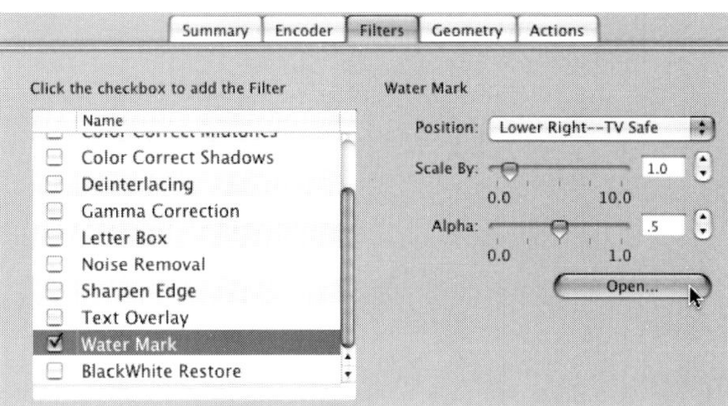

10. **Optionally adjust inset and cropping.** Click the Geometry tab to inset nonstandard-sized video. Options allow you to set cropping and output sizes. Inset videos will be surrounded by black and may appear small on your TV screen because they do not resize from their original sizes.

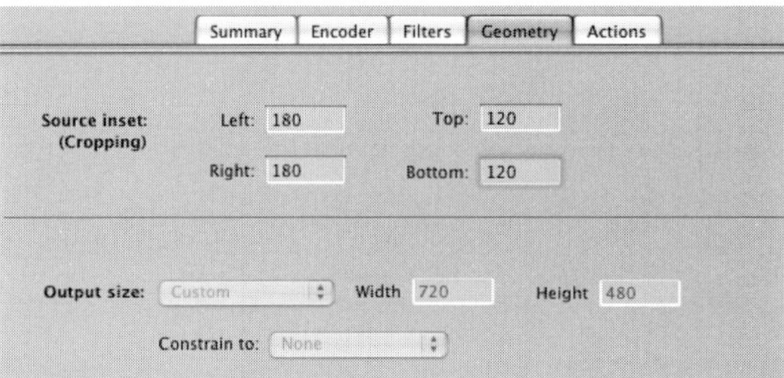

11. **Define any notification.** When finished with output, Compressor can e-mail you notification or execute a custom Apple-Script. Click the Actions tab to view the available options. Even if you're not a programmer, a simple AppleScript, such as Say "I am done compressing", might fit your needs. (Say instructs Applescript to use a voice synthesizer to vocalize the text between the quotes.)

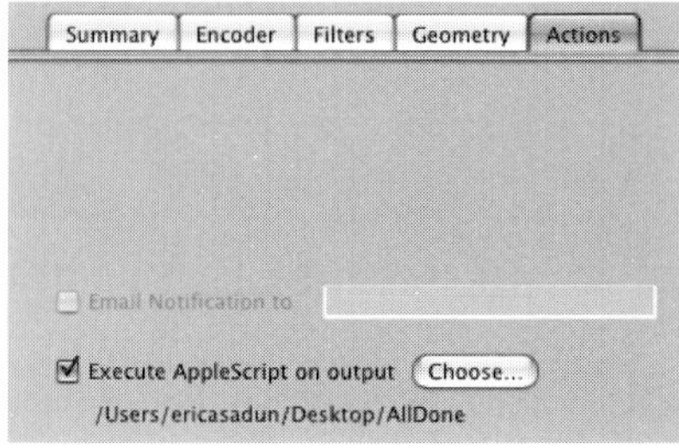

Use AppleScript ScriptEditor to define your scripts and save them to disk before assigning them in the Action tab.

Your new preset is now customized. You need not "save" or "apply" your work. Compressor notes all your changes as entered without further action and saves them to disk when you quit the program.

To find your new preset, quit Compressor and navigate to ~/Library/Application Support/Compressor. (It's in your home folder.) Your item appears with a .setting extension (for example, My MPEG-2 Preset.setting). This file uses XML (Extensible Markup Language) to store your settings. Simply drag it onto TextEdit's icon to view its contents.

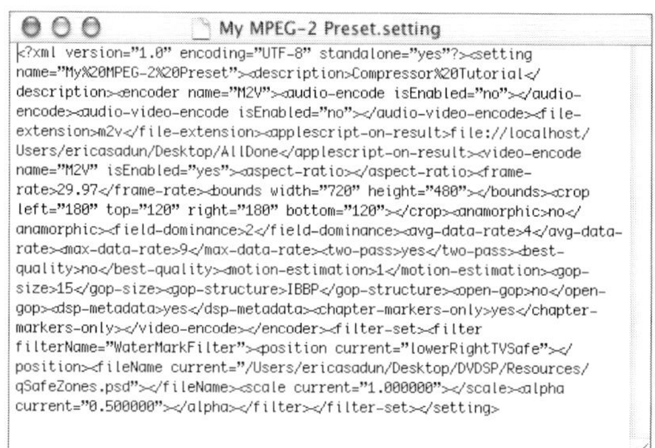

My MPEG-2 Preset.setting

```xml
<?xml version="1.0" encoding="UTF-8" standalone="yes"?><setting
name="My%20MPEG-2%20Preset"><description>Compressor%20Tutorial</
description><encoder name="M2V"><audio-encode isEnabled="no"></audio-
encode><audio-video-encode isEnabled="no"></audio-video-encode><file-
extension>m2v</file-extension><applescript-on-result>file://localhost/
Users/ericasadun/Desktop/AllDone</applescript-on-result><video-encode
name="M2V" isEnabled="yes"><aspect-ratio></aspect-ratio><frame-
rate>29.97</frame-rate><bounds width="720" height="480"></bounds><crop
left="180" top="120" right="180" bottom="120"></crop><anamorphic>no</
anamorphic><field-dominance>2</field-dominance><avg-data-rate>4</avg-data-
rate><max-data-rate>9</max-data-rate><two-pass>yes</two-pass><best-
quality>no</best-quality><motion-estimation>1</motion-estimation><gop-
size>15</gop-size><gop-structure>IBBP</gop-structure><open-gop>no</open-
gop><dsp-metadata>yes</dsp-metadata><chapter-markers-only>yes</chapter-
markers-only></video-encode></encoder><filter-set><filter
filterName="WaterMarkFilter"><position current="lowerRightTVSafe"></
position><fileName current="/Users/ericasadun/Desktop/DVDSP/Resources/
qSafeZones.psd"></fileName><scale current="1.000000"></scale><alpha
current="0.500000"></alpha></filter></filter-set></setting>
```

You can easily add preset groups (designated by the folder icon) as well as individual preset items. Click the folder button in Compressor's Presets window (on the top right, just below the toolbar) to create a new group folder. Drag preset settings onto the folder to group them.

Clean Up Your History

Compressor's History panel can become cluttered quickly when you're working on large projects. Follow these steps to empty the program's memory of past jobs.

1. **Quit Compressor.** The program cannot be running when you perform these steps.

2. **Navigate to ~/Library/Application Support/Compressor/History.** The Library is in your home folder.

3. **Drag the contents to the trash.** Select all the items in the History folder and delete them.

4. **Relaunch Compressor.** When you click History, all previous batch items have been removed, leaving you with a fresh start.

Create a Compression Droplet

Droplets are one of Compressor's handiest but most easily overlooked features. Compressor droplets create desktop icons, allowing you to drag and drop videos for instant batch submission. Follow these steps to create your own Compressor droplet.

1. **Open the Presets window.** Launch Compressor and click Presets.

2. **Choose a preset.** Select any of the presets. Your droplet will use these settings to compress files.

3. **Click Save Selection As Droplet.** The button appears at the top right of the Presets window, just below the toolbar. The icon looks like an arrow pointing down to a square. A Save dialog appears.

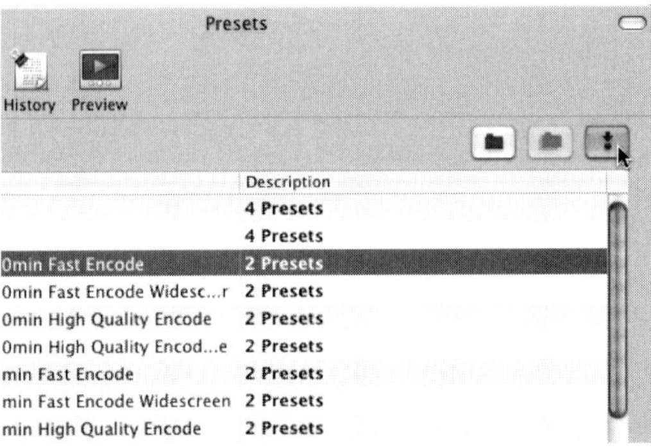

4. **Name your droplet.** Enter a name for your droplet, and navigate to where you want to save it.

5. **Choose a destination.** Select from Source, Desktop, or any other predefined destination. The destination you select specifies where the results of the droplet should be stored, not where the droplet appears. The default, Source, saves the compressed files in the same folder as your original items.

6. **Click Save.** Compressor creates a new droplet per your specifications.

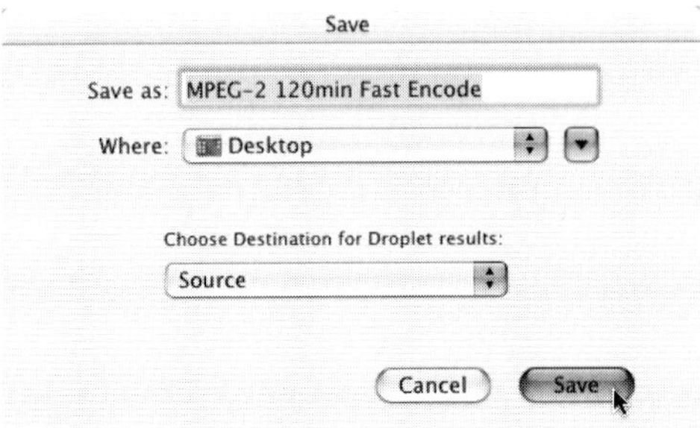

To use your new droplet, drag videos onto it. The droplet uses the settings you selected to add your videos as a new Compressor batch job.

Add New Destinations

Compressor lets you add custom destinations to the pop-up menu that appears in your Batch window.

1. **Open the Destinations window.** Click Destinations in the toolbar.

2. **Click +/Local.** Navigate to the folder you want to add (on a local computer), and click Open. (Clicking +/Remote lets you add a folder on a remote computer.)

3. **Name your destination.** Double-click the Name field to add an easily recognized title to your new folder.

4. **Optionally, make a default destination.** While your destination is selected, you can click Make Default to choose this new folder as the default destination.

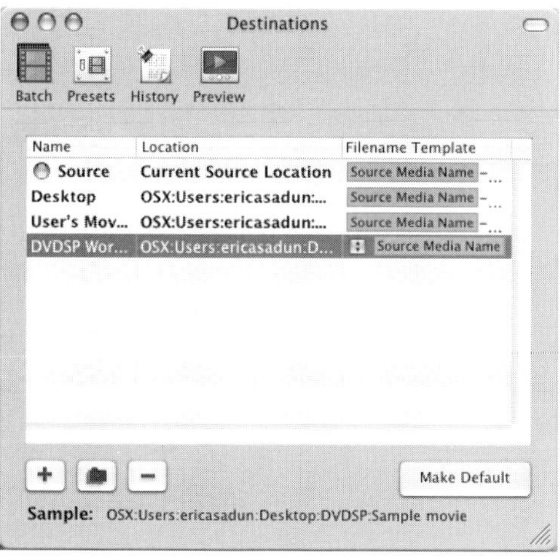

Encoding AC-3 Sound with A.Pack

A.Pack, which is part of the standard DVD Studio Pro 2 distribution, lets you encode audio to the Dolby Digital Audio format known as AC-3. A.Pack is not a sound editor. It does not "mix." As an encoder, it transforms your prepared audio source files into AC-3. A.Pack is Dolby certified (www.dolby.com) and produces fully compliant AC-3 files.

As you might expect, authoring sound is an art form, particularly when you intend to use surround sound to aurally "fix" sounds in space. With proper settings and prepared source material, A.Pack lets you assign your sounds to create a full surround-sound experience, complete with those rumbling low-frequency effects that make movie experiences so real.

Dolby's Tips

Dolby offers the following tips for DVD-video audio content, which are paraphrased from The Dolby Digital Professional Encoding Guidelines (www.dolby.com/tech/L.mn.0002.DDPEG1.pdf), more than 170 pages of professional how-to.

- **Start with silence.** Always begin your audio with at least two seconds of digital black silence.

- **Use proper bit rates and sampling.** Encode at 448Kbps for multichannel material. Encode at 192Kbps for two-channel stereo material. DVDs require a 48kHz sample rate.

- **Use quality audio.** The best audio quality produces the best encoded results. Dolby Digital accommodates both 16-bit and 24-bit audio.

- **Use Low Frequency Effects only when needed.** Don't enable LFE unless you've added dedicated low-frequency effects material in your original audio source.

- **Watch your flags.** Enable the proper flags for each parameter. For example, don't enable Dolby Surround unless the original material includes Dolby Surround encoding.

- **Save the SMPTE timecode when present.** It's used to synchronize with video.

If your audio demands are much simpler, you're not alone. Many DVD authors do not work with full 5.1 surround sound audio files (although its nice to know you can). A.Pack works just as well with single-channel and stereo files. It allows you to quickly specify and encode your sound files to produce these simple channel assignments.

To learn more about A.Pack and AC-3, refer to "Preparing Audio Sources" and "Using A.Pack to Encode AC-3 Sound" in your DVD Studio Pro 2 documentation.

Using A.Pack for Basic Encodes

A.Pack appears in the Applications folder of your OS X disk. Double-click the application icon to launch. If you are running the program for the first time, you'll be prompted for your name and serial number. Enter these, and you're ready to start encoding.

Follow these steps to encode your audio files.

1. **Open the Instant Encoder.** The A.Pack Instant Encoder window, shown in Figure 5.3, should appear by default. If you do not see it, choose Window > Instant Encoder (⌘-1). You use this window to take care of most basic encoding tasks.

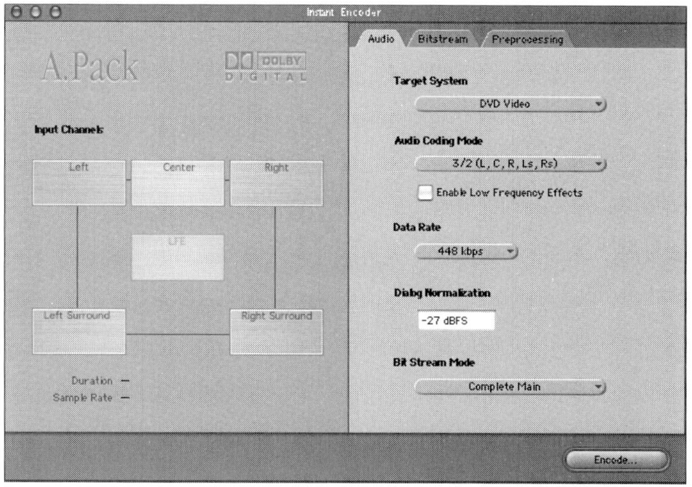

Figure 5.3 The A.Pack Instant Encoder window allows you to choose your audio coding, set your channels, adjust your encoding options, and launch your encode.

2. **Choose your audio coding.** Locate the Audio Coding Mode pop-up. Open it and select the coding you want to use. You have the following channel options: 1/0 (Center), 2/0 (Left, Right), 3/0 (Left, Center, Right), 2/1 (Left, Right, Center Surround), 3/1 (Left, Center, Right, Center Surround), 2/2 (Left, Right, Surround-Left, Surround-Right), and 3/2 (Left, Center, Right, Surround-Left, Surround-Right). In the simplest cases, choose 1/0 for mono tracks or 2/0 for stereo.

Always use 1/0 for a single, monaural audio track. With Dolby Digital selected and enabled, the sound plays from the center channel. With Dolby Digital disabled, the sound plays from the left/right speaker pair. With 2/0 audio, the audio plays from the left/right pair whether Dolby Digital is enabled or not. Dolby strongly recommends against encoding mono signals in 2/0 mode.

3. **Assign your channels.** You can assign audio to channels in two ways. Either drag an audio file onto the channel icon or click the icon and choose a file from the File Open dialog. When your audio file contains more than one channel, A.Pack prompts you to select the channel you want to assign, as shown in Figure 5.4. Be sure to use files with proper sample rates. DVD requires 48kHz audio.

A.Pack won't accept MP3 audio. Convert your MP3 audio to AIFF with QuickTime Pro before adding it to an A.Pack channel.

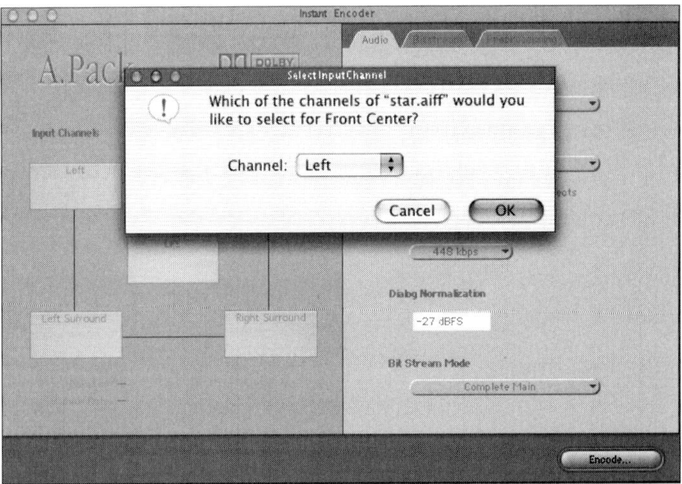

Figure 5.4 A.Pack lets you select the channel you want to assign when your sound file contains more than one audio channel. When setting left or right, be sure to match the file and encoder channels.

4. **Set encoding options.** Click the Audio tab. Choose DVD Video from the Target System pop-up, and choose 224 kbps from the Data Rate pop-up for a stereo stream. Change the Dialog Normalization setting from –27 dBFS to –31 dBFS. This leaves your audio at the levels you mixed them. Press Return to make the setting stick.

5. **Indicate the copyright.** Click the Bitstream tab. Check (or clear) Copyright Exists and Content Is Original to describe the content you're about to encode.

6. **Remove preprocessing.** Click the Preprocessing tab. Change the compression from Film Standard to None, and clear everything else. This keeps your audio stream exactly as mixed.

7. **Click Encode.** A.Pack opens a new Save As dialog. Select a location to save your file, enter a name, and click Save. Wait as A.Pack converts your file to the AC-3 format, saving the file with a .ac3 extension.

Solution: Create Motion Buttons for Your Menus from Your Compressed Movies

DVD Studio Pro 2 offers many convenient features. One of the best is the ability to create menu buttons from your footage. Use Compressor to process a series of video, and let DVD Studio Pro 2 build your menus.

1. **Create a new project.** Launch DVD Studio Pro 2, and start a fresh project.

2.   **Import your assets.** Import your compressed
     video and sound assets and a background
     still image. In the Solutions 5.1 folder on
     the companion DVD, you'll find three com-
     mercials for Cheerios , Ivory Soap, and Sun-
     beam Bread (cheerios.m2v, cheerios.wav,
     ivory.m2v, ivory.wav, sunbeam.m2v, sun-
     beam.wav)and a main menu image (cmenu
     .jpg). Copy these items to your disk, and
     drag them into the Assets tab.

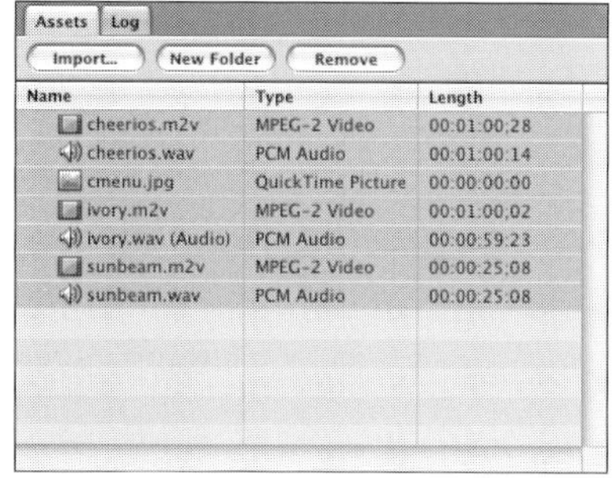

3.   **Select Menu 1.** It appears in the Outline tab. Click the Menu tab to open the
     Menu Editor.

4.   **Add the menu background.** Drag your still
     image (cmenu.jpg in this project) from the
     Assets tab onto the Menu Editor. While
     holding down the mouse button, choose
     Set Background and then release the
     mouse. DVD Studio Pro 2 adds the still
     image to the menu as a background.

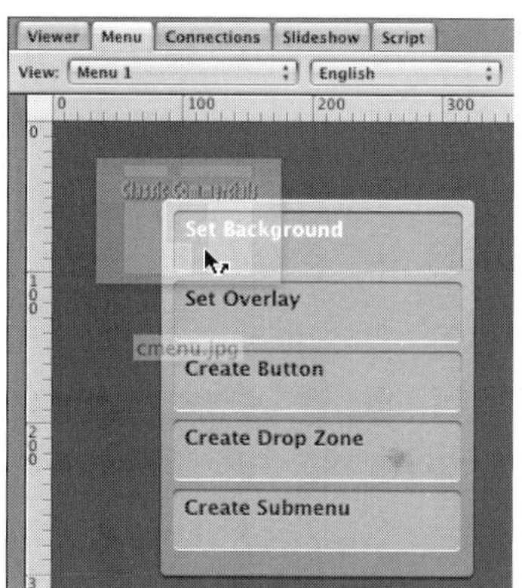

5.   **Add your videos.** Drag your first video (for
     example, cheerios.m2v) to the Menu Edi-
     tor. Do not release the mouse. When the
     drop palette appears, choose Create Button
     And Track (Connect To Track). DVD Stu-
     dio Pro 2 converts your video into a
     motion button, adds a new track with both
     audio and video (matching the names so
     that cheerios.wav adds with cheerios.m2v),

and sets all the appropriate links. When clicked, the button plays the new track.
When the track finishes playing, your new track returns to this menu. Repeat to
add your remaining videos.

6.   **Find a style.** Open the Palette (⌘-⌥-P). Choose Styles > Apple > Buttons. For
     this project, locate Frames Glass Small (the one that shows a frame with text
     underneath).

7. **Add the style to your buttons.** Drag the style (Frames Glass Small) onto your first button, and choose Apply To Button from the drop palette. Repeat for your remaining buttons. Click the text under each button to add an appropriate title.

8. **Arrange your buttons.** Choose View > Title Safe Area (⌘-Shift-E) to visualize the title safe overlay. Use the inner bounds of this rectangle to place your buttons. Avoid overlapping buttons; you might need to resize them to make them fit.

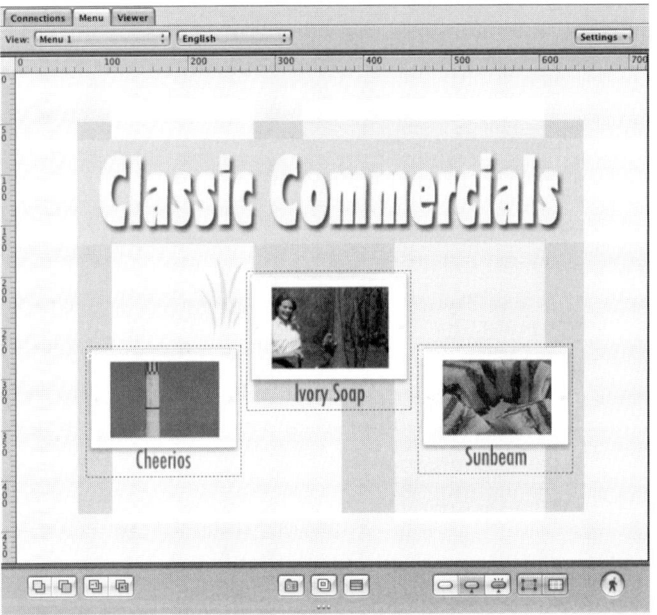

9. **Modify your highlights.** The default highlight (a yellow line under the button title) shows poorly against the pastel background. Open the Inspector (⌘-⌥-I). Select the first button and change the highlight color to bright orange. (This color change affects all buttons on the menu.) Then select each button in turn, and check Include Text In Highlight to extend the highlight to the button label.

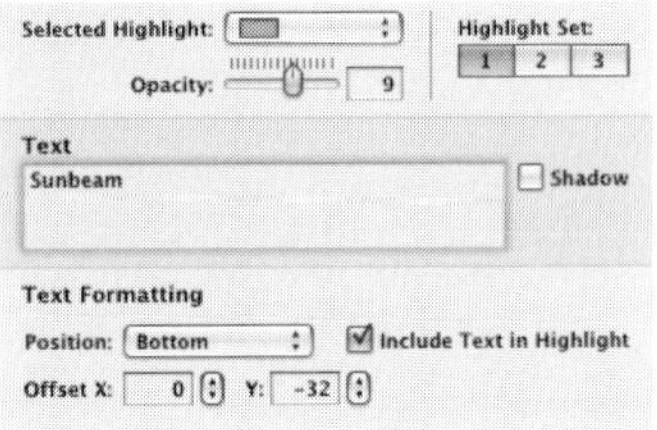

10. **Simulate.** Click the Simulator button in the toolbar. Your entire project should work correctly.

Solution: Add Background Audio to Your Menu

A well-chosen looping soundtrack can bring your menus to life. (A poorly chosen one can drive your audience to distraction.) In these steps, you'll add music from FreePlayMusic.com to your DVD Studio Pro 2 menus.

This project can follow up on the previous one, adding a music loop to the main menu.

1. Visit **www.freeplaymusic.com**. FreePlayMusic offers a variety of royalty-free tracks for personal, nonbroadcast use. (Broadcast rights are available for a fee.) Stop by their website, browse through their selections, and download a track or two to use in your projects. Thirty-second loops are particularly suitable for DVD projects. FreePlayMusic offers both MP3 and WAV files. Be sure to download WAV music for DVD Studio Pro 2 projects.

2. **Convert from WAV to AIFF.** Unfortunately, the FreePlayMusic WAV tracks are incompatible with A.Pack. Launch QuickTime Pro, and open your WAV file from within the program. Choose File > Export, and export to a new AIFF while preserving the PCM data. Use 16-bit stereo 48kHz samples.

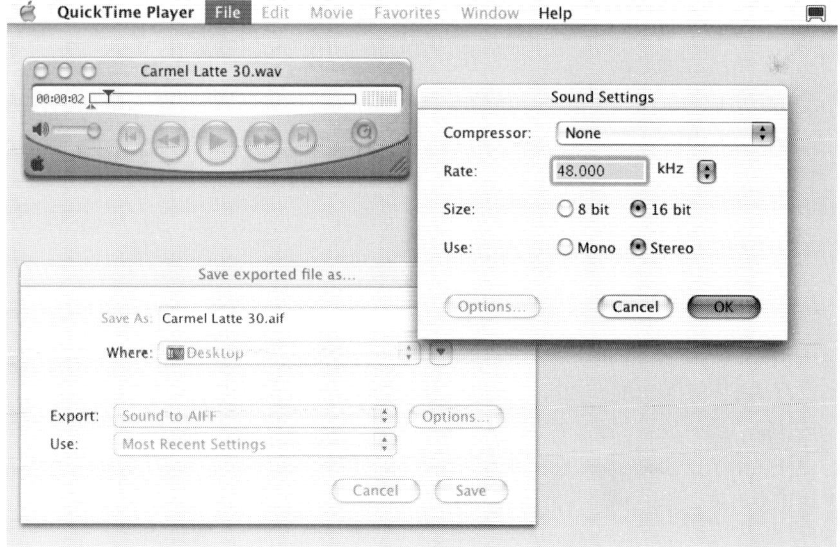

3. **Launch A.Pack.** The program appears in your OS X Applications folder. The Instant Encoder should appear when the program opens. If it does not, choose Window > Instant Encoder (⌘-1).

4. **Choose stereo output.** Click the Audio tab, and select 2/0 (l/R) for Audio Coding Mode.

5.   **Set the left input channel**. In the Input Channels pane on the left of the Instant Encoder window, click Left to open the Open File dialog. Navigate to your file, select it, and click Choose. A.Pack asks which channel you would like to select for front left. Select Left, and click OK.

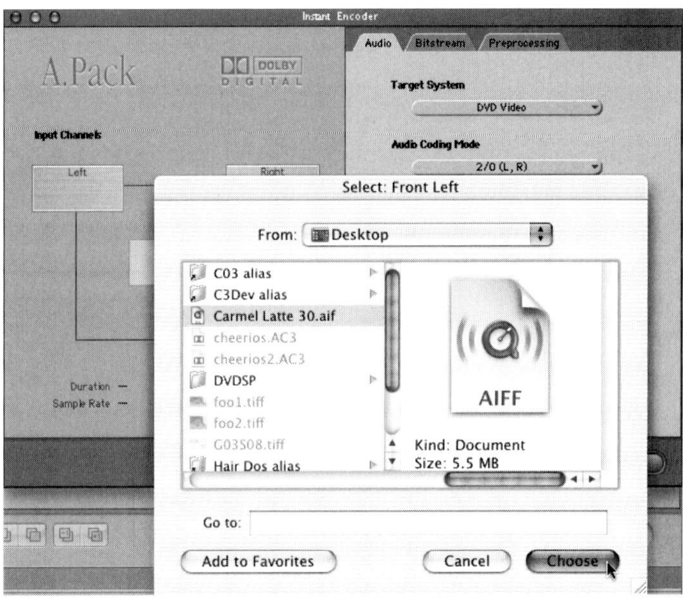

6.   **Set the right input channel**. Repeat the previous step, clicking Right. Select the right channel from your file.

7.   **Click Encode**. Use the default parameters for a DVD video target and let A.Pack encode your WAV to AC3. A.Pack opens the Save File dialog. Name your file and navigate as needed. Click Save, and then wait as A.Pack processes your file.

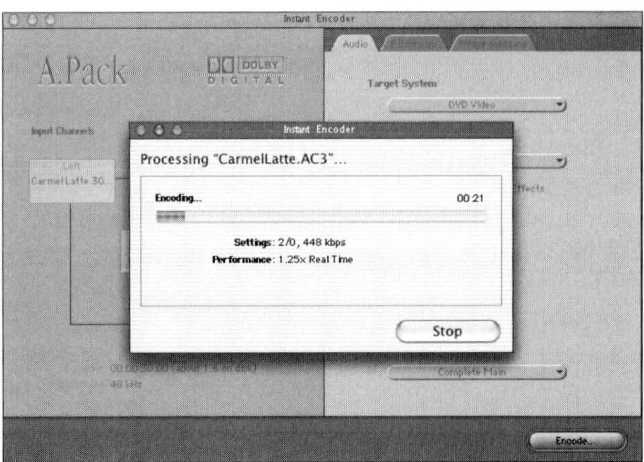

8.   **Add your AC3 file to DVD Studio Pro 2.** Open DVD Studio Pro 2 and load your project. Drag the newly converted AC3 sound to your Assets tab.

9.   **Select your menu.** Open the Outline tab, and select the menu to which you'll add the background audio loop. Click the Menu tab to open the Menu Editor and view the menu.

10. **Drag your audio.** Drag your background audio loop from the Assets tab onto your menu. Before releasing the mouse, choose Set Audio from the drop palette. By default, DVD Studio Pro 2 assigns your audio to the menu and automatically loops it so the audio clip restarts at the beginning after it finishes playing.

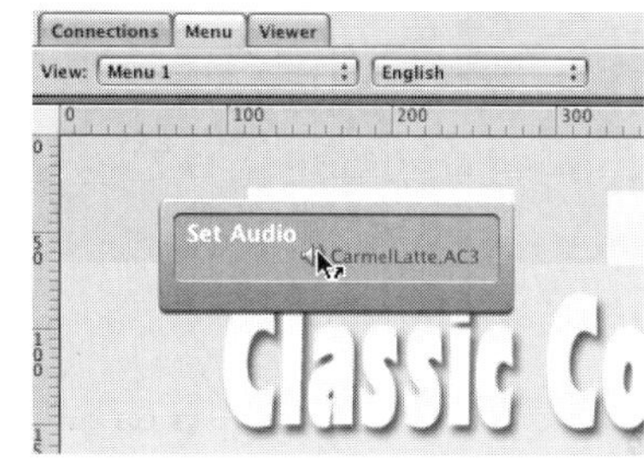

You have now downloaded, compressed, and added an audio loop to a menu in your DVD Studio Pro 2 project.

Track
00:00:00;00
Start:
Improved Styli
The Development of
00:02:59;29
00:03:59;29

are ever changing.

and colors to give to us
of our daily living.

Play
Original
Audio

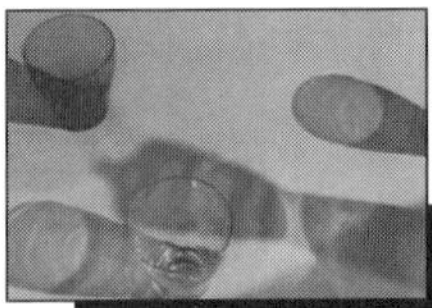

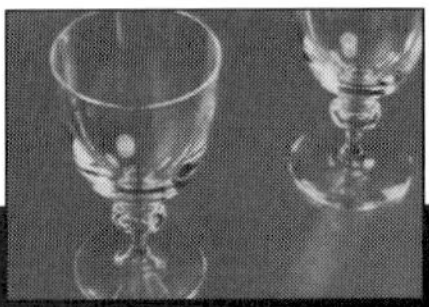

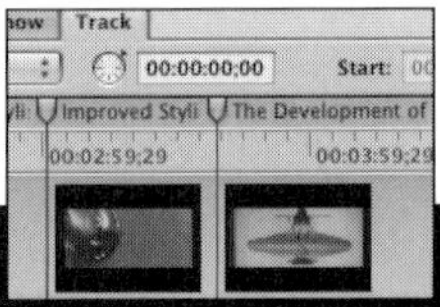

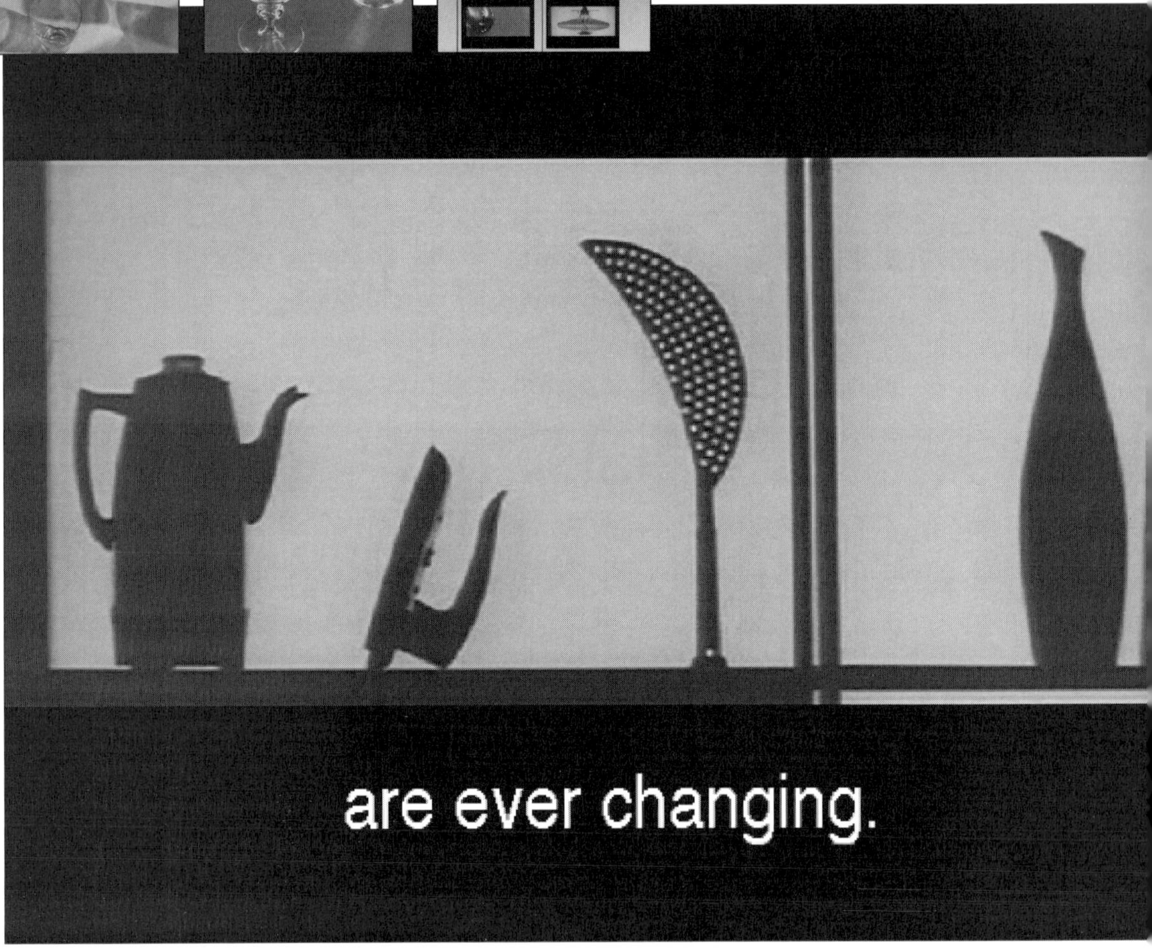

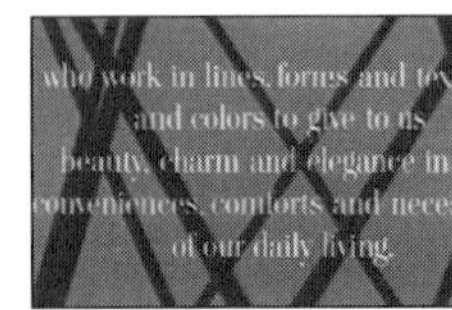

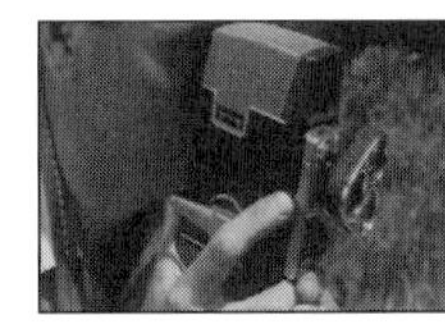

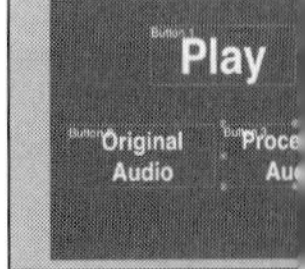

Building Tracks

In DVD Studio Pro 2, DVD tracks are built from coordinated blocks of video, audio, and subtitles, which work together to present a single programmed presentation much as the words and pictures in a book work together on each page. In this chapter, you'll learn how to create, populate, and use tracks in your DVD projects.

Chapter Contents

Track Essentials

If you've used movie-editing software, such as Final Cut or iMovie, the timeline-based Track tab should look familiar. Tracks consist of data called "streams" laid out over time, as shown in Figure 6.1.

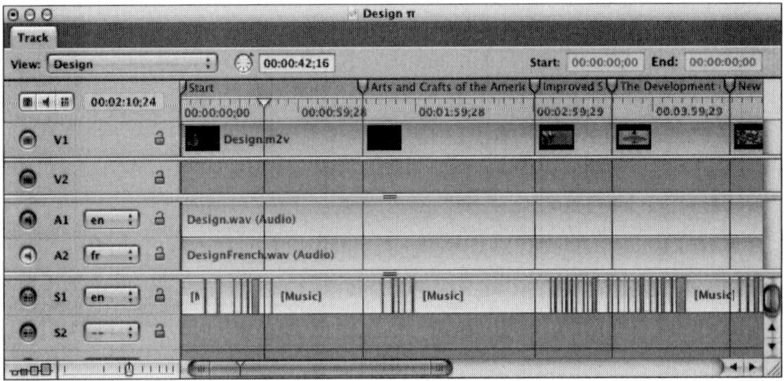

Figure 6.1 DVD tracks store the video, audio, and subtitle data that make up the bulk of your DVD presentation. Here you see a track consisting of four streams: one video, two audio, and one subtitle. At any time, DVD players can play back one instance of each stream type.

Stream types include the following:

Video Provide the visual component of your DVD movies, usually in the form of .m2v files. Each track can contain one or more video streams, allowing you to choose different "angles" to play back.

Audio Add the sound component to your movies. You can add extra audio streams to provide alternate sound tracks or skip audio entirely for a silent presentation. Audio streams are typically built from AC3 or PCM files.

Subtitle Let you overlay your movies with optional text and/or images. The subtitle buttons on your DVD remote control let you turn subtitles on and off at will. The Track Editor lets you add subtitles directly to your track, or you can import prepared text and image files. Like audio streams, subtitle streams are nonobligatory.

Unlike video-editing software, the DVD Studio Pro 2 timeline isn't used to merge assets but to align them for later playback selection. Well-prepared tracks ensure that audio and subtitles sync perfectly to video.

You can use the Track Editor to add as many as 9 video streams, 8 audio streams, and 32 subtitle streams to each track. These streams are named sequentially, such as V1, V2, and V3. The first letter of each stream refers to whether it's a video stream (V), audio stream (A), or subtitle stream (S).

Subtitles and Closed Captions

Subtitles are not the same thing as closed captions, although they may perform many of the same functions. Both allow your viewer to display speech as printed text, but subtitles go much further. Subtitles can use any font size, face, or style as well as pictures. Closed captions provide simple text, whose appearance cannot be customized. Closed captions usually add audio cues (such as doors slamming, phone rings, and so forth). Subtitles can add these cues, but they're not a standard presentation, as they are with closed captions.

Closed captions (also called Line 21 Closed Captions) embed text information into the video stream. To see them, viewers require a decoder chip in their television sets, distinct from the DVD player. Nearly all television sets sold in the United States now offer closed-caption compatibility, but you can't be sure that your audience will have access to this technology. Unlike closed captions, every standard DVD player supports subtitles.

DVD Studio Pro 2 can add closed captions to your tracks. Use the Other tab in the Track Inspector to select a Line 21 file. You can import closed captions in the .cc and .scc formats, but you cannot create these files within the program itself. Ccaption (http://www.ccaption.com/) offers closed-caption creation tools for the Macintosh.

For more information on closed captioning, visit the National Captioning Institute at http://www.ncicap.org/.

At any time, DVD players can play back one video, one audio, and one subtitle stream. Which streams are chosen usually depends on the player's language settings and, less typically, on programmed instructions you can add to your disc.

Use streams to build up your track's possibilities. Extra streams can add language support, audio choices, alternate movie angles, buttons over movies, or universal access.

Language Support Broaden your audience by adding languages to your DVDs. DVD Studio Pro 2 lets you add foreign-language audio streams for dubbed presentations and subtitles for visual translation, retaining the original audio. Use the approach that best suits your material and your audience.

Audio Choices Multiple audio streams let viewers choose from different audio qualities. You might add one stream using 2.0 PCM and another with 5.1 Dolby Digital. This approach lets you fine-tune your audio for each setup, ensuring that your audience hears the best sound their equipment can provide.

Angles Angles provide alternate video presentations using extra video streams. Typical angles might include less-graphic PG-rated footage, the wireframe models used to build the scene's animation, or original storyboard shots.

Movie Buttons Subtitle streams (more properly "subpicture" streams) let you place buttons over video, expanding DVD interaction. Buttons might branch off to alternate video presentations, lead to further product information, or allow your viewers to find "Easter eggs" (cleverly hidden bonus material).

Universal Access Extra streams let you open your DVD to wider audiences by offering various forms of universal access. Audio description tracks let visually impaired audiences augment their viewing experience by describing details, such as costumes, expressions, and gestures that might otherwise be missed by listening to the normal audio track. Subtitle captions and alternate video angles that embed sign language open your material to the hearing impaired. PBS is particularly committed to offering accessible media. Visit the Media Access Group at WGBH (http://main.wgbh.org/wgbh/pages/mag/about) for a more complete discussion of these issues.

Track Creation Tools

Although you build your tracks in the Track tab, other tools also play important roles. Here's a brief summary of the tools you'll use to create and customize tracks.

The Track Editor (⌘-9) Found in the Track tab, lets you lay out and customize your streams. You can add video and still images to the video streams, audio to the audio streams and text, and overlay art to the subtitle streams. The Track Editor coordinates asset duration and start times, so your material appears on time and in sync. The Track Editor also lets you assign languages to audio and subtitle streams so your tracks play back according to the language settings of your DVD player. See "Exploring the Track Editor" later in this chapter for more information.

The Outline Tab (⌘-5) Centralizes the creation and overview of project elements, including tracks. Use the Outline tab to add, name, and organize your tracks. See "Exploring the Outline Tab" later in this chapter for more information.

The Assets Tab (⌘-1) Acts as an audio-, stills-, and video-holding area and provides material you need to build your tracks. Populate tracks by dragging items from the Assets tab to your video and audio streams and, in the case of overlay stills, to your subtitle streams. See Chapter 1 for more information about the Assets tab.

The Viewer Tab (⌘-0) Plays a key role in creating tracks. Shown in Figure 6.2, it lets you see (and hear) exactly what you're building. As you move the playhead through your track, the Viewer updates to show the selected frame. Activate the video, audio, and subtitle streams you want to review, and then play them back in the Viewer. You'll

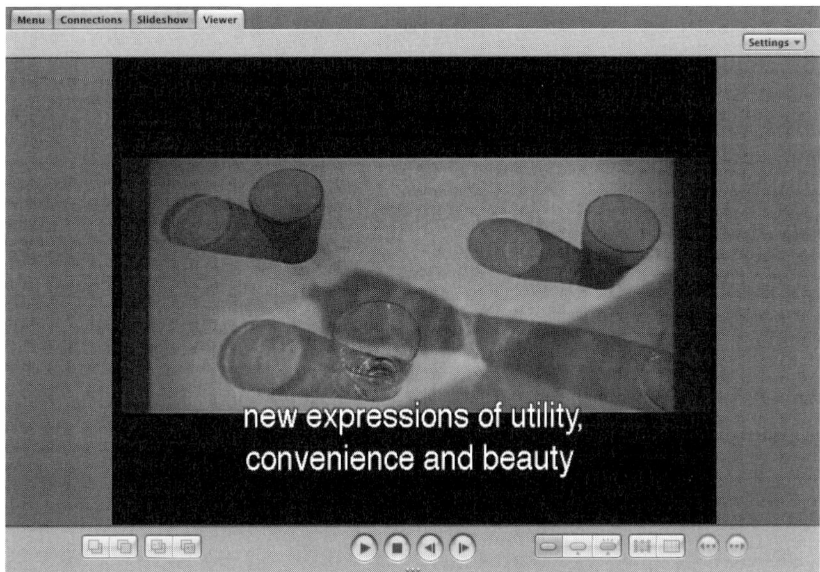

Figure 6.2 The Viewer tab offers an in-program monitor that transforms your tracks into watchable presentations. Use the Viewer to review subtitles or to ensure that audio and video remain in sync.

obtain immediate feedback to detect whether your track is in sync. See "Previewing with the Viewer Tab" later in this chapter for more information.

The Inspector (⌘-⌥-I) Lets you set many options related to the track itself; the video, audio, and subtitle clips that inhabit it, and the markers that break up this material into discrete sections. Various inspectors are available: for the track, for clips, and for markers. Typical track settings include the track's display mode (4:3 v. 16:9), its playback options (which scripts to run and how to respond to remote-control commands), and more.

Building Tracks

The process of building your tracks involves some assembly and some adjustment. Here's a step-by-step overview:

1. **Add tracks.** The Outline tab lets you create your tracks and add them to your project. Use the various methods described in this chapter to create new tracks.

2. **Open the Track Editor.** Select a track in the Outline tab, and then open the Track tab to view it.

3. **Populate the video and audio streams.** Drag assets from the Assets tab (or from the Finder) to the video and audio streams in your track.

When you drag QuickTime movie assets into your tracks, the video and audio lengths may appear different. According to Apple, this occurs when the frame rate of the audio does not divide evenly into the video frame rate and should not affect synchronization between the audio and video. Apple assures DVD Studio Pro 2 users that this problem is purely cosmetic.

4. **Set the display mode.** Open the Track Inspector and match the display mode to your stream assets. Specify whether you use 4:3 or 16:9 assets. For 16:9, choose how your track should display on a 4:3 monitor. Select from Pan Scan (shows just part of the picture) or Letterbox (adds black bars above and below the video).

By default, Pan Scan just shows the center portion of your 16:9 video. To make Pan Scan work more flexibly, displaying the key points of interest in your frames, you need to encode Pan Scan vectors into your MPEG assets.

5. **Organize.** If needed, fine-tune the material in your tracks. Adjust the start and end times for your clips, insert additional material or reorder items, and so forth. Do what it takes to lay out your audio and video in a way that best tells the story you're trying to express.

6. **Add and organize markers.** You can use markers to annotate your timeline at points of importance. Although you embedded chapter markers in your MPEG video, you might still want to add other markers to define when buttons appear over the video stream, to specify where dual-layer break points occur, to identify important times for scripts, and so forth. (Markers are discussed further in Chapter 7.)

7. **Add subtitles.** Use DVD Studio Pro 2 to add text subtitles to your track or import subtitles from a standard text format. Alternately, add subtitle overlays to apply pictures or other visual elements over your video. (Subtitles and languages are discussed at length in Chapter 8.)

8. **Specify languages.** Set languages for your audio and subtitle streams.

9. **Test.** Play your track in the Viewer. Use the track controls to enable and disable streams so you can test each combination of possible playback settings.

Unfortunately, early releases of DVD Studio Pro 2 tend to "hold on" to original versions of assets, even when you remove them and reload updated versions. If the Track Editor does not seem to be responding properly to your changes, save your work and relaunch the program.

Exploring the Outline Tab

When you're ready to add structure to your DVD project, look to the Outline tab. It's here that you build, name, and organize your project elements. The Outline tab, which is shown in Figure 6.3, provides a high-level overview of the components that make up your DVD project—the disc and its menus, tracks and stories, scripts, slideshows, and languages. In addition to this overview, the Outline tab helps you populate and organize project material. It's true that each element has its own Inspector and Editor, yet the Outline tab plays a central command role.

Chapters 2 and 3 introduced the Outline tab, discussing how to create and name menus. You discovered how to generate standard as well as layered menus and how to add extra menu languages. As you're about to see, menu management is just part of the power of this tab. In this section, you'll learn how to use the Outline tab to create and manage many other project elements.

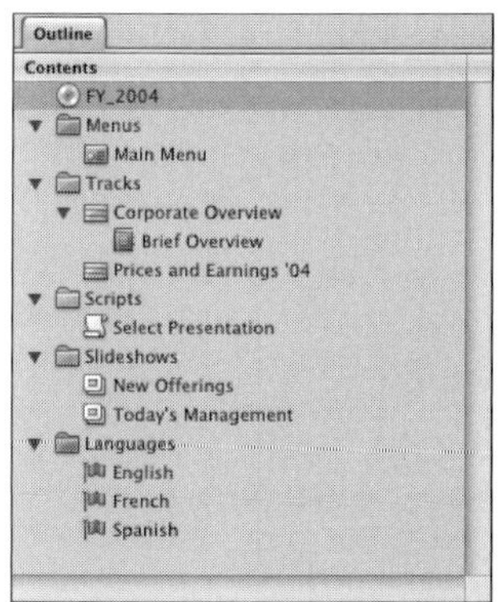

Figure 6.3 The Outline tab offers a folder-based overview of the elements that make up your project. Don't be deceived by this tab's apparent simplicity. The Outline tab offers more power and flexibility than it might appear.

Populating the Outline Tab

Build your project by adding menus, tracks, and so forth in the Outline tab. Here are several methods for adding items to your outline. Use these methods to add any project element with the exception of stories, which must be added directly to tracks.

Use the pop-up. Like most DVD Studio Pro 2 tabs, the Outline tab offers a context-sensitive pop-up. Ctrl-click (right-click) the Outline tab background, and then use the Add submenu to create menus, layered menus, tracks, slideshows, scripts, or languages.

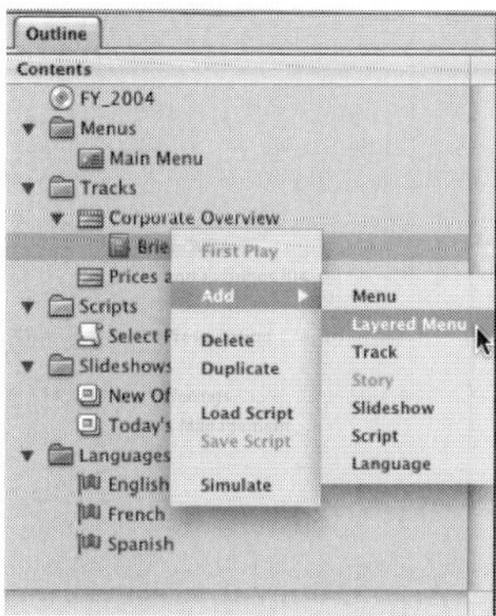

Click toolbar icons. The DVD Studio Pro 2 toolbar, which appears at the top of your main workspace, offers one-button creation for all outline categories. Simply click an icon, such Add Menu, Add Layered Menu, Add Track, and so forth.

Select from the program menu. Choose Project > Add To Project to create outline elements using the mouse or the keyboard. Choose from Menu (⌘-Y), Layered Menu (⌘-Shift-Y), Track (⌘-Ctrl-T), Slideshow (⌘-K), Script (⌘-'), and Language (⌘-/).

Adding Stories

Stories are elements that rearrange playback, describing how to play back parts of a track. Unlike other outline elements, you can only add stories to tracks. Chapter 7 discusses the story feature in depth.

To add a story, first select a track. Then choose Project > Add To Project > Story (⌘-Shift-T), *or* choose Add > Story from the pop-up, *or* click the Add Story icon in the toolbar. If you try to add a story to your project without a selected track, expect odd results. The story may appear randomly in any track.

Duplicating Elements

You can add exact copies of project elements by duplicating. Select any element then choose Edit > Duplicate (⌘-D) *or* ⌘-click(right-click) and select Duplicate from the pop-up.

Other ways to Add

In addition to these basic methods, DVD Studio Pro 2 offers a few more creative approaches for constructing new items. Table 6.1 shows some other ways to create new tracks, slideshows, and menus by dragging assets (from the Assets tab or from the Finder) to items in the Outline tab.

Here are a few things to note about dragging to the Outline tab:

Always enable matching audio. Choose Preferences > Track > Find Matching Audio when dragging.

Track and slideshow images use the default slide duration. You can set this duration by choosing Preferences > General > Slides.

Folders work too. You can drag folders as well as selections of items from the Assets tab.

All menus are standard. You can't create layered menus using the methods in Table 6.1.

▶ **Table 6.1** Ways to Populate Your Project in the Outline Tab

Asset(s) Dragged	To the Menus "Folder"	To the Tracks "Folder"	To the Slideshows "Folder"	To the Disc Icon
Image(s)	Creates a new menu for each image. Assigns each image to the menu background.	Creates one new track. Adds the image(s) to the V1 stream.	Creates a new slideshow and populates it with the images.	One image: creates a new menu. Assigns the image to the menu background. Several images: Creates a new slideshow using the images.
Video(s)	Creates one new menu per video. Assigns each movie as the menu background. Adds matching background audio when found.	Creates a new track for each movie. Adds the movie to the V1 stream. Adds matching audio to A1 when found.	No effect.	Creates one new track per video. Adds the movie to the V1 stream. Adds matching audio to A1 when found.
Audio (one at a time)	Creates a new menu. Assigns audio to menu background.	New track. Adds audio to Audio Stream 1 (A1).	No effect.	New track. Adds the audio to A1.
One video plus one audio	New menu. Assigns video and audio to menu background.	New track. Adds video to V1. Adds audio to A1.	No effect.	New track. Adds video to V1. Adds audio to A1.

Managing Project Elements

Once you've added your items, use the following methods to manage items in the Outline tab.

Naming Elements

Well-named outline elements allow you to organize and identify project items more effectively. Elements named "Jerry discusses FY 04 Profits," "New Offerings (Short Version)," and "Projected Earnings Viewgraphs" better describe their content and function than, say, "Track 3," "Story 1," and "Slideshow 5."

It's simple to change the names of your elements. Select the item you want to rename in the Outline tab, and then do one of the following:

Edit the name directly. Reclick the name to select the text and open the edit-view. Make your changes and press Return.

Use the Inspector. Open the Inspector (⌘-⌥-I). Select the Name field and edit its contents. When finished, press Return.

You can name any item in your outline, including your disc.

Reordering Elements

Use the Outline tab to organize your elements in the order that makes the most sense for you and your project. To move an item within a folder, simply drag it to its new position. (For obvious reasons, you cannot drag items between folders.)

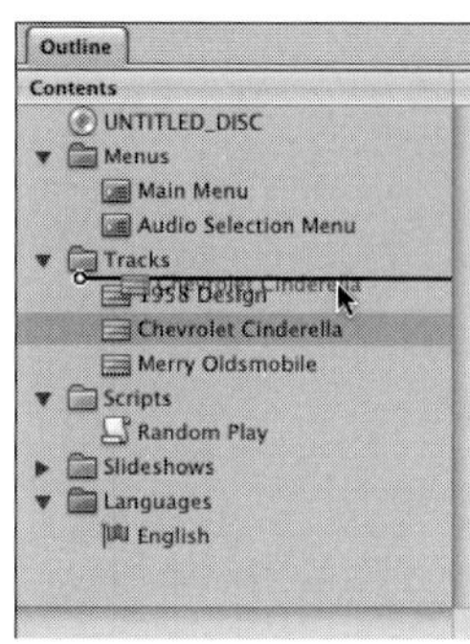

Deleting Elements

Remove unused and unneeded elements when possible. This helps keep your outline tight and avoids wasted space on your final disc. Items in your outline will appear on your disc, whether or not they are accessible by menus and other controls.

To delete an item, select its name in the Outline tab. Then choose Edit > Delete, *or* press the Delete key, *or* Ctrl-click(right-click) and choose Delete from the Outline tab pop-up.

Exploring Elements

DVD Studio Pro 2 offers a context-sensitive pop-up that appears when you point to an Outline element. Hover the mouse cursor over any element for a second or two to display a pop-up summary. The summary remains until you move the mouse.

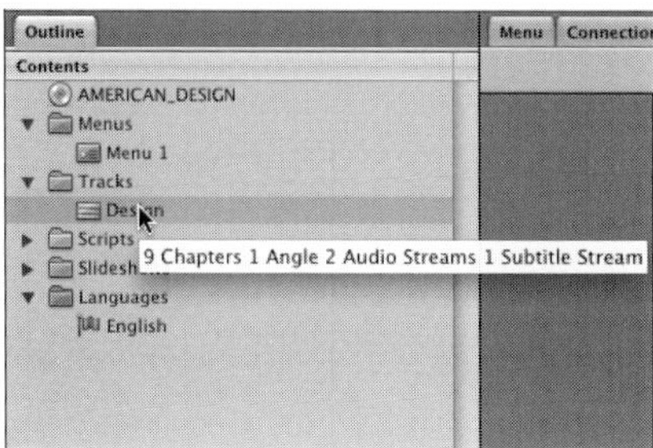

Adding Assets to Outline Elements

DVD Studio Pro 2 offers a number of convenient tricks that help you build outline items by dragging. The tricks listed in Table 6.2 work with assets dragged from both the Asset tab and from the Finder.

▶ **Table 6.2** Ways to Populate Your Project in the Outline Tab

Asset(s) Dragged	To Any Menu	To Any Track	To Any Slideshow
An image	Standard and layered menus: assigns the image to the menu background. If PSD file, selects and displays all layers.	Appends the image to the V1 stream. If PSD file, only displays those layers set as visible.	Adds the image to the end of the slideshow. If PSD file, only displays those layers set as visible.
Several images	Not applicable. Creates extra menus rather than affect the menu in question.	Appends the images to the V1 stream. If PSD file, only displays those layers set as visible.	Adds the images to the end of the slideshow. If PSD file, displays only those layers set as visible.
A video	Standard menu only: assigns the movie as the menu background. Adds matching background audio when found.	Appends the movie to the V1 stream. Adds matching audio to A1, at same start point, when found.	No effect.
An audio	Standard menu only: assigns audio to menu background.	Appends audio to audio stream 1 (A1) at the end of any existing audio.	No effect.
One video plus one audio	Standard menu only assigns video and audio to menu background.	Appends video to V1. Appends audio to A1 at the same start point.	No effect.

Exploring the Track Editor

The DVD Studio Pro 2 Track Editor is a cluttered but powerful window. A centerpiece of the DVD design process, it provides all the tools you need to assemble your tracks—marker layout, asset trimming, language selection, and more. Take time to understand the roles of the Track Editor components, and you'll be well rewarded.

The Track Editor Line by Line

For the most part, the Track Editor is laid out as a series of lines, as Figure 6.4 shows. Each plays a different role. Scan through these lines vertically to understand the tab components, and then scan horizontally to learn how each component works.

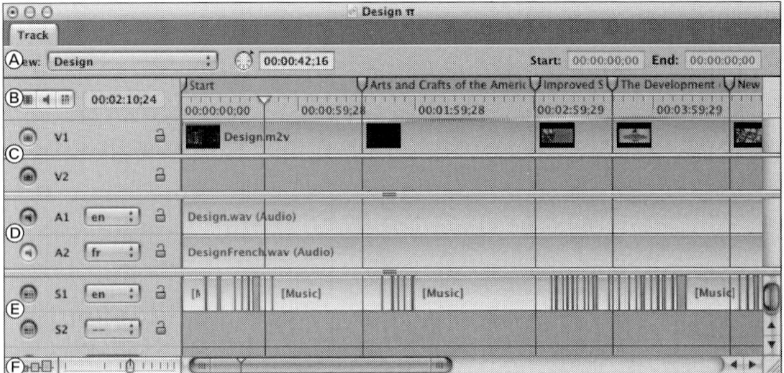

Figure 6.4 The Track Editor is best understood as a series of components, laid out one atop another. A line of controls (A) rests on top of the timeline (B). The timeline is followed by the video (C), audio (D), and subtitle (E) stream editors. Below the editors are more controls (F).

Top Control Line (A)

The top line of the Track Editor includes a number of controls that help you select and understand your track.

View Pop-Up At the left of the controls, the View pop-up selects which track to edit. Click to open the list of tracks, and then click the name of the track you want to edit.

Playhead Control The Playhead control appears just to the right of the View pop-up. Enter a time in the text box, and then click the stopwatch button to set the playhead. Use an HH:MM:SS;FF format for your time; colons separate the hours, minutes, and seconds. A semicolon separates the seconds and frames. This text box also updates whenever you drag the playhead, reflecting the current playhead time.

Clip Start and End Indicators These text boxes are at the right of the top control line. They display the start and end times for the selected clip (or clips) and are grayed out when no clips are selected. If you edit these boxes and press Return, the clip resizes to the edited times.

Timeline (B)

The track timeline (and assorted controls) appear below the control line just described. This line displays several viewing controls, some time feedback, and the timeline with its markers and playhead.

Streams Hide/View Buttons The three buttons, at the left of this line, let you collapse and show the three stream editor subpanes (C, D, and E). From left to right, these buttons hide and view the video, audio, and subtitles. Click each to collapse or reveal the subpane in question. Here, the video pane proves to be the odd man out. The V1 stream is always shown, regardless of whether the video streams subpane is open or closed.

Cursor Time Indicator The cursor time indicator is to the right of the hide/view buttons. When you move your cursor within any stream, this text field shows the track time at the position of your cursor.

DVD Studio Pro 2 lets you select either zero-based time codes (that start your track at 00:00:00;00) or asset-based time codes (that use the time code from the first clip in V1). To select, choose either View > Timescale > Zero-Based Timecode or View > Timescale > Asset-Based Timecode. Asset-based time codes may prove important when you import marker lists and subtitle files that use nonstandard starting times.

Timeline The timeline occupies the rest of line B, to the right of the controls just described. It consists of two lines. The top line contains the markers for your track: these might include purple chapter markers, orange button highlight markers, gray layer break markers, or green general (unspecified) markers. Each marker's name appears to its right. Below the markers is a ticked line, which displays the track times. The playhead, which is a small yellow-green inverted triangle, appears in this ticked line and can be dragged at will to set the current track time.

Dragging isn't the only way to set the playhead. Use the following shortcuts as well to navigate through your track:

Shortcut	Effect
Left arrow/Right arrow	Move one frame left or right.
Shift-Left arrow/Shift-Right arrow	Move one second left or right.
⌥-Left arrow/⌥-Right arrow	Move one GOP (group of pictures) left or right. The GOP structure depends on the way you compressed your data. See Chapter 5 for more details.
Ctrl-Left arrow/Ctrl-Right arrow	Move one marker left or right.
⌘-Left arrow/⌘-Right arrow or ⌥-E/Shift-E	Move to the start or end of the currently selected clip.
Home/End	Move to the start or end of the timeline.
Up arrow/Down arrow	Move to the previous or next timeline event. Events include clip edges and markers. (Clip edges includes all clips in all streams.)

Video, Audio, and Subtitle Editors (C, D, E)

The video-, audio-, and subtitle-editing subpanes appear just below the timeline. Two separator bars, found between the video and audio and between the audio and subtitle, let you apportion space between the three subpanes by dragging. This lets you set the number of video, audio, and subtitle streams that appear within the Track Editor at any time.

Each stream is configured the same way: several controls appear on the left side of each stream line followed to the right by the stream-editing workspace:

Stream Select Control The Stream Select control appears at the very left of each stream and selects the stream for playback. When selected, the controls glow blue (video), green (audio), or orange (subtitle). You can select at most one video, one audio, and one subtitle stream at a time. The video is not optional; you must select one video stream at all times.

Stream Name The stream name appears to the right of the Stream Select control. Named sequentially, the streams are prefixed with V for video, A for audio, and S for subtitles.

Stream Lock Click the lock to disable edits in the associated stream. When the streams are locked, you protect them from accidental changes. A diagonal crosshatch pattern overlays each locked track, as shown here. Click again to unlock.

Choose Project > Timeline > Lock All Streams (Shift-F4) to lock every stream in the timeline.

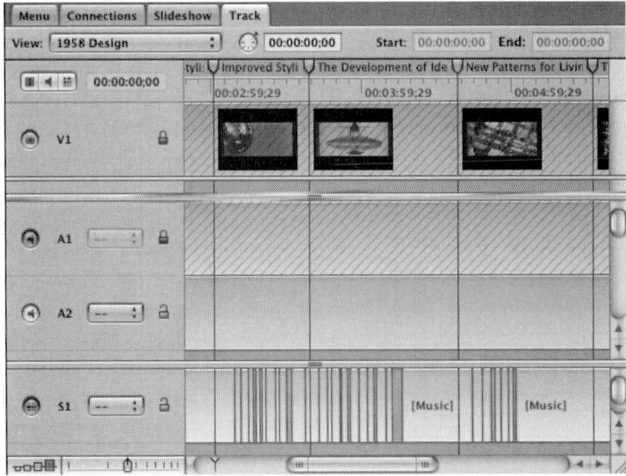

Stream Editor Each Stream Editor appears at the right of each line, starting just after the lock. This editor let you add, move, and trim material from your stream. Move your mouse over any clip and keep it there for a second or two to display the source asset filename.

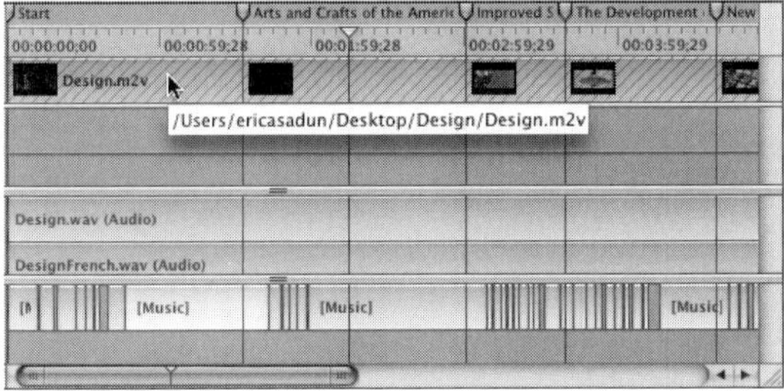

Bottom Control Line (F)

The bottom control line controls the visual presentation of your track. From left to right, this line contains the following controls:

Stream Height Appearing on the bottom left of the Track Editor, this control adjusts the vertical space apportioned to each stream, as shown in Figure 6.5. Click smaller boxes to compress the stream view, showing more streams at once. Click larger boxes to expand the stream view and show fewer, taller streams. (Press Shift-T to cycle through the four possible settings.)

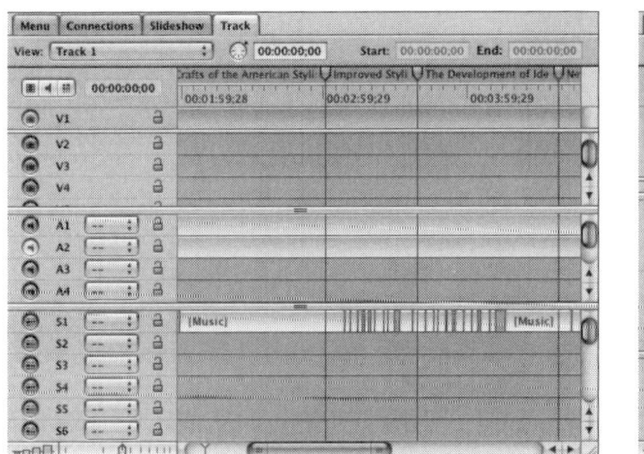

Figure 6.5 The Stream Height control lets you adjust the vertical height of your streams. As these two views show, there's a trade-off between better visual detail and the display of more streams.

Timeline Zoom This control appears just to the right of the Stream Height control. This slider adjusts the way the timeline appears, contracting or expanding the view to show greater or lesser detail. Drag the slider to the right to zoom out. At the smallest zoom, with the slider all the way to the right, you can view your entire track at once. Drag the slider to the left to zoom in, showing greater and greater project detail. Zooming in lets you set the playhead more accurately, providing better visual detail. Extra detail proves important when adding subtitles and markers to your project.

Timeline Scrollbar This control appears to the right of the zoom control and works more or less the way most scrollbars do—with two exceptions. Like other scrollbars, you can drag the scroller to select which part of the timeline to view. Unlike other scrollers, you can also drag the scroller ends out and in to set the timeline zoom. A downward pointing triangle with a line beneath it appears in the scrollbar, indicating the position of the playhead with respect to the portion of the timeline currently shown.

The following keyboard shortcuts augment the zooming controls just discussed:

Shortcut	Effect
⌘-hyphen	Zoom out from the timeline (jumping to the playhead if not visible).
⌘-Shift-hyphen (⌘-_)	Zoom out (without jumping to the playhead).
⌘-=	Zoom into the timeline (jumping to the playhead if not visible).
⌘-Shift-= (⌘-plus)	Zoom into the timeline (without jumping to the playhead).
Shift-Z	Zoom out completely to show the entire track at once.
Shift-⌥-Z	Zoom to fit the current selection. (In DVD Studio Pro 2.0, this feature works intermittently at best.)
Shift-T	Cycles through the various stream height settings.

Adding Material to Streams

Populating your streams couldn't be easier. Simply drag assets from the Assets tab, from the Palette, or from the to the video, audio and subtitle streams in your track. If you've enabled audio matching (choose Preferences > Track > Find Matching Audio when dragging), DVD Studio Pro 2 inserts the corresponding sound files when you add video.

Here are some points to ponder:

- Each line in the Track Editor, such as V1, A4, or S3, holds one stream. The stream can be composed of one asset or of several assets placed one after another.

- The V1 stream must be filled completely. Its first asset must start at the very beginning of the timeline and, unlike other streams, cannot contain any gaps between clips. When the V1 stream ends, the entire track ends.

- As far as the DVD specification is concerned, tracks are a kind of DVD "title." Each disc can contain a maximum of 99 titles. Other titles you'll encounter in DVD Studio Pro 2 include slideshows and stories. For example, when you add 70 slideshows to your project, you're left with 29 possibilities for either tracks or stories. Menus are not titles and are not affected by the 99-title limit.

- DVD players may pause when changing from one track to another, so plan your tracks accordingly. It may make more sense to add material to one extra-long track for start-to-end playback than to use several tracks for individual features.

Unfortunately, you cannot import segmented MPEG from third-party encoders into DVD Studio Pro 2. Some encoders break MPEG into 1GB pieces. Use a utility, such as MPEG Append (http://homepage.mac.com/ DVD_SP_Helper/MPEG%20Append/MPEGAppend.html) to combine the pieces into a single file before importing. MPEG Append can also fix timecode problems in your MPEG files.

Organizing Materials

Use the following methods to help organize the materials within your tracks:

Selecting Clips Click any clip to select it. Follow up by pressing ⌘-A to select all the clips within the same stream.

Moving Clips Moving lets you change the start times of your clips or reorder parts of your track. To move a clip, place the cursor in the middle of a clip and drag it to a new position. You can move clips within one stream or between streams.

DVD Studio Pro 2 offers an odd little trick for moving audio to a precise position. Set the playhead where you want the audio to begin, Ctrl-click(right-click) an audio clip, and choose Move Audio Clip To The Playhead.

Copying Clips You can copy clips to create duplicates in the same stream or in other streams. This lets you reuse the same material over and over within the same track. To copy, select a clip and choose Edit > Duplicate (⌘-D), *or* Ctrl-click(right-click) the clip and choose Duplicate Media clip, *or* ⌥-drag the clip to a new position and/or a new stream.

To duplicate a clip in a new stream at the same start time, use Shift-⌥-drag.

Removing Clips Remove clips from your tracks when they are no longer needed. Select a clip or clips and press Delete, *or* choose Edit > Delete, *or* Ctrl-click(right-click) and choose Delete Media Clip.

Inspecting Clips The Inspector provides a wealth of information about the clips in your streams. Select a clip and choose View > Show Inspector (⌘-⌥-I). The clip information presented depends on the type of clip selected.

Selecting Languages Use the pop-up to the left of each audio or subtitle stream to select a language for that stream.

Trimming Clips

You may encounter many reasons to trim clips. Trimming allows you to remove unwanted material from the start or end of a clip. It also lets you synchronize finish times or extract just part of a clip. To trim, select a clip, and then use one of the following methods:

Drag the clip ends. Move the cursor to either end of the clip until it changes into a square bracket (shown in Figure 6.6). Drag the clip end to shorten or lengthen it. The clip start and end indicators, found at the top-right of the Track Editor, update to reflect the new bounds.

Edit the clip start and end times. You can edit the clip start and end times directly to change the clip duration.

Use the Inspector. Each Clip Inspector offers Clip Start Trim and Duration fields. Select a clip, open the Inspector, and edit these fields to trim the clip as desired.

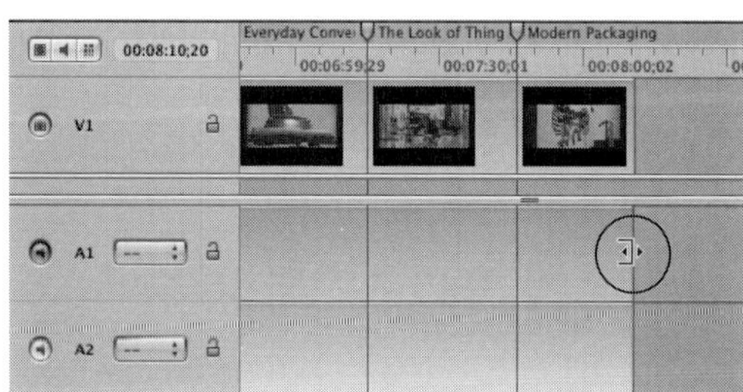

Figure 6.6 The square bracket appears when you move the cursor to the ends of a selected clip. The arrows indicate the directions you can drag; you cannot extend a clip beyond its natural length.

Moving the Playhead to the Start (or End) of a Clip

Here's a convenient way to place the playhead exactly where you need it. Select any clip in your track. Select the clip Start (or End) field (top-right corner of the Track tab) and copy it to memory. Select the Current Time field (towards the left, on the same line) and paste. Click the stopwatch button. The playhead jumps to the clip time you pasted.

DVD Studio Pro 2 offers a curious feature that allows you to create a merged MPEG file from your video stream. Ctrl-click(right-click) the stream and choose Export MPEG File from the pop-up, *or* choose File > Export > MPEG File to open the Save Stream As MPEG dialog. Enter a name for your new file, navigate to where you want to save it, and then click Save.

Unfortunately, this feature won't let you export stills or MPEG-1 files. That means you can't export your slideshow to MPEG, even if you first convert it to a track.

Even more unfortunately, in early releases of DVD Studio Pro 2.0, this feature does not work consistently. At times, it appears to export to disk, and no file is created. This happens particularly when you attempt to export trimmed clips or streams with gaps in the video.

Adding Angles

The angle button found on most DVD remote controls allows viewers to choose different video presentations without interrupting the audio stream. Extra angles provide any number of viewing variations from alternate camera shots to modified footage to bowdlerized visuals and beyond. Sports events recorded with multiple cameras offer a perfect opportunity to use angles. Angles might include wide shots over the entire field, the quarterback or tackle's Helmet Cam, shots from the goalposts down the center of the field, close-ups on particular players, and so forth. DVD Studio Pro 2 adds a maximum of nine video streams per track, allowing you to present nine unique video angles.

DVD angles have two forms:

Multiangle Tracks All streams in multiangle tracks, from V1 on up, have the same length. This creates angles that last the entire duration of the track. Unfortunately, this eats away at disc space. A 20-minute multiangle track with 4 angles occupies the same space as an 80-minute single-angle track.

Mixed-Angle Tracks Mixed-angle tracks offer partial video streams, providing alternate video at distinct times. This offers a way to provide small variations when most of the video remains the same. A typical use for mixed angles might include a scene reshot to omit profanity.

Figure 6.7 shows the look of typical multiangle and mixed-angle tracks.

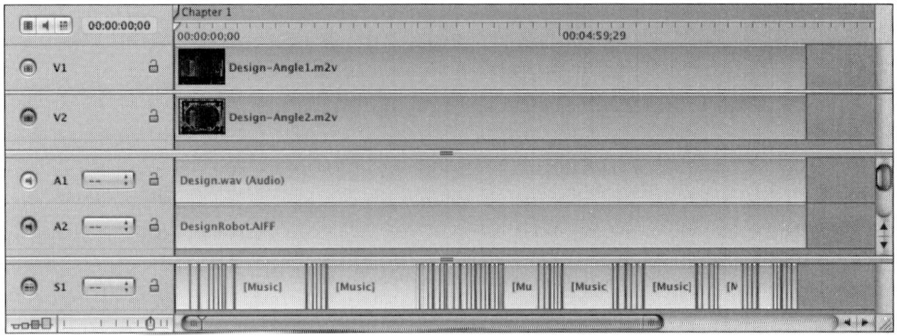

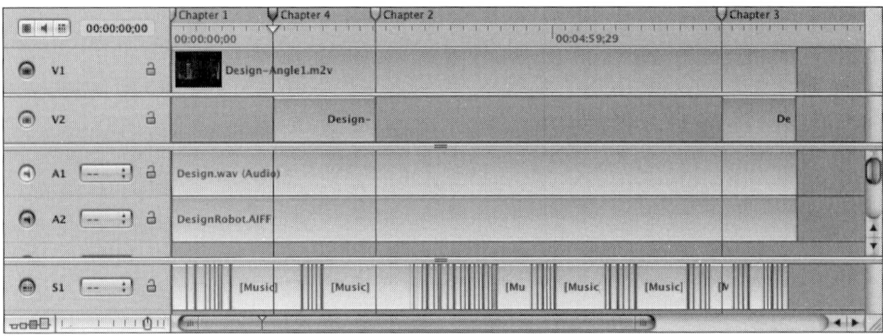

Figure 6.7 Multiangle tracks (top) use additional streams that last the entire duration of V1. Mixed-angle tracks (bottom) add extra camera angles at various points throughout the track. Although it may seem simpler to use multiangle tracks, they take up far more precious space on your disc. Mixed-angle tracks are a little harder to set up and synchronize, but they use less space.

To add extra angles to your project, follow these steps:

1. **Make room for extra streams.** In the Track tab, adjust the separator bars and the Track Height control to allow you to view the video streams you'll be working on.

2. **Populate V1.** Add assets to your first video stream to build the primary viewing angle.

Continue with the following steps when working with mixed-angle footage. When working with multiangle tracks, you need only add your extra streams, matching each to the length of V1.

3. **Add a marker.** Move the playhead to where you'll add the first mixed-angle footage. Press M to add a marker. The marker appears on the nearest GOP boundary—not necessarily at the exact location of the playhead. Select the

marker, open the Marker Inspector (⌘-⌥-I) and uncheck Chapter to transform the marker to a generic (nonchapter) marker.

4. **Drag the angle into place.** Add the new asset into place into V2 at the marker. It snaps into position. DVD Studio Pro 2 may complain that it can only use part of the asset. If so, click Use Anyway. DVD Studio Pro 2 will use as much of the material as possible, making sure to synchronize GOP structures and markers.

   If desired, add more clips of the same size and GOP structure to V3 and beyond, using the same start marker.

5. **Add an end marker.** Select the new clip you added to V2. Ctrl-click (right-click) the clip. Choose Add Marker To Clip End from the pop-up.

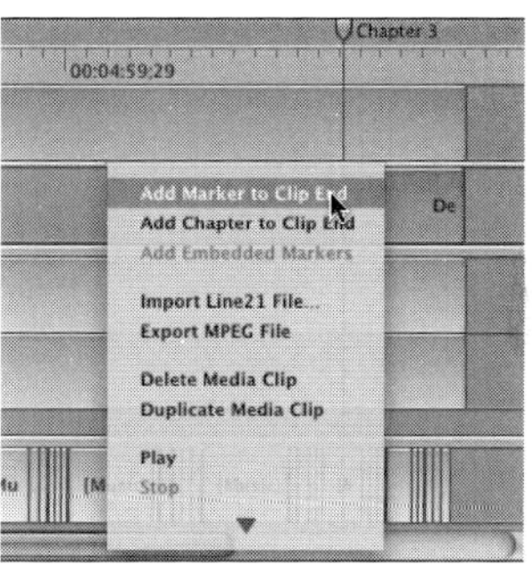

6. **Repeat.** Follow the previous steps to add more angles to your track. Make sure that streams V2 and above all use the same start and end positions for each angle clip.

   Here are some key points to note about adding angles:

- All alternate video, whether multiangle or mixed-angle, must match the GOP structure of your V1 stream exactly, with synchronized GOP boundaries.

- Depending on your encoder, GOP boundaries may not occur exactly at the times you'd expect, such as :00 or :15 for NTSC. Always add markers, as they set to natural GOP bounds. This ensures that your angle clips snap correctly into place.

- When working with mixed-angle tracks, you must synchronize V2 through V9. When you provide alternate video, you must provide it at exactly the same places for each extra video stream. If you have two alternate video streams and you add video from 00:02:00:00 through 00:07:00:00 in V2, you must do the same for V3 and so forth.

- Apple suggests that you only add stills to mixed angles when V1 includes a still at the same position, with the same length and with a marker set at the end of each still. When you add stills to V2–V9, they automatically match their length to the corresponding clip in V1.

Previewing with the Viewer Tab

The Viewer tab (⌘-0) plays an important role in creating tracks. It allows you to preview the tracks you create, watching them in real time to ensure that video, audio, and subtitles work together in synchrony. The Viewer is shown in Figure 6.8.

The Viewer works much as you'd expect, particularly if you're familiar with Final Cut or iMovie. It provides a screen to watch your movie and evaluate your track and provides several buttons that control playback.

You can use several keyboard shortcuts in addition to the controls found in the Viewer tab itself:

Shortcut	Effect
Spacebar or L	Play/pause
⌥-Spacebar	Stops playback and returns the playhead to its previous position
Home	Moves to start
End	Moves to end
K	Stops playback
Right arrow	Moves forward one frame
Left arrow	Moves back one frame

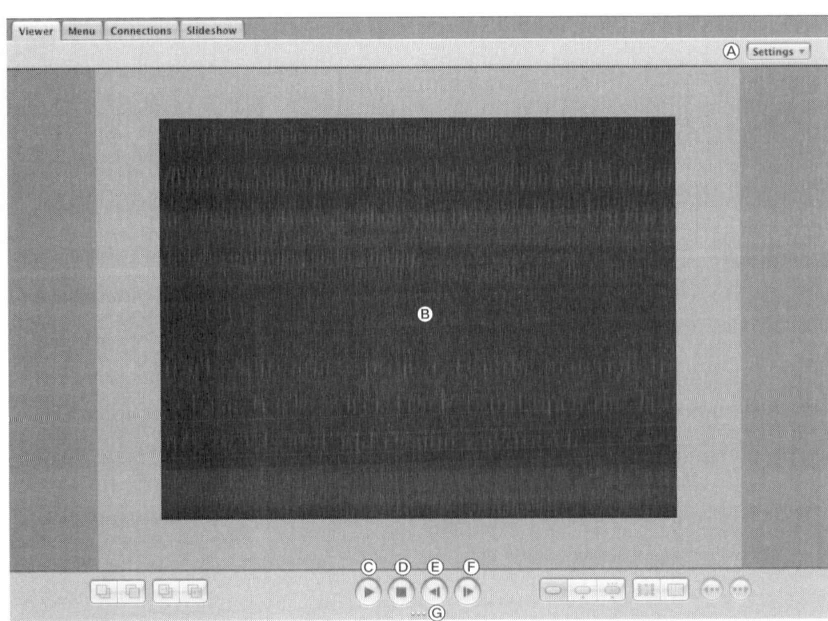

Figure 6.8 The Viewer tab provides an in-program monitor that helps you preview your tracks. The Settings pop-up (A) works just like the one in the Menu Editor, letting you select pixel shape and title-safe/action-safe overlays. The main viewing area (B) lets you watch your track. The Play/Pause (C) and Stop (D) buttons control track playback. Use the backward (E) and forward (F) step button to move through your track frame by frame. The small ellipsis at the bottom of the window is the the Show/Hide control (G). It allows you to hide the bottom toolbar to provide a bigger space for your main viewing area.

Take note of the following issues related to the Viewer:

Speed The Viewer may respond slowly, particularly on older, slower G4 systems. Always make sure to save your project before you use the Viewer for track playback, just in case you need to force quit DVD Studio Pro 2.

You'll generally get better Viewer response if you save your work and relaunch DVD Studio Pro 2 before using the Viewer, particularly after simulating.

Always-on Power   The Viewer keeps working even when you're not "playing" your movie track. This allows you to see frames at the playhead as you're editing your track.

Stream Selection Unfortunately, in early releases of DVD Studio Pro 2, the Viewer does not always keep up when you enable and disable video streams, often showing frames from recently selected (rather than currently selected) streams. When this happens, save your work and relaunch the program.

Track Navigation The navigation shortcuts that work in the Track tab work (for the most part) in the Viewer tab, although they tend to stop playback. For example, holding down the Ctrl key while pressing arrow keys steps through the markers in your project.

Subtitle Edits. The Viewer tab works both as a preview window and as a workspace when you edit subtitles. This second use is not its strength—you may do better to edit your subtitles in a text editor and import them rather than rely on the whimsical interactions of the Viewer tab.

Simulating from Tracks

Although the Viewer tab lets you preview your streams, it doesn't let you interact with them. You can't dynamically select from the available streams. The Simulator (⌘-⌥-0) can do that and more. Simulating allows you to test and verify all the interactive behavior in your project, including stream selection.

To simulate your track, Ctrl-click(right-click) within the Track Editor and choose Simulate From Track from the pop-up. (Alternately, you can select a track in the Outline Editor and choose Simulate from the Outline tab pop-up.) Figure 6.9 shows the Simulator controls you'll use while testing tracks.

Key Simulator shortcuts include the following:

Shortcut	Effect
Arrow keys (Up, Down, Left, Right)	Same results as the remote's button navigation arrows.
Return key	Activates the selected button. Same results as pressing Enter on the remote.
Shift-I	Hides/shows the Simulator's Information Drawer.
⌘-W	Closes the Simulator.

Figure 6.9 The Simulator allows you to interactively choose streams during playback. Features include the Play button (A), the Stop button (B), and the current playhead time display (G). The three stream selection pop-ups (C: video, D: audio, and E: subtitle) allow you to choose which stream to play. The View check box lets you turn subtitles on (checked) and off (unchecked). Here, the Simulator displays a subtitle track that has been translated into "Swedish Chef," per the solutions at the end of this chapter.

On older G4 Macintoshes and in early releases of DVD Studio Pro 2, the Simulator sometimes proves as hard as or harder to halt than the Viewer. When in doubt, press ⌘-W. The Simulator will eventually catch up to your keyboard commands and close itself.

The Simulator problem seems to be related to memory management. Repeated simulations may slow down DVD Studio Pro 2 performance more and more. When in doubt, save your project, quit, restart DVD Studio Pro 2, and then simulate. After simulating, you may want to quit and restart again, to ensure that all affected memory has been reinitialized.

Solution: Create a Multiangle Track with Alternate Audio

Multiangle tracks let you switch back and forth between video streams without interrupting the flow of the current audio stream. In this solution, you'll use real video, audio, and subtitle assets to build a working multiangle track.

The companion DVD includes a number of files you can use. You'll find full-length alternate tracks (Design-Angle1.m2v, Design-Angle2.m2v), alternate audio (Design.wav, DesignRobot.aiff, a robotized version of the original audio), and two ready-to-use subtitle files (Design.txt, ChefDesign.txt). ChefDesign.txt was automatically translated from English to Muppet Swedish Chef. Use these files to learn about building multiangle tracks with alternate audio.

1. **Adjust your Track Editor.** Start a new project. Open the Track tab and adjust the streams so you can see two video, two audio, and two subtitle streams. Use the Stream Height controls and the separator bars to create a well-proportioned workspace.

2. **Add the video and audio material.** Drag Design-Angle1.m2v to V1, and drag Design-Angle2.m2v to V2. Add Design.wav to A1, and add DesignRobot.AIFF to A2. With no matching names, DVD Studio Pro 2 does not automatically add audio when you place video. All four files have the same duration. Both video files use the identical GOP structure.

3. **Add subtitles.** Ctrl-click(right-click) in S1. Choose Import Subtitle File, as shown here. Navigate to Design.txt, select it, and click Choose. Wait as DVD Studio Pro 2 imports the 63 subtitles. Click OK. Repeat to add ChefDesign.txt to S2.

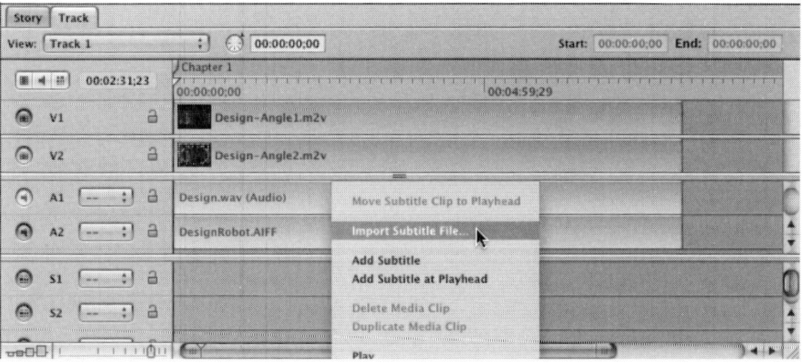

4. **Simulate.** Ctrl-click(right-click) in one of your video or audio streams, and choose Simulate From Track from the pop-up. DVD Studio Pro 2 opens the Simulator and begins to play the track.

5. **Choose streams.** Use the video, audio, and subtitle stream pop-ups that emulate the remote control to select which streams to play. You can change these in real

time as the simulation runs. In this project, you've added two streams of each kind. Check or clear the View check box to toggle subtitle playback on and off.

Solution: Use Mixed-Angle Footage

The pragmatic use of angles seldom works as cleanly in real life as Apple's documentation suggests. Your DVD Studio Pro 2 manual is full of good-looking track illustrations with beautifully even edges. They seem to imply that mixed-angle tracks should be as easy to assemble as LEGO toys. In real life, the results are often less elegant.

In this solution, you'll use actual mixed-angle footage to build a mixed-angle track. The source materials (Design.m2v, Design.wav, and Minute2Angle.m2v) all appear on the DVD that accompanies this book.

1. **Arrange your Track Editor.** Start a new project. Open the Track tab, and arrange the setup so that you can see two video streams and one audio stream. Use the Stream Height controls and the separator bars to create an easy-to-see workspace.

2. **Build your primary track.** For this solution, drag Design-Angle1.m2v to V1.Add Design.wav to A1.

3. **Move the playhead to minute 2.** The alternate track starts at minute 2. Enter 00:02:00;00 into the playhead control text box. Click the stopwatch. The playhead jumps to 00:02:00;00, more or less. A more likely destination might be 00:02:00;02.

4. **Add a marker.** Type **M**. DVD Studio Pro 2 adds a new marker at (or near) the location of the playhead, coinciding with the nearest GOP bounds.

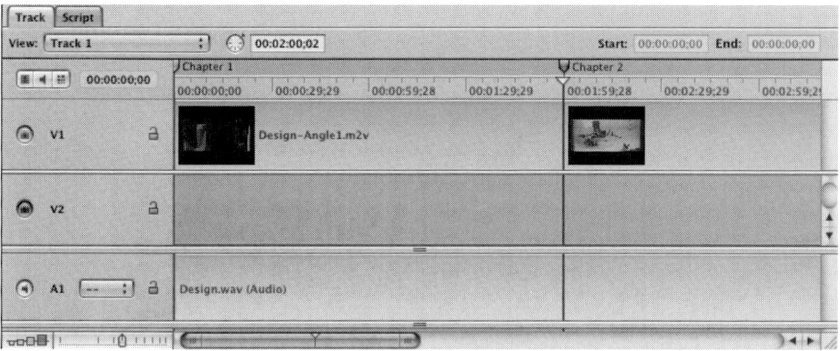

5. **Change the marker type.** Select the new marker (click it), and open the Marker Inspector (⌘-⌥-I). Clear the Chapter check box. The marker turns green. Edit the name to Angle1Start.

The Save Still button in the Marker Inspector allows you to produce a TIFF still of the frame at the position of your marker. Use this handy feature to collect thumbnails of your marked frames or for any other purpose.

6. **Add the angle.** Drag Minute2Angle.m2v into V2. Let it snap to the new marker. DVD Studio Pro 2 may alert you that the angle is only partially usable: click Use Anyway. The angle clip lasts for 1 minute. The last valid GOP bounds occur at 00:00:59;15.

7. **Add an end marker.** Ctrl-click(right-click) the new clip. Choose Add Marker To Clip End from the pop-up. DVD Studio Pro 2 adds a marker that coincides with the end of the clip, conforming to Apple's multiangle requirements. Rename the marker Angle 1 End.

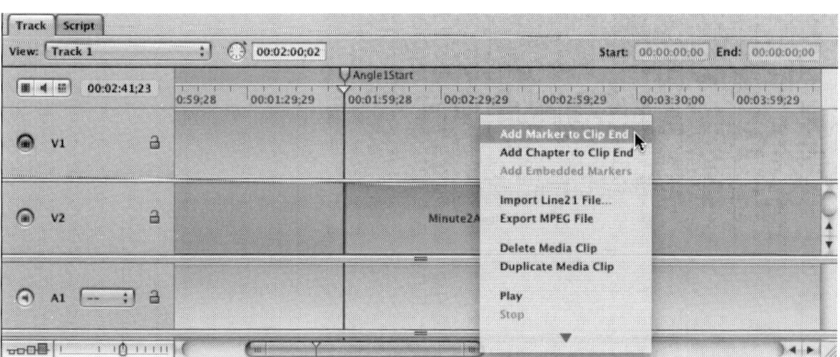

8. **Simulate**. Ctrl-click(right-click) within the track, and choose Simulate From Track. The Simulator opens and begins to play the track. Pause the playback. Select stream 2 from the video pop-up, and restart the playback. The Simulator plays back material from V1. At minute 2, V2 starts playing from your mixed-angle track, continuing until minute 3, where V1 resumes.

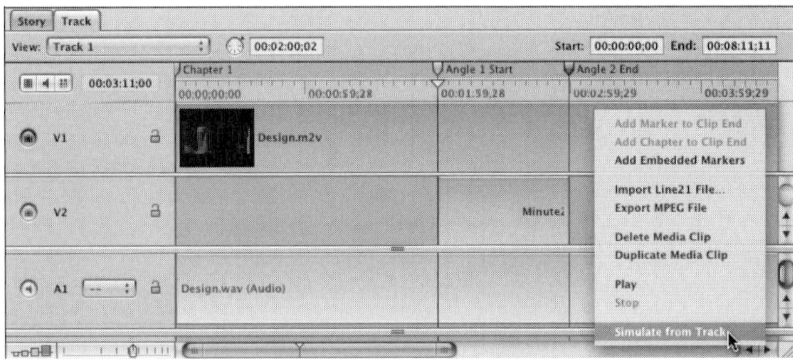

Solution: Build and Test a Wide-Angle (16:9) Track

DVD Studio Pro 2 allows you to import anamorphic (squeezed) wide-screen footage and use it in your 16:9 projects. It takes just a few steps to set the correct aspect ratio for your work. In these steps, you'll build and then test a wide-angle track.

1. **Create a new track**. In a new project, add Design-Wide.m2v to V1, and add Design.wav to A1 in the default Track 1 track. The Viewer shows the video in its squeezed, anamorphic form.

2. **Change the display mode.** Select Track 1 in the Outline tab. Open the Track Inspector (⌘-⌥-I), and choose 16:9 Letterbox from the Mode pop-up. The Viewer updates to show the correct 16:9 proportions. The Letterbox part of the aspect ratio instructs DVD Studio Pro 2 to use letterbox framing when playing this track back on 4:3 displays.

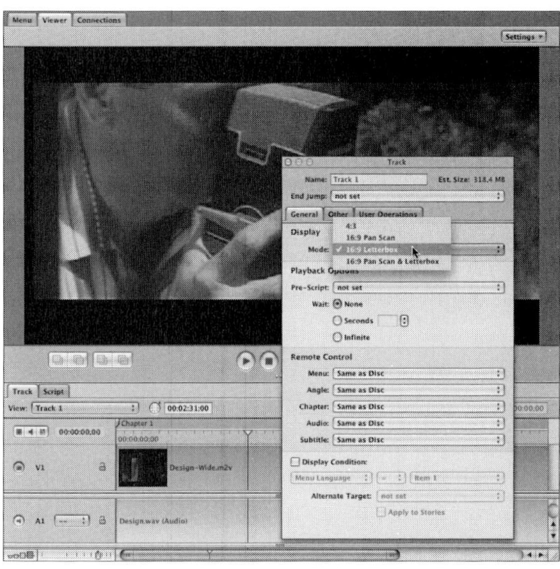

3. **Set the Simulator preferences.** Open the Preferences pane (choose DVD Studio Pro > Preferences or press ⌘-,). Click Simulator. Choose 16:9 Aspect (found toward the bottom of the pane), and click OK. This tells DVD Studio Pro 2 to simulate using a wide-screen display.

4.   **Simulate.** Ctrl-click(right-click) in the Track Editor, and choose Simulate From Track. The Simulator plays back your 16:9 footage using an extra-wide display.

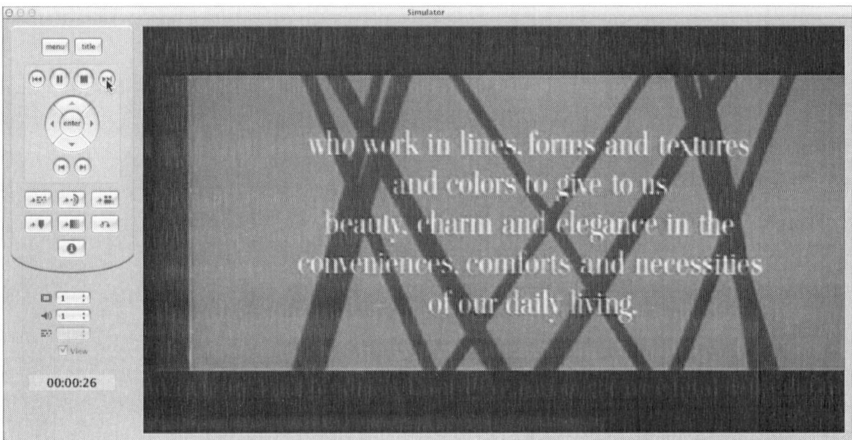

Don't forget to return the Simulator to a 4:3 aspect after finishing this project.

Solution: Connect a Menu Button to a Track

Connecting buttons to tracks makes your menus come to life. Unlike many of the sample menus in previous chapters, this solution creates a working menu that links to a real track.

Like many of the other solutions in this book, this one lets you take advantage of some new project defaults: Each fresh project contains one default track (Track 1) and one default menu (Menu 1). The disc's First Play too is set to Menu 1 by default.

Many older DVD players produce inconsistent results when you set First Play to a menu. As a rule of thumb, take precautions when you plan to distribute your DVDs widely. Set First Play to a track, even if it's a short dummy track, before continuing on to a menu.

1.   **Build a track.** Start a new project. Use the materials from the previous solutions to build a basic track. Select Track 1 and open the Track Editor. Add Design-Angle1.m2v to V1, and add Design.wav to A1.

2. **Build a menu.** Select Menu 1 in the Outline tab, and open the Menu Editor. Drag out a new button. Open the Button Inspector (⌘-⌥-I) and set the button text to Play. Center the text within the button (Position: Center), and check Include Text In Highlight. Select this new text, and use the Font dialog (choose Format > Font > Show Fonts or press ⌘-T) to make the letters large and bold.

3. **Connect the button to the track.** Locate Track 1 in the Outline tab, and drag it onto the Play button. Choose Connect To Track from the drop palette.

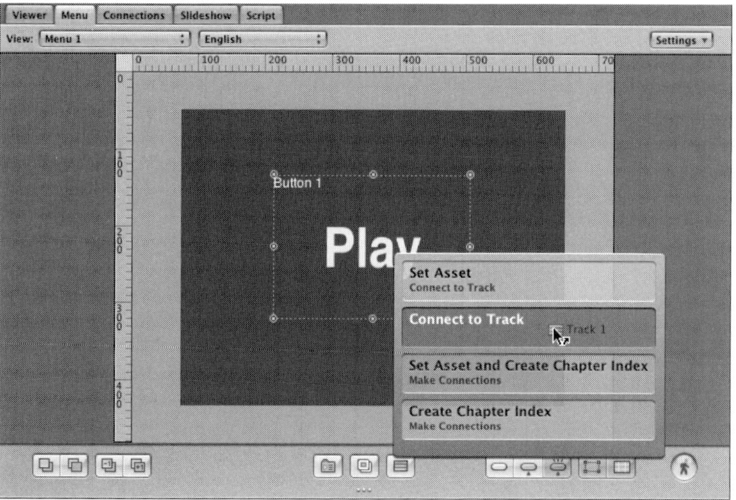

4. **Connect the track back to the menu.** Select Track 1 in the Outline tab, and open the Track Inspector. Set the End Jump pop-up to Menus > Menu 1 > [Menu]. This instructs DVD Studio Pro 2 to return to Menu 1 after playing the track.

5. **Simulate.** Save your project, and then click the Simulator button in the main toolbar. DVD Studio Pro 2 plays back your simple menu. Click Play to begin your track. Let the track play through, or click the Menu button (in the top left of the Simulator) to jump immediately to your main menu.

Solution: Choose an Audio Stream

Putting stream selection in the hands of your viewers allows you to bypass the DVD player's language selection system and opens new opportunities for audio choice. Let your viewers choose whether to listen to French or German, Dolby 5.1 or PCM Stereo, movie sound tracks or director's commentaries, and so forth.

 In this project, you'll use the materials on the companion DVD to create menu buttons that allow your viewer to select from a pair of audio streams. To accomplish this, you'll build some basic scripts. (Scripts are covered in detail in Chapter 11.) Although you can produce this functionality in other ways, the steps here demonstrate a quick and reliable method for stream selection.

1. **Build the track.** Start a new project. Use the materials on the companion DVD to build a basic track with two audio streams. Select Track 1 and open the Track Editor. Add Design-Angle1.m2v to V1, add Design.wav to A1, and add DesignRobot.AIFF to A2. Enable A1 and V1.

> A "robot" voice filter created the alternate track from the original.

2. **Add a chapter.** In the Track Editor, move the playhead to 00:01:45;00. The narration resumes at this point after a long musical interlude. Press M. DVD Studio Pro 2 adds a new marker, entitled Chapter 2.

3. **Build a menu.** Open Menu 1 in the Menu Editor. Drag out a new button, and open the Button Inspector (⌘-⌥-I). Set the button text to Play. Center the text within the button (Position: Center), and check Include Text In Highlight. Select this new text and use the Font dialog (choose Format > Font > Show Fonts or press ⌘-T) to make the letters large and bold. Duplicate and edit to create two new buttons: Original Audio and Processed Audio.

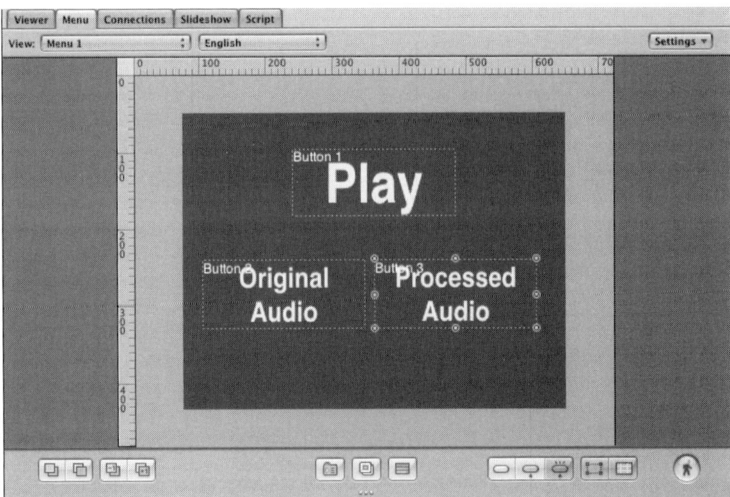

4. **Connect the Play button.** Select the Play button. Open the Button Inspector (⌘-⌥-I), and set the Target pop-up to Tracks > Track 1 > Chapter 2. This links the Play button to the narration that starts at Chapter 2 in your track. The pop-up selection reads Track 1::Chapter 2.

5. **Connect the buttons to streams.** Select Button 2 (Original Audio). Open the Button Inspector, and click the Advanced tab. Choose Audio Stream 1 in the Audio pop-up, select Button 3 (Processed Audio) in the Menu Editor, and Set the Audio to Audio Stream 2 in the Advanced tab of the Button Inspector.

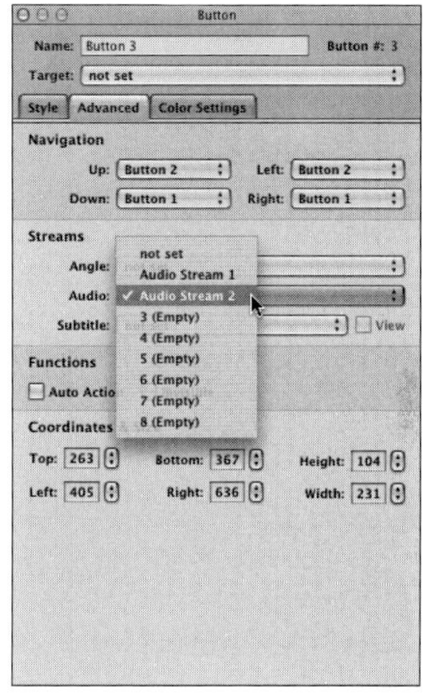

6. **Connect the track back to the menu.** Choose Track 1 in the Outline view. Open the Track Inspector, and use the End Jump pop-up to connect back to Menu 1. This step ensures that your viewer returns to Menu 1 after Track 1 finishes playing.

7. **Simulate.** Save your project, and click the Simulator button in the main toolbar. DVD Studio Pro 2 simulates your menu. Click Play, and your track begins to play back at the narration point you set in step 2. Let the track play through, or click the Menu button (in the top left of the Simulator) to jump immediately to your main menu. Click Processed Audio to switch to the roboticized version. Click Play, and the track begins to play again, this time using the filtered audio. Click Menu, Original Audio, and then click Play, and the audio returns to the original version.

In this project, you provide little real feedback that the selection has changed from original to processed audio (or back), although the button highlight returns to Play (the first button in the menu). You must play the movie in order to determine what change has occurred.

Tumacácori
National Historical Park
Printable Visual Guide

ROADS TO Romance
Play Movie

Markers and Stories

Markers and stories provide ways to organize and control the material within your tracks. These DVD Studio Pro 2 features allow you to subdivide your video into logical sections and access them in the manner that works best for you and your audience. In this chapter, you'll explore the role of markers and stories. You'll learn how to create them, why to use them, and how to use them to get the best results in your projects.

Chapter Contents

Understanding Marker Roles

Creating Markers

Creating Stories

Delving into the Connections Tab

Solution: Create a Story

Solution: Build Virtual Tracks, Adding More
   Videos Per Disc

Solution: Add DVD @ccess to Your Movie

Understanding Marker Roles

At times you need to divide your videos into segments for more precise positioning and playback. Markers define critical points in your tracks, providing ways to annotate and control track material. Markers split tracks into "cells," discrete portions with their own playback options. With markers, you can address the track as a whole, or you can index directly into cells, the discrete segments to which they point.

DVD Studio Pro 2 offers several kinds of markers, among which the chapter marker is most common. Markers appear above the timeline in the Track tab and are coded by color. Use the Marker Inspector to specify each marker's type.

Chapter Markers (purple) Chapter markers, which are often set in video-editing programs such as Final Cut and iMovie, organize tracks into discrete navigable sections. Chapters allow viewers to skip through portions of their tracks by pressing the Previous and Next Chapter buttons on a DVD remote. Chapter markers also let you create a DVD Studio Pro 2 feature called *stories*. Stories create predefined pathways through your chapter markers, to tell a unique story using the track material.

If you need to add scripting for more control over your DVD's interface, as discussed in Chapter 11, be aware that DVD Studio Pro 2 scripts can only refer to chapter markers. The other marker types are not recognized by scripting.

Button Highlight Markers (orange) Button highlight markers help you place buttons over your video, adding interactivity to your tracks. Buttons, which are properly a kind of subtitle, are produced with either text or overlay images. The button lasts through the duration of one cell, from one marker to the next.

Layer Break Markers (gray with a black dot) Dual-layer media (such as DVD-9 discs) use an extra physical layer to store more data per disc. DVD players can refocus their lasers to read data from both layers. The dual-layer breakpoint refers to the part of the track where your video splits between the first and second layer.

Layer breaks determine the outermost physical limit of playback on a disc. A DVD plays from the hub outward to the break; then, after switching layers, it plays from the break back in toward the hub.

General Markers, aka Cell Markers (green) Cell markers provide virtual boundaries in your track. Among other uses, cell markers help define DVD @ccess points (branches to web material for computer-based DVD playback) and mark the start and end of mixed-angle portions of the track.

Creating Markers

In DVD Studio Pro 2, you can add markers to your tracks in a number of ways. In this section, we'll look at some of the most common and useful ways. These methods range from using embedded markers to direct manipulation of the timeline to importing text files and beyond.

Dual-Layer Break Projects

Here are a few key points about projects that use layer breaks:

- Where possible, place entire tracks onto a single layer. Layer breaks always cause brief play-back delays. The laser must refocus from one layer to another before continuing. Fitting video material onto a single layer ensures that playback proceeds uninterrupted. When you must include dual layer breaks, always pick an unobtrusive location, where a slight freeze in the video won't interrupt the story flow.

- Fill the first layer as much as possible. A DVD-9 disc holds about 7.9Gb (binary gigabytes), or a little more than 3.9GB per layer. The larger your project, the more important it becomes for you to manage space properly. If you place the dual-layer break too early, you'll run out of space on the second layer.

- Replicators generally require you to submit layer-break material on Digital Linear Tape (DLT). This requires a DLT drive, which connects internally or externally via a SCSI (Small Computer System Interface) port. (Quantum, www.quantum.com, offers the most popular units.) Some replicators now accept disk images on portable hard drives. You build your project to disk, copy it to another drive, and submit that drive for replication. Always check with the replicator in advance to determine their standards.

- As with any replication service, always request a check-disc for your dual-layer productions. Some replicators will accommodate you, sending a disc to check before they press your order. Others will ask you to visit the facility and test the disc on an emulator (a software DVD player, such as the Apple DVD Player on your computer). Still others will refuse—the cost of preparing dual-layer check discs may not be economically feasible for them, particularly for small runs. Always check policies before you place an order. You don't want to be stuck with thousands of dollars of expensive coasters.

Some points to ponder:

- Although markers snap to GOP boundaries, many of the methods in this section allow you to add markers when there's no video (as yet) in the track. Without video, there are no GOP boundaries. You can add a marker at any frame. When you finally do add video, you must manually adjust the markers so they move to legal positions, at GOP boundaries.

- When video is present beforehand, new markers always snap correctly and legally to the nearest GOP boundary. Unfortunately, when you move a video clip, markers do not move automatically with it. Again, you'll need to manually adjust each marker. As a rule, it's best to add markers after the video has been fully positioned into its final track location.

- Always avoid adding markers within one second of each other or within one second of the start or end of any clip.

Using Embedded Markers

By far the most common way to add markers to your tracks is to import them in compressed material. Compressor, Final Cut, and iMovie all allow you to add markers to your footage before you compress to MPEG-2. (Chapters 4 and 5 discussed how to create chapter and compression markers in these programs.)

To use encoded chapter markers, drag an asset into your Track Editor. DVD Studio Pro 2 parses the MPEG-2 file and then loads its markers. A simple progress bar, shown in Figure 7.1, monitors this process.

Figure 7.1 Final Cut, iMovie, and Compressor all allow you to encode markers into your MPEG-2 files. When these files are added to your tracks, DVD Studio Pro 2 parses them, sequentially loads the markers from the new asset, and adds them to the track.

Adding Markers with the Track Editor

The Track Editor allows you to add markers via both direct manipulation and menu commands. Here are several ways to add markers in the Track Editor.

Click above the Timeline

A track marker area rests just above the track timeline. This area is slightly darker than the rest of the timeline, using the same background color as the individual streams. A default marker, Chapter 1, appears at the start of the track. (All tracks have a starting marker that can't be moved.)

To add another marker, place the cursor in the marker area. Move the cursor to the time where you want to add a marker. The cursor time indicator (properly called the pointer timecode display) at the left of the timeline helps you locate the exact time you're looking for. Click to add a new marker.

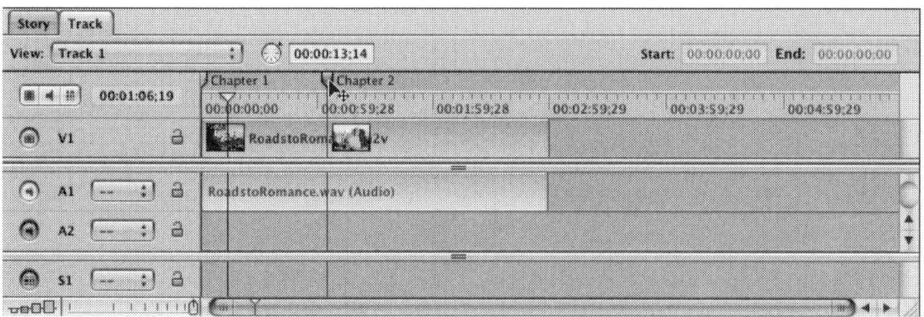

Marker Names

When you add new markers directly to tracks, DVD Studio Pro 2 names them sequentially as Chapter 2, Chapter 3, and so on. You can change the marker root name from Chapter by editing your preferences:

- Choose Preferences > Track and change the Marker Prefix Name. Check Check For Unique Name to ensure that no two markers have the same name.

- In some projects, you might want to use timecode ordering rather than numbers. Choose Preferences > Track and locate Generate Marker Names. Select Timecode Based, and check Auto Update. This ensures that timecodes update when you move markers to new positions.

- If you think you might have some illegal markers in your project, choose Preferences > Track and check Fix Invalid Markers On Build.

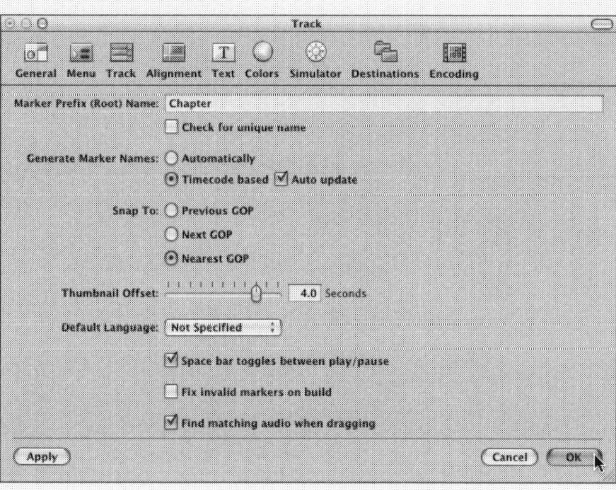

Press M

Both the Track Editor and the Viewer offer a convenient marker placement feature. Move the playhead to the time where you want to add a marker and press **M**. DVD Studio Pro 2 creates a new marker at the playhead position.

This method is more flexible than it might first appear. You can add markers while the playhead is still, as is typical in the Track tab, or while it's moving during playback, as is more typical in the Viewer. Figure 7.2 shows a typical Viewer marking setup.

Unfortunately, all caveats about Viewer delays apply to creating markers while viewing your footage. On older and slower G4s, such as the 733s and 800s, the Viewer may not respond promptly to your input—including play/stop commands and marker requests. You may want to save your work and restart DVD Studio Pro 2 before attempting to add markers in this fashion. Restarting reinitializes program memory and improves responsiveness.

Figure 7.2 The Viewer proves an important component when setting markers, offering instant visual feedback of the playhead's position in the video stream. You can add markers interactively as the Viewer plays. Press **M** to set a marker at the playhead. Press the spacebar to toggle playback on and off.

Add to Clip Ends

Using a simple shortcut, you can add a marker to the end of almost any clip in a video stream. Ctrl-click(right-click) any clip. Select Add Chapter To Clip End (chapter marker) or Add Marker To Clip End (cell marker). This method works for all video clips, except for the last clip in V1 and any clips whose end coincides with it.

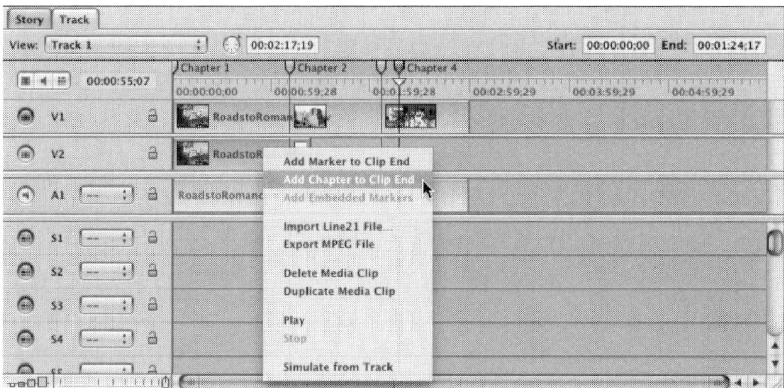

Adding Markers with Text Files

Text files offer another approach to adding markers. You can easily create a simple file that DVD Studio Pro 2 can read and import. Use TextEdit or some equivalent editor to create a new file with marker times and titles as follows:

Use plain text. In TextEdit, choose Format > Make Plain Text (⌘-Shift-T).

Use one line. Include one line per marker.

Set the marker time. Type the marker time, in the form HH:MM:SS:FF (hours followed by minutes, followed by seconds, followed by frames). Separate items with colons.

Add the marker name. After each time, add a space followed by the marker name. Keep the marker names short but meaningful.

Skip the comments. Apple claims that DVD Studio Pro 2 ignores lines with improper format, allowing you to add comments to your files. Practice shows that any deviation from the previous rules produce files that simply will not load.

Once you've created a text file in the correct format, follow these steps to import it as a marker list and add the markers:

1. **Choose Import Marker List.** Move your cursor to the gray marker space above the timeline and Ctrl-click(right-click). Choose Import Marker List. (Alternately, choose File > Import > Marker List.)

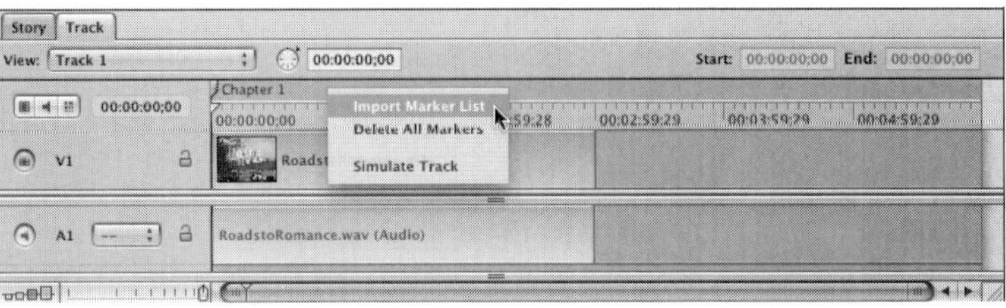

2. **Select your list.** In the Choose Marker File dialog, navigate to your list, select it, and click Choose.

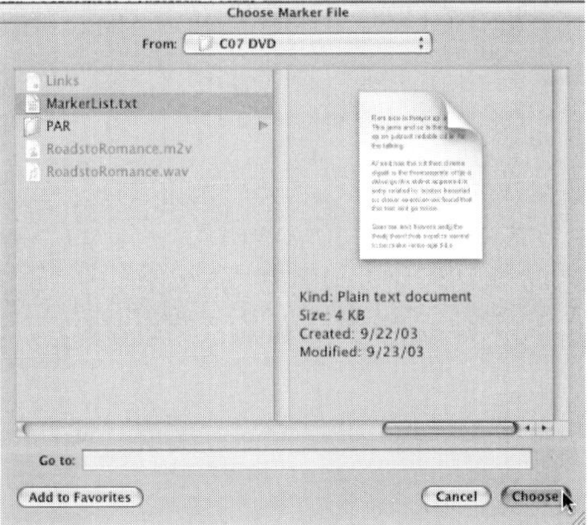

3. **Wait.** DVD Studio Pro 2 may take a few seconds to import your markers. This process may stop if you've made any errors in your text file. If so, go back to your text editor and check your formatting.

Managing Markers

The following techniques will help you manage the way markers work in your track.

Moving Markers

You can move markers by dragging them in the track marker area above the timeline. As Figure 7.3 shows, a ghosted bar follows your drag until you release the mouse. In addition, the cursor time indicator follows your progress, providing instant feedback as to the new marker position. When moved, markers snap automatically to GOP boundaries.

The Marker Inspector (see Figure 7.4) offers two other ways to move existing markers. Select a marker, and open the Inspector (⌘-⌥-I). You can change the time fields by editing the text within them, or you can adjust the slider found under the thumbnail. Both methods change the marker time.

Figure 7.3 When you drag a marker along the timeline, a light, ghosted line follows your progress along the V1 stream. The original, dark purple reference line remains in place until you release the mouse. Use these reference lines and the cursor time indicator to place your marker precisely. Markers always snap to GOP boundaries when moved.

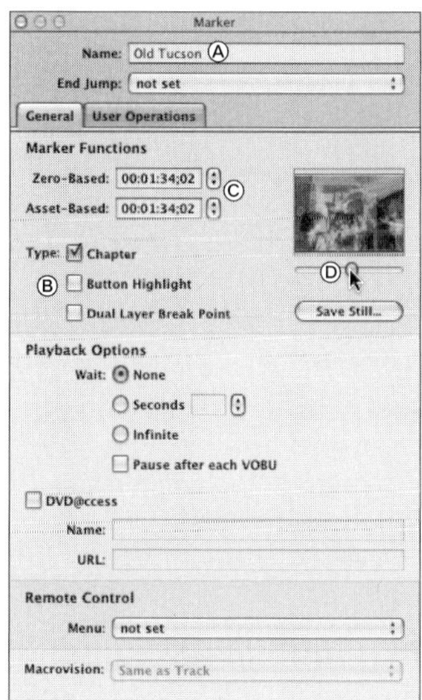

Figure 7.4 The Marker Inspector allows you to change many properties associated with a marker. Choose a new name by typing in the Name field (A). The Type check boxes (B) set the marker type. Edit either time field (C) (Zero-Based or Asset-Based) or adjust the slider (D) under the thumbnail to update the marker time.

Items in the Marker Inspector include the following:

Name Field (A) Use this text field to edit the marker name.

Type Check Boxes (B) These boxes specify the kind of marker in use. You can check more than one box at a time. For example, checking both Chapter and Button Highlight specifies a marker that's half purple (chapter) and half orange (button highlight). Leave all the check boxes blank to create a generic cell marker.

Time Fields (C) These text fields set the time at which the marker appears in the track. Use Zero-Based to set the track time from 00:00:00;00, or use Asset-Based to use the timecode from the clip in which the marker appears.

Time Slider (D) Drag the slider left or right to adjust the marker time. The thumbnail shows the V1 stream video at the current marker location.

Changing Marker Names

The Marker Inspector lets you change the name associated with a marker. Select any marker and open the Inspector. Edit the Name field, and press Return.

Deleting Markers

Select any marker and choose Edit > Delete (or press the Delete key) to remove it from your project.

To remove *all* markers from your project, choose Edit > Delete All Markers, or Ctrl-click(right-click) in the markers line and choose Delete All Markers from the pop-up.

You cannot select more than one marker at a time in DVD Studio Pro 2.

Changing Marker Types

The Marker Inspector offers a number of check boxes that let you set the type associated with your marker. Check Chapter, Button Highlight, or Dual Layer Break Point, or clear all boxes to use a cell marker.

Moving Among Markers

Here are a few tips about moving the playhead to your markers:

- To make the playhead jump to a marker, Ctrl-click(right click) any marker and choose Set Playhead Here.

- Hold down the Ctrl key and press the Right and Left arrow keysto jump between markers. Pressing Ctrl-Left arrow moves to the previous marker; pressing Ctrl-Right arrow moves to the next marker.

- Shift-M and ⌥-M also let you move between markers. Shift-M moves to the next marker; ⌥-M moves to the previous marker.

Creating Stories

At times, you may need to rearrange the way a track plays back. You might want to include deleted scenes for a director's cut or omit scenes for a PG version of your work. You might want to choose promotional material related to just one vacation package or provide a "random" playback order for more interesting tutorial material. Whatever your reasons, stories provide the solution. Stories rearrange the playback order of track cells, choosing which cells to play and in what order.

All stories are specific to tracks and appear subordinate to them in the Outline tab (see Figure 7.5). To add a story, first select a track. Then choose Project > Add To Project > Story (⌘-Shift-T), *or* choose Add > Story from the Outline pop-up, *or* click the Add Story icon in the toolbar. If you try to add a story to your project without a selected track, expect odd results. The story may appear randomly in any track.

Use stories the same way you use tracks. Add them to menus by connecting them to buttons. Refer to them in scripts or end jumps. If you can use a track at some point in your project, you can probably use a story just as well. Like tracks, stories are titles, occupying one of the 99 available titles per disc.

Looking at the Story Editor

The Story Editor, which is shown in Figure 7.6, is very basic. It contains two lists: on the left is a source list of track cells in their original order (B), and on the right is a story list, called the entry list (C). A view pop-up (A) lets you select which story to edit. A separator bar (D) apportions space between the source and story lists. Create stories by dragging items from the source list to the entry list in the order you want.

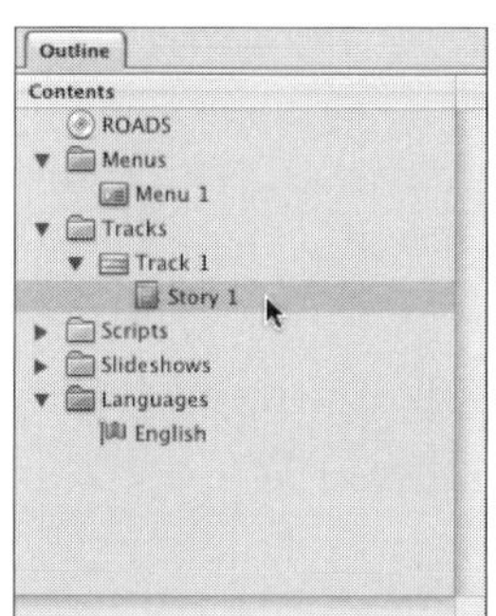

Figure 7.5 As the Outline tab reveals, all stories are associated with a particular track. Stories offer a way to rearrange the cells of a track to produce a unique presentation. Stories can contain all or just some of the cells found within a track.

Items in the Story Editor include the following:

View Pop-Up (A) Use the View pop-up to select the story you want to edit. The pop-up offers a list of all stories that appear in your project.

Source List (B) This list contains all the chapters in the story's parent track. You'll use these chapters as blocks to build your story.

Entry List (C) The list of entries contains chapters chosen from the source list to build the story. Entries can occur in any order and use only those chapters you need for your story. You can add chapters more than once or not at all.

Separator Bar (D) Apportion space between the source and entry lists by dragging the separator bar.

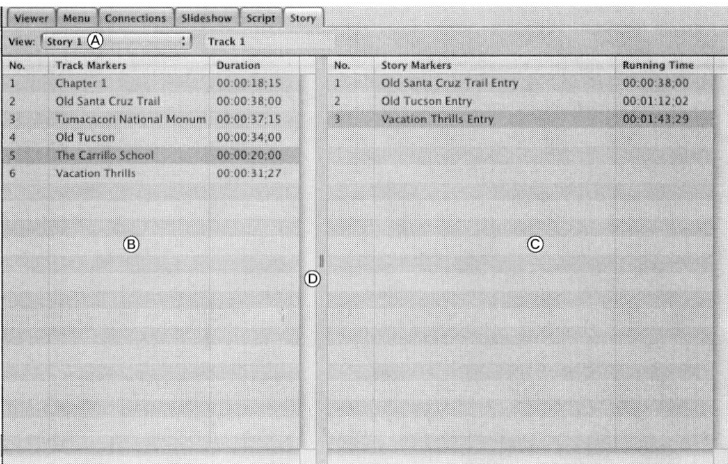

Figure 7.6 The Story Editor. View pop-up (A); source list (B); entry list (C); separator bar (D)

The right portion of the Story Editor holds the entry list. It shows the items that appear in your story: the order in which they will play (No., which is short for number), their starting marker (Story Markers), and their end time (Running Time). Populate this list by dragging items from the source list. Each dragged item creates a new entry.

Unfortunately, the Running Time column in the entry list does not refer to the duration of each entry. Instead, it indicates the time at which the entry completes in the story. To determine duration, you must subtract the running time of each entry from the running time of the entry that precedes it.

DVD Studio Pro 2 lets you add as many copies of a cell to your story as needed. Duplicate items are numbered, for example, Vacation Thrills Entry, Vacation Thrills Entry-2, and so on.

Managing the entry list couldn't be easier. Here's just about everything you can do with it:

Add Drag items from the story list to the entry list. Drop them at the position where you want the entry to appear.

Reorder Drag out-of-order entries to the position in the list where you need them to be.

Delete Select the entry or entries you want to remove, and press the Delete key. (Unfortunately, you cannot undo deletions. To restore entries, re-drag them from the source list.)

Change To change which chapter an entry refers to, Ctrl-click(right-click) the entry. Select Change Chapter, and choose a chapter from the sublist. The entry updates, reflecting the new chapter and running time.

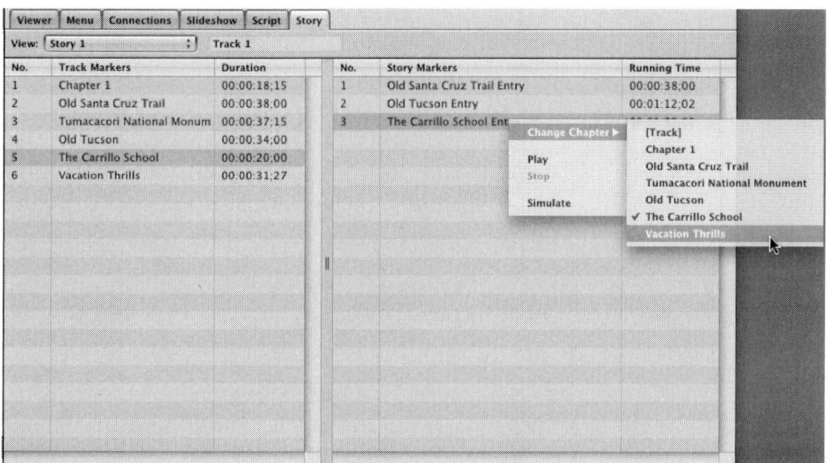

Editing Story Properties

The Story Inspector provides a few key properties that help you control your stories. Select a story in the Outline tab and open the Inspector to update these properties, which include the following:

Name Edit the Name field and press Return to change the name of your story. Story names default to Story 1, Story 2, and so on, but there's no reason you need to keep to this numbered sequence. Use whatever name best describes the role of the story in your project.

While the Story Inspector allows you to set end jumps for the story as a whole, the Story Marker Inspector allows you to set end jumps for individual entries. There's rarely any reason to do so. To access the Story Marker Inspector, select an entry from the entry list and open the Inspector.

End Jump As you can with tracks, you can specify the item to play after your story finishes. You can select Same As Track, or you can select a different destination.

Stream Options The Story Inspector offers a list of all available streams in a scrolling list just below the End Jump pop-up. At times, you might want to disable access to certain streams. For example, you might need to prevent viewers from bypassing parental controls and accessing objectionable audio material. Clear each stream that you want to exclude from your story.

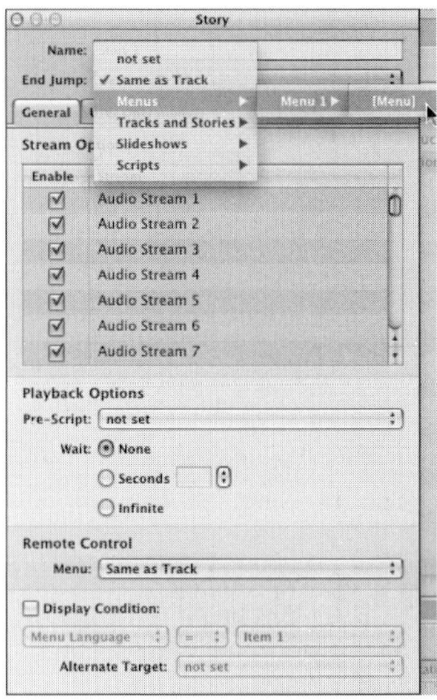

Testing Stories

DVD Studio Pro 2 lets you test stories by playing them back in the Viewer or the Simulator. You can also test stories by building projects and using the Apple DVD Player.

The Viewer

The Viewer (see Figure 7.7) provides the simplest testing capacity; it just lets you play back all or part of your story. When you want to preview how your story flows, use the Viewer.

- Ctrl-click(right-click) the entry list background and choose Play to view the entire story.

- Ctrl-click(right-click) any entry to start playback from that entry. (Playback will continue to the end of the story.)

- Press the spacebar or the Play/Pause button in the Viewer to control the playback.

The Simulator

To test story playback and interaction, Ctrl-click(right-click) the story name in the Outline tab or the background of the entry list to display a pop-up. Choose Simulate. The Simulator (shown in Figure 7.8) loads the story and plays it.

Unlike the Viewer, the Simulator allows you to test the way the story behaves as well as looks. Click the Next Chapter and Previous Chapter buttons to move back and forth through the entries in your stories.

Figure 7.7 The Viewer offers an interactive preview of your DVD Studio Pro 2 stories, showing the video in the active stream at the current position of the playhead. Use the controls at the bottom to play/pause, stop, move back by frame, or move forward by frame through your video. When playback reaches the end of each story chapter, it automatically jumps to the first frame in the next story chapter.

Figure 7.8 The Simulator lets you test your stories to see how they play back in sequence. Be sure to click the Next Chapter and Previous Chapter buttons to confirm for yourself that they stay within the story structure you built in the Story Editor.

The Apple DVD Player

Unfortunately, early releases of DVD Studio Pro 2 may cause problems when you use the Viewer and the Simulator. (As a rule, save your project and relaunch the program before and after using these tools to achieve the best program responsiveness.) The Apple DVD Player (see Figure 7.9) offers a convenient alternative for testing story interaction and playback:

1. **Build your project.** Set your disc's First Play to the story you want to test and build your project to disk. This creates a VIDEO_TS folder in the location you specify.

2. **Launch Apple DVD Player.** The DVD player lets you emulate the folder you just created to see how it would play back if burned to disc.

3. **Open the VIDEO_TS folder.** Choose File > Open VIDEO_TS Folder (⌘-O). Navigate to the VIDEO_TS folder, and click Choose.

4. **Start playback.** You must manually start playback by clicking the Play button on your virtual DVD remote.

Test your story by watching it and by using the controls on the virtual remote. In particular, notice how the Next Chapter and Previous Chapter buttons behave.

Figure 7.9 The chapter numbers in the Apple DVD Player refer to the chapter sequence found within this story, not to the sequence of the cell in the track. Here, Chapter 3 plays back the opening segment of the track—what would normally be the first chapter. Clicking the Previous Chapter and Next Chapter buttons moves through the story, not through the original track.

Delving into the Connections Tab

Connections define the way that DVD Studio Pro 2 project elements interact . A button might connect to a movie. A movie might connect to a script. A script might connect to a slideshow, and so on. Connections establish what happens when an element of your project is selected, plays, or finishes.

In DVD Studio Pro 2, you can make connections in many ways. In the chapters that led up to this one, you saw how to connect items using the Outline tab, the Menu Editor, the Track Editor, and the Inspector. And, as you probably discovered, it can be tedious to connect everything and hard to keep track of what's connected to what. For example, it's irksome to select a marker, open the Inspector, set a connection, and repeat. And repeat. And repeat.

The Connections tab centralizes many of the connection tasks you encounter when working with menus, tracks, markers, and more. In this section, you'll walk through an overview of the Connections tab and discover many of its best, most useful features.

Looking at the Connections Editor

The Connections tab, which is shown in Figure 7.10, looks superficially like the Story Editor. It consists of two panes, placed left and right. Further, you drag items from one side to the other. A closer look reveals the differences between the two and highlights some of the available features:

View Pop-up (A) DVD Studio Pro 2 offers three viewing styles: Basic, Standard, and Advanced. The Basic style shows only the crudest level of detail. The Advanced style shows every available connection and is the view of choice for serious DVD authors. Standard falls somewhere in between, offering more detail than Basic and less than Advanced.

Detail Pop-up (B) Choose the type of source items to view by selecting from All, Connected, or Unconnected. Connected shows items with a set target; Unconnected shows those without.

Element Identifier Field (C) This field shows the project item whose connections are displayed. To change it, choose another item from the Outline tab.

Connect/Disconnect Button (D) This button allows you to connect or disconnect items in the source list. To connect, select one item from the source list and one from the target list, and click Connect. To disconnect, select an already-connected item from the source list and click Disconnect.

Layout Selector (E) DVD Studio Pro 2 offers two layouts for the Connections tab. Click the first button for a side-by-side layout (source to the left, targets to the right). Click the second button for a top/bottom layout (source on top, targets on the bottom).

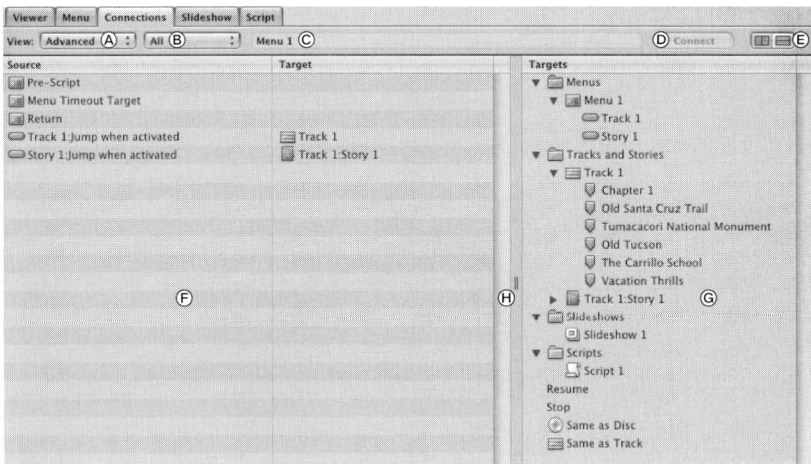

Figure 7.10 The Connections Tab. View pop-up (A); Detail pop-up (B); Element Identifier field (C); Connect/Disconnect button (D); layout selector (E); source list (F); project targets list (G); separator bar (H)

Source List (F) The source list shows the items in your project that you can connect. This list contains two columns. The first column, Source, shows the items in question. The second column, Target, shows any connection. At the basic level, there are five kinds of sources in your project, all of which can be found in the Outline tab: the disc and its menus, tracks, stories, and slideshows. The number (and detail) of the sources shown depends on the level you select from the detail pop-up.

Project Targets List (G) The targets list shows every item in your project to which you can possibly connect. These include all the menus, buttons, tracks, stories, markers, slideshows, slideshow stills, and scripts in the project. In addition, you may encounter four more special-purpose target commands: Resume, Stop, Same As Disc, and Same As Track.

Open and close the folders to see more or less detail in the targets list.

Separator Bar (H) The separator bar apportions space between the source and targets, regardless of whether the overall layout is horizontal or vertical.

Managing Connections

You can use the following methods to control connections.

Selecting an Item to Connect or View

In the Outline tab, select the item on whose connections you want to work. The Element Identifier field updates to show the item name. The source and targets lists show the sources and possible connections for that item.

Making Connections

You can make connections in several ways:

Connect by dragging. The easiest way to connect is to drag a target from the right pane onto the source on the left. A black box indicates that the target works with that source.

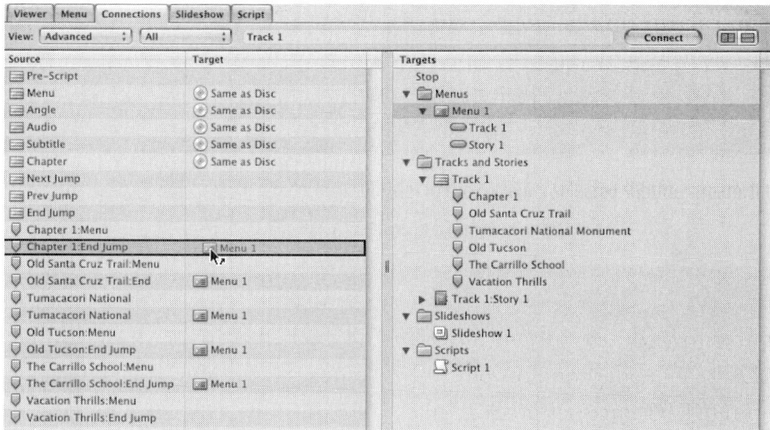

Click the Connect button. Select a source in the left pane, select a target from the right pane, and click Connect.

Connect via the Target pop-up. Move the cursor into the Target column of the source list. Ctrl-click(right-click) the background and choose a target from the pop-up.

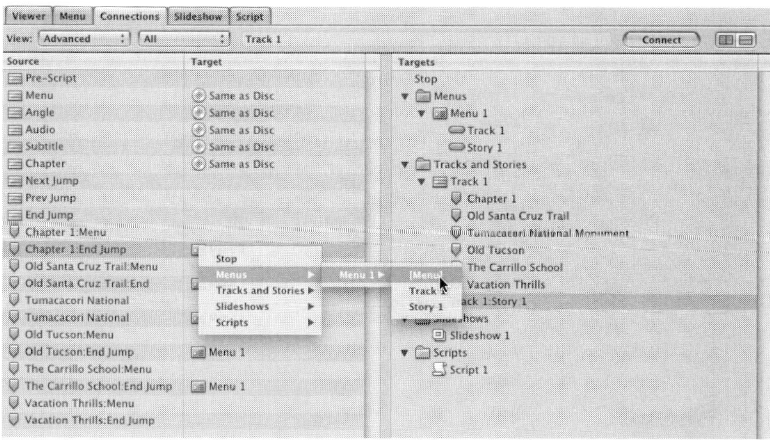

Replace Connections

Use any of the methods in the "Making Connections" section to replace an existing connection.

Removing Connections

To disconnect any source item, select it and click Disconnect or press Delete.

The Disconnect button is context sensitive, appearing only when you've selected an already-connected item.

Keyboard Shortcuts

Here are a few Connections tab shortcuts that may help you with your work:

↑↓	Move the source selection up and down
Ctrl-↑ and Ctrl-↓	Move the targets selection up and down
Return	Same as Connect/Disconnect
Delete	Disconnects the selected source item

Sources and Targets

One of the most important things to understand as you start working with the Connections tab is simply what all the sources and targets are. Table 7.1 summarizes the various sources you might encounter, and Table 7.2 lists the effects of the possible targets.

▶ **Table 7.1** Connection Sources

Source Name(s)	Where Found	What It Does
First Play	Disc	Sets the item that the DVD player begins to play when you first insert the disc. Typically set to a menu or a track.
Jump When Activated	Buttons	Defines the item linked to when the user activates the selected button.
End Jump	Track, chapter, marker, story, slideshow	Determines what action to take when the item finishes playing.
Pre-Script	Menu, track, story	Assigns a script that runs before playing back the menu, track, and so on.
Menu Timeout Target	Menu	Specifies the item linked to when a menu times out.
Next Jump, Prev Jump	Track, story	Sets the response to the Next Chapter and Previous Chapter remote buttons.
Title, Menu, Angle, Chapter, Audio, Subtitle, Return	Disc, track, story, slideshow, marker	Specifies what happens when you press these buttons on the DVD remote control. (Each of these—Title, Menu, Angle, Chapter, and so forth—refers to a standard button that may appear on your viewer's DVD remote.)

Target	Effect
Menu	Jumps to the menu
Button	Jumps to the button's menu and then selects this button
Track	Plays the track from the beginning
Story	Plays the story from the beginning
Marker	Starts playing from the marker
Slideshow	Starts the slideshow from the start
Slide	Starts the slideshow from the selected slide
Script	Executes the script
Resume	(menu buttons only) Returns to a particular point in a track or story, picking up where the viewer left off watching
Stop	(marker end jumps and slide end jumps) Forces the DVD player to discontinue disc playback
Same As Disc	(tracks, stories, markers, and slideshows) Sets the remote control button behavior as defined by the disc
Same As Track	(stories only) Sets the remote control button behavior as defined by the track

A few points to keep in mind about targets and Table 7.2:

- If the target has a pre-script, it's executed before playing the target. This may (or may not) interfere with the target's ability to actually play.

- You can link directly to a primary project element, such as a track, or to its component, such as a marker.

- Bolded items represent primary project elements. They are followed by their components.

- Italicized elements refer to special target functions that appear only for certain sources.

Solution: Create a Story

With stories, you can rearrange the way chapters play back in your tracks. In this project, you'll use real files to build a working story that reorders playback.

     You'll find a suite of supporting files on the DVD that accompanies this book. These files include a movie (RoadstoRomance.m2v, RoadstoRomance.wav), a list of markers (MarkerList.txt), a menu background (RoadsBG.psd), and a button style (Futura36.dspstyle).

1. **Build your track.** Select Track 1 in the Outline and open the Track Editor. Drag RoadstoRomance.m2v to V1. With name matching, DVD Studio Pro 2 automatically adds RoadstoRomance.wav to A1.

This and other projects in this chapter take advantage of the default track (Track 1) and menu (Menu 1) that DVD Studio Pro 2 adds to each new project. The disc's First Play defaults to Menu 1.

2. **Add markers.** Choose File > Import > Marker List. Navigate to MarkerList.txt, select it, and click Choose. DVD Studio Pro 2 adds the markers to your track.

3. **Add a story.** In the Outline tab, select Track 1. In the toolbar, click Add Story. DVD Studio Pro 2 adds a new story (Story 1) to Track 1.

4. **Open the Story Editor.** Select Story 1, and open the Story Editor (⌘-8). The five chapters you loaded (plus the default Chapter 1) appear in the source list.

5. **Create the story entries.** Drag Tumacori National Monument (No. 3) to the entry list on the right side of the Story Editor. Then drag The Carrillo School (No. 5) to the entry list, dropping it below the Tumacori National Monument. You've created a story with two entries and a running time of just under one minute.

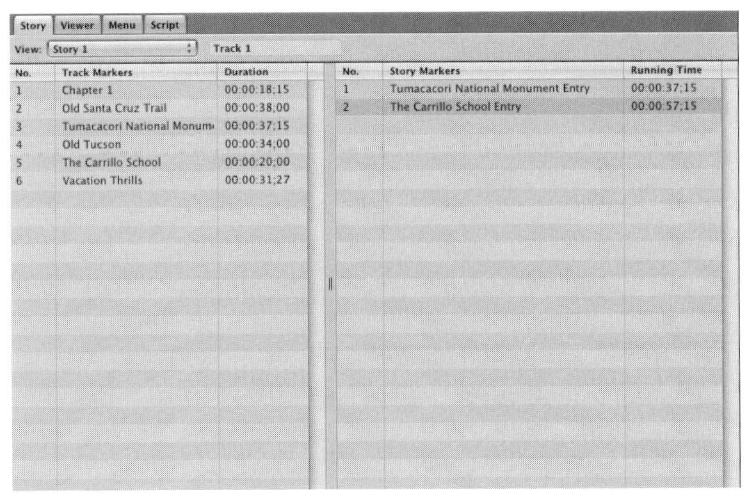

6. **Import a button style for this project.** Choose File > Import > Style. Navigate to Futura36.dspstyle. Select it, and click Import. DVD Studio Pro 2 reads the style and adds it to the Palette in Styles Custom:Buttons.

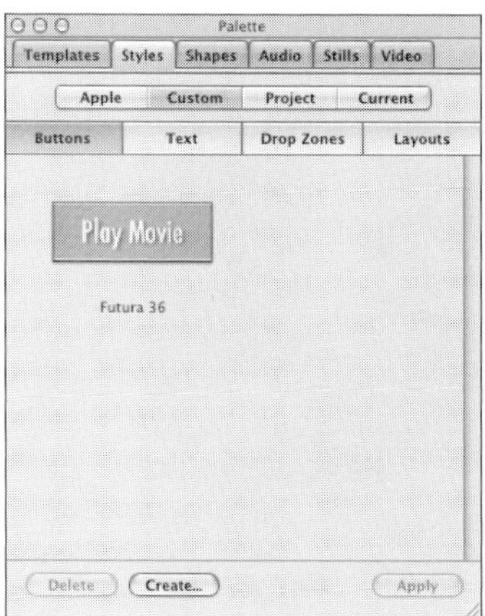

7. **Set the Menu button style.** Select Menu 1 in the Outline view, and open the Menu Editor. Drag your new button style from the Palette onto the menu. Choose Create Button/Set Default Button Style In Menu from the drop palette.

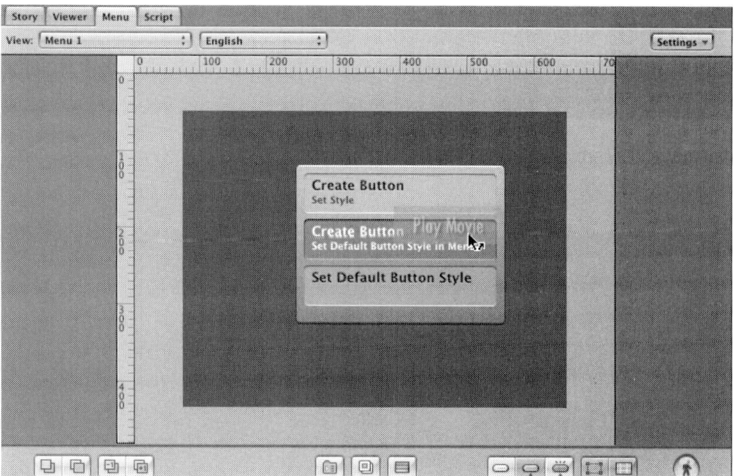

8. **Add a background and another button.** Drag RoadsBG.psd into the Outline tab, and drop it on Menu 1 to set the background. Drag out a second button, and change the text from Play Movie to Play Story.

9. **Connect the buttons.** Drag Track 1 onto the Play Movie button. Choose Connect To Track. Drag Story 1 onto the Play Story button. Choose Connect To Story.

10. **Connect the track and story.** In the Outline tab, select Track 1. Open the Inspector. Set End Jump to Menus > Menu 1 > [Menu]. In the Outline tab, select Story 1. In the Inspector, set End Jump to Same As Track. Return to the Outline tab, and select the disc. In the Inspector, confirm that First Play is set to Menu 1.

11. **Simulate.** Save your work to disk, and then click the Simulator icon in the toolbar. Use the Simulator to test the playback of your track and story. Be sure to try the Previous Chapter and Next Chapter buttons and see how they work in both situations.

Solution: Build Virtual Tracks, Adding More Videos Per Disc

Unfortunately, DVD Studio Pro 2 limits you to 99 tracks per disc (fewer, if you use stories and slideshows). Sometimes, you require more flexibility. Some projects can need 200, 500, or more video clips, putting you in an awkward situation if you plan to use a track for each video. Video-based sales catalogs and educational study review discs are both examples of the kinds of projects that might need many clips.

Fortunately, markers and chapters offer a way around this limit. Instead of adding one clip per track, you add one per chapter—up to 99 per track. This raises your possible number of videos from 99 to nearly 10,000.

The secret lies in adding end jumps to each chapter, returning control to menus or scripts without playing through to other chapters in the same track. In these steps, you'll use end jumps to play back each segment of your track one at a time.

These steps show how to create just a few buttons and segments, but you'll easily see how you might extend this method for more and more videos. The first three steps, building your A1 and V1 tracks, adding markers, and setting a button style, are the same as for building a basic story.

1. **Build your track.** Create a new project. Select Track 1 in the Outline tab, and open the Track Editor. Drag RoadstoRomance.m2v to V1. With name matching, DVD Studio Pro 2 automatically adds RoadstoRomance.wav to A1.

2. **Add markers.** Choose File > Import > Marker List. Navigate to MarkerList.txt, select it, and click Choose. DVD Studio Pro 2 adds the markers to your track.

3. **Import a button style.** Choose File > Import > Style. Navigate to Futura36.dspstyle. Select it and click Import. DVD Studio Pro 2 reads the style and adds it to the Palette in Styles :> Custom :Buttons.

4. **Add a menu background.** Drag RoadsBG.psd to the Outline tab and drop it on Menu 1. DVD Studio Pro 2 adds the art to the background of Menu 1. Open the Menu Editor to see the results.

5. **Set the Menu button style.** Drag the Futura 36 button style from the Palette onto the menu. Choose Create Button/Set Default Button Style In Menu from the drop palette. DVD Studio Pro 2 adds a new button using this style.

6. **Add more buttons.** ⌥-drag the new button to create three new copies, for a total of four buttons. Edit the text in your buttons to Santa Cruz Trail, Tumacacori, Old Tucson, and Carrillo School.

7. **Set end jumps.** In the Track Editor, select the chapter marker entitled Old Santa Cruz Trail. It's the second marker, appearing just after Chapter 1. Open the Marker Inspector (⌘-⌥-I). Set End Jump to Menus > Menu 1 > [Menu]. Repeat to set the end jumps for the following chapter markers: Tumacacori National Monument, Old Tucson, and The Carrillo School.

    Connecting the marker end jumps in this fashion can quickly prove tedious. (Also, you can accidentally move the markers when selecting them for inspection.) In the next steps, you'll use the Connections tab instead of the Inspector to link your buttons to your track. You can easily do the same for your end jumps—just select Track 1 rather than Menu 1 and drag Menu 1 to each end jump.

8. **Prepare to connect.** Select Menu 1 in the Outline tab. Open the Connections tab (⌘-2) and choose Advanced and All from the View pop-ups. Adjust the windows and folders so you can see all four Menu 1 buttons in the left panel and the complete list of Track 1 markers in the right panel.

9. **Make the connections.** Drag Old Santa Cruz Trail onto Button 1. Track 1: Old Santa Cruz Trail appears in the Target column next to Button 1:Jump when activated. In the same manner, drag Tumacacori National Monument onto Button 2, Old Tucson onto Button 3, and The Carillo School onto Button 4.

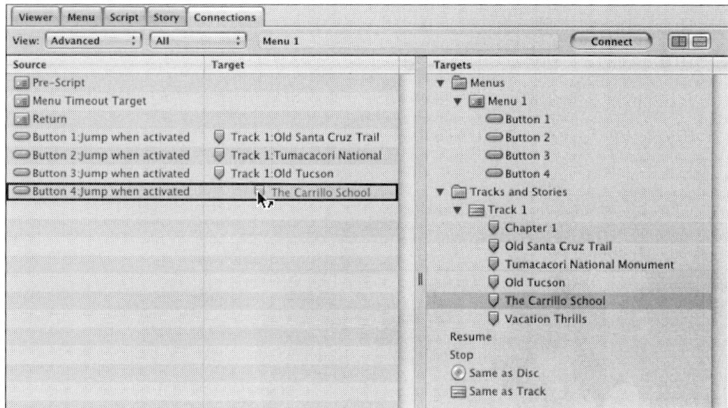

10. **Simulate.** Choose File > Simulate (⌘-⌥-0) to simulate your project. Ensure that each button works as expected, connecting to the linked chapter and returning control to the menu after each chapter finishes.

Solution: Add DVD @ccess to Your Movie

Apple's DVD @ccess feature allows you to connect items from your DVD to web links that open in your Internet browser. In this project, you'll set markers to build an automatic connection to a descriptive web page.

1. **Build the movie and menu.** Repeat steps 1 through 5 of the previous solution to create your track, add your markers, import a button style, set your menu background, and create a new button.

2. **Connect the button to the track.** Drag Track 1 from the Outline tab onto the button you just created. Choose Connect To Track from the drop palette.

3. **Connect the track back to the menu.** Select Track 1 in the Outline tab. Open the Inspector, and choose Menus > Menu 1 > [Menu] from the End Jump pop-up. This instructs DVD Studio Pro 2 to return to your menu after your track finishes playing.

The DVD @ccess name is strictly for your reference. It does not appear on your disc or to your viewer.

4. **Add a DVD @ccess point.** In the Track Editor, select the Old Santa Cruz chapter marker. In the Inspector, check DVD @ccess. (This option appears about two-thirds of the way down in the General tab.) Set the name to Old Santa Fe Trail. Set the URL to http://www.azstarnet .com/santacruz/. This tells DVD Studio Pro 2 to create a DVD @ccess link for the Old Santa Cruz Trail chapter marker that connects to a web page about the Santa Cruz valley.

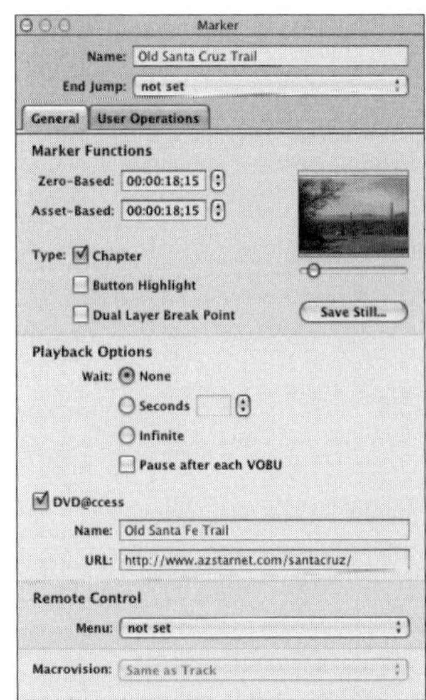

5. **Add more DVD @ccess points.** Select the Tumacacori marker and set the DVD @ccess to http://www.nps.gov/tuma/. Set the Old Tuscon marker link to http:// www.oldtucson.com/, and set the Carrillo School link to http://edweb.tusd.k12 .az.us/Carrillo/tour.html. Save your work to disk.

Always use a fully qualified URL for DVD @ccess. Valid protocols include http:, ftp:, file:, and mailto:.

6. **Build your project.** Click Build and compile your project to disk, creating VIDEO_TS and AUDIO_TS folders in the location you specify.

7. **Launch Apple DVD Player.** The program appears in the Applications folder of your OS X disk.

When links are in use, DVD Studio Pro 2 automatically adds a Windows DVD @ccess installer to your DVD during the burn. This installer allows most Windows computers and Windows software DVD players to process the connections in your movies.

8. **Enable DVD @ccess.** In the DVD Player, choose DVD Player > Preferences. Click the Disc tab. In the Features box, check Enable DVD @ccess Web Links, and then click OK.

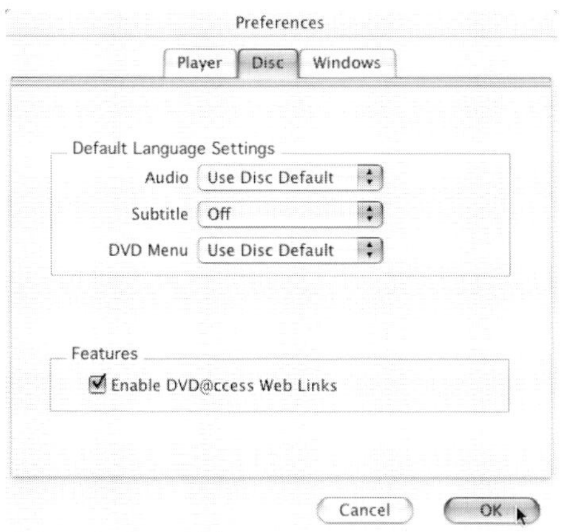

9. **Open your VIDEO_TS folder.** Choose File > Open VIDEO_TS Folder (⌘-O). Navigate to the VIDEO_TS folder you just created, select it, and click Choose.

10. **Play your "DVD."** Begin DVD emulation by clicking the Play button on your Apple DVD Player remote.

11. **Play your movie.** Ensure that Play Movie is selected, and then click Enter on your virtual remote. The movie track starts playback.

12. **Wait.** Watch your movie and wait. As each chapter begins, your default Internet browser launches and displays the page you set in the DVD @ccess link.

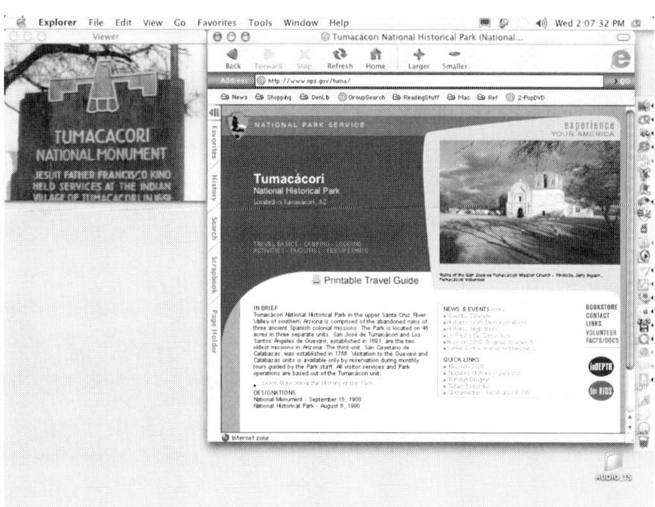

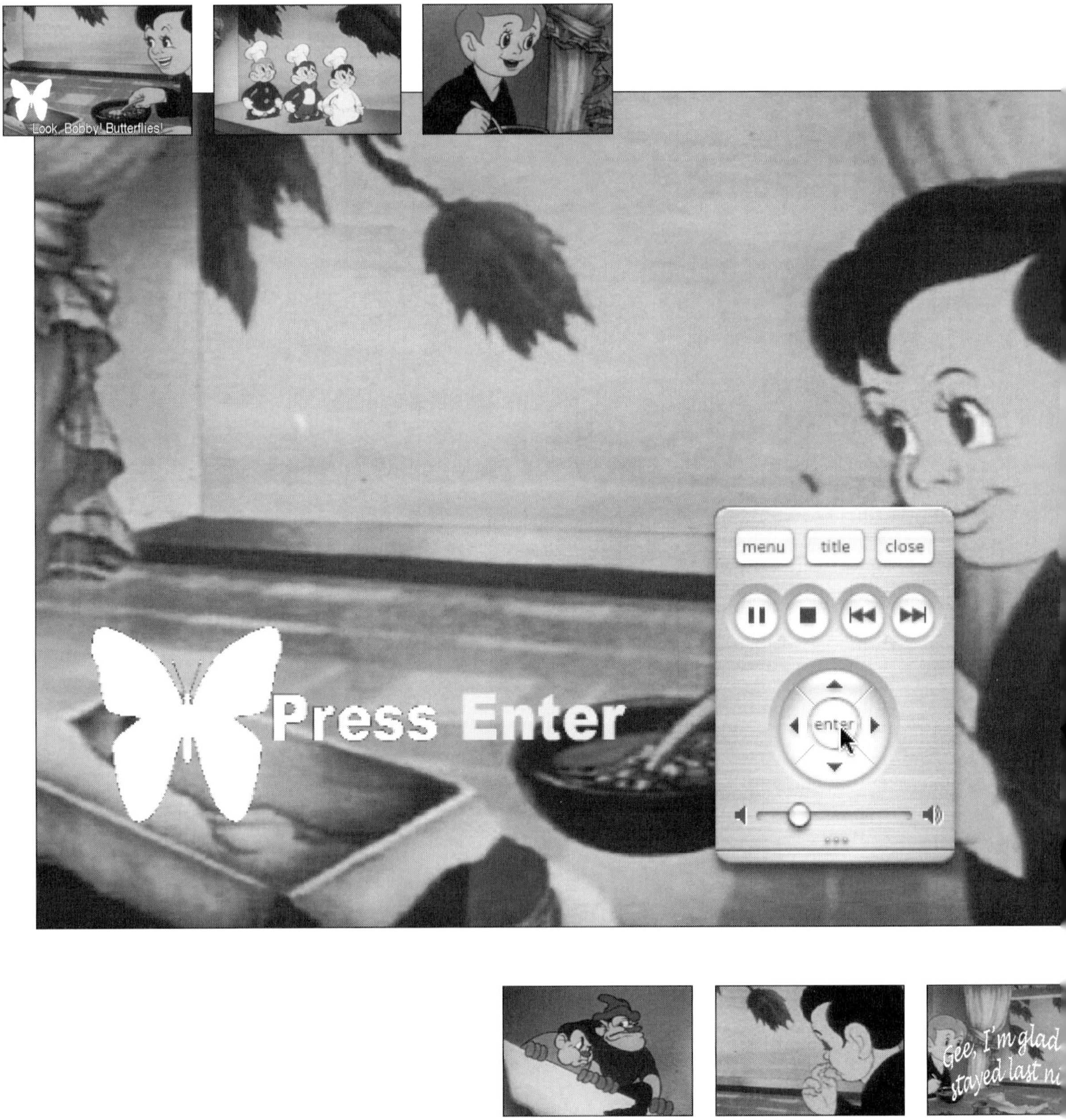

Press Enter

menu title close

enter

Subtitles

When you hear about subtitles, you probably think about overlaying video footage with text. Subtitles certainly do that. They let your DVD productions play back with understandable content in noisy environments such as gyms and tradeshows, with translations in foreign countries, and with visual clarity for hearing-impaired viewers. Still, you'd be wrong to think that subtitles just add words. Subtitles do a lot. They can add pictures, buttons, colors, animation, and more. In this chapter, you'll discover many of the ways to use subtitles in DVD Studio Pro 2. You'll learn about the roles and rewards of DVD subtitling and find out how to build these effects for yourself.

Chapter Contents

Subtitle Capabilities

If you think that subtitles are just white or yellow words splashed across the bottom of your screen, think again. DVD subtitles go way beyond simple captions, offering a wealth of visual styling. Subtitles can include the following:

Formatted Text Subtitles can be built out of any system font and text style, placed anywhere on your viewer's screen, and using any color you'd like.

Pictures Images as well as text can be subtitles, using the same kind of four-color art that you used for creating menu overlays.

Animation Clever use of subtitle progressions allows you to build simple animations over your video.

Fade Effects Fade your subtitles in and out as they appear and disappear from the screen to provide a softer visual feel.

Buttons Markers, subtitles, and jump conditions allow you to add buttons over video for advanced interaction.

In this chapter, you'll learn how to create subtitles for each of these features and how to make the most out of the subtitling capabilities of DVD Studio Pro 2.

Transcribing Text

Unless you have special-purpose transcription software, it's generally up to you and the resources you have on hand to build subtitles from your source video. It takes little more than a video player (such as QuickTime Player), a text editor (such as TextEdit—or a notebook and pencil), and a lot of time and patience to build a list of subtitles.

In their most basic sense, subtitles are made up of words and timing information. The words tell what the movie is saying. The timing specifies when the words are said. Unfortunately, many people attempt to collect both types of information together. This makes the subtitling process harder than it needs to be and less accurate than it can be.

Don't try to transcribe audio and work out subtitle timing at the same time. Transcription and timing are two very different tasks, best done sequentially. Transcribe your video first, and then worry about the timing. Already-transcribed text, in a copy-and-paste format (such as a text document), makes your job easier when you're ready to place subtitles in a timeline.

It's a rare thing in small business and personal DVD development to be handed a ready-to-use transcription. Be prepared to do the transcription work yourself. Playback tools, such as QuickTime Player, can help you play, stop, rewind, and review the audio track as you transcribe.

Build your transcription a line at a time, limiting your text for each line to what can be displayed at once in a single subtitle. Keep the process focused on accuracy. Pay special attention to completeness and spelling; try not to miss any words. Progress to the next subtitle after you're sure you've transcribed the current one correctly.

With the video fully transcribed, start looking at the timing. The Movie Info window in QuickTime Player (see Figure 8.1) can help you determine the start and end times for each subtitle. Make a note of these times yourself or use a utility (such as the one described in the next section) to create a timed list of subtitles.

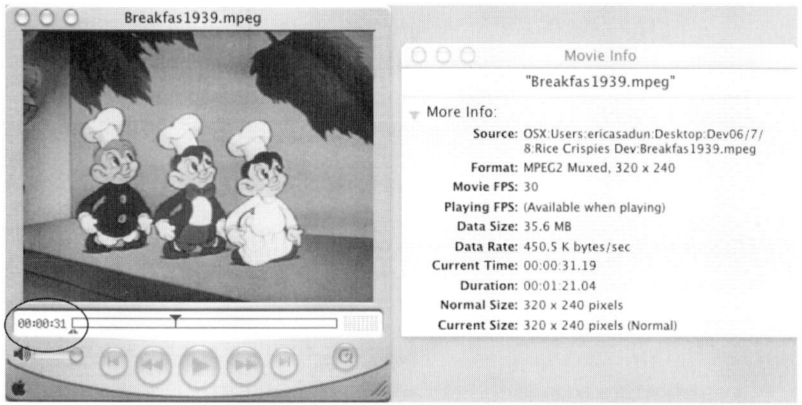

Figure 8.1 QuickTime Player's Movie Info window (choose Window > Show Movie Info or press ⌘-I) provides precise playback timing. The Current Time field displays the hours, minutes, seconds, and frames at the playhead.

The AppleScript Subtitling Utility

An exclusive AppleScript subtitling aid appears on the DVD that accompanies this book. You'll find it with the files for this chapter. This utility uses QuickTime Player to capture the start and end times for your subtitles, saving the results to Text-Edit. Follow these steps to use this program.

The AppleScript Subtitling Utility is included in source form, allowing you to inspect and modify the source as needed.

1. **Run the script.** Double-click SubtitlingUtility to open the AppleScript Script Editor. Click Run.

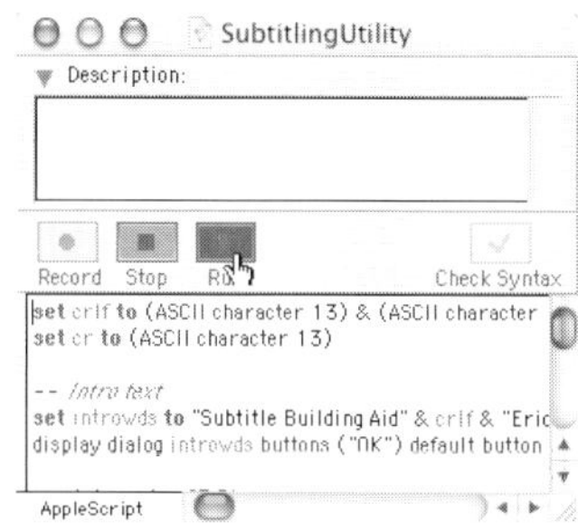

242

2. **Load your movie.** In the intro dialog, click OK. When prompted, launch Quick-Time Player and load the movie you need to subtitle. Click OK.

3. **Say Yes to the new text file.** The utility asks for permission to create a new file in TextEdit. Click Yes. TextEdit launches (if it is not already running) and opens a new window. Leave this window alone to let the utility do its work.

4. **Set the subtitle start time.** When prompted, move the QuickTime playhead to the start time of your subtitle, and then click OK. The subtitling utility reads the playhead time and remembers it.

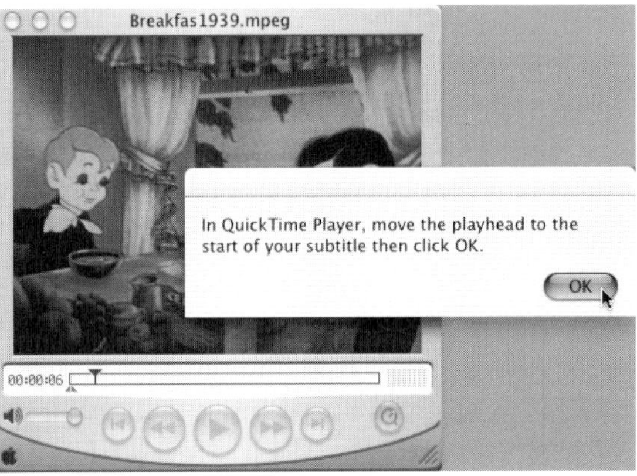

5. **Set the subtitle end time.** When prompted, move the playhead to the position where your subtitle ends, and then click OK. The utility remembers the playhead time.

6. **Enter the subtitle.** Type the subtitle text at the prompt, and then click OK. The script adds the new subtitle line to your script file using the start and end times you specified in the previous steps.

7. **Repeat.** To continue adding subtitles, click Yes when prompted. The script repeats the previous steps, asking you to set new start and end times and add another subtitle. Continue doing so as needed to build your subtitles up a line at a time. When finished, click No instead of Yes. The script saves your completed subtitle file to the desktop.

The Subtitles file you create using these steps is fully DVD Studio Pro 2–compliant. It can be imported using the steps described later in the "Importing Subtitle Files" section.

Creating Subtitles

DVD Studio Pro 2 offers many paths to subtitle creation, all of which produce workable and watchable subtitles. There's no "best" method. The approach you choose may depend on your mood, your needs, your comfort levels, and the advantages intrinsic to that technique.

In the next few sections, we'll look at three different approaches to creating subtitles in DVD Studio Pro 2:

Direct Manipulation Adding subtitles directly to the subtitle streams of the Track Editor by using the mouse and the Viewer

Importing Images Adding subtitles by overlaying your subtitle streams with four-color art

Importing Subtitle Files Adding subtitles by importing properly formatted subtitle files, particularly text

You'll learn how to use each method and some of the advantages (and drawbacks) involved.

Adding Subtitles by Hand

Direct manipulation is the simplest way to add subtitles to your DVD Studio Pro 2 projects. Double-click in the subtitle stream, type your text, and adjust the clip time. Repeat for each subtitle, and you're done.

Unfortunately, this simple method sometimes proves to be the most tedious approach for creating subtitles. The editing cycle may proceed slowly on older G4 computers; you may experience delays between typing text and the program acknowledging your keystrokes. Also, DVD Studio Pro 2 doesn't offer the best interaction for listening and transcribing.

Still, for quick-and-simple subtitles, this method can't be beat. For more complex projects, you probably should look elsewhere for your subtitling needs.

To add subtitles directly to your stream, follow these steps:

1. **Double-click in the subtitle stream.** In the Track Editor, move the cursor to the position where you want to add a new subtitle, and double-click. Alternately, choose Project > Timeline > Add Subtitle At Playhead (⌘-~). DVD Studio Pro 2 creates a new, selected subtitle track (bright yellow) at that spot. The Viewer opens if it is not already visible. A blinking cursor appears at the bottom-center of the current Viewer frame, just within the text safe zone.

The new subtitle is typically 5 seconds long. To change the default subtitle length, open the Preferences dialog (⌘-,) and click General. Enter a new subtitle length in seconds and click OK.

2. **Edit the subtitle.** Type the text of your subtitle into the field at the bottom of the Viewer. If the field loses focus, double-click to reselect. The selected text appears with inverted colors until you click away from the field.

You can also use the Text field in the Subtitle Inspector to edit subtitle text.

3. **Optionally, adjust the font and size.** Use the Fonts window (⌘-T) to adjust the text style for your subtitle. You can adjust all or just part of the subtitle.

Convenient shortcuts: ⌘-B applies a bold style to the selected text; ⌘-I applies italics; and ⌘-U underlines.

4. **Optionally, adjust the position.** If desired, drag the subtitle in the Viewer to any position. Alternately, open the Subtitle Inspector and set the horizontal and vertical placement.

5. **Adjust the duration.** You can adjust the length for your new subtitle clip using any of the methods discussed in Chapter 6. Either set the duration in the Subtitle Inspector or drag out the clip in the Track Editor.

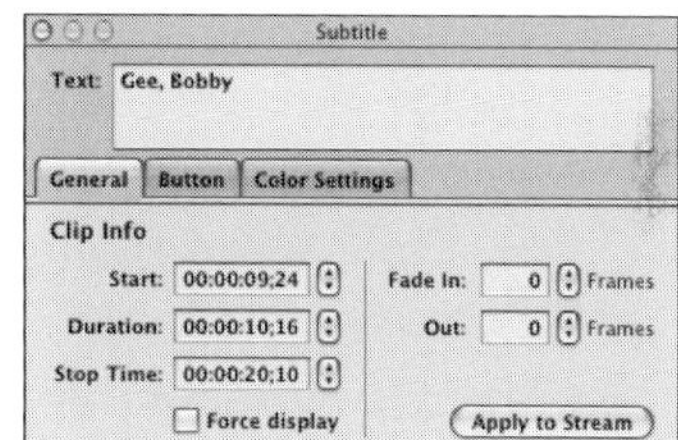

6. **Repeat.** Repeat the previous steps to add all the subtitles you need for the entire track.

7. **Set the stream language.** Use the pop-up just to the right of the stream name to select the language for the subtitle track.

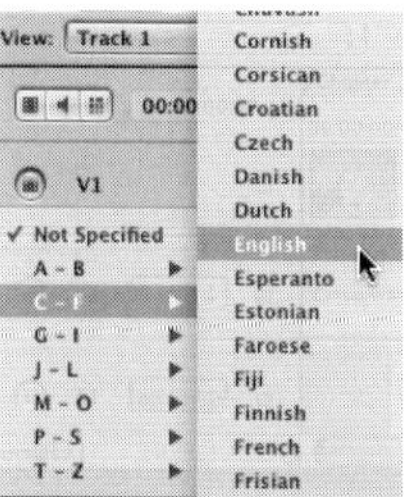

246
■

Adding Subtitles by Importing Graphic Files

Although subtitles seem like they're built around text, they're actually a kind of picture. DVD subtitle streams overlay your videos in exactly the same way that menu highlights overlay menus, using a four-color source with color mapping. In fact, subtitles and menu overlays are more or less the same thing, DVD-wise. The DVD name for subtitles is properly "subpictures," which better indicates the kind of material you're working with. These correspondences make even more sense when you discover that DVD Studio Pro 2 allows you to import images and add them to your subtitle streams.

Adding subtitle pictures couldn't be simpler. Follow these steps to create and import subtitle images:

1. **Create an overlay.** In Photoshop, create a four-color overlay, like the one shown in Figure 8.2. Legal colors include black, white, dark gray (66%), and light gray (33%). Save to disk as TIFF. See Chapter 3 for further details on creating four-color overlays.

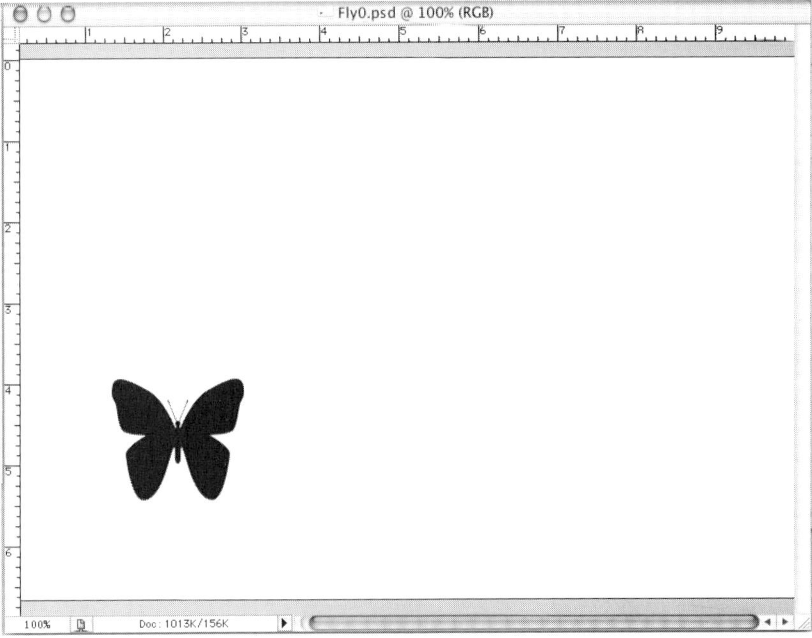

Figure 8.2 An overlay in Photoshop, ready to use for adding subtitles in DVD Studio Pro 2.

2. **Add the overlay to your subtitle stream.** Drag the overlay image onto your
    stream and release it near the point where you want the subtitle to start.

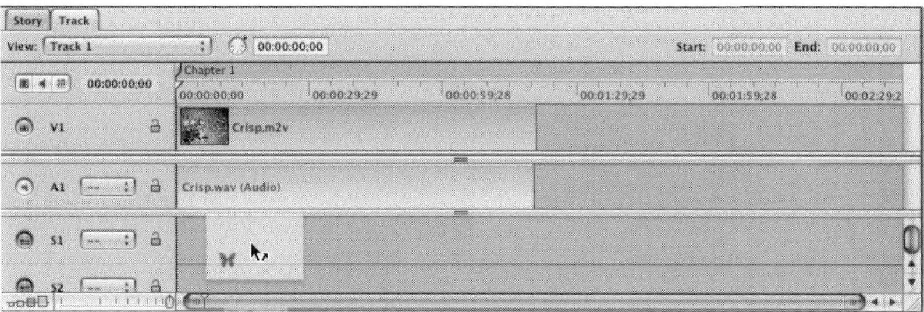

3. **Adjust the subtitle clip.** Resize and drag the new subtitle as needed to set its start-
    ing time and duration. (You can also use the Inspector to set these properties.)

4. **Test.** Move the playhead onto the subtitle. If needed, activate the subtitle stream
    by clicking the Stream Select control, to the left of the stream name. Use the
    Viewer to visualize your new subtitle and ensure that it fits properly within the
    title safe zone. If needed, use the Subtitle Inspector to adjust the position of your
    art. (See the next section for details.)

DVD Studio Pro 2 lets you mix graphics and text, adding images to your text subtitles. This produces the kind of subtitle display shown in Figure 8.3.

Figure 8.3 Mixing overlay graphics with subtitle text expands the range of your subtitle options, allowing you to mix and match pictures and words.

The secret lies in the General tab of the Subtitle Inspector, shown in Figure 8.4. This pane lets you assign an image to any text subtitle. Locate the Graphic section (it's toward the bottom) and click Choose to open a file browser. Navigate to your file, select it, and click Choose. DVD Studio Pro 2 loads the new overlay and combines it with the existing text.

The Offset X and Offset Y text fields let you fine-tune the placement of your new overlay. Use positive offsets to move the overlay right and down. Use negative offsets to move left and up. The small up and down triangles to the right of each field let you incrementally adjust the values by one, nudging the overlay a pixel at a time.

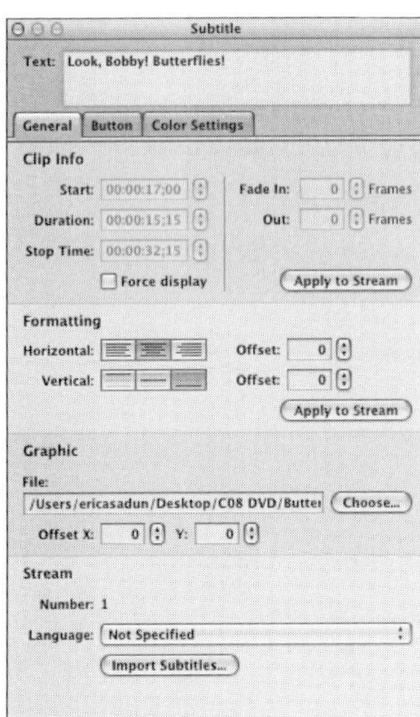

Figure 8.4 The Subtitle Inspector lets you add overlays to your existing text subtitles. Click the Choose button in the Graphic section to select the overlay file. The Offset X and Offset Y fields let you adjust the overlay placement.

Adding Subtitles by Importing Subtitle Text Files

DVD Studio Pro can import subtitle files created in other programs. The program supports the Spruce Technologies (STL) subtitle format, Sonic Solutions (SON) bitmap subtitles, Daiken-Comtec Laboratories Scenarist (SCR) bitmap subtitles, and plain text. Of these, the plain text format is easiest to create and use. No matter which format you choose, the method remains the same. Follow these steps to import subtitles into your project.

1. **Choose Import Subtitle File.** Ctrl-click(right-click) in any subtitle stream. Choose Import Subtitle File from the contextual menu to open the Choose Subtitle File dialog.

2. **Select a subtitle file.** In the Choose Subtitle File dialog, navigate to your file, select it, and click Choose.

3. **Wait.** DVD Studio Pro 2 imports the file you selected and reports the number of subtitles successfully imported. If this number does not match the subtitle count in your file, it may indicate a subtitle formatting error.

The Basic Subtitles Format

Plain text files often prove to be the most useful for many kinds of subtitling needs. They're easy to build, easy to import, easy to test, and easy to fix. The simplest form of subtitling looks like this (longer lines of dialog have been cut off to fit the page):

```
00:00:06:01 , 00:00:09:25 , Gee, I'm glad you stayed all night, Bobby
00:00:09:25 , 00:00:14:26 , Don'tcha like the cereal? [Bobby:] Oh…
00:00:14:26 , 00:00:19:03 , It's not crisp like the kind my breakfast…
00:00:19:03 , 00:00:20:16 , [Joey:] Breakfast Pals?
00:00:20:16 , 00:00:24:17 , [Bobby:] Sure. They come every morning as…
00:00:24:17 , 00:00:26:23 , [Whistle]
```

Here, each line contains a single subtitle with the following details:

- The subtitle is composed of a start time, an end time, and the subtitle itself.
- The start and end times and the end time and the subtitle text are separated by a space followed by a comma followed by a second space.
- The start and end times take the form HH:MM:SS:FF (hours, minutes, seconds, frames). Each two-digit number is separated by a colon.

You can edit imported subtitle text just like the subtitles created directly in DVD Studio Pro 2.

Command Lines

Subtitle text files can also include simple scripting. Lines with commands extend the power of subtitle text files, allowing you to change subtitle settings such as fonts, sizes, and positions. Commands also let you add fade in and fade out times. Command lines start with a dollar sign ($) and are followed by a variable name and assignment, for example, $FontName = Arial. You can intersperse these lines throughout your subtitle text file. Here is a typical subtitle file with embedded command lines.

```
$FontName = Arial
$FontSize = 20
$HorzAlign = Center
$VertAlign = Bottom
$XOffset = 60
$YOffset = -80
$FadeIn = 15
```

```
00:00:06:01 , 00:00:09:25 , Gee, I'm glad you stayed all night, Bobby
$Bold = True
00:00:09:25 , 00:00:14:26 , Don'tcha like the cereal? [Bobby:] Oh…
$FontSize = 30
00:00:14:26 , 00:00:19:03 , It's not crisp like the kind my breakfast…
$ForceDisplay = True
00:00:19:03 , 00:00:20:16 , [Joey:] Breakfast Pals?
$Bold = False
00:00:20:16 , 00:00:24:17 , [Bobby:] Sure. They come every morning as…
00:00:24:17 , 00:00:26:23 , [Whistle]
```

A few points to remember:

Settings persist until you change them. If you set the font size via a subtitle command, that size continues throughout your subtitles until you use another size command. When you turn on the bold attribute, every subtitle is bolded until you issue a $Bold = False command.

Spelling matters. As with any programming or specification language, DVD Studio Pro 2 offers no room for typing mistakes in the subtitle commands.

Use existing fonts. You must select a font that currently appears on your system—correctly spelled! DVD Studio Pro 2 will not load subtitle files that contain "missing" fonts.

$ForceDisplay might not force display—at least in DVD Studio Pro 2 itself. Most subtitleß commands display correctly in the Viewer and the Simulator, but for some reason $ForceDisplay doesn't produce reliable results unless you build your project and emulate in Apple DVD Player.

Restart the program as needed. DVD Studio Pro 2 has a bad tendency to hang on to previous settings when you load new subtitle files. You may need to save your work and restart the program to make the program acknowledge the current set of subtitle commands.

The following are the most commonly used commands; see your DVD Studio Pro 2 manual for a complete list of supported commands.

$FontName Sets the font family name. You *must* select a font that appears on your system. If you don't, the subtitle file will stop loading. Example:

```
$FontName = Arial
```

$FontSize Sets the size of the font. Example:

```
$FontSize = 32
```

$Bold, $Italic, $Underlined Turns the font's bold, italic, or underlined attribute on or off. Set to either True or False. Examples:

```
$Bold = True
$Underlined = False
```

$TextContrast Sets the text opacity from 0 (transparent) to 15 (opaque). Example:

```
$TextContrast = 7
```

$Outline1Contrast, $Outline2Contrast Sets the opacity for the two text outline colors. Example:

```
$Outline1Contrast = 15
```

$HorzAlign, $VertAlign Sets the horizontal and vertical aligment. Valid alignments include left, center, right, top, and bottom. Example:

```
$VertAlign = Center
```

$Xoffset, $YOffset Sets the horizontal and vertical offsets in pixels. Positive offsets move right and down. Negative offsets move left and up. Examples:

```
$YOffset = 20
$Xoffset = -15
```

$ForceDisplay When set to True, this command forces subtitles to display—whether or not subtitles are switched on by the DVD player. Example:

```
$ForceDisplay = True
```

$FadeIn, $FadeOut Sets the fade time (in frames) during which the subtitle gradually appears on or disappears from the screen. Example:

```
$FadeOut = 15
```

Embedded Controls

In addition to the commands listed previously, you can actually embed certain controls directly into the subtitle text itself. These inline controls add a bit of visual style with a minimum of annotation.

```
00:00:06:01 , 00:00:09:25 , Gee, I'm ^Bglad^B you stayed all night…
00:00:09:25 , 00:00:14:26 , Don'tcha like the cereal? [Bobby:] Oh…
00:00:14:26 , 00:00:19:03 , It's not ^Icrisp^I like the kind my…
00:00:19:03 , 00:00:20:16 , [Joey:] ^UBreakfast Pals^U?
00:00:20:16 , 00:00:24:17 , [Bobby:] Sure. They come every morning as…
00:00:24:17 , 00:00:26:23 , [Whistle]
```

The following are the most important controls that can be embedded into subtitle text:

^B Turns bolding on and off. Example:

```
00:00:06:01 , 00:00:09:25 , Gee, I'm ^Bglad^B you stayed all night…
```

^I Turns italics on and off. Example:

```
00:00:14:26 , 00:00:19:03 , It's not ^Icrisp^I like the kind my…
```

^U Turns underlining on and off. Example:

    `00:00:19:03 , 00:00:20:16 , [Joey:] ^UBreakfast Pals^U?`

| Forces a line break. Example:

    `00:00:38:14 , 00:00:40:27 , Let's get 'em. | C'mon Mushy.`

Importing Graphics through Text Subtitle Files

DVD Studio Pro 2 allows you to import graphics files via your text-based subtitle files as well as text. To reference an image from your subtitle file, follow these steps:

1. **Create an overlay.** In Photoshop, create a four-color overlay, like the one shown in Figure 8.5. Legal colors include black, white, dark gray (66%), and light gray (33%). Save to disk. (See Chapter 3 for details on creating four-color overlays.)

Figure 8.5 A four-color overlay in Photoshop, ready to import into DVD Studio Pro 2 through a subtitle text file

2. **Edit the subtitle file.** Open your subtitle file in your favorite text editor, such as TextEdit.

3. **Define a file token.** The token you define tells DVD Studio Pro 2 to load a file rather than read text from the rest of the line. In this example, the token is *GFILE*, for example, $SetFilePathToken = *GFile*. Any syntactically distinct token will do the job. Select one that's easy to recognize and simple to type.

```
$SetFilePathToken = *GFile*
00:00:06:01 , 00:00:09:25 , *GFile*GeeGlad.tif
00:00:09:25 , 00:00:14:26 , Don'tcha like the cereal? [Bobby:] Oh…
00:00:14:26 , 00:00:19:03 , It's not crisp like the kind my breakfast…
00:00:19:03 , 00:00:20:16 , [Joey:] Breakfast Pals?
```

4. **Add the file references.** After the start and stop times, begin with the file token followed by the name of the file.

```
00:00:06:01 , 00:00:09:25 , *GFile*GeeGlad.tif
```

This tells DVD Studio Pro 2 to use GeeGlad.tif as the subtitle overlay starting at minute 6.

To work, each overlay file must reside in the same folder as the subtitle text file.

5. **Load the text file.** Return to DVD Studio Pro 2. Import your subtitle file into a stream. Test to make sure that your overlay or overlays work as desired.

When Subtitle Text Files Go Wrong

Subtitle files can fail to import correctly for any number of reasons. Here are the most common. When errors crop up, DVD Studio Pro 2 stops importing and creates either a partial load of subtitles or no subtitles at all.

Wrong Timecodes Make sure that your subtitle timecodes match the timecodes for your video assets. The timecodes must be correctly formatted, must be nonoverlapping, and must finish with or before the video.

Missing Fonts Always make sure that the font names you use in your text files appear on your system. (Press ⌘-T to open the Fonts palette and check.) Also be sure that the font name is correctly typed, for example, Arial, not Ariel.

Missing Graphics Keep your graphics files in the same folder as your text file. Ensure that you've typed their names precisely. For example, don't confuse TIF with TIFF.

Command Errors Avoid typos in your commands. Make sure you've typed $Force-Display, for example, and not $ForceDsplay.

At times, you may encounter stray characters that don't seem to belong in your subtitles, for example, a trailing } or \ at the end of your video. Often these strays are created by extra characters in your text file. Converting from rich text to plain text may help. In TextEdit, choose Format > Make Plain Text (⌘-Shift-T). Delete the final carriage return and linefeed from your file. This often fixes the problem.

Setting Subtitle Color

As you learned earlier in this chapter, subtitles are similar to menu overlays. DVD subtitles overlay videos just like menu highlights overlay menus. Both use a four-color source with color mapping, and both use the Inspector's Color Settings tab to select overlay colors and opacities.

The Subtitle Inspector sets properties for both the selected subtitle itself and for all the subtitles in your stream. Subtitle color settings are one of those properties that affect the entire stream, just like button color settings affect all buttons within a menu. Figure 8.6 shows the Subtitle Inspector's Color Settings tab.

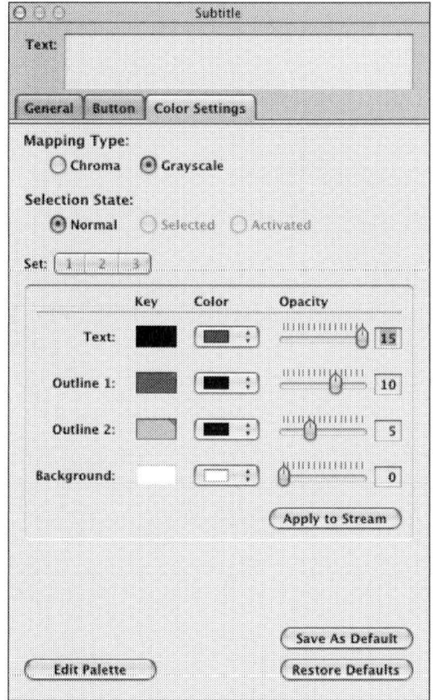

Figure 8.6 You use the Color Settings tab of the Subtitle Inspector to set the color mappings and opacity for each of the four colors used in the subtitle stream. These changes affect all subtitles within the selected stream.

Follow these steps to update the color settings for your subtitles:

1. **Select a subtitle.** Select any subtitle within the stream you want to work on.

2. **Open the Inspector.** Click the Inspector button in the toolbar *or* choose View > Show Inspector (⌘-⌥-I).

3. **Open the Color Settings tab.** It is the last of the three tabs in the Subtitle Inspector. The other two are General and Button.

4. **Choose Grayscale and Normal.** This book assumes that you develop all your subtitle overlay art using four colors of gray. Selection State only applies to buttons-over-video.

5. **Choose overlay colors.** The name next to each key color (Text, Outline 1, Outline 2, and Background) indicates the role of each color in your subtitles. To select a new text overlay color, use the black (Text) key pop-up and choose from the 16 available colors.

If you can't find the color you need from the existing 16 hues, click Edit Palette, and use the system color picker to choose a new shade. Chapter 3 discusses the Edit Palette feature in detail.

Exploring Other Subtitle Features

The Subtitle Inspector's General tab (see Figure 8.7) offers many useful features for your subtitling tasks. Here's an overview of those features—and how you can use them in your projects.

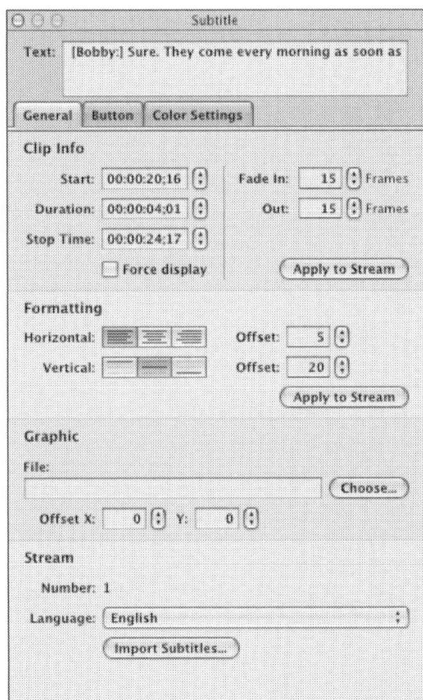

Figure 8.7 The Subtitle Inspector's General tab allows you to configure your subtitle clips and streams, offering a diverse set of features.

Subtitle Text In the Text field you can directly edit the subtitle text without using the Viewer. You might want to paste directly into this field to avoid the lag times that can occur when you type directly into DVD Studio Pro 2.

Start and Duration Times Avoid the hassles of direct manipulation by editing the Start and Duration fields. These fields let you set times using frame-accurate precision.

Force Display Viewers normally turn subtitles on and off by clicking the subtitle button on their DVD remote. When you want to bypass your viewer's subtitle settings and force a subtitle clip to display, check Force Display.

The Force Display feature affects only subtitles in the currently selected subtitle stream. If the viewer is watching Subtitle Stream 2 (S2), the Force Displays in S1 have no effect.

Subtitle Fades Adjust the Fade In and Out times to dissolve your subtitle clips in and out. The fields indicate the number of frames to apply the fade. Click Apply To Stream to apply these fade settings to all the clips in your stream. DVD Studio Pro 2 uses, at most, 16 levels to display subtitles, so plan accordingly.

You can't add fades to subtitles that work as buttons over video.

Alignment The Horizontal and Vertical formatting boxes let you align your subtitle text with the text safe zone. Click any of the six boxes, choosing from left, center, and right horizontal alignment and top, center, and bottom vertical alignment. The Offset boxes let you nudge the alignment away from these settings pixel by pixel. Use positive offsets to move your subtitles right and down. Use negative offsets for left and up. Click Apply To Stream to apply the alignment and offset settings to the entire subtitle stream.

Overlays You can overlay subtitle clips with an image by clicking the Choose button and selecting a four-color picture from disk. This procedure is described in "Adding Overlay Graphics to Text Subtitles," earlier in this chapter.

Language Use the Language pop-up to select a language for the stream in which your subtitle clip appears.

Subtitle languages are distinct from those enumerated in the Outline tab. You can select any language for your subtitles, regardless of whether the language appears in the Outline tab. Viewers cycle through subtitle streams by clicking the Subtitle button on their remote control.

Import Subtitles Clicking the Import Subtitles button in the Subtitle Inspector loads a new set of subtitles for the currently selected stream. This feature entirely overwrites the existing subtitles in the stream.

You can set defaults for several subtitle features via preferences windows in DVD Studio Pro 2 (choose DVD Studio Pro > Preferences or press ⌘-,). There are subtitle options in the General (see Figure 8.8), Text (see Figure 8.9), and Colors (see Figure 8.10) preferences windows.

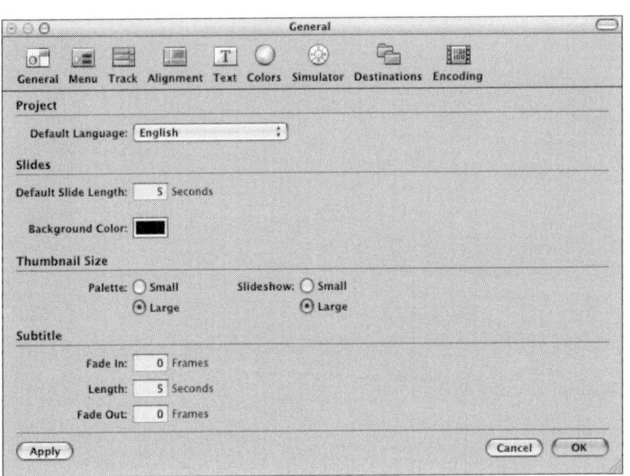

Figure 8.8 Use the General preferences window to set the default length of your subtitles as well as the default fade times. Adjust the length in seconds and the fade-in and fade-out times in frames.

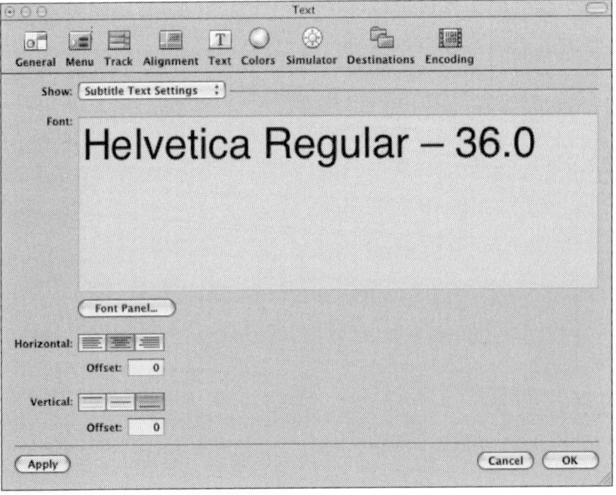

Figure 8.9 Use the Text preferences window to set the default text and alignment for your subtitles. Choose Subtitle Text Settings from the Show pop-up. Click Font Panel to change the default font face and size. Click the Horizontal and Vertical alignment buttons to set how subtitles align with title safe. Use the Offset fields to add pixel offsets to the alignment to nudge the default subtitle positions. Other settings available from the Show menu include Menu Button Defaults and Menu Text Defaults.

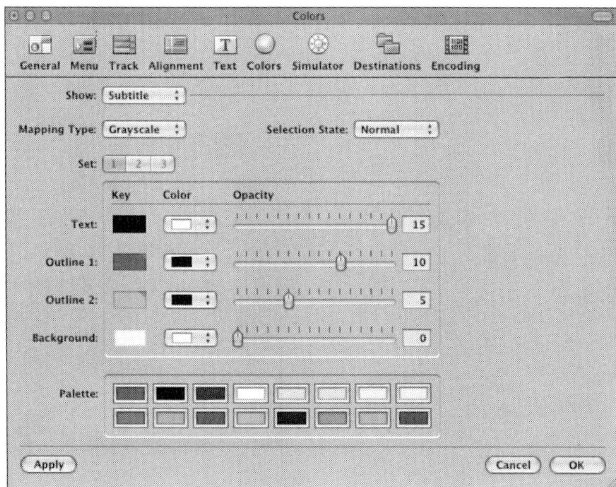

Figure 8.10 Choose Subtitle from the Show pop-up in the Colors preferences window to set the default color mappings for your subtitles. Use the color pop-ups and opacity sliders to choose new defaults.

Other Things to Know About Subtitles

Here are a few other points to keep in mind when working with subtitles:

- Viewers can't switch streams mid-subtitle. Each subtitle must finish displaying before your viewer can switch to a new subtitle or turn subtitle display on or off.

- Subtitles won't display mid-subtitle. When your viewer switches from S1, say, to S2, they must wait for a new subtitle to begin. If S2 contains a subtitle clip in progress, a visible subtitle won't appear until the start of S2's next subtitle clip.

- Subtitles can't cross chapter markers. Add your markers first, before adding subtitles. At build, DVD Studio Pro 2 automatically clips subtitles to marker boundaries. Unfortunately, in early releases of DVD Studio Pro 2, this clipping is not always reflected in the Simulator. The Simulator may incorrectly play subtitles that cross markers.

- 16:9 subtitles will stretch. All subtitles appear normally when played back on a 4:3 display but will stretch on 16:9 monitors. Apple suggests that you choose narrow fonts when working with subtitles placed over 16:9 tracks. To make graphic overlays work correctly with 16:9 tracks, make sure to squeeze them anamorphically before importing into DVD Studio Pro 2. They'll stretch vertically when played back on 4:3 displays.

- When there's a language mismatch between the A1 and S1 streams, some DVD players automatically show subtitles by default. They assume you're using subtitles to translate from one language to another. This automatic display can provide exactly the functionality intended. When you want to leave subtitle display in the hands of the viewer, try to match the languages in A1 and S1.

Adding Buttons Over Video

DVD interactions shouldn't be limited to menus. You can expand the way your DVDs connect with your viewers by adding buttons over video. DVD Studio Pro 2 makes it simple to configure your subtitle streams to add interactive elements. Follow these steps:

1. **Add a marker.** Move the playhead to the point where you want to add the button over video. Press **M**. DVD Studio Pro 2 adds a new chapter marker at the nearest GOP boundary.

You can also change the marker type in the Track Editor. Ctrl-click(right-click) the marker, and choose Button Highlight Marker from the pop-up.

2. **Change the marker type.** Select your new marker and open the Marker Inspector (⌘-⌥-I). Check Button Highlight in the General tab. DVD Studio Pro 2 updates your marker, changing the color to half purple and half orange.

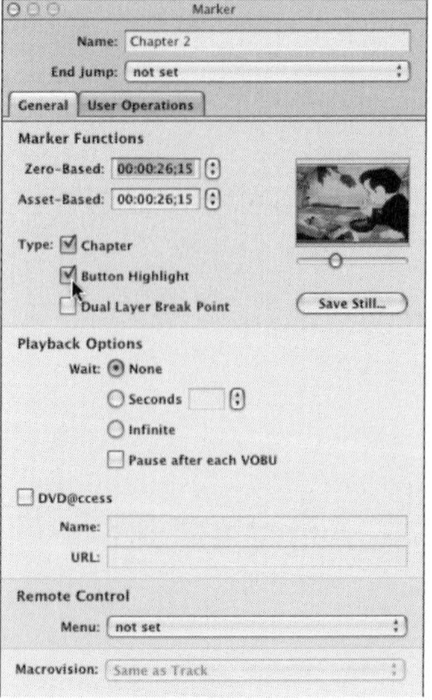

3. **Add another marker.** Subtitle buttons must be bounded on both sides by markers. Move the playhead to the position where your button display ends. Press **M**. A second chapter marker appears.

4. **Create the subtitle.** Double-click in the subtitle stream (S1) between the two markers. DVD Studio Pro 2 creates a new subtitle clip that fits precisely between the markers. The clip is selected, and a text-editing cursor appears in the Viewer.

5. **Edit the subtitle contents.** Use the Subtitle Inspector (⌘-⌥-I) to set the text or graphics for this subtitle button or directly edit the text within the Viewer.

6. **Draw a button.** Drag within the Viewer background to create your new button.

At times, early releases of DVD Studio Pro 2 simply refuse to add buttons to the Viewer. When this happens, delete the new subtitle and return to step 4.

You can add more than one button at a time to your subtitle overlays, just as you can use more than one button with your menu overlays.

7. **Set the selected and activated highlight colors.** Return to the Subtitle Inspector, and open the Color Settings tab. Provide a bright, high-contrast color (such as yellow or green) for your selected or activated text.

Unlike regular subtitles, button subtitles allow you to set highlight colors for Selected and Activated states as well as Normal.

8. **Link your button.** In the Subtitle Inspector, open the Button tab. Use the Target pop-up to link your button to a menu, track, story, slideshow, or script.

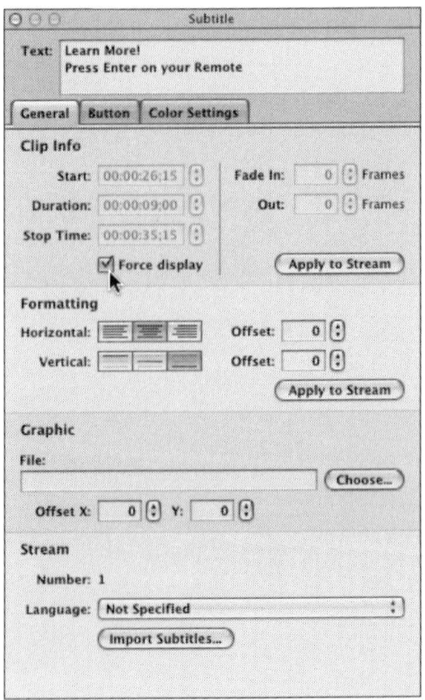

9. **Check Force Display.** Open the General tab in the Subtitle Inspector, and check Force Display. This step ensures that your viewers will see the button whether subtitles are enabled or not.

A few key points of interest:

Number of Buttons You can add as many as 36 buttons per subtitle for 4:3 display, as many as 18 buttons for 16:9 Pan Scan and 16:9 Letterbox, and as many as 12 buttons for 16:9 Pan Scan & Letterbox mode.

Button Navigation Button navigation works just like it does in menus. Use the Remote section in the Subtitle Inspector to set the way your buttons react to up, down, right, and left clicks from your viewer's remote.

Text and Overlays With subtitles, you can create text-only buttons, image-only buttons, or a combination of the two. Use the Subtitle Inspector to set the text and image file.

Button Targets You can link to the same kinds of targets with subtitle buttons as with any other DVD Studio Pro 2 element. Choose from menus, tracks, stories, slideshows, and scripts.

16:9 Button Highlights and 4:3 Displays Unfortunately, overlay highlights don't compensate when you move between 16:9 and 4:3 displays. As a rule, create separate graphics for each kind of display, and add each to a separate subtitle stream. Use scripting to choose which stream to display. When in doubt, stick to text buttons and oversize your button areas.

Testing Subtitles

You can test subtitled tracks by using the Viewer, the Simulator, and the Apple DVD Player. Of these three, only the DVD Player provides reliable feedback, particularly on older G4 computers. Unfortunately, it's also the tool that takes the most time to load and use. When you can, test your work with the Viewer and the Simulator. When you can't, rely on the Apple DVD Player. It will show the real behavior of your subtitles.

The Viewer

You must enable subtitle streams before you can see them in the Viewer. Activate the stream by clicking the Stream Select control—it's to the left of the stream name—and then move the playhead within the track to see the subtitles.

The Simulator

Before you've fully built a project, it's easier to simulate a track than the project as a whole. Ctrl-click(right-click) within the track and choose Simulate From Track. Test your subtitles by choosing a stream from the Subtitle Select pop-up. Make sure to check View to enable subtitle playback.

The Apple DVD Player

The Apple DVD Player lets you emulate a DVD from the project files you build. Set your disc's First Play to the track you want to test, and build your project to disk. Launch DVD Player and open the VIDEO_TS folder (⌘-O) you just built. Click Play to start playback.

Locate the small three-dot ellipsis at the bottom of the virtual player remote control. Click it to display the advanced remote buttons. The Subtitle button, at the bottom left, cycles through each of the possible subtitle settings: Subtitles Off, Subtitle Stream 1, and so on. The player will note the language whenever you've assigned one to a subtitle stream.

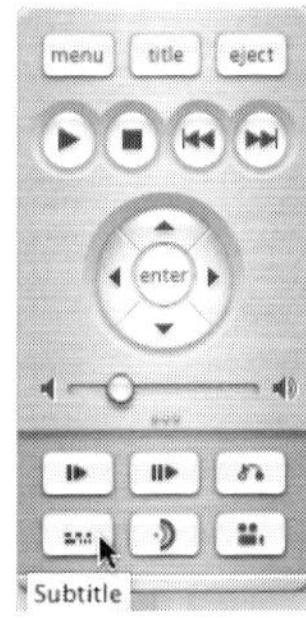

Solution: Build an Animated Subtitle Sequence

 Small, quick changes in overlays can create simple animated effects. Follow these steps to build a simple subtitle animation. As usual, you can find all the files for this project in this chapter's folder on the companion DVD. The animation frames were created in Photoshop, using simple black-on-white RGB images.

> Each new DVD Studio Pro 2 project contains a default track (Track 1). The solutions in this chapter use this ready-to-use project element.

1. **Build your track**. Add audio and video to Track 1 to build the base content of your track. For this project, add Crisp.m2v to V1. (It's in this chapter's folder on the companion DVD.) With title matching, DVD Studio Pro 2 automatically adds Crisp.wav to A1.

2. **Add the first animation image**. Drag the first butterfly (Fly1.psd) onto S1. Select it and open the Subtitle Inspector. Set Start Time to 00:00:15;00, set Duration to 00:00:00;03, and check Force Display. The subtitle resizes and moves into place. Adjust the track zoom so you can see the new subtitle.

3. **Add more animation images**. Drag the second butterfly (Fly2.psd) onto S1. In the Inspector, set Start Time to 00:00:15;03, set Duration to 00:00:00;03, and check Force Display. Repeat for the remaining images, advancing the start time by 3 frames each time. This animation uses 4 pictures.

4. **Duplicate each image**. Zoom in closely, until you can easily select each subtitle clip. Select the first of the four clips. ⌥-drag it just a little to the right. A copy of the clip appears to the right of the fourth clip, before the cursor even moves off the original clips. Release the mouse and let the clip snap into place.

5. **Repeat.** ⌥-drag the second clip to the right. Again, a copy appears. Let it snap into place. Repeat this process, advancing one clip at a time until you've created several copies of all four subtitles in sequence. This is a lot easier to do than it may first appear. The bright yellow selection always shows which clip was last copied.

6. **Set your overlay colors.** Select one of the subtitle clips, and open the Subtitle Inspector. Click the Color Settings tab, and set the Text key to White/15. You can leave the other settings as is (Outline 1 Black/10; Outline 2 Black/5; and Background Black/0), or you can anti-alias your art by choosing white instead of black. Click Apply To Stream to use these settings for every subtitle in your stream.

7. **Build your project.** Ctrl-click(right-click) the disc in the Outline tab. Choose First Play > Tracks And Stories > Track 1 > [Track]. Click Build, and build your project to disk.

8. **Emulate.** Launch Apple DVD Player. Choose File > Open Video_TS Folder (⌘-O). Navigate to the VIDEO_TS folder you just built, select it, and click Choose. Click

Play and watch your movie. At second 15, your butterfly appears. (Recall you set Force Display for each subtitle clip.) The butterfly flaps its wing for a second or two (depending on how many copies you made of the animation images) and then disappears.

Solution: Add a Button to an Animation

In this project, you'll add a button to the end of the animation sequence you built in the previous solution. A short animation makes a great introduction for interactive elements.

1. **Add a new marker.** Select the last subtitle clip in your animation sequence. Copy the end time from the Clip End field at the top right of your Track Editor. Paste it into the Playhead Time field, and click the stopwatch. The playhead jumps to the end of your clip. Type **M** to add a marker. A marker will appear near (not necessarily on) the playhead.

2. **Edit the clips.** Adjust your animation clips so the last clip end coincides with your new marker. You may need to lengthen the last clip or remove a clip or two to achieve this.

3. **Change the marker type.** Select your new chapter marker, and open the Marker Inspector. Check both Chapter and Button Highlight. The marker updates, becoming half purple and half orange.

4. **Add another marker.** Move the playhead to the right, leaving about 8 seconds after your new marker. Type **M** to add a second marker. Adjust the track zoom so you can see both markers at once.

5. **Add the subtitle and assign the art.** Double-click between the markers. DVD Studio Pro 2 creates a new subtitle clip, snapping it precisely to the two markers. Select the new clip, open the Subtitle Inspector, and check Force Display. Locate the Graphic section, and click Choose. Navigate to FlyLast.psd in the Chapter 8 folder on the DVD. Select it and click Choose.

6. **Drag out a button.** Move the playhead onto the new clip so you can see the button art in the Viewer. Drag on the background of the Viewer to create a new button.

At times, DVD Studio Pro 2 simply refuses to add buttons to a button highlight subtitle clip. When this happens, delete the clip and repeat steps 5 and 6.

270

7. **Set the button highlight colors.** Return to the Subtitle Inspector, and open the Color Settings tab. Set the selected colors to Text: Yellow/15, Outline 1: White/10, Outline 2: White/5, and Background: Black/0. Set the activated colors to Text: Light Green/15, Outline 1: White/10, Outline 2: White/5, and Background: Black/0.

These colors are just suggestions. Use any color settings you like.

8. **Emulate.** Once again, build your project to disk and test it in the Apple DVD Player. Your new button won't actually do anything, but it will respond to the Enter key on the virtual remote.

If you like, create a second track and link your button to it. Use the files in "Crackle's Secret" on the companion DVD. For a nice loop, link Track 2 back to Tracks and Stories > Track 1 > Chapter 2.

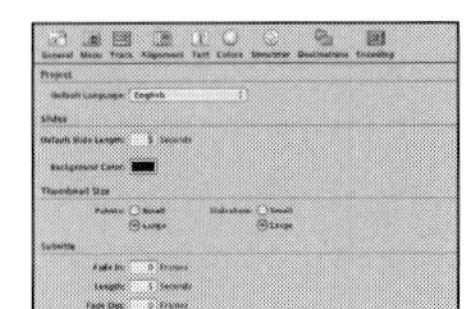

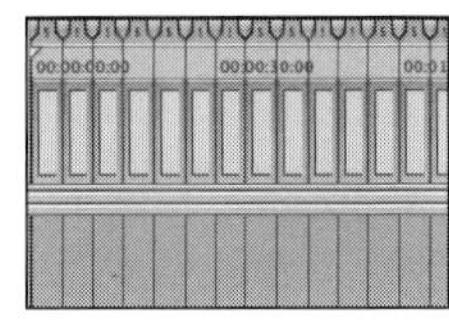

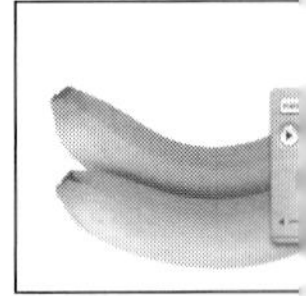

Building and Using Slideshows

DVD slideshows produce exactly what you might expect—a series of still image, optionally accompanied by audio. DVD Studio Pro 2 makes it simple to build and customize slideshows. You might add a single audio track for your entire show or customize each slide with sound. You can set the time of each slide or leave navigation control in your viewer's hands. In this chapter you'll learn what kinds of DVD slideshows you can—and cannot—build with DVD Studio Pro 2.

Chapter Contents

Slideshow Pros and Cons

Setting Slideshow Preferences

Understanding the Slideshow Tab

Managing Slides and Slideshows

Understanding How Pauses Work in Tracks

Solution: Create a Slideshow with Arrows

Solution: Create a 16:9 Slideshow

Solution: Create a Slideshow with Transitions

Solution: Create a Video "Slideshow"

Slideshow Pros and Cons

In Chapter 6, you learned how to add images to tracks and to produce a sequence of stills that play one after another. So why use slideshows? Why not just build tracks? The answer is that slideshows and the Slideshow Editor do more for you. Here are some reasons:

Slideshows provide the right tool. The Slideshow Editor helps you to control timing, ordering, and slide navigation; the Track Editor does not. The Slideshow Editor is designed to do one job and do it well.

Slideshows use audio intelligently. With tracks, audio plays no role in laying out the video stream. Sideshows use audio more sensibly. The Editor can adapt slide duration to match audio duration and provide audio looping as needed.

Slideshows have manual advance. Slideshows offer better ways to interact with still material. Viewers can watch the slideshow at their own pace, returning to previous slides or proceeding to new material as needed. It takes a lot of tedious work—adding markers and setting playback options—to achieve the same effect in the Track Editor.

That said, there are things that slideshows can't do. Sometimes tracks do provide the best solution. Here is a list of common slideshow limitations, for which tracks—not slideshows—offer a better answer:

Slideshows don't transition. If you're looking for fancy PowerPoint-style slide transitions, DVD Studio Pro 2 won't oblige; slideshows present one slide after another without custom visual wipes. Use video-editing software, such as Final Cut or iMovie, to add slide transitions and then import as a track.

You cannot add more than 99 slides to a show. If you want to move beyond this limit, you'll have to add your stills to a track or create additional slideshows.

 Tracks have limits too. You cannot add more than 99 chapters per track—an important consideration if you want to include pauses in your tracks.

Slideshows don't do 16:9. All DVD Studio Pro 2 slideshows use a 4:3 aspect ratio. If you want to create a 16:9 slideshow out of anamorphic stills, you'll have to use a track.

Slideshows don't support subtitles or languages. When you want to add language support or subtitles to your slideshows, you must convert them to tracks.

Slideshows don't intermingle video with stills. Only tracks provide the support you need for combining these two asset types.

Setting Slideshow Preferences

Before you start building slideshows, you might want to configure a few defaults. The General dialog (choose DVD Studio Pro > Preferences, or press ⌘-,), shown in Figure 9.1, allows you to set the following useful slideshow properties:

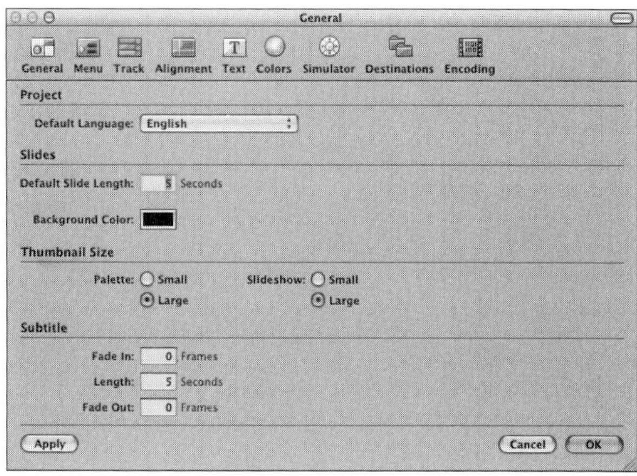

Figure 9.1 The General dialog offers several default settings for your project. Slideshow-related preferences include default slide length, background color, and thumbnail size.

Default Slide Length Enter a default still duration in seconds. This default applies to images you add to both slideshows and tracks.

Background Color Sometimes you import stills with odd aspect ratios. DVD Studio Pro 2 pads these with the default background color, fitting them to the proper 4:3 display. (The geometry of the original image determines whether the padding uses horizontal or vertical bars.)

Thumbnail Size Set the slideshow thumbnail viewing size by choosing Small or Large. Small thumbnails fit more slides into the visible workspace of the Slideshow Editor. Large thumbnails offer greater visual detail for each slide listing.

Understanding the Slideshow Tab

The Slideshow Editor, shown in Figure 9.2, provides an interface that lets you develop, modify, and review DVD Studio Pro 2 slideshow presentations. Features of the Slideshow tab include the following:

View Pop-up (A) Select the slideshow you want to work on from this pop-up.

Convert To Track Button (B) Click to transform the slideshow into an ordinary track. You can undo the transformation, but you can't, as a rule, convert tracks into slideshows.

Slideshow/Audio Duration Controls (C) Choose whether to fit the slideshow duration to the length of the audio or to use the intrinsic slide lengths. Check Loop Audio to provide a continuous soundtrack throughout the slideshow, no matter its length.

Figure 9.2 The Slideshow Editor helps you create and control your slideshow presentations. View pop-up Ⓐ, Convert To Track button Ⓑ, Slideshow/Audio Duration controls (overall) Ⓒ, Audio Well Ⓓ, Slide Duration control Ⓔ, Manual Advance check box Ⓕ, Slide list Ⓖ.

Audio Well (D) Drag an audio file to this well to assign it as the background audio for the entire slideshow. (Drag the audio from the well to clear it.)

Slide Duration (E) Choose one of the predefined times (1, 3, 5, or 10 seconds) to change the duration for the currently selected slide(s).

Manual Advance (F) Check this box to pause after displaying the selected slide(s) until the viewer clicks the Next or Previous button on the remote control.

Slide List (G) The central portion of the Editor contains a list of slides. Each line of this list includes the slide number, a thumbnail, source filename, the audio attached to the slide (if any), the starting time for the slide, its duration, and whether the slide uses manual advance ("pause").

Managing Slides and Slideshows

Slideshows are like menus and tracks in that they are named elements of your DVD project. Like these elements, you can add them to your project by using the Outline tab and then using an Editor to customize them, in this case the Slideshow Editor. This section presents the basic slideshow operations.

Slideshow Management

You can create, manage, and test your slideshows in DVD Studio Pro 2 in many ways. Use these techniques to work with slideshows at their highest level, as elements of the project.

Adding Slideshows

To create a new, blank slideshow, choose one of the following options:

- Click Add Slideshow in the toolbar.
- Ctrl-click(right-click) in the Outline tab and choose Add > Slideshow.
- Choose Project > Add To Project > Slideshow (⌘-K).
  You can also use the following shortcuts to begin creating a slideshow:
- When you drag images to the Slideshows folder in the Outline tab, DVD Studio Pro 2 creates a new slideshow from those images. You can drag a selection of images or an entire folder.
- When you drag images to the Menu Editor, a drop palette appears. Choose Create Button And Slideshow to create a slideshow from your pictures and a button that links to them.

  "Adding Slides" later in this section shows how to add content to your new slideshow.

Removing Slideshows

To remove a slideshow from your project, select it from the Outline tab and choose Edit > Delete (or press the Delete key).

Renaming Slideshows

To change a slideshow's name, select it in the Outline tab and click its name again. A text field lets you edit its name. (Alternatively, open the Slideshow Inspector and edit the Name field.)

Editing Slideshows

To begin editing a slideshow's content, double-click the slideshow in the Outline tab, or open the Slideshow Editor and select a slideshow from the View pop-up. See "Managing Slides" for the operations you can perform on individual slides within a slideshow once it's open for editing.

Setting Options

Like tracks, you can add end jumps to your slideshows, instructing the DVD to play another asset when your slideshow completes. To set the jump, select the slideshow in the Outline tab. Open the Slideshow Inspector, and use the End Jump pop-up to set your target.

Other options in the Inspector allow you to set a pre-script and connect the Menu, Track, Audio, Chapter, and Subtitle buttons on your viewer's remote to targets within the project.

Converting Slideshows to Tracks

"Slideshow Pros and Cons," earlier in this chapter, summarized some of the reasons you might need to convert a slideshow to a track. Click the Convert To Track button in the Slideshow Editor to convert your slideshow into a track. Alternatively, select a slideshow in the Outline tab and choose Project > Slideshow > Convert To Track.

The new track uses the same name as the original slideshow. A slideshow called, for example, Slideshow 2, becomes a new track called Slideshow 2.

Unfortunately, if you already have a track that consists of a series of stills, you cannot convert it into a slideshow.

If you're just playing around or experimenting, you might want to convert a copy of your slideshow to a track, rather than convert the original.

Testing Slideshows

You can test slideshows using the Viewer, the Simulator, and Apple DVD Player:

- To view, select a slide, open the Viewer, and click Play. Viewing allows you to watch and listen to project content.

- To simulate, Ctrl-click(right-click) the slideshow (in the Outline tab), or Ctrl-click(right-click) the background of the Slideshow Editor and choose Simulate. Simulation lets you test the way your project elements behave on a simulated DVD player using a simulated remote control.

- To emulate, set the slideshow as your disc's First Play. Build the project to disc, open the Video_TS folder (⌘-O) in DVD Player, and click Play. Emulation allows you to use the DVD-playing software on your computer to play DVD content from folders on your hard drive rather than from a burnt or pressed DVD.

Managing Slides

The Slideshow Editor and Slide Inspector let you author and customize your slide presentations; in other words, they let you control the contents of your slideshows. In addition to the basic operations of adding, deleting, selecting, and viewing slides, you can reorder their sequence or change a slide's duration, and you can set manual advance and add DVD @ccess points.

Adding Slides

To populate your slideshow, drag stills to the Slide list from the Assets tab or the Finder. In the slideshow, move the dragged cursor to where you want to add the new images. A black line indicates the position of the new slides during the drag. Release the mouse to add the new slides to that position.

DVD Studio Pro 2 offers a particularly handy feature for adding slides: It lets you drag folders from the Finder. When you drop the folder onto the slideshow, the program loads the image files found inside.

Selecting Slides

In DVD Studio Pro 2, you can create slide selections in the following ways:

- Click a slide to select it.
- Shift-click to select a continuous range of slides.
- ⌘-click to select nonadjacent slides.

Removing Slides

To remove items from your slideshow, select one or more slides, and choose Edit > Delete (or click the Delete key). Choose Edit > Undo (⌘-Z) to restore just-deleted slides.

Viewing Slides

When you double-click a slide, the Viewer *should* open and display your slide. In practice (at least in early versions of DVD Studio Pro 2), the Viewer may display your slide or may not display anything at all.

For more consistent behavior, open the Viewer before you select a slide to display. Click Play or press the spacebar to hear the audio associated with the selected slide.

Reordering Slides

After adding slides, you might want to reorder them. Select one or more slides, and drag them to a new position in the Slide list. The black line shows where the slides will appear when you release the mouse.

Changing Slide Duration

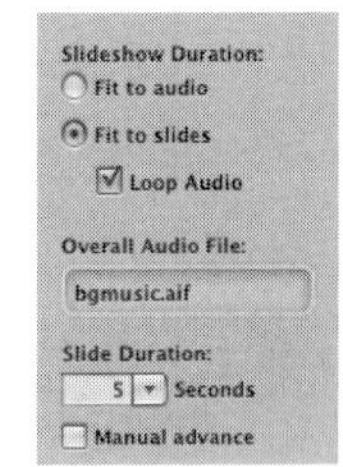

To change timing, select a slide, double-click the time in the Duration column, edit the duration, and press Return. Alternatively, select a slide or slides and choose a duration from the Slide Duration control or enter a value in the Slide Duration text box. The change applies to all selected slides.

Setting Manual Advance

Manual advance places playback control in the hands of your viewer. To add this feature, select a slide or slides, and check Manual Advance. This sets the Pause feature for the set of selected slides. Alternatively, check each Pause box.

To set manual advance for the entire show, use Select All (choose Edit > Select All or press ⌘-A) to select the entire collection of slides, and then check Manual Advance.

Viewers must press the Next or Previous chapter button on the remote control to manually advance through a slideshow. The regular arrow buttons on the remote won't work; these remote buttons work only for selecting menu items on the TV screen. If you want your viewers to use arrows to advance to the next and previous slides, you must convert the slideshow to a track and add auto-activating menu items (Next Slide and Previous Slide) to each slide. (Auto-activating menu buttons are discussed further in Chapter 11.)

Adding DVD @ccess to a slide

Slide-based DVD @ccess points work just like the marker-based ones discussed in Chapter 7. Select a slide, open the Slide Inspector, check the DVD @ccess box, and add a URL. (The Name field is optional, used strictly for your own reference).

When enabled, this feature works during computer-based playback, tasking your Internet browser to load the URL as the slide displays.

 DVD @ccess is discussed further in Chapter 11.

Audio and Slideshows

Slideshow sounds augment slide visuals, providing an audio component for your presentations. DVD Studio Pro 2 offers a couple of ways to use sound: with a single background track or individual audio clips.

Adding a Background Audio Track

Drag a sound file into the Audio Well to assign it to the entire slideshow as an overall background. If the well is already occupied, the new file replaces the old one. The Slideshow Duration controls are enabled only when the well is full.

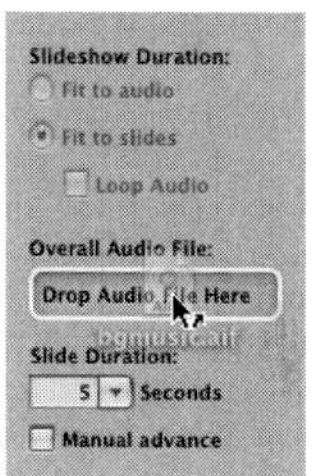

Removing Background Audio Tracks

You can easily detect an empty Audio Well. It reads Drop Audio File Here. Filled wells display filenames instead. To remove background audio, drag out from the well. DVD Studio Pro 2 creates a puff-of-smoke animation, indicating a newly cleared well. Alternatively, Ctrl-click(right-click) the well and choose Remove from the pop-up.

Fitting Audio

You can set Slideshow Duration options whenever you've assigned an overall background audio file.

- Choose Fit To Audio to set each slide's duration to an equal portion of your audio track.

- Choose Fit To Slides to use the individual times set in the Duration column.

    When working with Fit To Slides, keep the following in mind. If the audio ends first, the slideshow finishes in silence. If the slideshow ends first, the last slide remains onscreen until the audio finishes.

    When you want your music to continue playing throughout the slideshow, no matter how long it takes for the viewer to finish watching, consider looping your audio. This option appears only when the background track is Fit To Slides.

Adding Audio to Individual Slides

To add sounds to slides, you'll need to drag any sound (if one exists) out from the Audio Well. Then drag a sound file from the Assets tab or from the Finder onto the Audio column of any slide. A black outline appears around the slide listing, showing where the sound will appear.

OS X contains a number of built-in sounds in /System/Library/Sounds. These sounds, such as Morse and Tink, can add a pleasant but subtle touch to your DVD slideshow presentations.

Things to Know About Slideshows

Here are a few important facts you need to know about creating and using slideshows:

You can't duplicate slides. You can't copy slides the way you copy other project elements. When you want two copies of a slide to appear in your slideshow, add the slide twice.

There are no built-in arrows. Unlike iDVD, DVD Studio Pro 2 does not offer prebuilt arrow navigation menu buttons for slideshows. In iDVD, you can easily add special buttons with arrows on them by checking a box in iDVD's Slideshow Editor. These buttons let your audience navigate by selecting the onscreen arrows. When you build a slideshow with arrow buttons in iDVD, they don't import into DVD Studio Pro 2 with your project. If you miss the look of iDVD arrows, edit your artwork with arrows, add helpful text such as "Click Next to continue…," or add your own auto-activation buttons to each slide—unfortunately, a time-consuming and tedious process.

Avoid too-quick slides. Set each slide's duration to at least 12 frames (NTSC) or 10 frames (PAL). Some DVD players don't handle quick-changing slideshows in a graceful manner.

The final slide may stick. Where possible, don't add manual advance to your final slide. Many DVD players won't react to the Next button, leaving your viewer in indefinite limbo. For better compatibility and playback, either use the Connections tab to set the slideshow's Next Jump (see Chapter 7) or duplicate the last slide and leave the Pause box unchecked. (If you do duplicate the slide, keep it short. Limit the duration to a second or so.)

Tracks can't become slideshows. You can't convert tracks into slideshows, but you can undo your conversion of a slideshow into a track.

Tracks retain settings. When you convert slideshows to a track, the track retains each slide duration and pause setting.

Understanding How Pauses Work in Tracks

When you convert slideshows into tracks, you create a series of stills punctuated by chapter markers (see Figure 9.3). Each chapter marker holds the key to the slideshow pause: it contains a playback control that pauses indefinitely after playing the chapter. This pause allows the viewer time to navigate using the Previous and Next chapter buttons on their remote.

Figure 9.3 A slideshow converted to a track appears as a series of still images and chapter markers. The chapters control the navigation, allowing the converted track to pause after each slide.

Follow these steps to add a pause to any chapter in your DVD project:

1. **Select a chapter marker.** Choose the chapter marker at the start of the cell you want to pause.

2. **Open the Marker Inspector.** Press ⌘-⌥-I.

3. **Locate the Playback controls.** They appear in the General tab, about halfway down the pane, as shown in Figure 9.4. Wait options include no waiting (None), waiting for a certain number of seconds (Seconds), and an indefinite pause (Infinite).

4. **Click Infinite.** This instructs the DVD to pause after playing the chapter and wait for the viewer to use the remote.

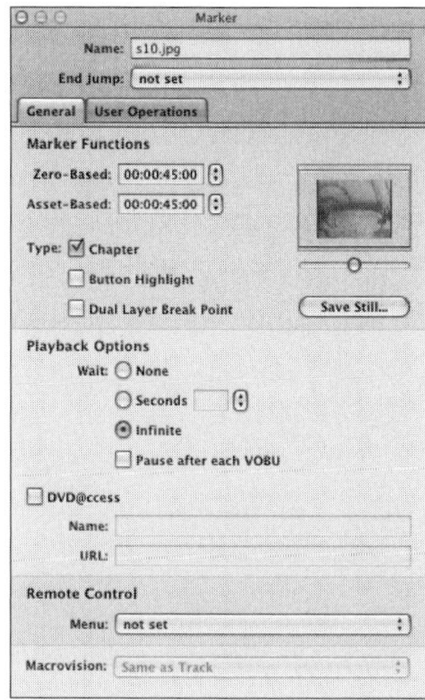

Figure 9.4 Playback options allow you to create an indefinite pause after playing each chapter. Viewers can use the Next and Previous chapter buttons to navigate beyond this pause, creating a slideshow effect.

You can use this method to create a kind of pseudo-slideshow with moving footage, in which you add a pause after each video segment in a track. Adding subtitles or buttons can prompt the viewer to use the remote for navigation.

Paused presentations created in this manner demonstrate the same playback problems as paused slideshows. Always add a nonpaused segment to the end of a track to allow the track to finish playing.

Analyzing Tracks: Chapters, Cells, and VOBUs

As you saw in Chapter 7, chapter markers (all markers, for that matter) divide tracks into segments called cells. The chapter marker for each track cell appears at the beginning of its segment, not at the end. If you want to jump to another element after playing a chapter, you must update the marker found at the start of that chapter. The chapter will play through to its end (the chapter's "out point") and then perform the jump. Select the starting marker, and then use the Inspector or Connections window to set the target for the jump. This explains why each new track contains a Chapter 1 marker at the start. You can rename the marker, but you can't delete it. Each track must contain at least one cell.

VOBU Slideshows

DVD Studio Pro 2 actually offers two ways to pause in tracks: after each chapter and after each video object unit (VOBU). The Pause After Each VOBU check box appears below the Wait radio buttons in the Inspector (see Figure 9.4 earlier in this chapter).

Track cells are composed of one or more VOBUs, a component of DVD playback. Still-image VOBUs last for the duration of the still. The pause after each VOBU option provides another way to create DVD slideshows, stopping at the end of each still.

Pause After Each VOBU allows you to create slideshows with hundreds of slides per show. This feature lets you advance manually through each slide, each one a VOBU. Normal slideshows, which use chapter markers to control navigation, are limited to 99 slides. Pause After Each VOBU works past this limitation, using as many stills as desired.

Video VOBUs, which last a second or less, correspond to the I-frames found in the MPEG-2 video stream. Typically, they occur about twice a second.

You can prepare a Pause After Each VOBU slideshow in a nonlinear editor, such as Final Cut, or by dragging your stills onto the V1 stream in DVD Studio Pro 2's Track Editor.

Solution: Create a Slideshow with Arrows

At times, you might want to add graphic arrows to your slideshows to provide visual feedback to your viewers, a la iDVD. At the same time, you might not want to alter your original artwork. Overlays provide a simple solution. Follow these steps to add overlay subtitles to your slideshows.

1. **Create a slideshow.** Locate the Commo Slides 4x3 folder on the companion DVD. Drag the folder onto the Slideshows folder in the Outline tab. This creates a new slideshow, Slideshow 1, using the default time of 5 seconds per slide.

2. **Set Manual Advance.** Double-click Slideshow 1 to open the Slideshow Editor. Select all the slides in the slideshow (⌘-A), and then check Manual Advance to set the Pause option for each slide in your show.

> You might want to either uncheck the Pause box for the final slide in your show or add a second copy of that slide without a pause to avoid DVD player playback issues. 

3. **Click Convert To Track.** This converts your slideshow to a new track, named Slideshow 1. The Track Editor opens if it is not already visible and displays your new track.

4. **Add the arrows.** Ctrl-click(right-click) within S1, the first subtitle track. Choose Import Subtitle File, navigate to arrowsubs.txt (it's in the Arrow Overlays folder), select it, and click Choose. DVD Studio Pro 2 loads the file and creates a series of arrow subtitles for your track.

> The arrowsubs.txt file, which was created by hand, contains a list of subtitles at 5-second intervals that load the arrow graphics. The file also contains a line that sets the Force Display attribute for all the subtitles in the file. 

5. **Set the colors.** Choose any of your new subtitle clips. Open the Subtitle Inspector (⌘-⌥-I), and click the Color Settings tab. Set each overlay color to white, using opacities of 15, 10, 5, and 0 for the text, outline 1, outline 2, and background keys. Click Apply To Stream. This creates smooth anti-aliased arrows that stand out from the yellow ochre background used in this project.

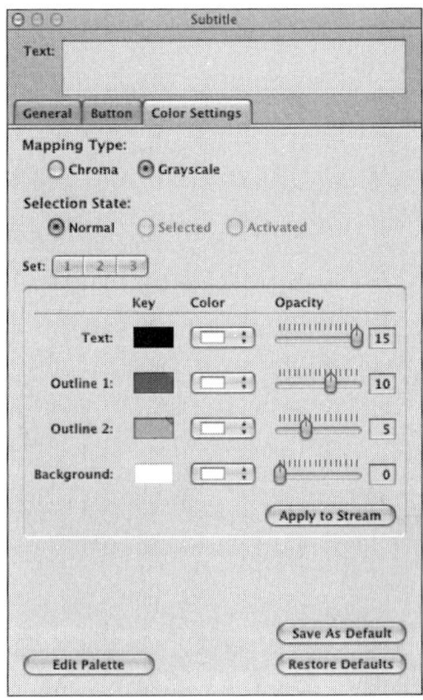

6. **Simulate.** Ctrl-click(right-click) within V1, and choose Simulate From Track. Test your slideshow. The arrows should appear whether or not the View Subtitles check box is checked.

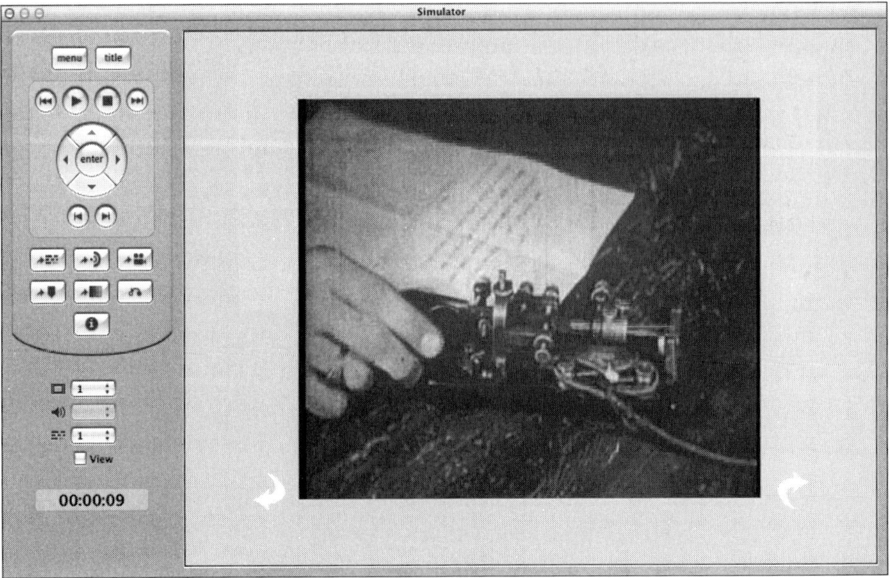

You might want to add interactive buttons to your arrow overlays for better playback on computers.

Solution: Create a 16:9 Slideshow

In this solution, you'll build a widescreen slideshow that plays back correctly on both standard and widescreen televisions.

1. **Build a slideshow.** Create a new project. Locate the Commo Slides 16x9 (Anamorphic) folder on the companion DVD and drag it onto the Slideshows folder in the Outline tab. DVD Studio Pro 2 adds a new slideshow (Slideshow 1) to the project using these stills. Double-click this slideshow to open the Slideshow Editor.

2. **Add a sound track.** Locate BGMusic.AIFF in the Audio folder for this chapter's support files on the companion DVD. Drag it to the Overall Audio File well and drop it there. Find the Slideshow Duration controls, and select Fit To Duration. Each slide duration updates to 00:00:06:10.

3. **Convert to a track.** Click Convert To Track. DVD Studio Pro 2 transforms the slideshow into a track and opens the Track Editor and Viewer. The new track appears in the Outline tab under the Tracks folder using the original name of Slideshow 1.

4. **Change the display mode.** In the Outline tab, select Slideshow 1 (it's a track) and open the Track Inspector (Command-Option-I). Locate the Mode pop-up and change it from 4:3 to 16:9 Letterbox. This tells DVD Studio Pro 2 to use widescreen presentations when possible and a letterbox-style display on 4:3 aspect televisions. The Viewer updates to reflect the new aspect ratio.

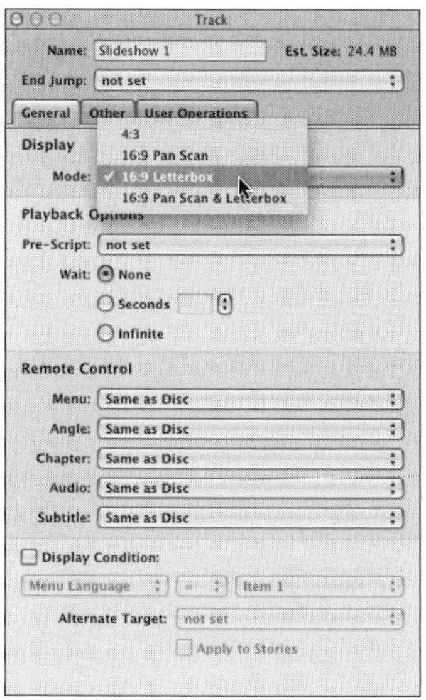

288

5. **Set Simulator preferences.** Choose DVD Studio Pro > Preferences (⌘-,) and click the Simulator icon to load the Simulator preferences. Locate the Aspect options at the bottom of the pane, choose 16:9, and click OK to close the Preferences pane. This allows you to test your project using a simulated widescreen display.

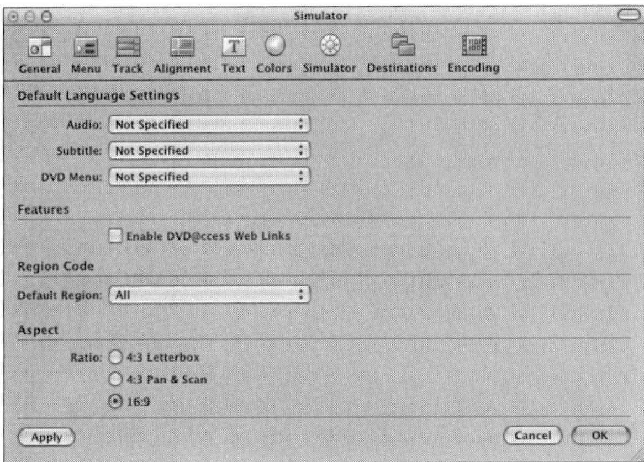

6. **Simulate.** Ctrl-click(right-click) in V1. Choose Simulate Trom Track, and test your 16:9 slideshow playback. It should look as shown here. Optionally, return to the Simulator preferences pane, set the aspect ratio to 4:3, and ensure that the slideshow plays back correctly using letterbox on 4:3 displays.

Solution: Create a Slideshow with Transitions

Although DVD Studio Pro 2 does not offer slideshow transitions, you can easily create them in a video-editing program such as Final Cut or iMovie. In these steps, you'll build a slideshow with transitions and discover their great weakness—returning from one slide to a previous slide.

1. **Build your movie.** Use your favorite video editor to create a series of slides with transitions between them. Add chapter markers before the start of each transition.

2. **Compress your movie.** Import your movie into Compressor and convert to MPEG-2. A compressed version of this fruit and transition slideshow (Fruits.m2v) appears on the companion DVD.

3. **Import into DVD Studio Pro 2.** Create a new project in DVD Studio Pro 2. Double-click Track 1 to select it, and open the Track Editor. Drag Fruits.m2v onto V1. The markers you created automatically load.

Unfortunately, when you drag video files onto tracks in the Outline tab, embedded markers do not automatically load. To add markers, open the track, Ctrl-click(right-click) the new video clip, and choose Add Embedded Markers.

4. **Set your pauses**. In the Track Editor timeline, select Chapter 1. Open the Marker Inspector, and set the playback wait to Infinite. Repeat for every chapter marker in your project: select each marker and set an infinite wait.

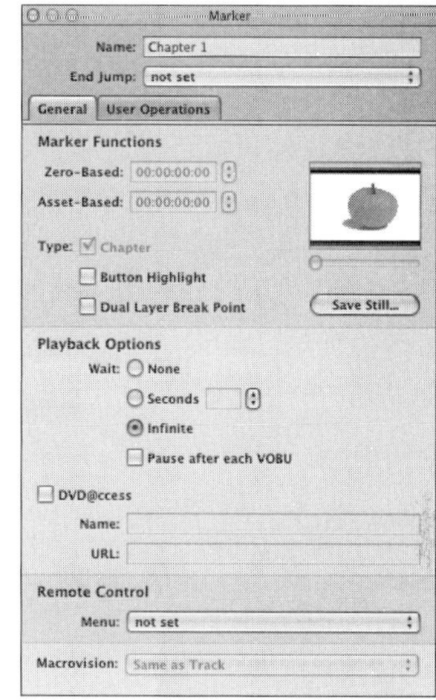

5. **Add a final marker**. Enter 00:00:33:00 in the Playhead text box, and then click the stopwatch to move the playhead to the time. Type **M** to add a new marker, Chapter 2. Do not set a pause for this marker.

6. **Set First Play**. In the Outline tab, select your disc. Open the Disc Inspector, and choose Tracks And Stories > Track 1 > [Track] to set First Play.

7. **Build.** Click Build in the toolbar to build your project to disc. Navigate to where you want to save your project, and click Choose. Wait as DVD Studio Pro 2 creates the VIDEO_TS and AUDIO_TS folders for your project.

8. **Emulate.** Launch Apple DVD Player. Choose File > Open VIDEO_TS Folder. Navigate to the folder you just created, select it, and click Choose. Click Play on your virtual remote control to display the apricot.

9. **Experiment.** Click Next Chapter. The apple slides into place. Click Next Chapter again, and the banana moves into position. Next, you discover the big drawback of this method of slideshow creation: click Previous Chapter. You might expect

the banana to slide back to the apple. It does not. Instead, the player returns to the previous chapter marker and shows the apricot sliding to the apple.

A clever use of scripting and extra footage can produce the more appealing and expected visual effect, but it takes a lot of work and goes beyond the scope of this chapter.

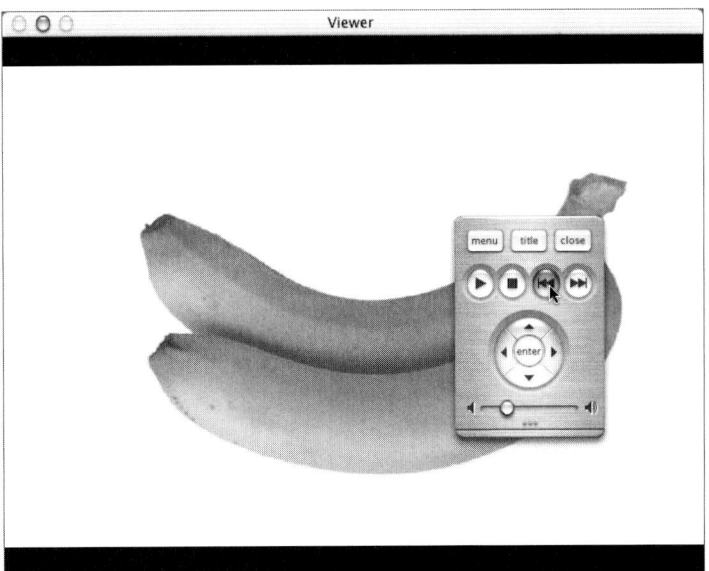

Solution: Create a Video "Slideshow"

The same foundation that produces slideshows in tracks can create a slideshow made up of videos rather than stills. In these steps, you'll create a slideshow out of a series of video segments.

1. **Start a new project in DVD Studio Pro 2.** The program automatically creates a fresh new track, Track 1, and adds it to your project. Select Track 1 from the Outline tab, and open the Track Editor.

2. **Add your movies to Track 1.** Add the videos from the Individual Fruit Movies folder on the companion DVD. (Unfortunately, you cannot add the folder. Instead, you must select the movies and drag them to the track.)

3. **Add markers.** Ctrl-click(right-click) each clip in Track 1 (except for your final clip), and select Add Marker To Clip End.

4. **Set marker properties.** Open the Inspector. Select each marker in your project, and set the marker type to Chapter Marker. Set the wait to Infinite for every marker except the final one.

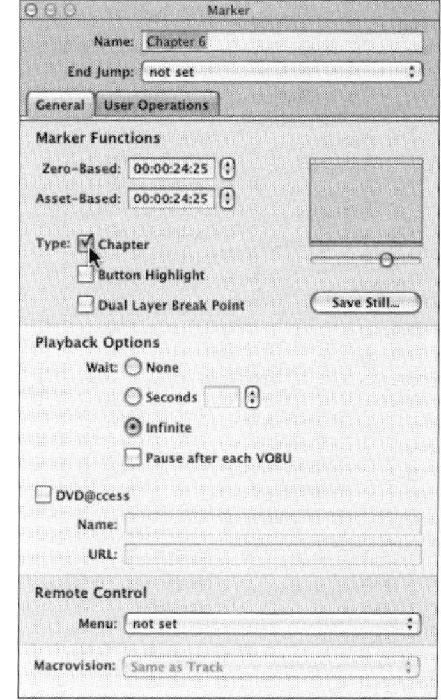

5. **Set First Play.** In the Outline tab, Ctrl-click (right-click) the disc. Choose First Play > Tracks And Stories > Track 1 > [Track].

6. **Build.** In the toolbar, click Build. Select a folder and click Choose. DVD Studio Pro 2 builds the VIDEO_TS and AUDIO_TS folders for your project.

7. **Emulate.** Launch Apple DVD Player. Choose File > Open VIDEO_TS Folder (⌘-O). Navigate to the VIDEO_TS folder you just built, and select it. Click Choose. On the simulated remote, click Play. Click the Next Chapter and Previous Chapter buttons to navigate through your video slideshow.

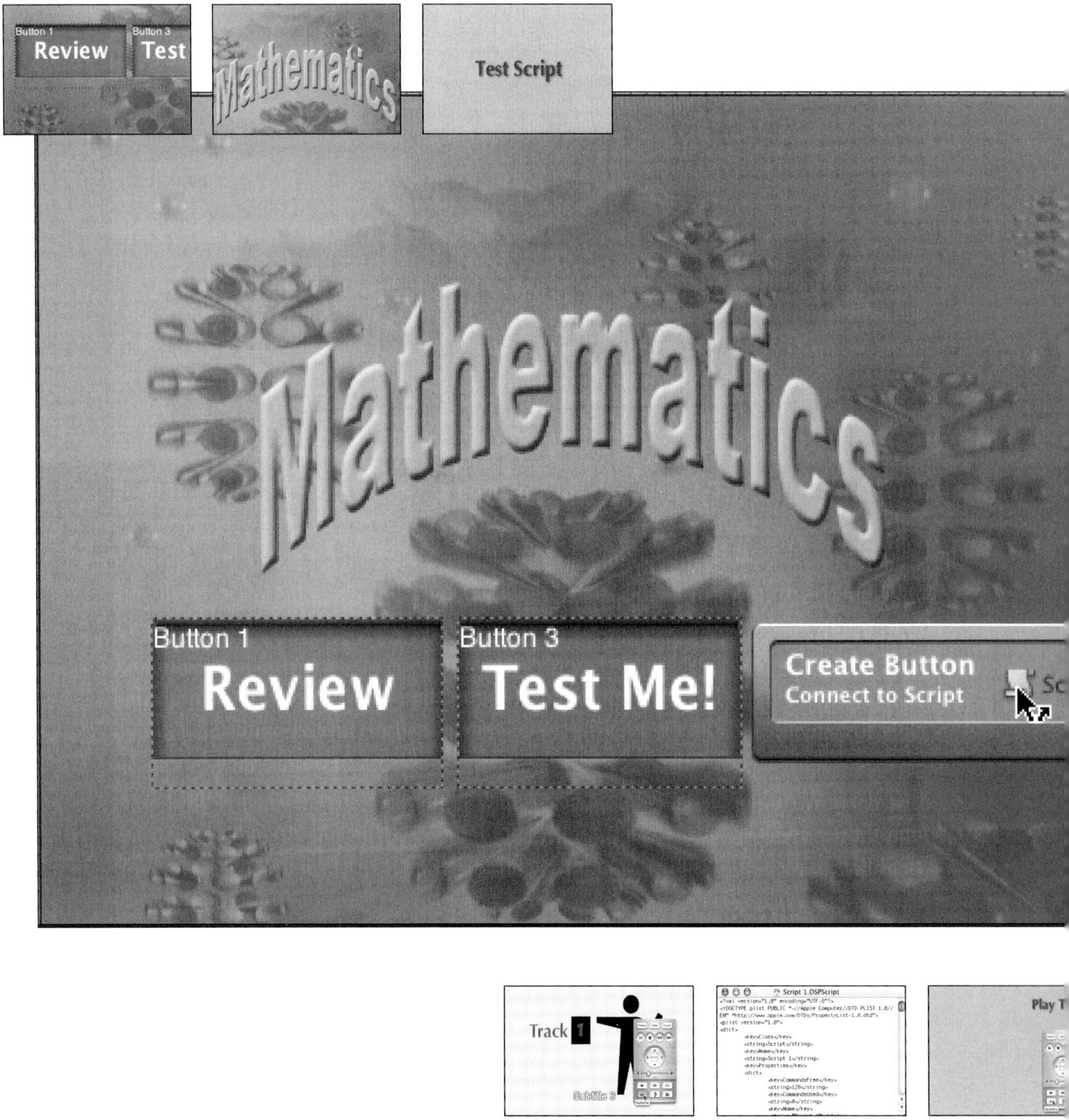

Button 1
Review
Button 3
Test
Mathematics
Test Script
Mathematics
Button 1
Review
Button 3
Test Me!
Create Button
Connect to Script

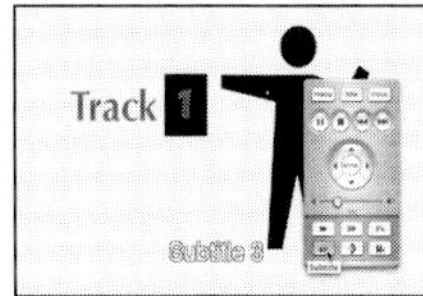

Track 1
Subtitle 2

Script 1.DSPScript
<?xml version="1.0" encoding="UTF-8"?>
<!DOCTYPE plist PUBLIC "-//Apple Computer//DTD PLIST 1.0//
EN" "http://www.apple.com/DTDs/PropertyList-1.0.dtd">
<plist version="1.0">
<dict>
        <key>Class</key>
        <string>Script</string>
        <key>Name</key>
        <string>Script 1</string>
        <key>Properties</key>
        <dict>
                <key>CommandsFree</key>
                <string>128</string>
                <key>CommandsUsed</key>
                <string>0</string>
                <key>Name</key>

Play T

Scripting DVDs

When you need to program the way your DVDs behave, scripting offers the answer. Scripting provides complex and creative ways to connect with viewers and control the presentations they watch. As you've seen in previous chapters, DVD menus and buttons allow viewers to interact with DVDs in a variety of ways. Scripting takes interaction a step further. Scripts let you customize DVD behavior, using a simple programming language. Language commands let you select destinations, store state information, create pseudorandom results, and more. With just a few lines of code, you can make your DVDs act the way you need them to.

Chapter Contents

Adding Scripts to Projects

DVD Studio Pro 2 scripts are project elements, just like menus, tracks, stories, and slideshows. While other elements contain video or audio, scripts contain programming commands (as many as 128 commands per script), which you specify and edit using the Script tab. Scripts appear in the Outline tab and are created, named, ordered, and removed in the same manner as all other elements. (See Chapter 6 for an overview of the Outline tab and its functions.) You treat scripts as you would treat any other element, playing them and connecting to them.

DVD scripting, like any programming language, requires a certain set of sequencing and logic skills, which should be familiar to anyone with programming experience. This chapter assumes you have a certain familiarity with programming, although the steps and solutions can be followed regardless. C-language equivalents are provided wherever possible. Most programmers study C at some point, and, along with Assembly language, C provides excellent equivalents to DVD scripting.

Scripts play two roles in DVD Studio Pro 2: as normal targets of other elements—you can link to a script, just as you'd link to a menu, a track, or a slideshow, and as prescripts, a feature that executes script-based instructions before a track, slideshow, menu, or story plays back. Here are some of the ways you can connect to and use scripts in your DVD Studio Pro 2 projects:

Connect end jumps to scripts. You can use the Inspector and the Connections tab to connect an element's end jump to a script, as Figure 10.1 shows. When the track, slideshow, or story finishes playing, the DVD player runs the selected script. End jump scripts might choose which element to play next, keep track of the already-played items seen by the viewer, or choose which button to highlight before moving on to a menu.

Connect buttons to scripts. Menu buttons can target scripts, just as they'd link to tracks, slideshows, and so forth. Use the Target pop-up in the Button Inspector to link a button to a script or drag a script onto a button to connect directly. The script plays back when the button is selected and activated. Figure 10.2 shows how to create a button by dragging a script onto the Menu Editor. Button scripts might set playback options or select an element to play.

Set the disc's First Play. You can connect your disc's First Play option to a script, just as you might connect it to a menu or a track. The Options tab contextual menu and the Disc Inspector both offer ways to set First Play. First Play scripts might initialize playback settings, select a random element to play, or customize playback to match the parental management configuration found on the DVD player.

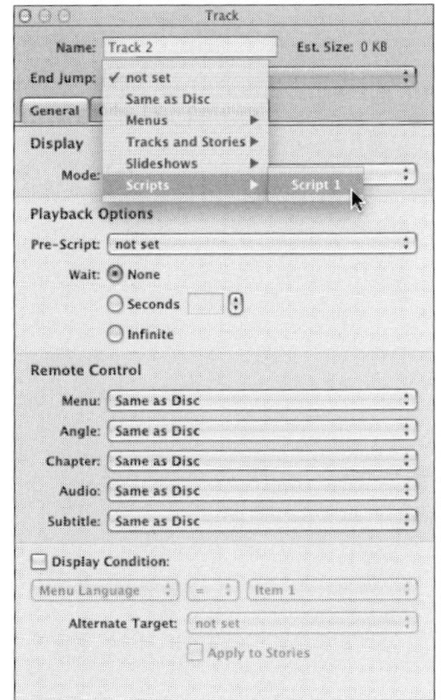

Figure 10.1 DVD Studio Pro 2 lets you link your end jumps to scripts, just as you would link to any other element. Use the End Jump pop-up in the Track, Slideshow, and Story Inspectors to connect. The script will run after the element finishes playing.

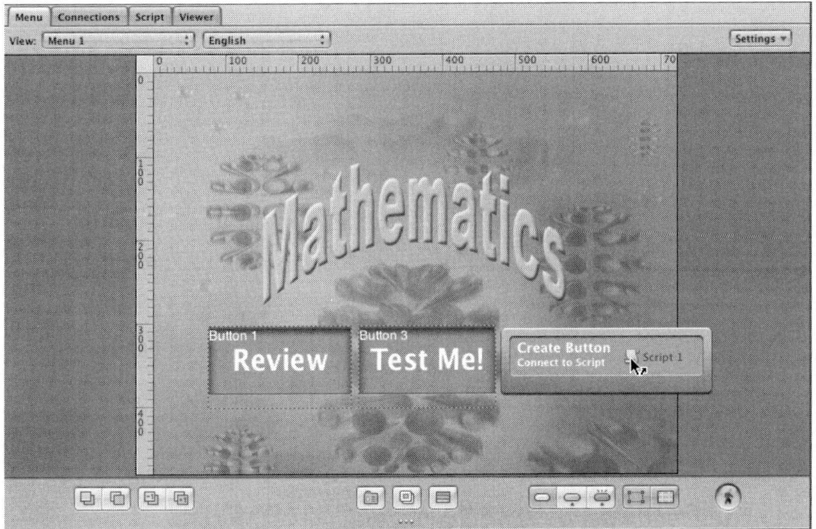

Figure 10.2 DVD Studio Pro 2 lets you create a button and connect it to a script all in one step. Drag a script onto the background of the Menu Editor, and choose Create Button/Connect tTo Script from the drop palette. This creates a new, targeted DVD button using the default menu style.

Add prescripts to project elements. Tracks, menus, stories, and slideshows all allow you to designate a feature called prescripts, as shown in Figure 10.3. Prescripts are DVD Studio Pro 2 scripts that execute before an element begins to play. A prescript might choose a chapter or slide to begin playback, or it might adjust the stream settings based on language preferences.

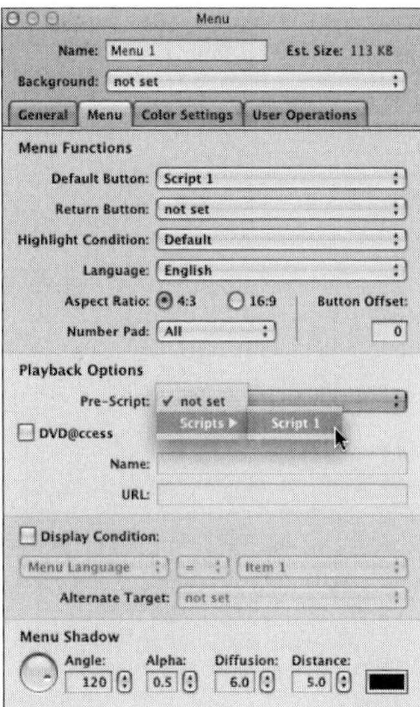

Figure 10.3 The Playback Options area in the Menu, Track, Story, and Slideshow Inspectors allow you to select a prescript. Prescripts execute before these program elements begin playback. The Pre-Script pop-up appears in the Menu tab for menus, in the General tab for tracks and slideshows, and in the main Slideshow Inspector, which has no tabs.

The Script Editor and Inspectors

The Script Editor (see Figure 10.4), which appears in the Script tab, lets you build programs for your DVD projects.

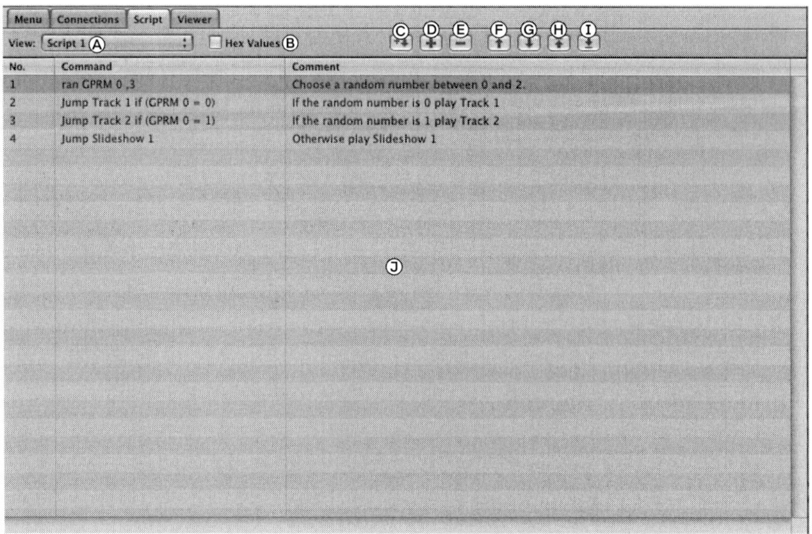

Figure 10.4 The Script Editor lets you build custom programming to control the way your DVD behaves. View pop-up Ⓐ; Hex Values check box Ⓑ; Command Insert button Ⓒ; New Command button Ⓓ; Remove Command button Ⓔ; Move Command Up button Ⓕ; Move Command Down button Ⓖ; Move Command To Top button Ⓗ; Move Command To Bottom button Ⓘ; Command List Ⓙ

The Script Editor includes the following features:

View Pop-Up (A) Choose the script you want to edit from this pop-up, or select a script in the Outline tab. The Editor updates to reflect the selected script.

Hex Values Check Box (B) Check this box to view and specify all numbers using hexadecimal (base 16) notation (recommended).

Insert Command Button (C) Click to insert a new command line after the selected line (alternately, ⌘-+ or ⌘-Shift-=).

Add Command Button (D) Click to add a new command at the bottom of the Command List (alternately, ⌘-=).

Remove Command Button (E) Click to remove the selected line or lines from the Command List. (Alternately, choose Edit > Delete or press Delete.) Choose Edit > Undo (⌘-Z) to restore just-deleted commands.

Move Command Up Button (F) Click to move the selected line above the line that precedes it, causing the two lines to switch positions.

Move Command Down Button (G) Click to move the selected line below the line that precedes it, causing the two lines to switch positions.

Move Command To Top Button (H) Click to move the selected line to the top of the Command List.

Move Command To Bottom Button (I) Click to move the selected line to the bottom of the Command List.

Early releases of DVD Studio Pro 2 produce uneven results when you attempt to move a selection of more than one line. When commands suddenly seem to double incorrectly, reselect each line to display the true contents. If this does not solve the problem, save your work and relaunch the program.

Command List (J) Forming the main portion of the Script Editor, the Command List shows all the current script commands. Each command is numbered and contains an optional comment.

You can reapportion space between the Command and Comment columns by dragging the line between the names in the Command List title bar.

Each DVD Studio Pro 2 script can contain as many as 128 commands.

The Script Command Inspector

The Script Editor lets you add, reorder, and delete commands, but it does not let you specify what those commands are. The Script Command Inspector fills that role, letting you choose and customize the commands you use in the script. Shown in Figure 10.5, the Script Command Inspector uses a series of pop-ups and text fields to build each command.

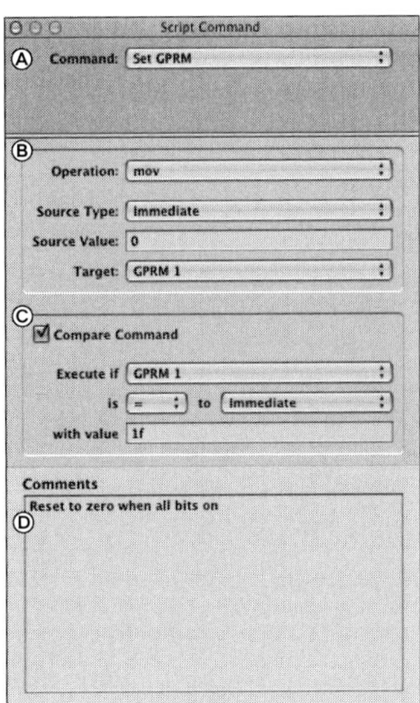

Figure 10.5 The Script Command Inspector lets you select and customize script commands. Command selection pop-up Ⓐ; Command customization area Ⓑ; Comparison configuration area Ⓒ; Comments area Ⓓ

Features of the Inspector include the following:

Command Selection Pop-Up (A) Use this pop-up to choose from one of the 11 possible commands.

Command Customization Area (B) The customization area offers many command parameters. This area might contain no controls or many, depending on the selected command. Use these controls to set the way the command behaves.

Comparison Configuration Area (C) Many commands offer conditional execution. Use this area to define which conditions allow your command to execute.

Comment Area (D) This text field allows you to annotate your scripts so that you and others can better understand the logic behind them. Clear comments are an essential part of effective script development and maintenance.

As with other Apple programs, you can add carriage returns to your comments by pressing ⌥-Return as you type. Unfortunately, you'll only be able to see the complete comment in the Inspector. The Comments area in the Command List does not resize to show multiple lines.

The Script Inspector

In addition to the Script Command Inspector, DVD Studio Pro 2 also offers a limited Script Inspector that sets options that apply globally to your script, rather than to individual commands. Figure 10.6 shows the features of this Inspector, which include the following:

Name Field (A) The Name field lets you edit the script's name.

Commands Used and Commands Remaining Indicators (B) These indicators do exactly what you might expect. Unfortunately, in early versions of DVD Studio Pro 2, the math sometimes gets a bit wonky, as you can see in Figure 10.6. In theory, the used plus remaining numbers should always equal 128.

GPRM Variable Names (C) The eight GPRM Variable Name fields let you rename GPRM 0 through GPRM 7 to more meaningful variable names.

Although the Script Inspector allows you to rename variables, in the interest of clarity, this feature is not used in this chapter.

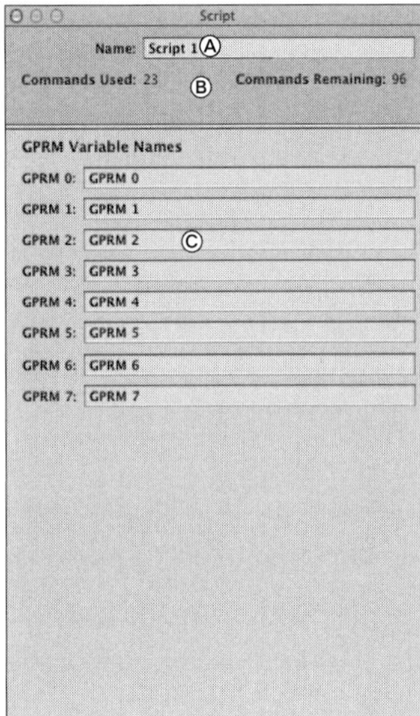

Figure 10.6 The Script Inspector offers limited ways to customize your script as a whole. Name field Ⓐ; Commands Used and Remaining indicators Ⓑ; GPRM Variable Names Ⓒ

Discovering the Elements of Scripting

DVD Studio Pro 2 scripting allows you to access programming features that are universally available in commercial DVD players. The language is based on the properties and capacities of these players, which are built to conform to the DVD specification. Here are a few key concepts to keep in mind about scripting:

Each DVD player contains a simple on-board microprocessor. This processor loads and executes your scripts from your DVD.

Programs are compact. Scripts can contain a maximum of 128 command lines and no more.

Programs are simple. There are precisely 11 commands plus a set of conditionals available in the scripting language. These commands are closest in form to Assembly language, although they'll also feel familiar to anyone versed in C-language programming.

You must explicitly transfer control from scripts. Unlike prescripts, scripts don't have a natural place to go after they end. Jump or exit commands tell the DVD player what to do after finishing a script. Otherwise, the DVD processor will sit at the end of your script and wait. Forever.

Data is all register based. You might want to acquaint (or reacquaint) yourself with register-based math and bitwise operations. All data use 16-bit registers with no underflow or overflow flags. If you add 1 ($0001) to 65535 ($FFFF), the result will be 0 ($0000), not 65536.

In this section, you'll learn about the basic commands, data types, operations and so forth that constitute the DVD Studio Pro 2 scripting language.

Commands

DVD Studio Pro 2 scripts are built from the 11 commands listed in Table 10.1. This limited language, augmented by the conditionals (compare conditions), provides the complete set of operations for DVD scripting.

▶ **Table 10.1** DVD Studio Pro 2 Scripting Commands

Command	Description	Arguments and Conditions
NOP	No Operation. As the name suggests, NOP commands do nothing. They allow you to add comments without function or insert placeholders for later command development.	No arguments. No compare conditions.
Jump	Leaves the script and transfers control and playback to a new project element such as a menu, track, script, and so forth.	Uses two arguments: the jump target and optional GPRM-based button selection. Can use compare conditions.
Jump Indirect	Works like Jump but uses the value stored in a register to select the program element to jump to. Project element addresses are just one of the data types that you can store in registers.	Takes one argument, a GPRM that stores the target destination. Can use compare conditions.
Set GPRM	Stores the result of an operation in a GPRM register. Operations include math, bitwise logic, simple assignment, and more.	Four arguments include an operation, a source type, a source value, and a destination. Can use compare conditions.
Goto	Jumps within the script to another command line, referenced by a line number, that can range from 1 through 128. Goto commands allow you to transfer control from one part of your script to another, creating blocks of related commands.	Takes one argument—a command line number. Can use compare conditions.

Command	Description	Arguments and Conditions
Set System Stream	As the name suggests, this command sets the current video, audio, or subtitle stream.	Arguments include the choice of stream types and the requested stream number, which can be a constant or GPRM based. Can use compare conditions.
Resume	Instructs the DVD player to resume playback where it last left off. (Primarily for use in scripts. The results of this command are unpredictable when used in prescripts.)	No arguments. Can use compare conditions.
GPRM Mode	Toggles a register between normal operations and countdown mode. In countdown mode, the register decrements once per second from the value input, until it reaches zero. In normal mode, the GPRM acts as a variable, storing data until that data is overwritten or reset.	Uses two arguments: the GPRM to affect and the mode. Can use compare conditions.
Exit	Stops playback, preventing the viewer from watching the disc. This command is typically used with parental control authorization and playback region checks. When executed, it denies the viewer further access to the material on the disc.	No arguments. Can use compare conditions.
Exit Prescript	Not related to Exit, this command simply transfers control back to the element whose prescript this is. Exit Prescript offers a well-behaved stopping point for prescripts.	No arguments. Can use compare conditions.

DataTypes

DVD Studio Pro 2 scripts use a combination of variable and literal data called Element Types. Each of these data types uses 16-bit words to store values. Types include the following:

GPRMs The eight General Purpose Register Memories (GPRMs) act as program variables, allowing you to store information however you want. Each register acts independently. Changes to a value in one register will not affect the values in any other.

And, theoretically, each general register reinitializes to 0 when a new disc is inserted into a DVD player. (Pedants may want to zero out their GPRMs using First Play scripts.)

Although the general register names default to GPRM 0 through GPRM 7, you can add meaning by assigning variable names in the Script Inspector.

SPRMs The 24 System Parameter Register Memories (SPRMs) provide predefined system information, including language settings, items currently being played, and DVD player configurations. The appendix provides a list of SPRM values and uses. Advanced scripts often spend a lot of time querying SPRM values, extracting bitwise-encoded data from those values, and deciding how to act based on the extracted data.

Immediates Immediate values are simply constants, integers that range between 0 ($0000) and 65535 ($FFFF).

Jump Targets Jump targets let you choose from the available menus, buttons, tracks, stories, chapters, slideshows, slides, and scripts in your project.

Specials Specials allow you to select from the Current Item (the menu, track, slideshow, or story for prescripts; otherwise the script itself), Last Item (the item that targeted this script and caused it to run), and the Last Track (the last played track).

The last track is stored correctly and works, even when you link from a menu button.

Operators

The Set GPRM command can use any of the operators shown in Table 10.2 to compute values, which are stored in GPRM registers.

▶ **Table 10.2** Operators for the Set GPRM Command

Command	What It Does	Example	C-Equivalent
MOV	Copies the contents of the source register to the destination register	MOV GPRM 2, GPRM 0	GPRM2 = GPRM0;
SWP	Swaps the contents of the source and destination registers	SWP GPRM 1, GPRM 2	TMP = GPRM1; GPRM1 = GPRM2; GPRM2 = TMP;

Command	What It Does	Example	C-Equivalent
ADD	Copies the sum of the source and destination values into the destination register	ADD GPRM 4, GPRM 0 ADD GPRM 5, $24	GPRM4 += GPRM0; GPRM5 += 0x24;
SUB	Subtracts the source value from the destination value and stores the result in the destination register	SUB GPRM 2, GPRM 0 SUB GPRM 0, $FF	GPRM2 -= GPRM0; GPRM0 -= 0xFF;
MUL	Multiplies the source value with the destination value and stores the result in the destination register	MUL GPRM 1, GPRM 2 MUL GPRM 4, $8	GPRM1 *= GPRM2; GPRM4 *= 0x08;
DIV	Divides the destination value by the source value and stores the result in the destination register	DIV GPRM 2, GPRM 1 DIV GPRM 3, $4	GPRM2 /= GPRM1; GPRM3 /= 0x04;
MOD	Divides the destination value by the source value and stores the remainder (the modulus) in the destination register	MOD GPRM 0, GPRM 5 MOD GPRM 7, $12	GPRM0 %= GPRM5; GPRM0 %= 0x12;
RAN	Generates a random value between 1 and the source value and writes the results to the destination register	RAN GPRM 1, GPRM 3 RAN GPRM 0, $3	GPRM1 = (rand( )%GPRM3)+1; GPRM0 = (rand( )%0x03)+1;
AND	Performs a bitwise AND operation on the source and destination values, storing the results in the destination register	AND GPRM 2, GPRM 0 AND GPRM 1, $10	GPRM2 &= GPRM0; GPRM1 &= 0x10;
OR	Performs a bitwise OR operation on the source and destination values, storing the results in the destination register	OR GPRM 3, GPRM 4 OR GPRM 2, $04	GPRM3 |= GPRM4; GPRM2 |= 0x04;
XOR	Performs a bitwise exclusive or (XOR) operation on the source and destination values, storing the results in the destination register	XOR GPRM0, GPRM3 XOR GPRM5, $07	GPRM0 ^= GPRM3; GPRM5 ^= 0x07;

Compare Conditions

The comparison configuration area (see Figure 10.5, letter D, earlier in this chapter) allows you to add conditional execution to your script commands. This area appears for every command except NOP. When selected, it allows you to compare a GPRM register with any other data element (including GPRMs, SPRMs, constants, and so forth). If the results are true (or nonzero), the command executes. If not, the script proceeds to the next numbered line. Check the Compare Command check box to enable this feature for the selected command.

DVD Studio Pro 2 provides seven ways to compare two data items: greater-than (>), greater-equal (>=), less-than (<), less-equal (<=), equal (=, although it should properly be ==), not-equal (!=), and bitwise-and (&). Each of these operates as it would in any traditional programming language.

The bitwise-and comparison lets you check whether a bit (or bits) have been set. For example, you might want to know whether bit 3 is on or off. A C-language test might check if (GPRM0 & 0x08) (or if (GPRM0 & 1<<3), for bit-shifting gurus). In DVD Studio Pro 2, you'd check if (GPRM 0 & $8) instead.

Recall that bits are counted from zero. A 16-bit word contains bit 0 (least significant) through bit 15 (most significant).

Building Scripts

Apple's introduction of the Script Command Inspector was meant to improve scripting reliability, preventing users from making syntax errors. DVD Studio Pro 2 scripting tries to strike a balance between programming flexibility and ease of use. Sadly, it does not. In the current release, scripting may prove too limiting for experienced programmers and too complex for novice DVD authors. Unfortunately, in DVD Studio Pro 2, you cannot do a lot of things that you might expect to do in other programming language editors.

You cannot edit the command text or comments directly. You must use the Script Command Inspector to create and modify your commands and comments.

You cannot copy, paste, or duplicate command lines. You must reenter each line by hand.

You cannot print. DVD Studio Pro 2 offers no printing capability. (⌘-P burns discs.) If you cannot live without a script listing, use a screen utility such as Grab (/Applications/Utilities/Grab) to capture the display. This limits you to the small screen font and display intrinsic to DVD Studio Pro 2. Longer scripts may require several screen shots as you scroll through the program.

You cannot save a simple text listing to disk. DVD Studio Pro 2 allows you to save item descriptions and XML representations of your scripts, but not the script commands themselves in a simple list.

In addition to these concerns, the delay times between setting a parameter in the Inspector and having it change in the Command List can be mind-boggling, particularly on older G4 systems. This makes programming a slow and tedious task. Fortunately, most DVD scripts are short—rarely requiring more than a dozen or two lines.

Sonic Scenarist Professional, at a mere $22,000, allows you to move beyond DVD Studio Pro 2's built-in limitations to access all 16 GPRMs, all SPRMs, and so forth. Scenarist, which is considered the de facto industry standard for DVD authoring, runs exclusively on Microsoft Windows.

Adding Commands

In DVD Studio Pro 2, each script command line must be customized with the Script Command Inspector. To add new commands to your DVD Studio Pro 2 scripts, follow these steps:

1. **Add a command.** Click the + button (⌘-+) in the Script Editor to add a new command to the end of your script. All new commands are set to NOP by default. Select the new command.

2. **Open the Script Command Inspector.** Press ⌘-Option-I. The Inspector opens and displays the default NOP settings pane.

3. **Choose a new command.** Select a command from the Command Selection pop-up at the top of the Inspector pane.

4. **Configure the arguments.** Commands can take no arguments, one argument, or several. Use the controls in the command customization area to set the way your command behaves.

5. **Optionally add a compare condition.** If desired, check Compare Command. Select a GPRM, a comparison operation, and a data item to compare to.

6. **Add a comment.** Finish customizing your command by adding a meaningful expository comment. Press Return to transfer your new comment into the Script Editor.

7. **Repeat.** Repeat as necessary to build your script, a command line at a time.

Sample Commands

In this section, you'll see some example of commands and how they are built.

Jump Track 1 if (GPRM 0 = $0) Leaves the script and starts playing back Track 1 if GPRM 0 is set to 0. To create this command, choose Jump from the Command pop-up. Choose Tracks and Stories > Track 1 > [Track] from the Jump To pop-up. Check

Compare Command. Choose GPRM 0 from the Execute If pop-up, = from the Is pop-up, and Immediate from the To pop-up. Set with value to 0.

Set System Stream Au(Audio Stream 2) An(1) Sets playback to A2 (Audio Stream 2) and V1 (Angle 1). To create this command, choose Set System Stream from the Command pop-up. Select Parameters: Immediate Value. Check Audio and Angle. (Leave Subtitle unchecked.) Choose Audio Stream 1 from the Audio pop-up. Choose 1 from the Angle pop-up.

mul GPRM 2, $4 Multiply the contents of GPRM 2 by 4 and store the results in GPRM 2. To create this command, choose Set GPRM from the Command pop-up. Choose mul from the Operation pop-up and Immediate from the Source Type pop-up. Set the Source Value to 4. Select GPRM 2 from the Target pop-up.

mov GPRM 1, Last Item Stores the last played item in GPRM 1. To create this command, choose Set GPRM from the Command pop-up. Choose mov from the Operation pop-up, Special from the Source Type pop-up, Last Item from the Source Value pop-up, and GPRM 1 from the Target pop-up.

Goto 20 if (GPRM 1 = Current Item) Move to Command Line 20 in the current script if the currently playing item has been stored in GPRM 1 To create this command, choose Goto from the Command pop-up. Enter **20** in the Line Number field. Check Compare Command. Choose GPRM 1 from the Execute If pop-up, = from the Is pop-up, Special from the To pop-up, and Current Item from the value pop-up.

Jump Indirect GPRM 4 if (GPRM 0 & S8) Jump to the target stored in GPRM 4 if bit 3 is set in GPRM 0. To create this command, choose Jump Indirect from the Command pop-up. Choose GPRM 4 from the Set To pop-up. Check Compare Command. Choose GPRM 0 from the Execute If pop-up, & from the Is pop-up, and Immediate from the To pop-up. Enter 8 in the With Value field.

swp GPRM 2, GPRM 1 Swap the contents of GPRM 1 and GPRM 2. To create the command, choose Set GPRM from the Command pop-up. Choose swp from the Operation pop-up, GPRM from the Source Type pop-up, GPRM 1 from the Source Value pop-up, and GPRM 2 from the Target pop-up.

Saving Scripts

DVD Studio Pro 2 offers two ways to save your scripts to disc. Neither produces a particularly readable listing, but both can be reloaded into projects as needed.

Saving Item Descriptions

DVD Studio Pro 2 allows you to save item description files for any project element, including scripts. Description files use a proprietary format (shown in Figure 10.7) to store information. The program can re-create these elements in other projects by reading the files.

Figure 10.7 DVD Studio Pro 2 item description files can store (and later recover) scripts using a proprietary text-based format.

Follow these steps to save your script descriptions to disk.

1. **Select a script.** Open the Outline tab and select the script you want to save.

2. **Export the script.** Choose File > Export > Item Description to open a File dialog.

3. **Save.** Navigate to the folder where you want to save your script. Enter a name and click Save. DVD Studio Pro 2 saves the script to disk using a .dspScript extension. You can view the contents of this new file by dragging it onto the TextEdit application.

DVD Studio Pro 2 uses lowercase .dspScript files to save script item descriptions and uppercase .DSPScript files to save XML script renditions.

Saving XML Script Files

In addition to item descriptions, DVD Studio Pro 2 allows you to save your scripts to disk using XML (Extensible Markup Language), as shown in Figure 10.8. Like item descriptions, you can use these files to load your scripts into other projects. XML is a platform-independent markup language that stores script information using custom tags and data. Apple uses XML extensively in OS X.

To save an XML script file, Ctrl-click (right-click) a script in the Outline tab, and choose Save Script from the contextual menu to open a File dialog. Navigate to where you want to save your script, enter a name, and click Save. DVD Studio Pro 2 saves your script to a new .DSPScript file.

To view the contents of the new file, drag it onto the TextEdit application. Alternately, create a copy and change the extension to .plist. Use the Property List Editor (available free from http://developer.apple.com) to browse the XML data stored in the file.

Figure 10.8 DVD Studio Pro 2 uses XML to store scripts in a recoverable format.

Loading Scripts

The way you save your scripts determines how you must load them. If you saved to an item description, load the file by choosing File > Import > Item Description. If you saved to an XML file, in the Outline tab right-click and choose Load Script from the contextual pop-up. Either way, navigate to your file, select it, and click Open.

Once the script is loaded, you must reconfigure it for your new project, matching it to the current project elements. All jump targets reset to not set, for example, mov GPRM 0, not set, or Jump not set. Use the Script Editor to relink targets to the elements in your new project. Use your script normally after updating the jump targets.

Discovering Advanced Simulator Features

To better track the behavior of your project elements and scripts, you can use a few "hidden" features of the Simulator (⌘-⌥-0). To access these features, open the Info Drawer, and press Shift-I or click the circled I button. Figure 10.9 shows the Simulator with the following hidden features displayed:

Info Button (A) Click the Info button or press Shift-I to open or close the Info Drawer.

Item Properties List (B) Shows a list of properties associated with the currently playing element, including the menu name, prescript, and so forth.

Current Register Values List (C) Lists all registers (including SPRMs and GPRMs) and their current values. Use this list to monitor register settings and their changes as your project plays back.

SPRM and GPRM Hide/Show Check Boxes (D) Check or clear these two boxes to toggle the display of each kind of register.

Hex Check Box (E) Check this box to view all register and property values using hexadecimal (base 16) notation. As a rule, leave this box checked unless you have some pressing need to use decimal (base 10) notation in your work.

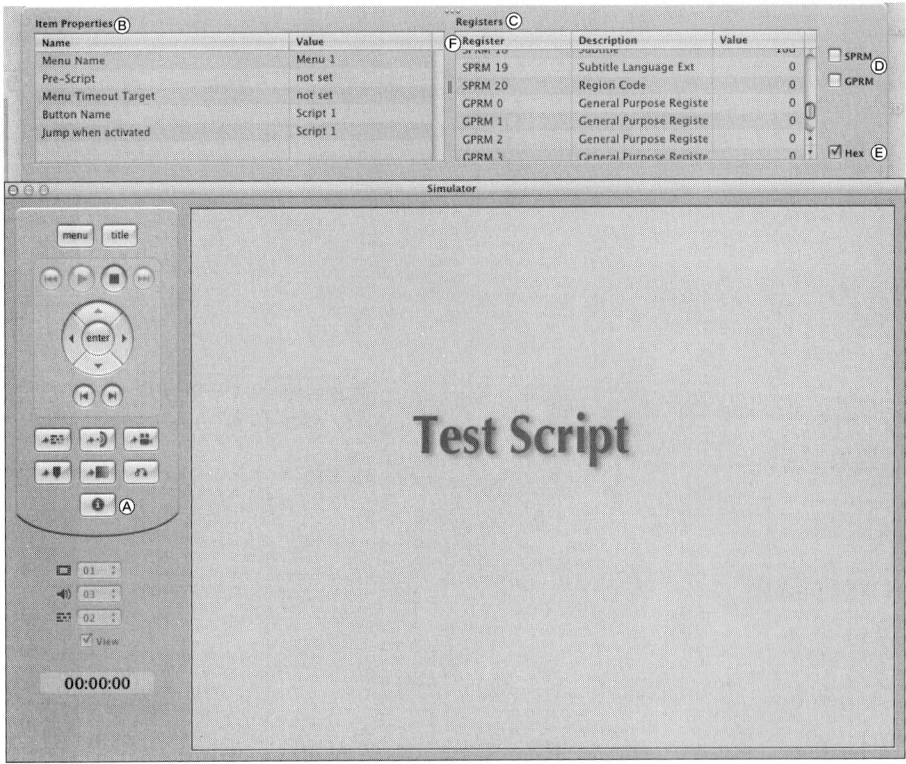

Figure 10.9 The Info Drawer in the Simulator helps you debug your DVD projects and track the progress of your scripts. Info button Ⓐ; Item Properties List Ⓑ; Current Register Values List (SPRMs and GPRMs) Ⓒ; SPRM and GPRM hide/show check boxes Ⓓ; Hex check box Ⓔ; Interface Controls Ⓕ

Interface Controls (F) Two interface controls appear near the center of the Info Drawer. Use the separator bar to apportion space between the Item Properties and Register lists. Drag the three dots on the drawer edge to resize the entire drawer. With the drawer at its largest size, you'll be able to see 26 registers (out of the possible 29) at once; with the drawer at its practical smallest, you'll be able to see about 5 registers.

Solution: Use the Info Drawer to Monitor Registers

The Info Drawer allows you to monitor the values stored in the SPRM and GPRM registers as your project executes. As with any debugging tool, the stored values let you peek inside your variables and track how they change over time. Use the Info Drawer to ensure that your program executes as expected, producing meaningful data values. In these steps, you'll use a script that increments GPRM 0 each time you run the script.

 The chapter materials on the companion DVD contain all the resources and assets you need to build and test the scripting solutions. Be sure to import Optima48.dspstyle before working through the solutions. Choose File > Import > Style. Navigate to the file, select it, and click Import. Once imported, the style remains for all future projects.

1. **Set up a new project.** Create a new DVD Studio Pro 2 project. Select the prebuilt Menu 1 element in the Outline tab, and delete it. Choose File > Import > Item Description, and navigate to AddOne.dspMenu. Select it and click Import. Repeat to import AddOne.dspScript. In the Outline tab, drag BG1.psd onto Test Menu. Save your new project.

> Item descriptions use absolute path names for stills, video, and audio. For this solution, you must add BG1.psd by hand because the path name would reference my computer. In your own projects you can simply store item description files without stripping out assets in advance, as I did here.

2. **Connect the script to the button.** Double-click (the newly imported) Test Menu to open the Menu Editor. Drag the imported script onto your Menu button, and choose Connect To Script from the drop palette.

3. **Examine the script.** Double-click the AddOne script in the Outline tab to open the Script Editor. This script has two lines. The first increments the value of GPRM 0 by 1, and the second returns control from the script to Test Menu.

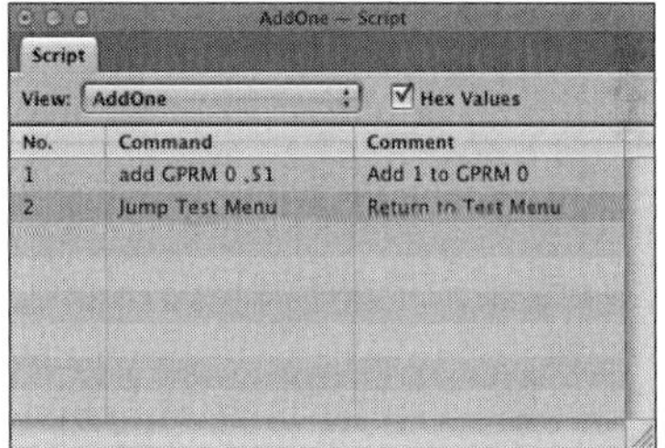

> Is the second line set to Jump not set? If so, you probably imported the Item Description files in the wrong order. To fix, set the jump target by hand.

4. **Set First Play.** In the Outline tab, Ctrl-click (right-click) the disc. Choose First Play > Menus > Test Menu > [Menu] from the pop-up.

5. **Simulate.** Click the Simulator icon in the toolbar to open the Simulator, and open the Info Drawer. Check the SPRM box to hide the SPRM values. Scroll until you can see GPRM 0, which should start at 0.

6. **Test.** Click Run Script. GPRM 0 increases by 1. Click Run Script again. Each time you click the button, GPRM 0 increases by 1. When you're satisfied that the script works as expected, close the Simulator.

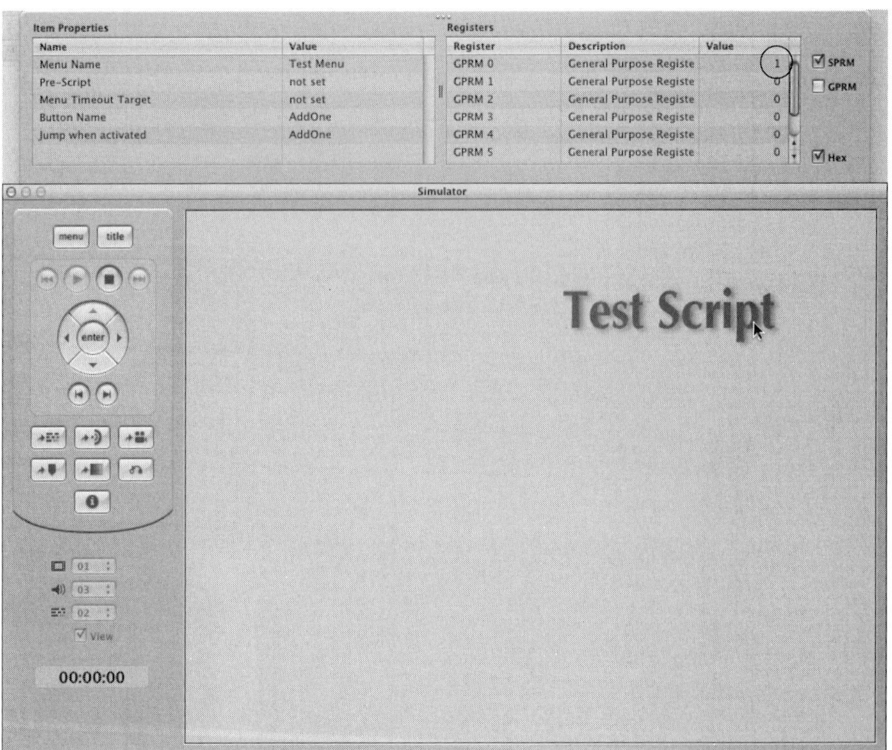

Solution: Play a Random Track

The DVD standard allows the microprocessor on board the DVD player to use a special algorithm to select pseudorandom numbers. In this project, the script sets GPRM 0 to a random number between 1 and 3. Each subsequent command tests the value in GPRM 0 to decide which track to play.

1. **Create a new project.** Delete the default Menu 1 and Track 1 elements.

2. **Build tracks.** Drag Track1.m2v, Track2.m2v, and Track3.m2v onto the Tracks folder in the Outline tab. Reorder the new tracks so they appear in the following order: Track1, Track2, Track3.

Building tracks 1 through 3 first allows the PlayRandom script to refer to these tracks.

3. **Import a menu and a script.** Choose File > Import > Item Description. Navigate to PlayRandom.dspMenu. Select it, and click Import. Repeat to import PlayRandom.dspScript. These files create Random Menu and PlayRandom in the Outline tab.

4. **Finish the menu.** Drag BG1.psd onto Random Menu in the Outline tab. Double-click Random Menu to open it in the Menu Editor. Drag the PlayRandom script from the Outline tab onto the Play A Random Track button. Choose Connect To Script from the drop palette.

5. **Set the track end jumps.** Open the Inspector (⌘-⌥-I). Select each track and set the end jump to Menus > Random Menu > [Menu]. This returns playback control to the menu after each track finishes playing.

6. **Examine the script.** Double-click the PlayRandom script in the Outline tab to open the Script Editor. This script has four lines. The first line assigns a random number between 1 and 3 to GPRM 0. The next three lines decide which track to select. If the random number is 1, the second line jumps to Track 1. If the number is 2, the third line jumps to Track 2. The last line simply jumps to Track 3, as all other possibilities have been exhausted.

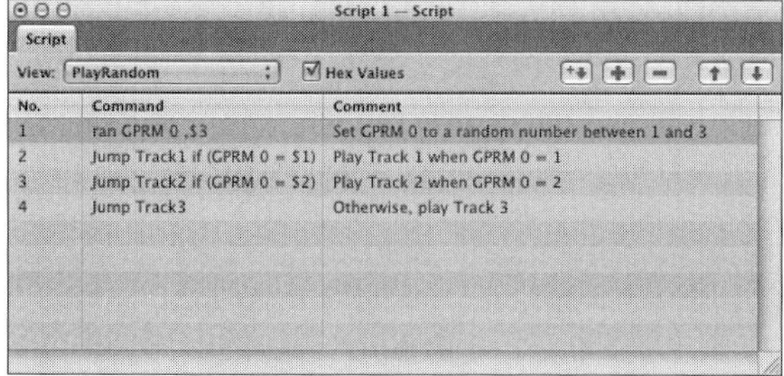

No.	Command	Comment
1	ran GPRM 0 ,$3	Set GPRM 0 to a random number between 1 and 3
2	Jump Track1 if (GPRM 0 = $1)	Play Track 1 when GPRM 0 = 1
3	Jump Track2 if (GPRM 0 = $2)	Play Track 2 when GPRM 0 = 2
4	Jump Track3	Otherwise, play Track 3

7. **Set First Play.** In the Outline tab, Ctrl-click (right-click) the disc. Choose First Play > Menus > Test Menu > [Menu] from the pop-up. When a viewer inserts your disc into their DVD player, Test Menu immediately starts to play.

8. **Simulate.** Click the Simulator icon in the toolbar to open the Simulator, and open the Info Drawer. Check the SPRM box to hide the SPRM values. Scroll until you can see GPRM 0, which should start at 0.

9. **Test.** Click Play A Random Track. GPRM 0 changes to a number between 1 and 3. The corresponding track plays back. (It's short. Each track lasts only

8 seconds.) Click again to choose another track, repeating until you're convinced that the selected track truly is random.

Solution: Use a Prescript to Control Subtitles

Some DVD players automatically (and inappropriately) enable subtitles without regard to the viewer's desires. (My Apex AD-660 is one such villain.) In this project, you'll use a prescript that initially disables subtitles for your track. Your viewer can then decide whether to view subtitles.

1. **Create a new project.** Delete the default Menu 1. Drag Track1.m2v onto the default Track 1 in the Outline tab. The track name updates to Track1 (no space).

2. **Add subtitles.** Open Track1 in the Track Editor, and right-click the S1 stream. Choose Import Subtitle File, and navigate to Subtitles.txt in the Chapter folder. Select it, and then click Choose. DVD Studio Pro 2 imports four rather dull subtitles. Click OK.

3. **Import the script.** Choose File > Import > Item Description. Navigate to NoSub .dspScript, select it, and click Import. A new script, UnsetSubtitles, appears in the Outline tab.

4. **View the script.** Open UnsetSubtitles in the Script Editor. This script contains two lines. The first line sets GPRM 0 to 62 ($3E). The second line sets the system stream to the value stored in GPRM 0. The number 62 is special and instructs the DVD player to turn off subtitles.

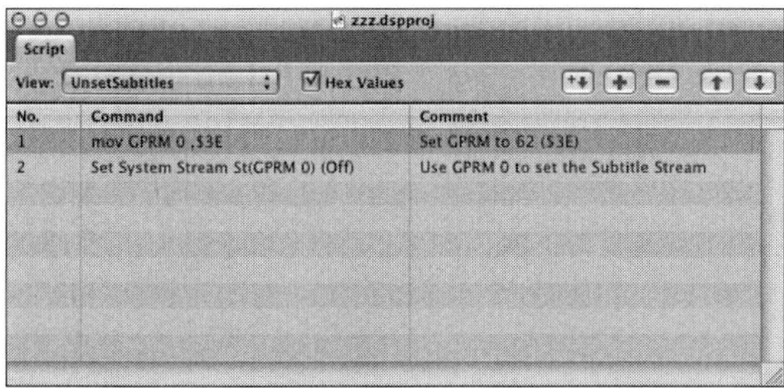

Use 63 ($3F) instead of 62 to force subtitles on instead of off.

For prescripts, you need not jump at the end. Control returns automatically to the program element whose prescript this is. If you jump to this script as an element, the two lines play back, and then the script hangs forever—or until you press the Menu button on your DVD remote.

5. **Add a menu.** Choose File > Import > Item Description. Navigate to NoSub.dsp-Menu, select it, and click Import. PlayMenu is added to the project. Its one button should automatically be targeted to Track 1. Drag BG1.psd onto PlayMenu in the Outline tab to set the background.

6. **Set the track properties.** Select Track1. Open the Track Inspector, and set End Jump to Menus > PlayMenu > [Menu]. Set Prescript to Scripts > UnsetSubtitles. This script plays before the track begins to play back. In the Track Editor, enable S1.

7. **Set First Play.** Ctrl-click (right-click) the disc in the Outline tab. Choose First Play > Menus > PlayMenu > [Menu]. Save your project.

8. **Build your project.** Click the Build icon. Navigate to your desktop, and click Choose. DVD Studio Pro 2 creates Video_TS and Audio_TS folders on your desktop. Wait for the program to finish this process, and then click OK.

9. **Open your project in DVD Player.** Launch Apple DVD Player. Choose File > Open Video_TS Folder (⌘-O). Navigate to the Video_TS folder on your desktop, and click Choose. Locate the virtual remote control, and click Play.

10. **Display the entire remote control.** In DVD Player, click the ellipsis (three dots) at the bottom of the virtual remote control to open the button drawer. The lowest left button controls subtitles. Click it until you have turned on subtitles.

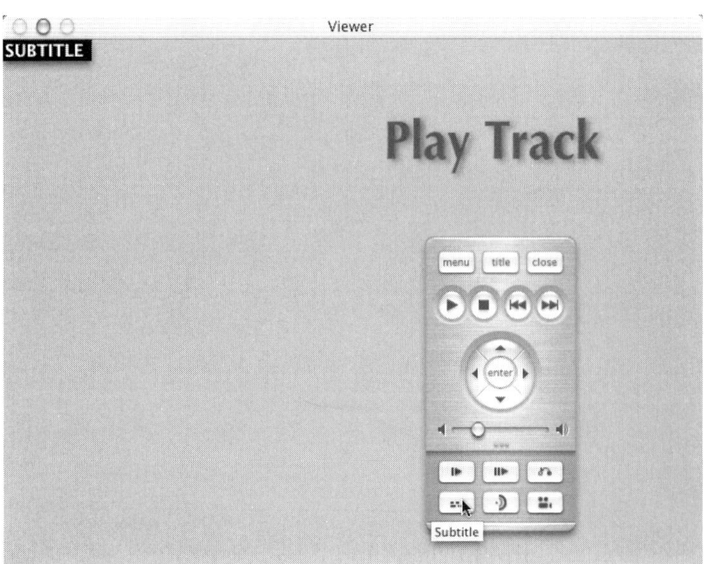

11. **Test.** Click Enter on the virtual remote control. Your track begins to play, without subtitles. Click the Subtitle button. The subtitles appear and play until the track ends. Click Enter on the remote, and the track plays one more time, but again the subtitles are disabled until you select them.

Solution: Count Menu Timeouts and Send a Message

In this project, you'll play a motion menu a set number of times before providing the viewer with a visual hint about selecting buttons. This menu uses both a prescript, to initialize a counter, and a script set for timeouts, which increments that counter each time. When the counter exceeds 3, a special track plays.

1. **Start a new project.** Drag SpecialTrack.m2v onto the default Track 1 in the Outline tab. DVD Studio Pro 2 assigns the video to the track and renames the track to SpecialTrack. Delete the default Menu 1.

2. **Create tracks.** Select Track1.m2v and Track2.m2v, and drag them onto the Tracks folder in the Outline tab. DVD Studio Pro 2 creates two new tracks, adding the video and matching audio. You'll now have three tracks in your project: Special-Track, Track1, and Track2.

3. **Create a menu.** Choose File > Import > Item Description. Navigate to impat.dsp-Menu, select it, and click Import. DVD Studio Pro 2 creates ImpatientMenu, complete with two buttons that link to Track1 and Track2.

4. **Import the scripts.** Choose File > Import > Item Descriptions to import impat1.dspScript, impat2.dspScript, and impat3.dspScript. This creates three new scripts: Add And Test, Init GPRM 0, and Init GPRM 0 And Go.

5. **Set the track end jumps.** Set SpecialTrack's End Jump to Menus > ImpatientMenu > [Menu]; set Track1's End Jump to Menus > ImpatientMenu > Track1; and set Track2's End Jump to Menus > ImpatientMenu > Track 2. Each track remembers its button and returns to it after play.

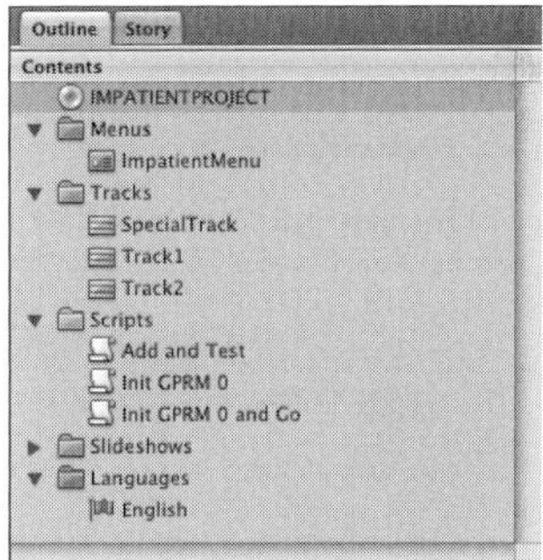

6. **Set the track prescripts.** Set all three prescripts to Scripts > Init GPRM 0. The track Pre-Script pop-up appears in the General tab of the Track Inspector, just a bit below the End Jump pop-up. Each prescript resets the menu counter, so the menu starts fresh after playing a track.

7. **Set First Play.** Set the disc's first play to Scripts > Init GPRM 0 And Go. This script initializes the menu counter and jumps to the menu. This is an actual script with a jump at the end, rather than the prescript used in the previous step.

8. **Edit the menu.** Drag ImpatMenu.m2v onto ImpatientMenu in the Outline tab. This assigns the video to the menu background. Select ImpatientMenu, and open the Menu Inspector. In the General tab, set the At End pop-up to Timeout. Leave Seconds at 1 Secs. Set Action to Scripts > Add And Test. This runs the Add And Test script each time the menu's motion finishes.

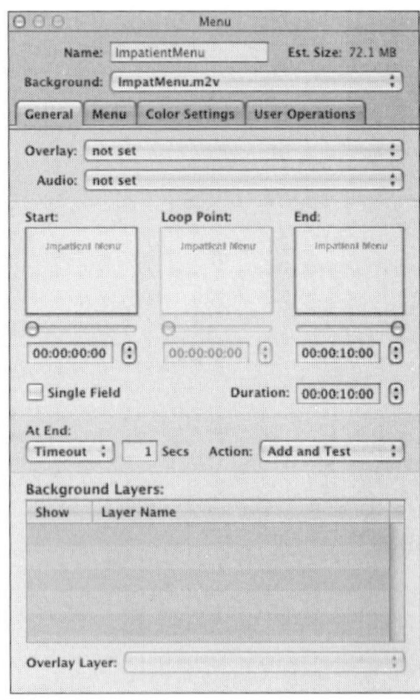

9. **Look at Init GPRM 0.** In the Outline tab, double-click Init GPRM 0 to open this script in the Script Editor. It contains just one line, mov GPRM 0, $0, which sets GPRM 0 to 0. This script runs before each track is played, ensuring that the menu is reset correctly after the track finishes playing.

10. **Look at Init GPRM 0 And Go.** Open Init GPRM 0 And Go in the Script Editor. Identical to Init GPRM 0, it adds one extra line, Jump ImpatientMenu. This script provides a nonprescript variation on the Init GPRM 0 script, transferring control directly to ImpatientMenu. As First Play, this script initializes GPRM 0 and then links to ImpatientMenu.

11. **Look at Add And Test.** This script runs each time the menu times out. It stores SPRM 8's current value in GPRM 1. This lets you know which menu button was last selected. Next it increases the value of GPRM 0, indicating that the menu has timed out again. The script tests to see if GPRM 0's value is greater than 3. If so, it jumps to the special track. If not, it replays ImpatientMenu, highlighting the most recently selected button.

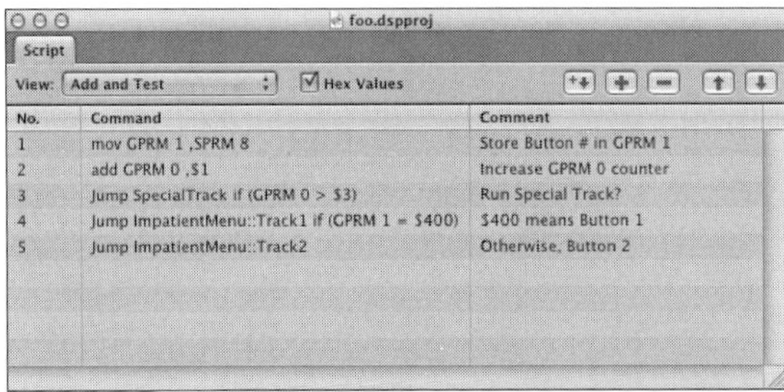

12. Build your project. Save your work. Click the Build icon, and build your project to your desktop.

13. Test in Apple DVD Player. Launch DVD Player, and choose File > Open Video_TS Folder (⌘-O). Navigate to the new Video_TS folder you just created. Select it, and click Choose. On the virtual remote control, click Play. Make sure that the project works as expected, jumping to the timeout video after playing the menu four times.

You can also test this project in the Simulator, but the intense motion and scripting may overwhelm older G4 units. The Simulator allows you to better track the values stored in the GPRM and SPRM registers as the project plays.

Solution: Create a Shuffle Play

Randomly playing tracks is all well and good, but sometimes you'd rather play each track in a project before repeating any video. Although the DVD specification allows you to create "shuffled" play, that feature is not available in DVD Studio Pro 2. Instead, here's a solution that uses bitwise operands to store the tracks that have already played. You can adapt this project to work with as many as 16 tracks, the maximum number of bits available in a register.

1. Start a new project. Delete the default Menu 1 and Track 1 elements in the Outline tab.

2. Build new tracks. Select Track1.m2v through Track5.m2v, and drag all five files from the Chapter folder onto the Tracks folder in the Outline tab. DVD Studio Pro 2 creates five new tracks, adding the video and matching audio. Drag the tracks into numeric order.

3. Import the shuffle script. Choose File > Import > Item Description. Navigate to shuffle.dspScript. Select it and click Import. A new script appears in the Outline tab.

4. Build the menu. Choose File > Import > Item Description to load shuffle.dsp-Menu. Drag BG1.psd onto ShuffleMenu in the Outline tab to add the background. ShuffleMenu contains a single button, which links to the Shuffle script.

5. Set the end jumps and First Play. Select each track in turn, and set the end jump to Menus > ShuffleMenu > [Menu]. Then set the disc's First Play to Menus > ShuffleMenu > [Menu] as well.

6.   **Examine the script.** Open the Script Editor and view your new script. This is by far the longest and most complicated script in this book and is described in the following paragraphs in detail.

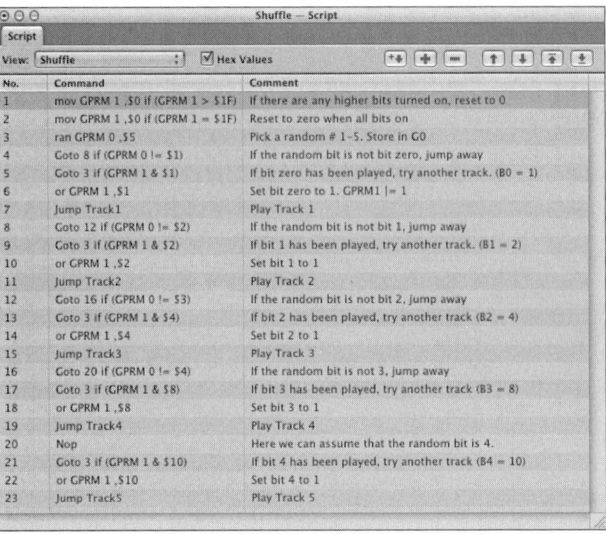

No.	Command	Comment
1	mov GPRM 1 ,$0 if (GPRM 1 > $1F)	If there are any higher bits turned on, reset to 0
2	mov GPRM 1 ,$0 if (GPRM 1 = $1F)	Reset to zero when all bits on
3	ran GPRM 0 ,$5	Pick a random # 1–5. Store in G0
4	Goto 8 if (GPRM 0 != $1)	If the random bit is not bit zero, jump away
5	Goto 3 if (GPRM 1 & $1)	If bit zero has been played, try another track. (B0 = 1)
6	or GPRM 1 ,$1	Set bit zero to 1. GPRM1 |= 1
7	Jump Track1	Play Track 1
8	Goto 12 if (GPRM 0 != $2)	If the random bit is not bit 1, jump away
9	Goto 3 if (GPRM 1 & $2)	If bit 1 has been played, try another track. (B1 = 2)
10	or GPRM 1 ,$2	Set bit 1 to 1
11	Jump Track2	Play Track 2
12	Goto 16 if (GPRM 0 != $3)	If the random bit is not bit 2, jump away
13	Goto 3 if (GPRM 1 & $4)	If bit 2 has been played, try another track (B2 = 4)
14	or GPRM 1 ,$4	Set bit 2 to 1
15	Jump Track3	Play Track 3
16	Goto 20 if (GPRM 0 != $4)	If the random bit is not 3, jump away
17	Goto 3 if (GPRM 1 & $8)	If bit 3 has been played, try another track (B3 = 8)
18	or GPRM 1 ,$8	Set bit 3 to 1
19	Jump Track4	Play Track 4
20	Nop	Here we can assume that the random bit is 4.
21	Goto 3 if (GPRM 1 & $10)	If bit 4 has been played, try another track (B4 = 10)
22	or GPRM 1 ,$10	Set bit 4 to 1
23	Jump Track5	Play Track 5

The Shuffle script uses GPRM 0 to select a random number between 1 and 5 and uses GPRM 1 to store the already-played tracks. This depends entirely on bit arithmetic. The | (or) and & (and) operations allow you to set and test certain bits in a register without affecting any of the other bits.

```
1: mov GPRM 1, $0 if (GPRM 1 > $1F)
```

This line uses a special number $1F (31 in base 10), which is the value of a register with the 5 lowest bits turned on and the top 11 bits turned off. This project uses 5 tracks. If the project used 2 tracks, you'd need to use 3 ($3) instead. If the project used 8 tracks, you'd need to use 511 ($1FF). In other words, for N tracks, the magic number equals $(2^{\wedge}(N+1) - 1)$.

As far as this line is concerned, any values in GPRM 1 above 31 for a 5-track project indicate that something is wrong—probably that the register was not initialized correctly.

```
2: mov GPRM 1, $0 if (GPRM 1 = $1F)
```

Whenever GPRM 1 reaches a value of $1F, all 5 tracks have played. This line resets GPRM 1 so that the tracks are free to replay.

```
3: ran GPRM 0, $5
```

Here, the script "rolls the dice." It selects a random number between 1 and 5 and stores it in GPRM 0. (As with $1F, you can adjust $5 to reflect the actual number of tracks in your project.)

```
4: Goto 8 if (GPRM 0 != $1)
```

This line checks whether the script has rolled a 1. If not, control passes to line 8, where the script checks for a 2, and so on.

```
5: Goto 3 if (GPRM 1 & $1)
```

This line checks whether the script already played Track 1. GPRM 1 stores the already-played tracks by turning on bits. Bit 0 corresponds to $1 (2^0 is 1). If this &-compare is true, the script returns to line 3 to select another random number.

```
6: or GPRM 1, $1
```

Here, the script sets bit 0 in GPRM 1 using an or operation. Next time through, this bit tells the script that Track 1 has been played.

```
7: Jump Track 1
```

The script ends, passing control to Track 1, which starts to play.

Lines 8–11, 12–15, 16–19, and 20–23 perform exactly the same tests and actions as lines 4–7. Each group of lines tests for a matching random number, determines if the track has already been played (if so, the script returns to line 3), sets the bit for the track that's about to play, and plays the track. The only distinction occurs in line 20, a NOP operation, which does nothing. By the time the script reaches line 20, you can be assured that the random number is 5, corresponding to Track 5 and bit 4. All other possibilities are exhausted.

7. **Simulate.** Click the Simulation icon in the toolbar, open the Info Drawer, and watch the progress of GPRM 0 and GPRM 1. If you like, use one hand to keep track of playback. Curl the finger that corresponds to each track as it plays. When all your fingers are bent, open the hand and allow the process to begin again. If you think of your fingers as bits, this is exactly the process that the script is performing.

General
Menu
Color Settings
User Operations
Overlay: not set
Audio: not set
Start:
Loop Point:
End:
00:00:00:00
00:00:03:00
00:00:07:29

Play Movie
Director's Commentary
Theatrical Trailers

3: An Evil Plan

1: Our Story Begins
2: Enter a Ship
3: An Evil Plan

Playback Options
Pre-Script: not set
DVD@ccess
Name:
URL:
Display Condition:
Parental Level
Alternate Target: Track 1
Not Rated
1 - G
2
3 - PG
4 - PG-13
5
6 - R
7 - NC-17

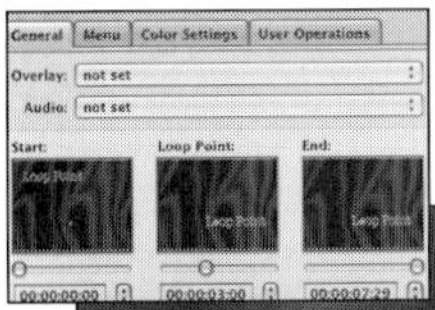

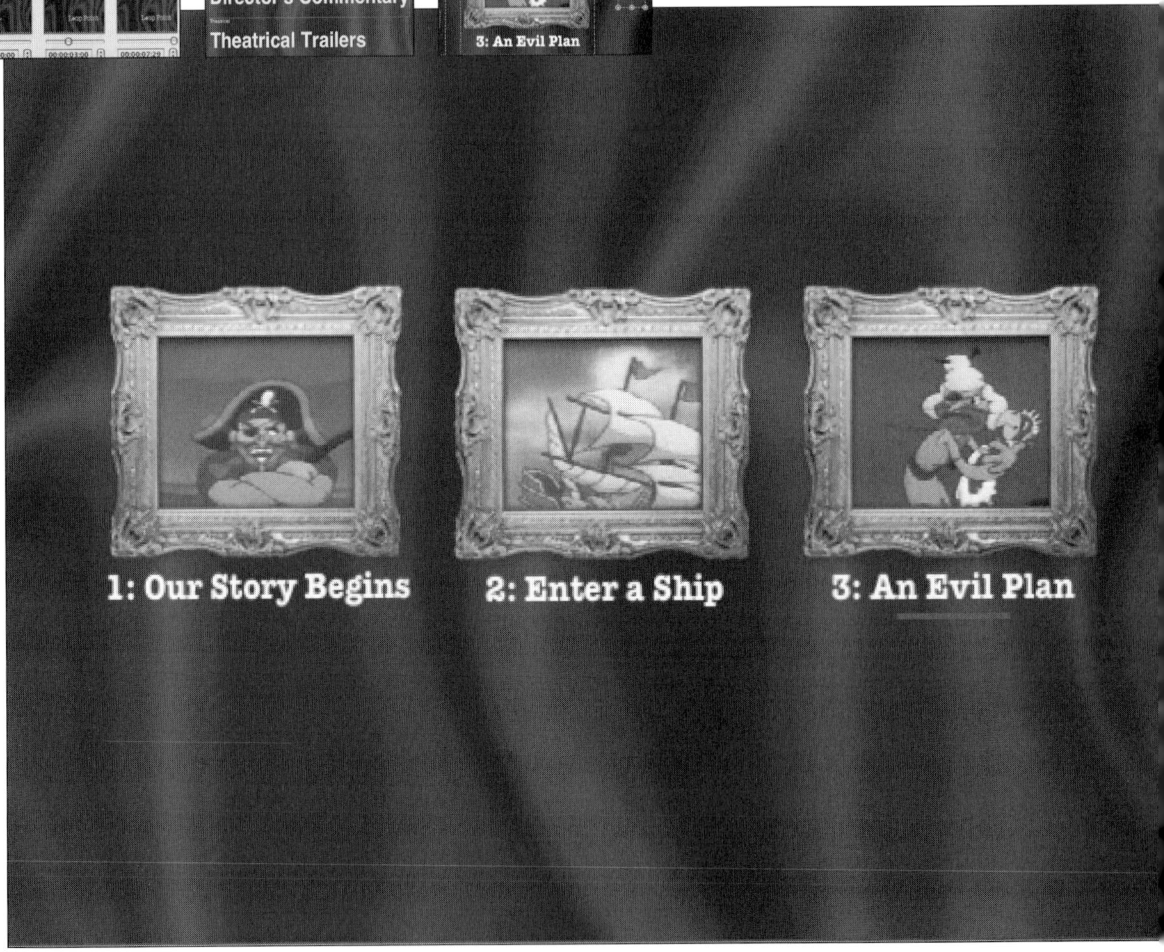

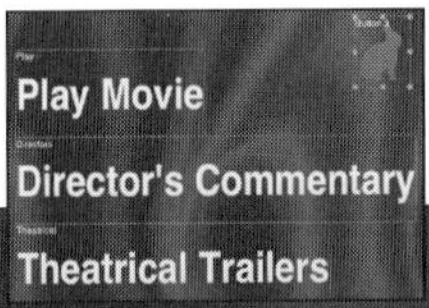

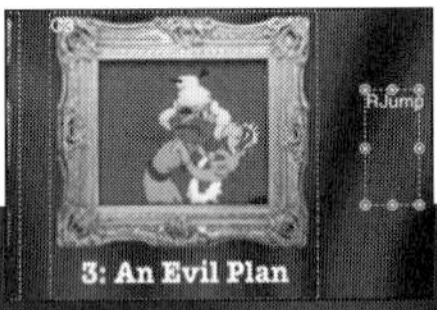

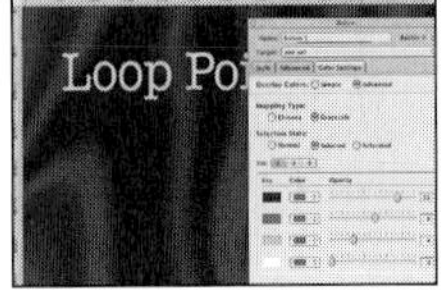

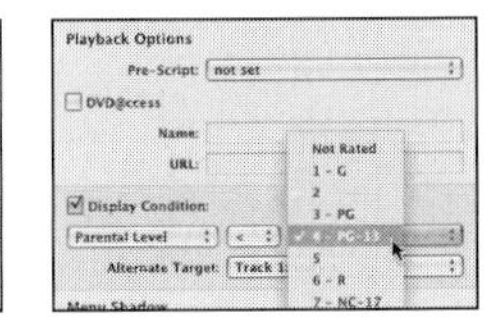

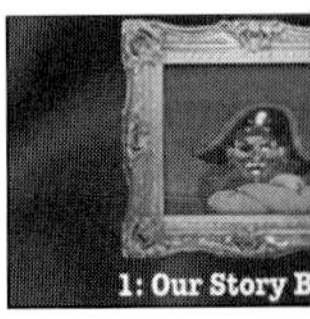

Advanced Interaction Menus and Methods

Sometimes you'll want to go beyond simple menus and buttons to use some of the more advanced features of DVD Studio Pro 2. In this chapter you'll discover many of the styles that produce the professional-level interactions you find on Hollywood DVDs. This chapter discusses less-known and less-used, but more powerful, features scattered throughout the program. These advanced styles range from invisible buttons and display conditions to loop points and Easter eggs.

Chapter Contents

Auto Action and Invisible Buttons

Selecting a Menu Button

Setting the Menu Drop Shadow

Customizing Motion Menu Loops

Using Display Conditions

Reviewing DVD @ccess Features

Controlling User Interactions

Solution: Navigate through Menus with Arrows

Solution: Build a Simple Easter Egg

Solution: Create a Loop Point

Solution: Add a Copyright Notice Screen to
   Your Movies

Use the techniques discussed in this chapter to enliven your DVD productions in ways you might not have thought you needed. You might discover that you do need them after all.

Auto Action and Invisible Buttons

The Advanced tab of the Button Inspector (see Figure 11.1) allows you to attach two special properties to your DVD Studio Pro 2 buttons: Auto Action and Invisible. These two settings provide advanced ways to use buttons, often working hand in hand.

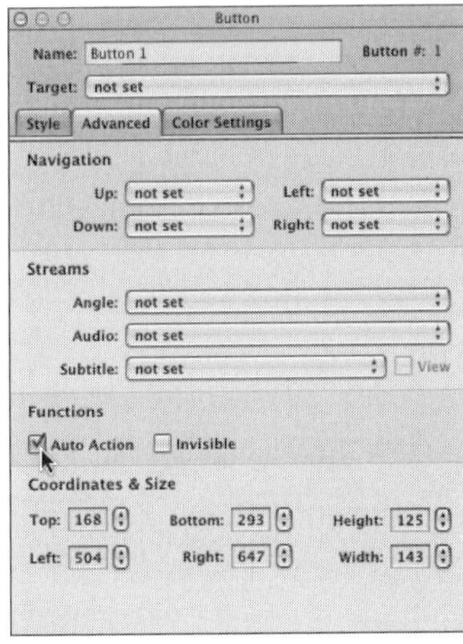

Figure 11.1 Open the Button Inspector's Advanced tab to set advanced button styles. Check the Auto Action or Invisible option to enable that style.

Auto Action Buttons Auto action buttons activate whenever they're selected. They link immediately to their target; viewers need not press Enter on their DVD remote. Auto action buttons create a different way to interact. With regular DVD menu buttons, your viewer must navigate to a button to select it and then press Enter to make things happen. With auto action buttons, you can create menus and button overlays that respond to arrow presses on your viewer's remote. As soon as an auto action button is selected, something happens.

Invisible Buttons As the name suggests, viewers cannot see invisible buttons, even when they are selected. This allows you to place hidden buttons in your menus or on your video, providing additional possibilities without visual clutter. Invisible buttons can add secret links to extra video material or provide a slideshow-style way of moving between menus and clips.

Be sure to enable Button Outlines in the Menu Editor when working with invisible buttons. Choose View > Show Button Outline And Name.

Selecting a Default Menu Button

DVD menus always contain one menu button selected by default. Which button is first selected depends on the way you configure or link to the menu. In DVD Studio Pro 2, you can indicate the menu button to select when displaying a menu in the following ways.

Setting the Default Button

Use the Menu Editor's Menu tab to select the default button for your menus. Locate the Default Button pop-up and select a menu button. Figure 11.2 shows the Menu Inspector with a default button set. Alternatively, choose Not Set to leave the default button feature unselected.

Although you can easily override this default (by targeting a specific button, using highlight conditions, and so forth), this feature provides a consistent selection starting point.

Avoid adding default buttons to motion menus. The loop point forces the selected button back to any selected default. This can jar viewers who have selected another button in the meantime.

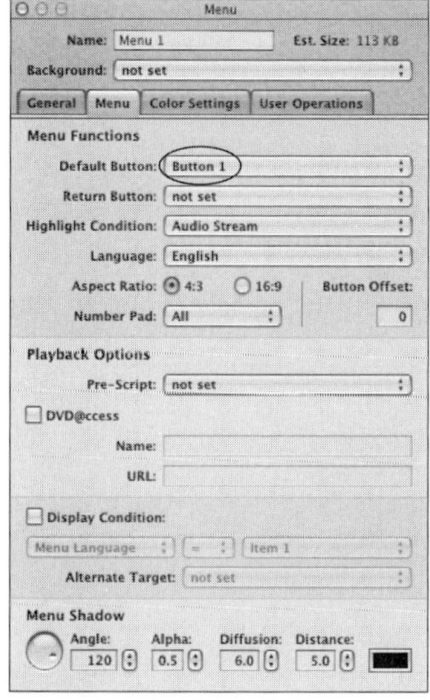

Figure 11.2 Open the Menu Inspector and its Menu tab to find the Default Button pop-up. Choose a button to set the menu default.

Targeting Buttons

The same pop-ups that let you link to menus, tracks, slideshows, and so forth allow you to link to specific buttons on menus. Just choose a button to select when the menu displays.

Targeting buttons is simple enough. The End-Jump, Jump-To, or Target pop-ups found in the Inspector list all menu buttons. For example, you might choose Menus > Menu 1 > Button 3 instead of Menus > Menu 1 > [Menu].

When you set a link in this fashion, DVD Studio Pro 2 shows it as Menu 1::Button 1, with a double colon between the menu and the button. This is similar to the way it displays links to a chapter (for example, Track 1::Chapter 4) or slide (for example, Slideshow 1::Slide5.tif).

Here are some ways to use this feature.

- **Return to the original button.**   Choose the button that links to the most recently played track. This allows the viewer to return to the menu in exactly the same state as it was left.

- **Proceed to the next button.**   Choose the button that follows the most recently played track. This allows you to guide the viewer through a series of videos.

- **Select a related track.**   Choose the track that you think the viewer might want to use next. Consider an educational DVD title. After playing a concept track, you might place the selection on a button that links to a review or a testing track.

Using Highlight Condition to Select a Button

The awkwardly named Highlight Condition provides another way to select a button. When set, it selects the button that corresponds to the last-played stream number for video, audio, or subtitle streams. Figure 11.3 shows the pop-up that lets you select the stream type for this feature.

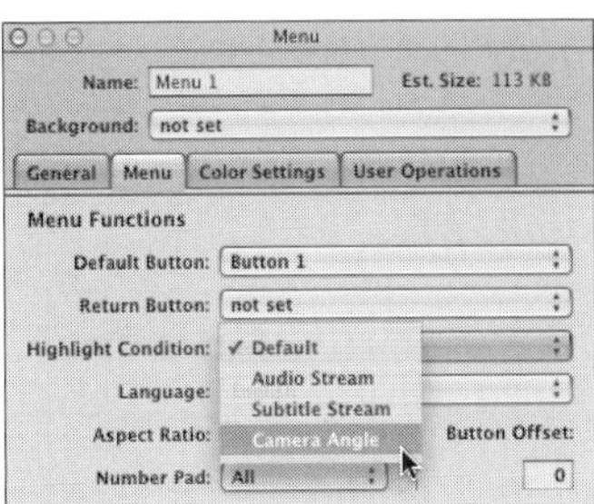

Figure 11.3 Use the Highlight Condition pop-up, found in the Menu tab of the Menu Inspector, to select menu buttons based on the most recently played audio, subtitle, or video (Camera Angle) stream.

328

Imagine that your animated movie contains a regular video angle and one that reveals the underlying wireframes used to create the graphics. When the wireframe version finishes playing, a menu appears with its Learn More About Animation button preselected. Highlight conditions make this scenario possible.

Highlight conditions are particularly sensitive to button order. When you add two buttons one after another, the first button has a higher rank than the second, even if the placement on-screen has the first button below or to the right of the second. To see each button listed in order, select the menu and open the Connections tab. This ordering sets the way that buttons match to stream numbers.

As with default buttons, the highlight condition behavior is overridden by button targeting.

To change angles in Apple DVD Player, you must access the controls in the hidden drawer. Click the three dots on the virtual remote to display the drawer, and locate the Subtitle, Audio, and Angle buttons.

Allowing or Disallowing Button Number Access

You can author DVDs so that viewers can use the numbers on the remote control to select menu buttons. The Number Pad pop-up in the Menu Inspector's Menu tab allows you to permit or deny access to buttons in this fashion. The pop-up offers three choices:

All Permits access to every button in the menu via the remote's numeric keypad.

None Denies access via the remote's numeric keypad.

(Number) Instructs DVD Studio Pro 2 to allow the viewer access to some but not all buttons.

Using numbers rather than All or None takes some extra thought and planning. The number you select sets the highest allowed number key. For example, if you choose 2 on a menu with 5 buttons, the viewer can press 1 or 2 to access buttons 1 or 2. Pressing 3 or higher does nothing. The viewer cannot access buttons 3 through 5 in this way. This approach works particularly well when you use more than one logical kind of button on a menu. For example, you might want to use numbers to select scenes, but not for choosing languages.

As with highlight conditions, the button order in the Connections tab matters. Select the menu in the Outline tab and open the Connections tab (see Figure 11.4). The list of buttons shows the underlying numbering.

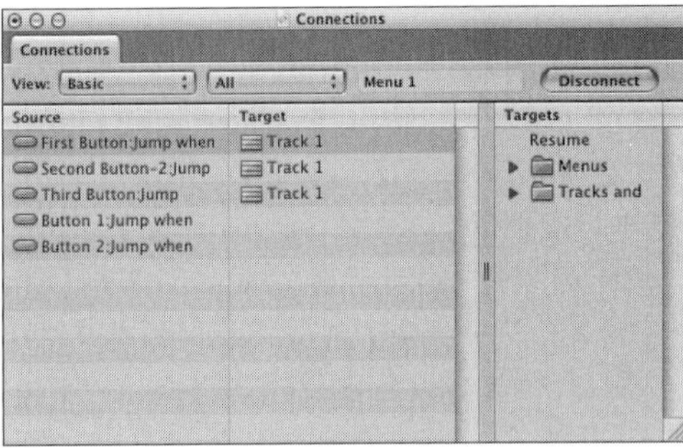

Figure 11.4 When you select a menu and open the Connections tab, the button ordering found there indicates the number sequence each button will use. The first button (First Button) corresponds to button 1; the last (Button 2) corresponds to button 5.

You can offset the starting button number so that numbers make better sense to your viewer. Say, for example, that you're listing catalog numbers or scene-selection numbers. The menu might link to catalog item 35 or movie scene 51. Use the Button Offset field to accommodate these higher numbers. If 35 refers to the first item in your menu, set the offset to 34. If the first item is 51, use 50. Use an offset number that's one less than the first menu item. Figure 11.5 shows an example. This feature allows your viewers to use more meaningful numbers when making menu selections.

 The Menu Inspector's Menu tab also allows you to set a target for the Return button on your viewer's remote. Use the Return Button pop-up to choose from any of the elements in your project.

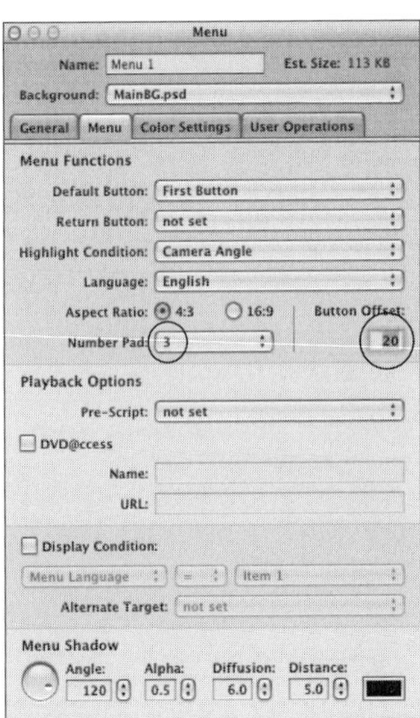

Figure 11.5 The Menu tab in the Menu Inspector allows you to set number pad options and offsets. In the example shown here, the settings allow viewers to access the first three buttons by entering 21, 22, and 23 on their remote controls.

Setting the Menu Drop Shadow

Many menu components—button text, button shapes, drop zone shapes, and menu text—allow you to add drop shadows. Drop shadows are a common effect used in print publishing as well as video. Shadows provide a three-dimensional look for your menus, adding a subtle visual flourish. With them, parts of your DVD menu appear to "float" above the background. Drop shadow check boxes appear in the Inspectors for each item. When these check boxes are checked, DVD Studio Pro 2 applies a drop shadow that falls from the item onto the menu beneath. You use the Menu Shadow section of the Menu Editor's Menu tab to configure how the drop shadows appear throughout the menu. Figure 11.6 shows the various controls involved.

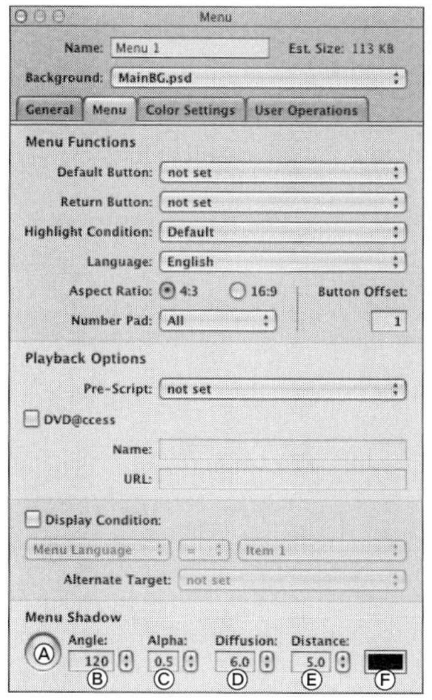

Figure 11.6 Menu Shadow controls appear at the bottom of the Menu Editor's Menu tab: Rotary Angle control Ⓐ; Angle setting Ⓑ; Alpha setting Ⓒ; Diffusion setting Ⓓ; Distance setting Ⓔ; Shadow Color control Ⓕ.

Rotary Angle Control (A) Sets the position of the drop shadow with respect to the center of the item. Rotating the dot to the top position (12:00) sets the shadow above the item. Setting the dot at 3:00 places the shadow to the right, and so on.

Angle Setting (B) Reflects the current setting for the Rotary Angle control—and vice versa. Enter an angle between 0 and 360 degrees to place the drop shadow around an item. A setting of 12:00 corresponds to 0 (or 360) degrees; 3:00 corresponds to 90, 9:00 to 270.

Alpha Setting (C) Controls shadow translucency. Set this control between 0.0 (completely transparent, invisible) and 1.0 (completely opaque, dark shadow).

Diffusion Setting (D) Controls the shadow's softness. Choose a setting between 0.0 (hard, sharp edges) and 15.0 (very soft, diffuse edges).

Distance Setting (E) Sets the distance from the item to the shadow. Choose a setting between 0.0 (under the object, with the "light source" directly above) to 15.0 (offset to the maximum position, with the "light source" at a sharp angle).

Shadow Color Control (F) Shows the currently selected shadow color. Click to open the Color Picker to select another color to use.

 Diffusion and distance settings above 15.0 are treated as if they were 15.0.

 Alpha settings and Distance settings of 0.0 produce drop shadows that cannot be seen. A zero Alpha setting is invisible. A 0.0 distance appears under each object.

Customizing Motion Menu Loops

Whenever you create an introductory track for a motion menu, you encounter pauses. These pauses occur when the track ends, just before the menu loop begins. The DVD player must switch from the track to the menu, causing a slight but noticeable delay during playback.

Fortunately, DVD Studio Pro 2 provides a solution. Using its menu loop feature, you can set a custom loop point in your menu video, allowing you to build a single video asset that includes both an introduction (displayed only once) and repeating menu material. The video starts with the introduction, plays through the normal menu motion, and then loops back to a point that you set. It's simple. It's elegant. And it causes few playback disturbances. Follow these steps:

1. **Build the loop.** Use your favorite video-editing or animation software to build your introduction and loop.

2. **Create the menu.** Build a menu in DVD Studio Pro 2. Add the new video to the menu background and build your buttons. (See the list following these steps for some caveats about button type.)

3. **Set the loop.** Open the Menu Inspector (⌘-⌥-I), click the General tab, and locate the At End pop-up, as shown in Figure 11.7. Choose Loop. This instructs the menu to loop each time it finishes playing the motion video.

4. **Set the loop point.** Adjust the Loop Point slider or enter a value in the text box just below to set the loop point. When the background video finishes playing, the menu loops back to this point.

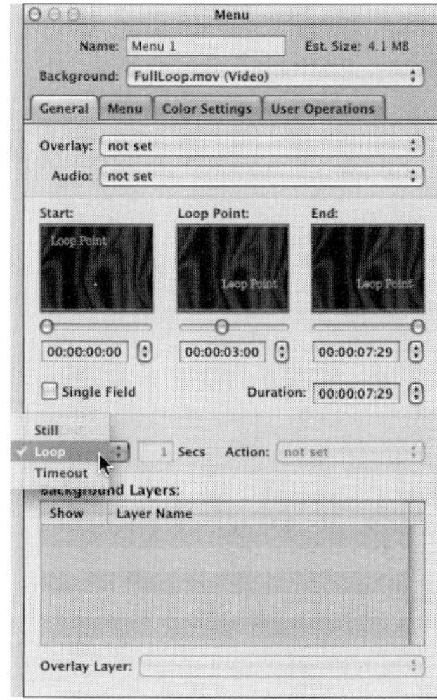

Figure 11.7 The General tab in the Menu Inspector allows you to loop your menu video. Choose Loop from the At End pop-up, and then set the video's start, end, and loop points. Make sure to use overlay buttons, or your loop point menus won't work.

Keep the following points in mind when building motion menus with loop points:

You must use overlay buttons. Unlike normal motion menus, menus with loop points do not work with shapes, drop zones, text, or button assets. Stick to overlays, and, whenever possible, design any button art or text into the motion footage.

Use natural GOP boundaries when building video. Be aware of the length of the animation and the time of the loop. Use these to set the boundaries for the introductory material and to plan for the overall loop length.

The loop point controls the appearance of button highlights. Highlights appear the first time the loop point is passed. This allows the introduction to proceed without the distraction of buttons.

The introduction plays each time you link to the menu. When you want to play just the looping portion after returning from a track or slideshow, consider linking to a second copy of the menu without the introduction.

Other Ways to Build Menu Loops

Some projects simply cannot do without shapes, drop zones, text, or button assets. In these cases, you'll have to use one of the following approaches. Add a track or a second menu with the introductory material, and then link. This lets you use these other items and bypass the issue of loop points.

Introductory Tracks

Creating an introductory track is simple enough. Add your introductory video material to V1 and any supporting audio to A1. Target the track's End Jump to your menu. If needed, add buttons over the video. Be sure to relink your project elements to the introductory track rather than to the menu itself.

If you want to get extra clever, you can place the entire video (introduction plus loop) into a track. Set a chapter marker for the loop point and end jump to that marker. Add buttons over the video, and you're set. This produces a menu that works almost exactly the same way as the Loop Point menu described previously, but gives you extra flexibility when adding overlay art in addition to your buttons.

Introductory Menus

A second menu can provide a well-behaved introduction to your motion menu. Create a new menu, add the introductory video, and set the At End pop-up (see Figure 11.7 earlier in this chapter) to Time Out. After the menu video plays once, it links to the target set in the Action pop-up, which you set to the Loop menu.

Links from one menu to another proceed with fewer pauses than links from tracks to menus or menus to tracks. All menus use the same Video Title Set (VTS), allowing the DVD player to move quickly from one menu to another.

Use these same methods—linked tracks and menus—when you want to add button transitions. Button transitions are videos that play after a viewer activates a button. Create one properly linked transition video for each button. You cannot reuse a track for more than one transition unless you plan to link to the same project element or you're willing to use scripting to provide different destinations.

Using the At End Pop-Up

The At End pop-up (see Figure 11.7 earlier in this chapter) provides three ways to customize the way your menus behave after the motion video finishes playing.

Still Plays the motion video (and audio) once and then freezes on the last frame. The last frame displays for the duration of the menu.

Loop Plays the motion video continuously, restarting whenever the end is reached. After the first time through, the menu plays from the optional loop point. When no loop point is defined, the menu plays again from the beginning.

Timeout Works like Still but sets a time (in seconds) after which the DVD links to the element set in the Action pop-up. When using a motion background, the timer starts when the motion video finishes playing once. For still backgrounds, the timer begins as the menu first displays.

Follow these steps to add a timeout to your menu.

1. **Build your menu.** Add your background, buttons, and so forth.

2. **Open the Menu Inspector.** Click the General tab.

3. **Set the timeout.** Choose Timeout from the At End pop-up. Specify how long to wait and enter that value (in seconds) in the Secs text field.

4. **Set a target.** Use the Action pop-up to link to a project element. The DVD jumps to this element when the timeout is reached.

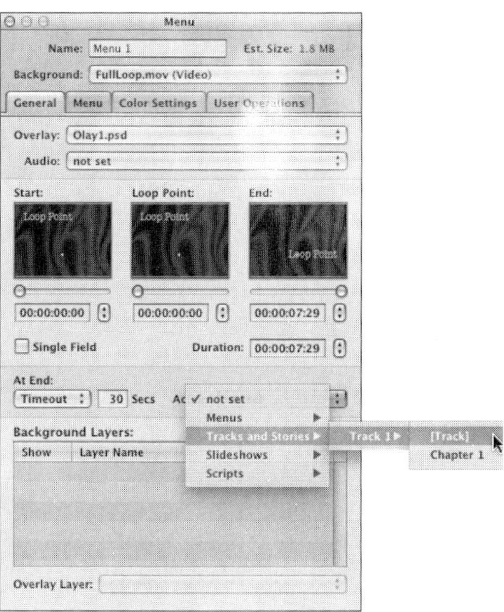

Using Display Condition

The Display Condition check box control access to menus, tracks, and stories without scripting. the condition consists of a simple comparison. If the comparison is true, the element plays. If not, you provide an alternate target, which the DVD links to instead.

Follow these steps to add a display condition.

1. **Select a menu, track, or story.** In the Outline tab, choose the item with which you want to work.

2. **Open the Inspector.** Press ⌘-⌥-I.

3. **Locate the display conditions.** The Display Condition controls appear in the Menu Inspector's Menu tab, the Track Inspector's General tab, and the Story Inspector's General tab.

4. **Choose a condition type.** Use the Display Condition pop-up (shown in Figure 11.8) to select from the list. Table 11.1 describes the available condition types.

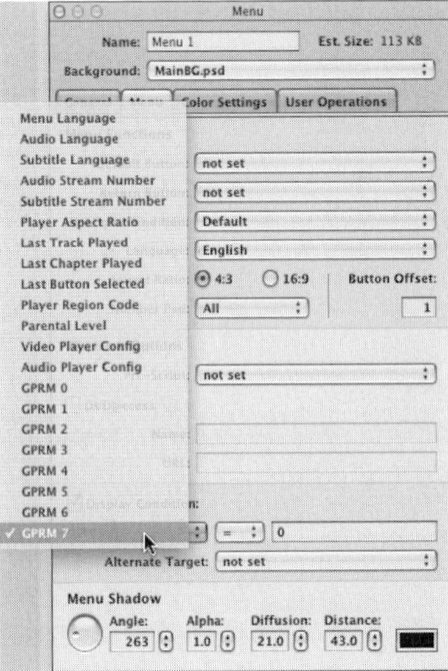

Figure 11.8 Use display conditions to customize DVD presentations to the needs and settings of your audience. DVD Studio Pro 2 offers 21 display conditions that allow you to control whether your viewers can access tracks, stories, and menus and provide alternate destinations, where needed. These conditions let you regulate on the basis of parental rating (such as PG-13), regions (the United States is in Region 1), player language, and more.

5. **Choose a conditional relationship.** These use the same comparisons discussed in Chapter 10: is greater than (>), greater-equal (>=), less-than (<), less-equal (<=), equal (=, although it should properly be ==), not-equal (!=), and bitwise-and (&). Each of these operates as it would in any traditional programming language.

6. **Choose a value to compare to.** All the values (Apple calls them Conditional States) associated with display conditions are constants. The type of condition you selected in step 4 determines the control presented in the Inspector. Table 11.1 details the kinds of settings you may use to set a comparison value. Some conditional states include predefined lists (such as language, region code, and parental rating); others allow you to enter integer values. Figure 11.9 shows the parental rating pop-up.

Unlike scripting, display conditions always use base 10 (decimal) numbers.

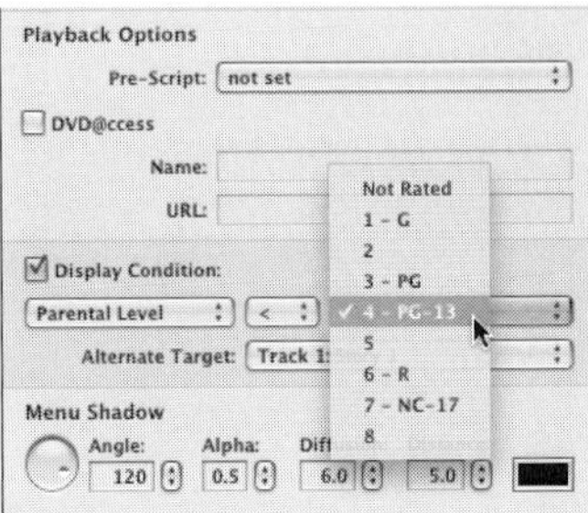

Figure 11.9 All display conditions compare a GPRM or SPRM register to a constant. Here, the condition checks to see if the Parental Level (SPRM 13) is less than PG-13 (4). If so, this menu jumps to an alternate target.

7. **Select a target.** In the Alternate Target pop-up, choose an element from your project to which to link.

You can add display conditions directly to stories, or you can check the Apply To Stories check box in the Track Inspector's General tab. This feature applies the Track's display condition to each of its stories.

▶ **Table 11.1** DVD Studio Pro 2 Display Condition Types and Possible Settings

Display Condition Type	Possible Condition Settings
Menu Language (SPRM 0), Audio Language (SPRM 16), Subtitle Language (SPRM 18)	Choose from the list of recognized two-character language codes, just as you'd select a language for an audio or a subtitle stream. Compares against the initial language settings defined by the DVD player.
Audio Stream Number (SPRM 1), Subtitle Stream Number (SPRM 2)	Choose from A1 through A8 or S1 through S32.
Player Aspect Ratio (SPRM 14)	In theory, you choose from a pop-up to select from 4:3, 16:9 Pan-Scan, 16:9 Letterbox, and 16:9 Pan-Scan And Letterbox. In actuality (at least in early versions of DVD Studio Pro 2), you don't select anything. This option is broken.
Last Track (SPRM 4), Last Chapter (SPRM 7)	Enter a base 10 integer in the text field. Chapter numbers start with 1 and increase by 1 for each subsequent chapter. Track numbers, which also start with 1, reflect the ordering in the Outline tab.
Last Button Selected (SPRM 8)	Select from a pop-up, offering values in the range 1 through 36. If you're unsure of button ordering, select the menu and view the Connections tab. The buttons are numbered in the order found there, starting with 1.
Player Region Code (SPRM 20), Parental Level (SPRM 13)	Use the pop-up to select from the eight worldwide regions or the eight parental levels (plus not rated). Surprisingly, you cannot test for Region Not Set (Region 0) with display conditions.
Video Player Config (SPRM 14), Audio Player Config (SPRM 15	Enter a base 10 integer in the field provided. See the Appendix for details about the possible values in these SPRMs.
GPRM 0 through GPRM 7	Enter any base 10 integer in the field. Values can be in the range 0 through 65535.

Display conditions are not prescripts. Here are a few points to keep in mind.

You can use both. DVD Studio Pro 2 allows you to assign both a prescript and a display condition to each menu, track, and story in your project.

Prescripts offer more power. Prescrips can do everything that display conditions can do—and a whole lot more.

Display conditions don't require any programming. This is often a blessed convenience and a simpler alternative to prescripts.

Prescripts run first. Both display conditions and prescripts execute before the element begins to play back. Prescripts execute before the display condition is performed.

Prescripts run when you link to root elements. You must target a menu, track, slideshow, or story to ensure that a prescript will execute. Linking to buttons, chapters, or slides bypasses element prescripts.

Display conditions always run. It doesn't matter whether you target a button, a menu, a chapter, or a track. Display conditions always execute before project elements play back. This allows you to block access to materials, no matter how the link is made.

Prescripts can introduce delays. DVD Studio Pro 2 places all scripts into Video Title Set 1. The DVD player may need to jump from the part of the DVD that stores a track, story, or slideshow to the prescript.

Display conditions execute rapidly. DVD Studio Pro 2 stores all display conditions in the same part of the disc as the project element. Display conditions thus run quickly, allowing your audience to view elements without delay—unless the display condition is violated. In that case, the DVD player must jump to another program element.

Reviewing DVD @ccess Features

DVD @ccess allows you to link menus, markers, and slides to URLs. This lets you add further interactive content to your DVD for when it plays back on a personal computer. Several previous chapters in this book have discussed and demonstrated the ways to use DVD @ccess. The review provided here summarizes material scattered throughout the book.

Using DVD @ccess on Windows and Macs

DVD Studio Pro 2 automatically includes a DVD @ccess installer in the DVD-ROM portion of your disc whenever you use DVD @ccess in your project. This installer lets you install DVD @ccess on Windows-based computers. Unfortunately, the software compatibility with Windows is, at best, iffy. Emerging standards, such as Web-DVD, may pave the way for a true multiplatform solution for DVD/World Web Web coordination.

DVD @ccess software comes installed on all current Mac systems, although you must enable it in Apple DVD Player. Choose DVD Player > Preferences to open the Preferences dialog. Click the Disc tab, locate the Features box, and check Enable DVD @ccess Web Links. Click OK to close the Preferences dialog.

Adding DVD @ccess to Project Elements

Follow these steps to add a DVD @ccess link to your project.

1. **Select a menu, a marker, or a slide.** These are the only three DVD Studio Pro 2 elements that support DVD @ccess.

2. **Open the Inspector.** Locate the Playback options. For menus, click the Menu tab. For markers, click the General tab. The Slideshow Inspector has no tabs— DVD @ccess appears in the main Inspector pane.

3. **Check DVD @ccess.** This tells DVD Studio Pro 2 to use the link information you provide.

4. **Enter a name and a URL.** The URL specifies the item to which you want to link. The Name field offers nothing more than a helpful comment. The information you enter is not actually used by DVD Studio Pro 2.

Valid URLs

URLs that are valid to use with DVD @ccess include the following types:

*   Standard Internet links, for example, http://www.ericasadun.com

*   File links, for example, file://MY_DVD/InfoFolder/info.txt

*   E-mail links, for example, mailto:nospam@spam.com

    Use special care when linking to files on your DVD. Use the exact name of your disc, folders, and files. In the General tab of the Disc Inspector, you can define a folder to use for the DVD_ROM portion of your disc. The folder you select does not appear on the disc you build. Instead, all the materials within that folder appear at the disc's top level. Keep this in mind when setting up your file URLs.

Enabling DVD @ccess for the Simulator

Follow these steps to enable DVD @ccess features when you simulate your project.

1. **Open the Preferences dialog.** Choose DVD Studio Pro > Preferences (⌘-,).

2. **Open the Simulator Preferences pane.** Click the Simulator icon in the top Preferences toolbar.

3. **Enable DVD @ccess.** Locate the Features section, find the Enable DVD @ccess Web Links check box, and check it.

4. **Click OK.** This saves your changes and closes the Preferences dialog.

Controlling User Interactions

The DVD standard defines a number of operations (informally known as User Ops) that you can allow or disallow to restrict the way viewers can use their remote controls. These take the form of flags (1-bit switches with on and off settings) that DVD Studio Pro 2 encodes into the elements of your disc. The User Operations tab appears in the Inspectors for menus, tracks, stories, and markers and allows you to disable or enable these responses.

You might want to control the way your DVD responds to commands for two reasons—to avoid errors produced by pressing the wrong remote control buttons and to force viewers along certain viewing paths. Uses might include the following:

- Confine students to the lesson flow you design into the disc

- Prevent customers from fast-forwarding through a sales pitch

- Keep viewers from accessing "unauthorized" portions of the DVD without proper access methods

- Add "Easter egg" capabilities to only parts of your disc

- Prevent viewers from leaving the FBI warning screen before it finishes playing

Contrary to what you might expect, DVD Studio Pro 2 employs user operations to *deny* access to certain remote control buttons rather than to allow access. As Figure 11.10 shows, the User Operations pane lets you select which items to disable during playback of your project elements.

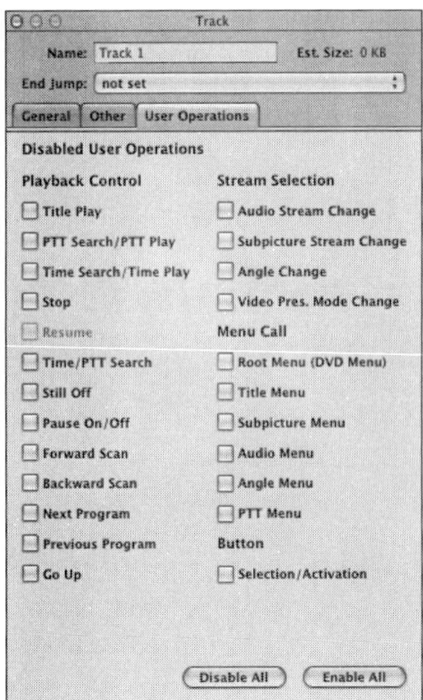

Figure 11.10 DVD Studio Pro 2 provides User Operations panes for tracks, stories, menus, and markers. This Inspector pane disables ways that viewers can interact with DVDs. Common uses include forcing viewers to watch FBI warnings and preventing viewers from skipping ahead through sales pitches and tedious academic lectures.

User operation lockouts are widely seen as an inconvenience by the DVD-viewing public. More and more, people are modifying their DVD players to bypass these authoring decisions. The DVD-authoring community has responded (in part) by skipping user operation denials in some newer commercial productions, allowing viewers to retain control over their watching habits.

The User Operations pane can disable as many as 24 kinds of user interactions on the DVD player's remote control. DVD Studio Pro 2 divides these UOPs (user operations) into four types:

Playback Control (13 controls) Controls the ways that viewers watch and interact with DVD content

Stream Selection (4 controls) Responds to user requests to change streams

Menu Call (6 controls) Handles viewer requests to display particular menus

Button (1 control) Determines whether on-screen buttons react to viewer responses

Table 11.2 lists the UOPs that DVD Studio Pro 2 can control. Follow these steps to disable UOPs in your project.

1. **Select a project element.** In the Outline tab, choose a track, story, or menu, or select a chapter in the Track tab.

2. **Open the Element Inspector.** Choose View > Show Inspector (⌘-⌥-I).

3. **Open the User Operations tab.** Click the tab to bring the pane to the front.

4. **Select which UOPs to disable.** Use the check boxes to disable those operations you want to deny the viewers. The items you check affect only the project element you selected in step 1. To disable all operations, click Disable All. Click Enable All to clear every check box in the pane.

▶ **Table 11.2** DVD Studio Pro 2 User Operations

User Operation	Type	Role	Effect when disabled
Title Play (UOP2); Part of Title (PTT) Search/PTT Play (UOP1); Time Search/ Time Play (UOP0)	Playback Control	Allows the number keys on the remote control to jump to (or play from) a new title, chapter marker, or time.	Prevents those jumps.
Stop (UOP3)	Playback Control	Stops movie playback before the end of the movie is reached.	Prevents any premature stop.

User Operation	Type	Role	Effect when disabled
Resume (UOP16)	Playback Control	Resumes movie playback after jumping to a menu.	Prevents resumption from the menus to a track or story.
Time/PTT Search (UOP5)	Playback Control	Locates and plays video in stream by entering exact times.	Prevents those jumps.
Still Off (UOP18)	Playback Control	Disables paused stills in slideshows.	Allows viewers to pause slideshows.
Pause On/Off (UOP19)	Playback Control	Pauses movie during playback.	Prevents viewers from pausing movie.
Forwards / Backwards Scan (UOP8, UOP9)	Playback Control	Provides fast forward/fast reverse.	Prevents fast forward/ fast reverse.
Next Program / Previous Program (UOP7, UOP6)	Playback Control	Moves to next chapter/ previous chapter.	Prevents skipping between chapters.
Go Up (UOP4)	Playback Control	Returns one level higher in navigation path. This important remote key is not supported by DVD Studio Pro 2 during track playback.	Prevents response to the Return button.
Audio Stream Change, Subpicture Stream Change, Angle Change (UOP20, UOP21, UOP22)	Stream Selection	Changes streams in response to the Audio, Subtitle, and Angle buttons.	Prevents response to these buttons.
Video Presentation Mode Change (UOP24)	Stream Selection	Switches between 4:3 and 16:9 presentations.	Prevents response to the button.
Root Menu (DVD Menu), Title Menu, Subpicture Menu, Audio Menu, Angle Menu (UOP11, UOP10, UOP12, UOP13, UOP14)	Menu Call	Requests specific menus: main DVD menu, Title menu, Subtitle menu, Audio menu, and Angle menu. The Root Menu and Title Menu keys are used most often.	Prevents response to the buttons during movie playback.
PTT Menu (UOP15)	Menu Call	Requests the Chapter menu.	Prevents response to the button during movie playback.
Selection/Activation (UOP 17)	Button	Chooses (and activates) on-screen menu buttons.	Prevents selecting and activating button highlight areas.

Solution: Navigate through Menus with Arrows

Auto-activating invisible menu buttons makes it possible to navigate between menus using only the arrows on your viewer's remote control. Follow these steps to build a pair of menus that use this navigation scheme. You'll find the files for this project on the companion DVD.

1. **Start a new project.** Remove the default menu (Menu 1) from the project.

2. **Populate the track.** Drag PegLeg.m2v onto Track 1 in the Outline tab. The track renames to PegLeg. Double-click the track to open it in the Track Editor.

3. **Add chapter markers.** Locate the Markers area, above the timeline. Ctrl-click(right-click) this area, and choose Import Marker List from the pop-up. Navigate to Markers.txt in the chapter folder. Select it, and click Choose. DVD Studio Pro 2 adds 9 markers to your project. Click OK.

4. **Add the menus.** Choose File > Import > Item Description. Navigate to Menu1.dspMenu. Select it and click Import. Repeat to import Menu2.dspMenu. Locate MainBG.psd, and drag it onto Menu 1 in the Outline tab. Repeat for Menu 2.

5. **Look at the menus.** Open the Menu Editor, and choose View > Show Button Outline And Name. Look at the menus. Each menu contains three scene buttons plus one extra button. Menu 1's extra button is RJump, located to the right of C3. Menu 2's extra button is LJump, to the left of C4.

At times DVD Studio Pro 2 does not properly reload the button assets from the menu description file. When this happens, select each menu button, set its asset to PegLeg.m2v, and clear the Motion check box.

6. **Customize the Auto Action button.** Use the Menu Editor's View pop-up to open Menu 1. Select RJump, open the Button Inspector, and click the Advanced tab.

Check Auto Action, and check Invisible. Set the target to Menus > Menu 2 > C4. When selected, RJump automatically targets C4 on Menu 2.

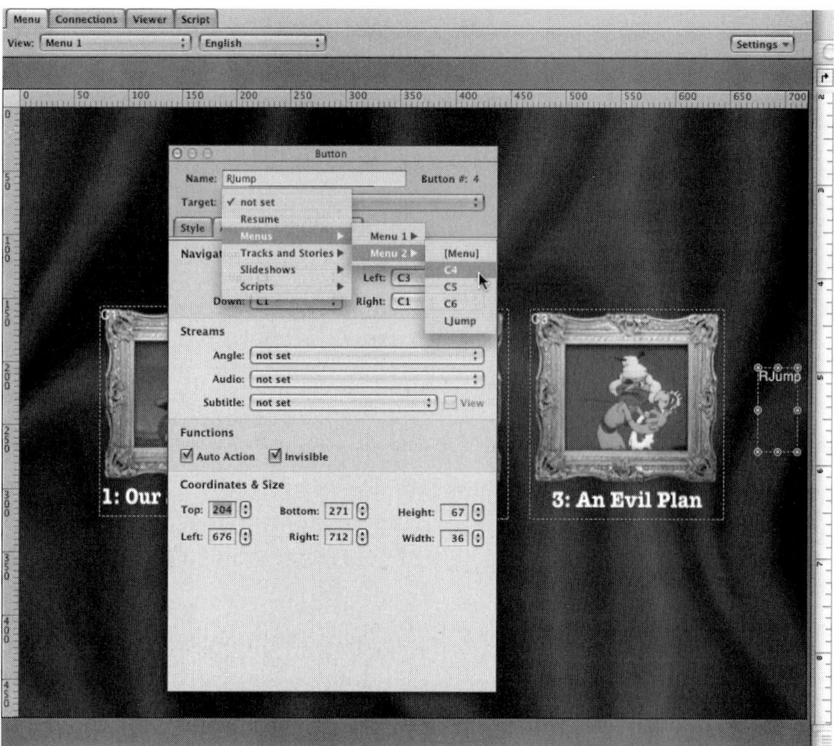

7. **Limit the navigation from C1.** Select Menu 1's leftmost button, C1. In the current layout, your viewer might accidentally activate RJump by pressing the left or up remote arrow buttons from C1. To fix this, open the Button Inspector's Advanced tab, and set the Up and Left pop-ups to C1.

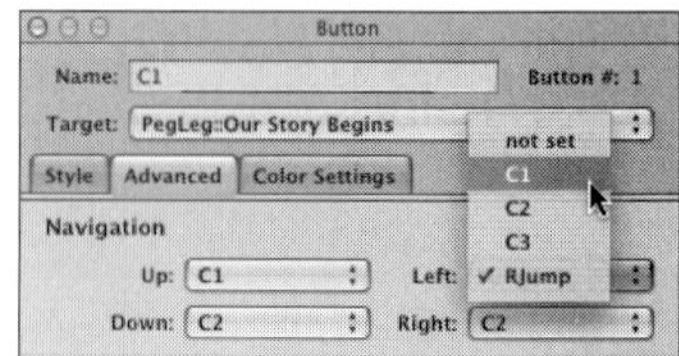

8. **Customize LJump.** Choose Menu 2 from the Menu Editor's View pop-up. Select LJump, and open the Button Inspector's Advanced tab. Check Auto Action and Invisible. Set the Target to Menus > Menu 1 > C3.

9. **Limit the navigation from C6.** Select C6, the rightmost button in Menu 2. Open the Button Inspector's Advanced tab. Set the Down and Right pop-ups to C6. Again, this prevents accidental navigation to LJump.

10. **Set First Play.** In the Outline tab, Ctrl-click(right-click) your disc. Choose First Play > Menus > Menu 1 > C1. When your disc begins playback, Menu 1 will display with the C1 button selected.

11. **Simulate.** In the Outline tab, Ctrl-click(right-click) Menu 1, and choose Simulate from the pop-up.

12. **Test.** Use the arrow keys to navigate through your menus and confirm that they work as expected. Clicking the Right arrow on the third scene selection button (3: An Evil Plan) takes you to Menu 2 and Scene 4. Clicking the Left arrow takes you back.

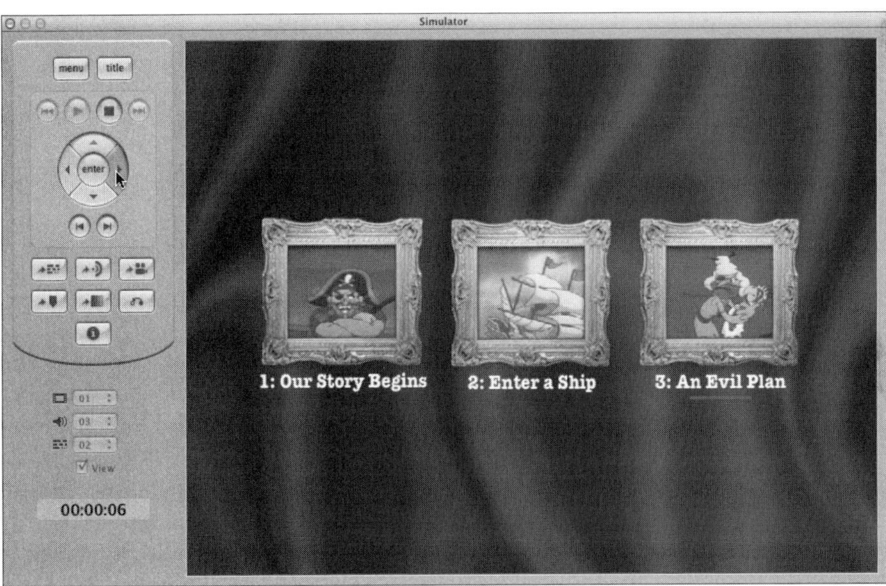

Solution: Build a Simple Easter Egg

The phrase *Easter egg* refers to a hidden, undocumented feature added to DVD menus or tracks. Hollywood blockbusters are well known for DVD Easter eggs. It seems like most commercial DVD releases now contain at least one egg-stra. Sites, such as www.dvdeastereggs.com, let egg devotees share their discoveries.

You can add eggs to your projects in many ways. Here's one of the simplest. Use the following steps to build a menu with an egg surprise. Again, you'll find all the files on the companion DVD.

1. **Start a new project.** Remove the default Menu 1.

2. **Create the menu.** Choose File > Import > Item Description. Navigate to EggMenu.dspMenu, select it, and click Choose. DVD Studio Pro 2 adds EggMenu to the Outline tab.

3. **Review the menu.** Open the new menu in the Menu Inspector. It contains six buttons: Three use normal text (Play Movie, Director's Commentary, Theatrical Trailers), and three do not. Button 1 and Button 2 appear outside the title safe zone, and Button 3 appears in a blank space within it.

4. **Add the overlay.** Drag Egg.psd onto the Menu Editor's background. Choose Set Overlay from the drop palette. Egg.psd contains a single highlight, a rabbit, at the position of Button 3. Select Button 3 to see it.

5. **Add a background.** Add a background by dragging MainBG.psd onto EggMenu in the Outline tab.

6. **Set the navigation.** Open the Button Inspector's Advanced tab. Use the following chart to set the navigation for each button. These settings create a secret path from Director's Commentary to Button 3: left, up, left.

Button	Up	Down	Left	Right
Play	Play	Directors	Play	Play
Directors	Play	Theatrical	Button 1	Directors
Theatrical	Directors	Theatrical	Theatrical	Theatrical
Button 1	Button 2	Directors	Directors	Directors
Button 2	Directors	Directors	Button 3	Directors
Button 3	Directors	Directors	Directors	Directors

7. **Simulate.** In the Outline tab, Ctrl-click(right-click) EggMenu, and choose Simulate from the pop-up to open the Simulator window. Use the arrow keys on the simulated remote to test the navigation for this project. Confirm that the project works as expected and that the secret sequence leads you to the hidden bunny.

Solution: Create a Loop Point

Motion Menu loop points allow you to combine an introduction and a loop into a single video asset. In this solution, you'll use create a motion menu and set the loop point. Again, you'll find the files on the companion DVD.

1. **Create a new project.** Double-click Menu 1 to open it in the Menu Editor.

2. **Add a background and an overlay.** Locate FullLoop.mov, and drag it onto the menu background. Choose Set Background from the drag palette. Then find LoopOlay.psd, drag it onto the menu background, and choose Set Overlay from the drag palette.

3. **Create a button.** Drag out a button in the lower-left corner of the menu window to display the Play Movie button, and select it. Open the Button Inspector (⌘-⌥-I), and click the Color Settings tab. Choose Advanced, Grayscale, and Selected. Set each key color to red, and set the opacities to 12, 8, 4, and 0.

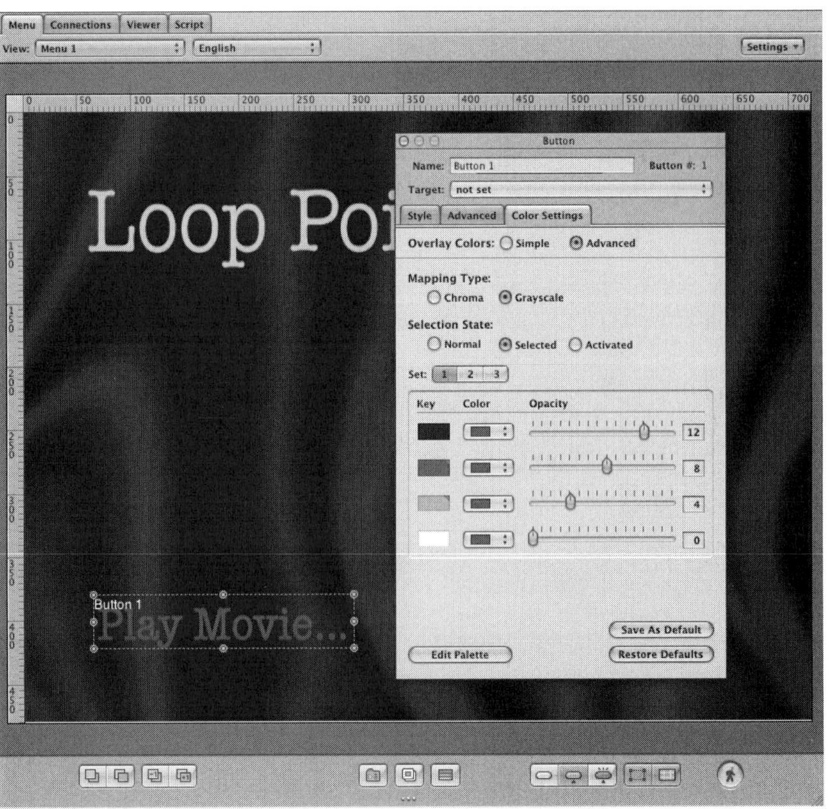

4. **Set the loop point.** Click the menu background to select the menu. Open the Menu Inspector's General tab, locate the Loop Point slider and text box, and set the Loop Point time to 00:00:03:00.

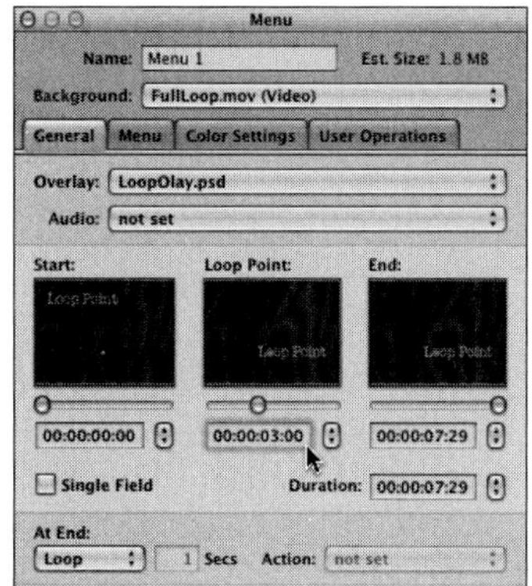

5. **Simulate.** Ctrl-click(right-click) the menu background, and choose Simulate from the pop-up. The Simulator opens, and the menu begins to play. The button does not appear until the loop point is reached. Once reached, the loop repeats. You will not see the introductory video material again until you reload the menu. To do so, click the Stop button on the virtual remote, and then click Title.

Solution: Add a Copyright Notice Screen to Your Movies

Locking viewers out of their remote controls for a short time prevents your audience from skipping important parts of your video, such as an FBI Warning screen and crucial training segments, and lets you keep the viewer from leaving the track by a remote control action any time you have reason.

FBI warnings are not required by law, even for professional DVDs. They are entirely an invention of the Hollywood video industry. They have little or no practical value in protecting the author's copyright. Those rights are guaranteed by national and international convention, whether a notice appears or not.

To add a copyright notice, follow these steps. You'll find the files on the companion DVD.

1. **Create a new DVD Studio Pro 2 project.** Each new project automatically contains a track, Track 1. Click Add Track to add a second track, Track 2, to your project.

2. **Populate your tracks.** Locate Warning.psd and Fruits.m2v on the DVD. Drag Warning.psd onto Track 1, and drag Fruits.m2v onto Track 2. DVD Studio Pro 2 adds the materials to each track and automatically renames the two tracks to Warning and Fruits.

3.   **Lengthen the warning clip.** Double-click the warning track to open the Track Editor. Select the Warning.psd clip and open the Inspector. Set the duration to 10 seconds (00:00:10:00).

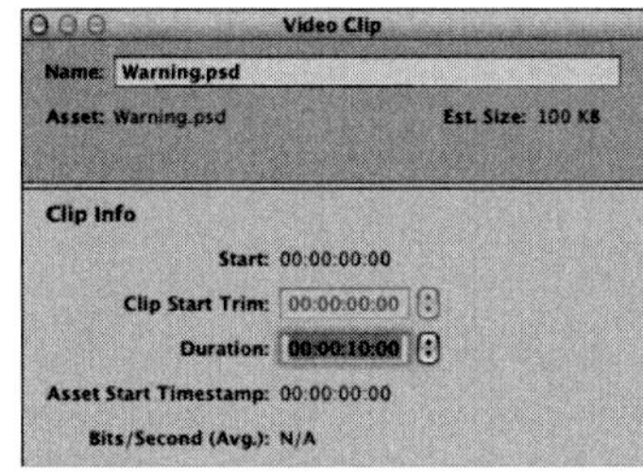

4.   **Customize the user operations.** In the Outline tab, select the warning track. Open the Inspector, and click the User Operations tab. Click Disable All to disable all operations associated with the track.

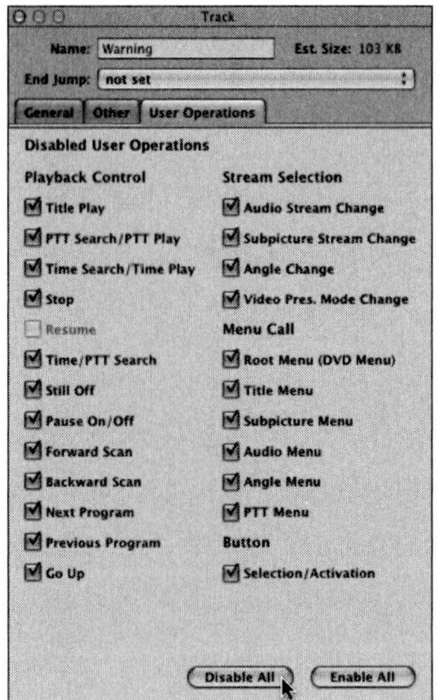

5.   **Set First Play.** In the Outline tab, Ctrl-click(right-click) the disc, and then choose First Play > Tracks And Stories > Warning > [Track].

6.   **Set Warning's end jump.** Select Warning in the Outline tab. Open the Inspector, and click the General tab. Set the End Jump to Tracks and Stories > Fruits > [Track]. This does nothing more than provide a movie to play at the end of your FBI warning.

7. **Simulate.** Click the Simulator icon in the toolbar, and open the Simulator window. The Warning track begins to play. The remote control buttons are grayed out, indicating that the DVD will not respond to those controls. (A bug in DVD Studio Pro 2 may allow the Track Skip buttons to play in the Simulator.) Once the FBI warning finishes playing, controls return to their normal state.

Toast Titanium
roxio
Data
Audio
Video
Copy
DVD-ROM (UDF)
Drag files and folders
into this area
New Disc
Add
Remove
Pioneer CD-RW/DVD-RW 103

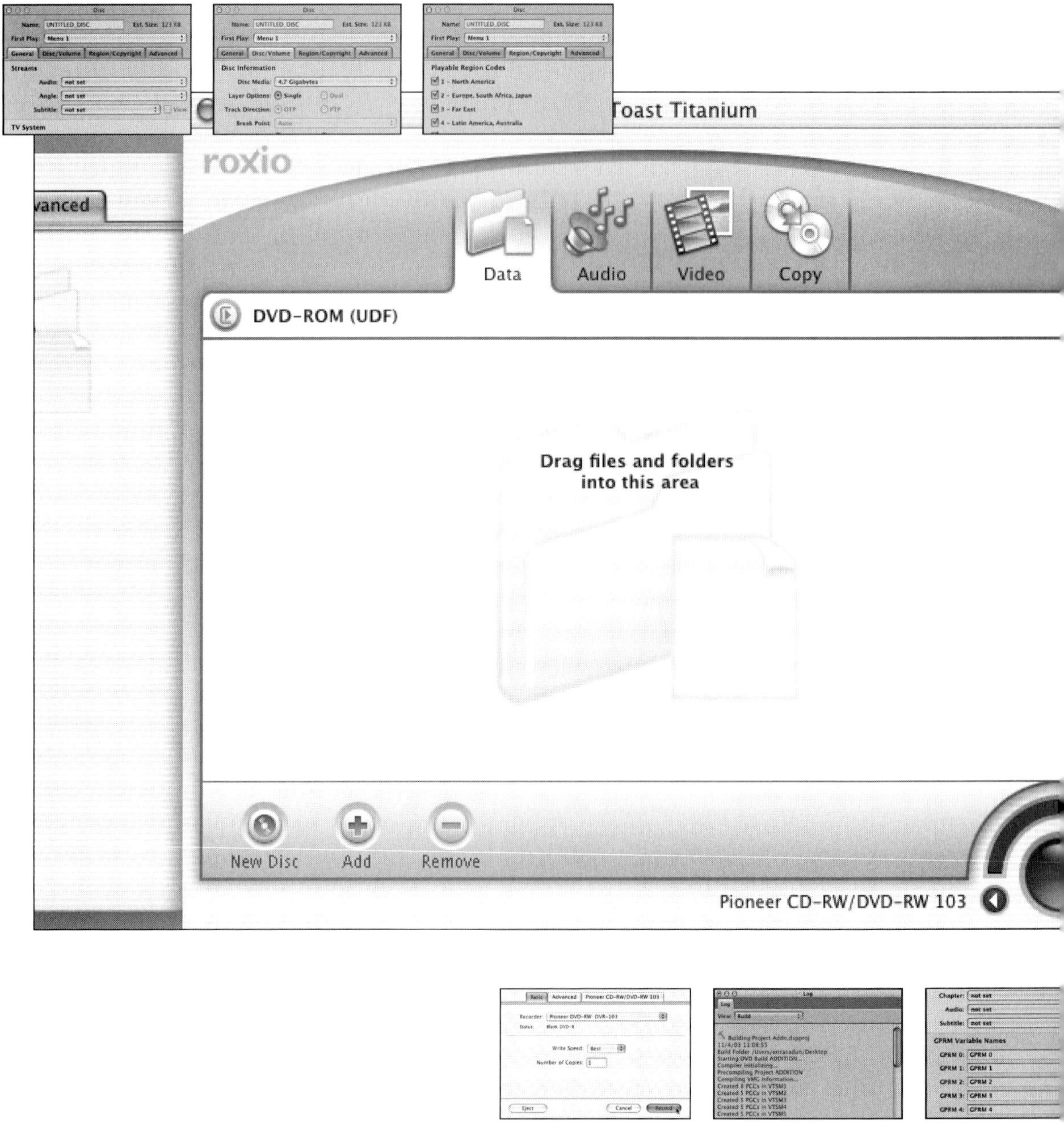

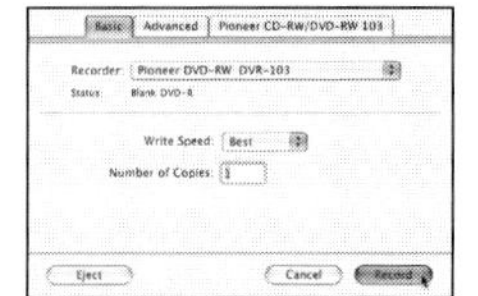

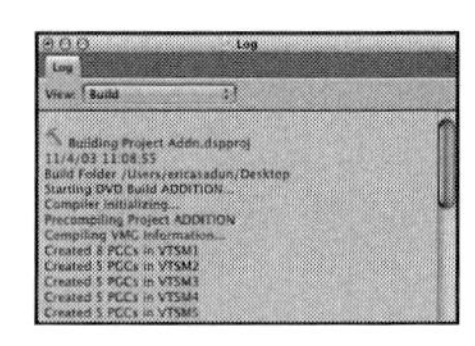

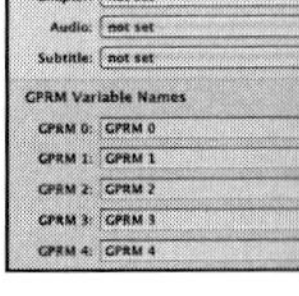

Building and Burning

The difference between a properly built DVD and one with playback errors lies in the attention to detail. It takes lots of careful effort to ensure that the DVDs you produce work exactly as intended. DVD authoring involves linking, naming, navigation layout, remote button assignment, scripting, and other detail-heavy preparation. (Of course, it all starts with proper asset preparation, as discussed in Chapter 4.) Errors in any of these areas affect final DVD playback. In this chapter, you'll learn about the final stages of DVD production: building and burning. You'll find out what it takes to transform your DVD Studio Pro 2 project into a properly working DVD.

Chapter Contents

Building DVDs That Work

Throughout this book, you've learned how to author and build DVDs. As you've discovered, when creating DVDs, designing and authoring occupies the majority of the creative effort. Building and burning your work uses a different set of skills—diligence and proofing. Here's a summary of the advice you've found in the chapters leading up to this one. Use the following tips to keep on top of your DVD Studio Pro 2 projects.

Plan carefully. Plan before you author. A well-designed project will come together more smoothly and more reliably than one authored in a slapdash manner. Plan your menus, work through the navigation, and think about the ways your viewer will interact with your DVD. Work these decisions out on paper or in a diagramming program such as OmniGraffle Professional, and use your design document as a basis for your DVD Studio Pro 2 work.

Think inclusively. Know your audience. Make sure your planning accommodates their age-appropriate and linguistic needs as well as any physical limitations they might have.

Build incrementally. Don't feel that you must build your entire project at once. As with programming, incremental design proves valuable to the DVD author. Build, test, and debug one element at a time before moving on to the next track, menu, script, or so forth.

Check every detail. Verify every element in your project. Open the Inspector, and look through each available Inspector tab. Scan the Connections tab. Make sure that every menu button, every remote control button, every prescript, and so forth has been properly assigned. Dot every *i*. Cross every *t*.

Test each project component. Use the Viewer, the Simulator, and DVD players (stand-alone or the Apple DVD Player) to test your components. DVD Studio Pro 2 allows you to simulate each component independently for a reason. Make sure your components both look right and play right.

Reviewing Disc Properties

The settings in the Disc Inspector (see Figure 12.1) allow you to customize overall properties associated with your DVD project. Always review these settings as you start to wrap up your project and prepare to output your work. Table 12.1 provides an overview of the settings that apply to authors who intend to burn 4.7GB discs with the Apple SuperDrive (or equivalent).

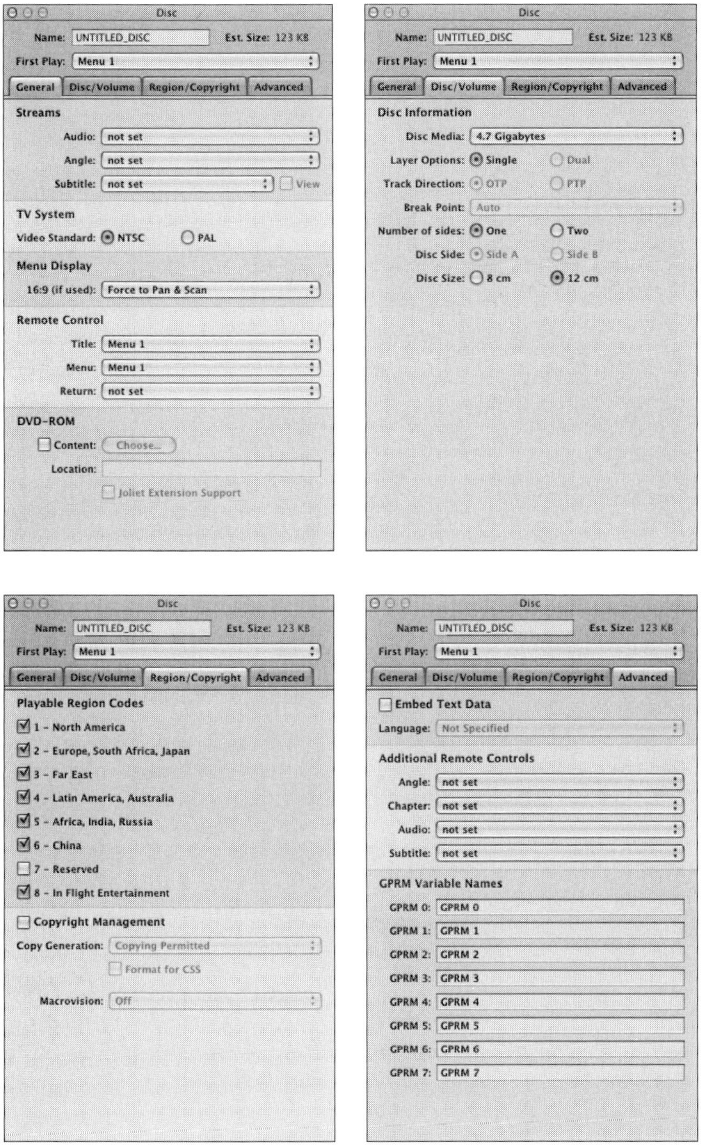

Figure 12.1 The Disc Inspector offers four tabs of property settings.

► **Table 12.1** he Disc Inspector Properties for 4.7GB Projects.

Property	Description
Name (all tabs)	Legal names contain a maximum of 32 characters, including uppercase letters (A–Z), the numerals 0–9, and the underscore character (_). Enter the disc name in the Name field.
First Play (all tabs)	Specifies the project element that starts to play when your disc is inserted in a DVD player.
Streams (General tab)	Allows you to set the initial audio, video (angle), and subtitle streams. Check View to force the subtitle stream to display.
TV System (General tab)	Each project can use either NTSC or PAL assets, but not both. Always set your video system before you begin to build your projects.
Menu Display (General tab)	Specifies how 16:9 menus will display on a 4:3 screen. Choose between Force To Letterbox and Force To Pan & Scan.
Remote Control (General tab)	Sets how the Title, Menu, and Return remote control buttons behave in your project.
Additional Remote Controls (Advanced tab)	Sets how the Angle Menu, Chapter Menu, Audio Menu and Subtitle Menu remote control buttons behave in your project. Although part of the official DVD specification, these buttons actually appear on very few commercial DVD player remote controls.
DVD-ROM (General tab)	Check Content to add a DVD-ROM portion to your disc. Click Choose and select the folder you want to include. Each item in the folder appears at the top level of your DVD disc. Click Joliet Extension Support to allow Joliet filenaming. Joliet is a standard developed by Microsoft to support long filenames. Adding Joliet support allows your DVD-ROM filenames to use an extended character set, spaces, punctuation, and names longer than 26 characters. Using Joliet filenames may confuse certain older DVD players, so use this option only when necessary.
Embed Text Data, Language (Advanced tab)	Used to support DVD@ccess and DVD-Video Text Extensions. (The latter adds your track names to the disc.) Use the Language pop-up to specify the language for the text extensions. Choose Not Specified to allow the text to appear regardless of language.
GPRM Variable Names (Advanced tab)	Use these text fields to rename your GPRM registers for scripting.

For years, Digital Linear Tape (DLT) has been the standard way to submit DVD projects to replicators. Even now, with the wide availability of recordable DVDs, DLT is used for complex projects. Many of the advanced features in the Disc Inspector apply only to those projects created on DLT. These features set flags in the DLT data that replicators detect and use to manufacture your discs. For example, you cannot burn discs on your Apple SuperDrive that use Macrovision or CSS (Content Scrambling System) encoding. They have to be pressed at a replication facility with the proper Macrovision and/or CSS licenses. Table 12.2 details the disc settings for a DLT project. As a rule, you need not invest in DLT technology unless you have a pressing need to use these features.

▶ **Table 12.2** Disc Inspector Properties for DLT Projects

Property	Recommendation
Disc Media (Disc/Volume tab)	Choose the type of medium you intend to create. When working with Apple SuperDrives, always choose 4.7GB. For DLT output, choose from 1.46GB (single-layer 8cm discs), 2.66GB (dual-layer 8cm discs), 4.7GB (single-layer 12cm discs, DVD-5), and 8.54GB (dual-layer 12 cm discs, DVD-9). For 3.95GB discs, choose the 4.7Gb setting.
Layer Options, Track Direction, Break Point (Disc/Volume tab)	Use these settings to control whether the disc will use single or dual layers. For dual layer projects (DLT only), always choose OTP, the opposite track path for DVD-9. This allows the second layer to play from the break point back to the hub, making for a smoother layer break pause. Choose the marker for the dual-layer break point, being sure to set it as a layer break beforehand, in the Marker Inspector.
Number of sides, Disc Side (Disc/Volume tab)	Specify whether your project will use single-sided (choose One) or double-sided (choose Two, DLT only) disc sides. The Disc Side control lets you indicate to the replicator which side the DLT describes. Always choose the one side "Side A" settings for DVD-5 and DVD-9 projects.
Disc Size (Disc/Volume tab)	Select either 8cm or 12cm disc size.
Playable Region Codes (Region/Copyright tab)	Check the regions in which your disc is authorized to play back. This option does not affect discs burned in your SuperDrive. The replicator must detect this setting using a DLT.
Copyright Management, CSS, Macrovision (Region/Copyright tab)	Check Copyright Management to add CSS copy protection flags to DLT output for replication. Choose No Copy Permitted, and check the Format For CSS check box.

Building and Formatting Your Project

After you finish creating, testing, and inspecting your project, it's time to build and format. Building creates the files that will appear on your DVD. Formatting places those files onto storage media, including DVD-recordable discs, DLT, and disc images.

Make sure you've left enough disk space on your hard drive to accommodate your entire project—it can occupy 4.7GB (or more for DLT dual-layer projects).

To build your project, click the Build button in the toolbar to open the Choose Build Folder dialog. Navigate to a folder on your hard drive, select it, and click Choose. As DVD Studio Pro 2 builds your project, the progress appears in the Log window (see Figure 12.2). Wait for the build to finish ("Compile Completed Successfully"), and then click OK.

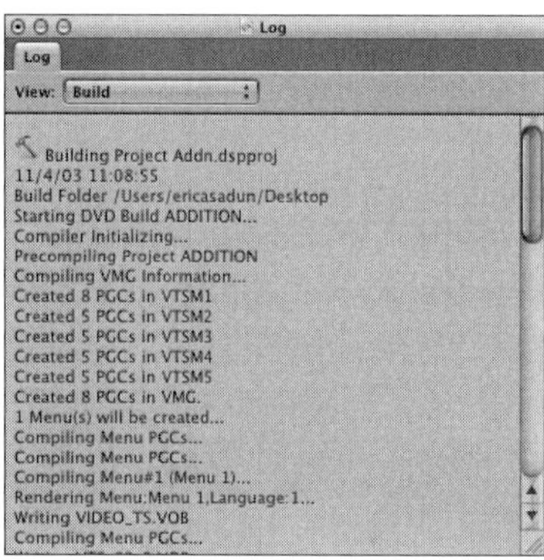

Figure 12.2 The Log Window (⌘-3) provides a blow-by-blow review of the build process. Follow the progress of your build by watching the text updates. Any project build errors will be reported here in detail.

Building your project creates both audio and video titleset folders (Audio_TS and Video_TS). Some DVD players will not play discs without Audio_TS folders. DVD Studio Pro 2 creates an empty Audio_TS folder for each project.

You can emulate your newly built project by opening it in Apple DVD Player. Launch the player, choose File > Open VIDEO_TS Folder (⌘-O), select the folder, and click Choose. When loaded, the project data does not automatically start playing. Click the Play button on the virtual remote control to start playback.

Formatting places your Video_TS and Audio_TS folders onto compliant data storage, which can either be played back directly or used to replicate discs. Follow these steps to output your project to disc, DLT, or disc image.

1. **Open the Format dialog**. Click Format to open the Format dialog, as shown in Figure 12.3. It contains three tabs: General, Disc/Volume, and Region Copyright. For the most part, these tabs reproduce the settings in the Disc Inspector, offering one last chance to update your disc settings. Only the Source and Destination settings are unique to this dialog. Review your disc settings, and make any necessary changes.

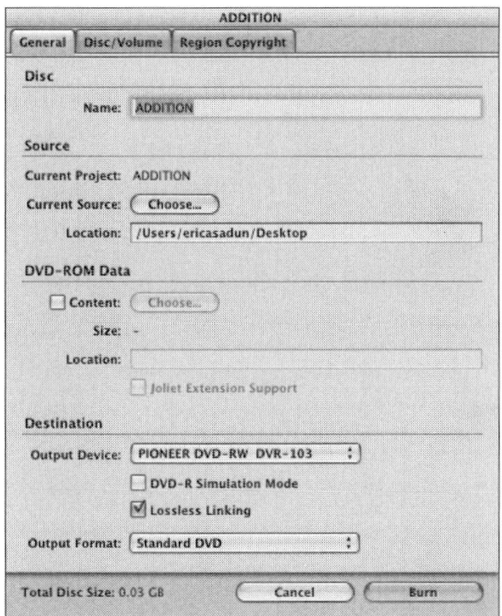

Figure 12.3 The Format dialog helps you copy your project data to disc, DLT, or a disc image. Use the destination settings to choose the output device and format. The title bar in this dialog reflects the disc name.

2. **Choose the source data.** Click the Source setting's Choose button to select the folder that contains the Video_TS and Audio_TS folders you want to use. These are set by default to the last location you used to build your project.

3. **Choose an output device.** Devices include recordable DVD drives, DLT drives, and hard drives. The Simulation check box allows you to test your recording DVD drive for buffer underruns without actually writing to disc. Leave this option unchecked to burn a disc. The Lossless Linking check box adds further underrun protection—albeit at a cost. This feature can produce discs that are incompatible with replication. Always uncheck Lossless Linking when you plan to replicate.

4. **Choose an output format.** The available formats depend on the selected output device. For SuperDrives (and near equivalents), choose Standard DVD. For DLT, choose Cutting Master Format (CMF version 1). (CMF has replaced the Data Description Protocol (DDP) as the DVD-video format of choice for replication.) Choose .img to create a DVD disc image on your hard drive.

5. **Click Burn (or Format).** The button label depends on whether you output to disc (Burn) or to DLT/disc image (Format). DVD Studio Pro 2 prompts you through the remainder of the burning or formatting process.

When burning to DVD-RW, always insert the disc before attempting to burn with DVD Studio Pro 2. Tell OS X to "ignore" it, and then proceed with your normal format. This bypasses the tendency of DVD Studio Pro 2 to balk when given a DVD-RW rather than a DVD-R disc.

Burning with Toast

Roxio Toast Titanium 6.0 (www.roxio.com) offers an excellent alternative to DVD Studio Pro 2 for basic burning needs. Unlike DVD Studio Pro 2, Toast has no issues with DVD-RW media—or CD media, for that matter. Toast is fast and reliable. Here are several approaches to creating your discs with Toast.

Building a UDF-Formatted Data Disc

Surprisingly, DVDs are little more than Video_TS and Audio_TS folders saved to a DVD blank using the Universal Disc Format (UDF). DVDs with ROM material simply add extra files and folders in addition to the two basic DVD folders. Toast lets you burn the Video_TS and Audio_TS folders to disc (as well as any extra material you care to add) to produce a compliant DVD that plays back in your computer and on set-top units.To build a UDF-formated data disc, follow these steps:

1. **Build your project to disk.** Use DVD Studio Pro 2 to build your Video_TS and Audio_TS folders todiskas described earlier in this chapter.

2. **Launch Toast Titanium.** Toast opens a main window that has four tabs. Click the Data Disc tab. If the Disc Settings Drawer is not open, click the button at the top left of the Toast window, just below the tabs. The button is labeled with an angle bracket and a triangle.

3. **Choose DVD-ROM (UDF).** Click the Advanced tab in the Disc Settings Drawer. Click DVD-ROM (UDF). Toast updates the Content area for a new DVD-ROM disc.

4. **Add the Video_TS and Audio_TS folders.** Drag them onto the Content area to add them to your disc, as shown in Figure 12.4. Optionally, add any other ROM files you want to include on the DVD. Be sure to add them directly to the disc and not to the Video_TS and Audio_TS folders.

5. **Remove extra files.** DVD Studio Pro 2 normally removes certain files from the build folders before burning. Open the Video_TS folder in the Content area. Locate the .layout (for example, myproject.layout) and the VOB_DATA.LAY files. Select each file and delete it from the disc contents. (This does not affect the folders on your hard drive.) Search through the listed content folders for any .DS.Store metafiles created by OS X, and remove those as well.

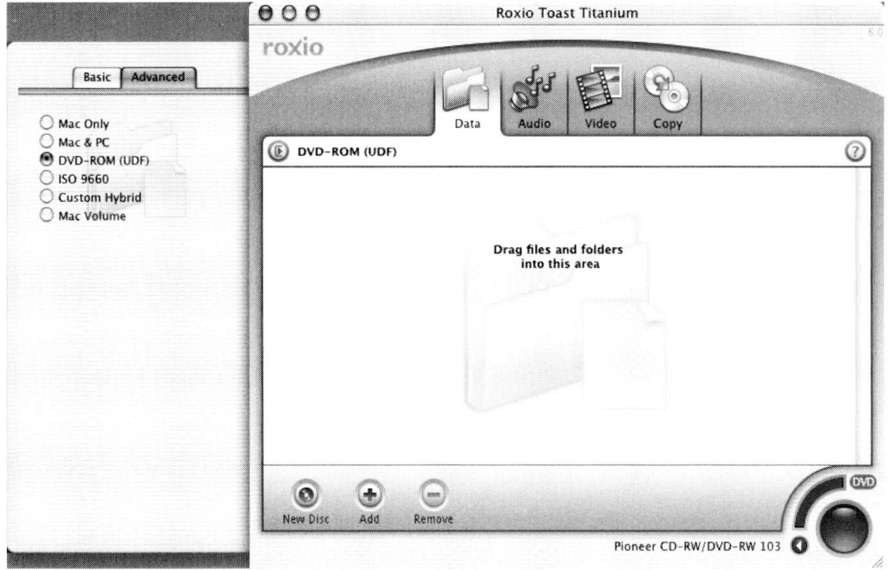

Figure 12.4 Toast Titanium's Content area, ready to receive Video_TS and Audio_TS folders

6. **Rename the disc.** New discs are named My Disc by default. To change the name, select My Disc to open a text edit box. Update the name as desired, using DVD-compliant naming (a maximum of 32 characters, uppercase letters, 0–9, and the underscore character). Match this name to any DVD @ccess "file:" URLs used in your project.

7. **Record.** Insert a blank DVD-R or DVD-RW disc. Locate the large red Burn button, which appears in the lower-right corner of the Toast window. Click it to open the Settings dialog. Verify that the settings are correct, and then click Record. Wait as Toast records your new DVD.

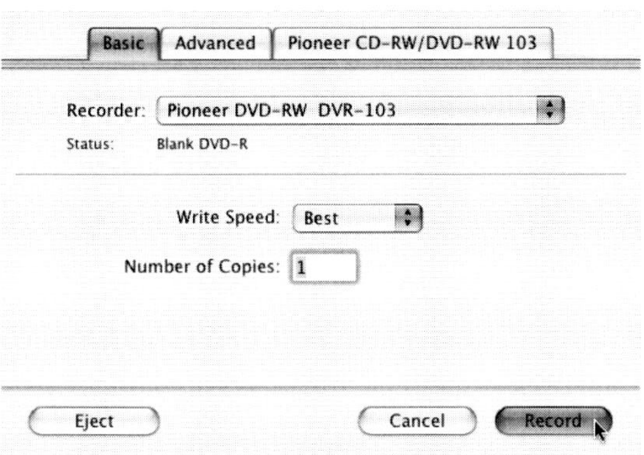

Copying a DVD from a Disc Image

In addition to building new UDF formatted data discs, you can also use Toast to transform a DVD image (.img) into an actual disc. Disc images allow you to build and format a DVD on one machine and burn it on another. The following steps describe how to use an image file created in DVD Studio Pro 2 to burn a DVD in Toast.

1. **Create an Image.** Use DVD Studio Pro 2 to create a DVD disc image file as described earlier in this chapter. Build your project and click Format. Set your output device to Hard Disk and your output format to .img.

2. **Set up Toast.** Launch Toast. Click the Copy Disc tab, open the Disc Settings Drawer, choose Advanced, and select Image File. You'll see the message "Drag a disc image into this area" in the Content area.

3. **Add the .img file.** Drag the image file onto the Content area.

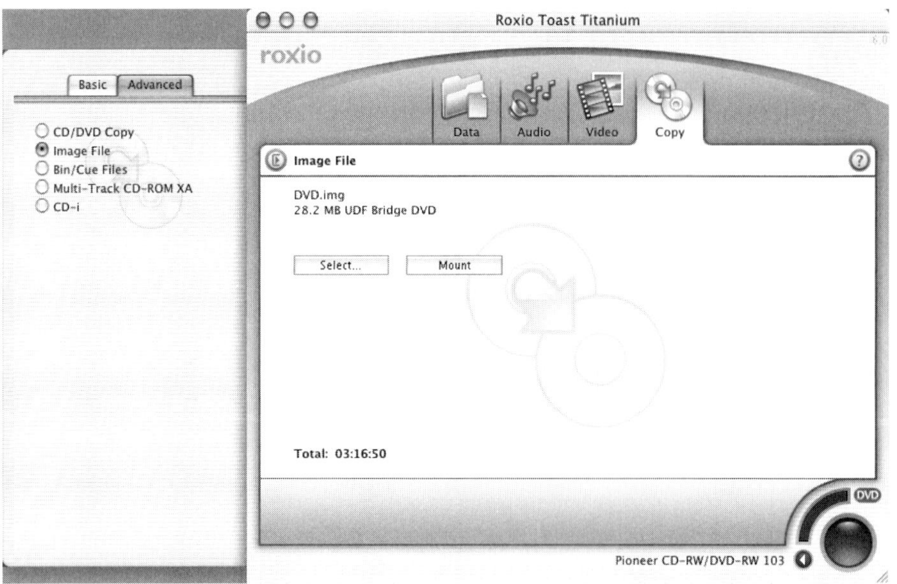

4. **Record.** Insert a blank DVD-R or DVD-RW disc. Locate the large red Burn button, which appears in the lower-right corner of the Toast window. Click it to open the Settings dialog. Verify that the settings are correct, and then click Record. Wait as Toast records your new DVD.

Writing DVD Data onto Compact Discs

By inserting a blank CD-R or CD-RW disc instead of a DVD-R or DVD-RW disc, you can create a format called DVD on CD, miniDVD, or cDVD. This format stores DVD data on CD-ROM, which is a quick and inexpensive way to produce short projects. The discs are compatible with most computer systems, although with only a minority of set-top DVD players. Less than one-third of available commercial players support DVD on CD. Consult the player compatibility list at www.dvdrhelp.com to see which players support the miniDVD format.

Purists may argue that miniDVD refers to the 8cm DVD-1 format. The consumer DVD player marketplace has ruled otherwise.

Copying Your DVDs

You can use Toast to quickly and easily duplicate your recordable DVDs. Click the Copy Disc tab, open the Disc Settings Drawer, and choose CD/DVD Copy. Insert a disc, click the Burn button, and follow the prompts. Toast reads your original disc, prompts you to insert a blank, and copies the disc contents to the new DVD.

Backing Up Your Work

Unfortunately, DVD Studio Pro 2 .dspproj project files are not ideal for backup. For example, when moved from the original save folder, they sometimes fail to load—potentially crashing the program and losing your work. Here are some tips for archiving your work safely.

Keep your project files in their original folder. When possible, do not move projects from one folder to another. For that matter, avoid moving assets. Although DVD Studio Pro 2 allows you to relink missing assets, doing so can be a pain.

Always copy your project files. Prevent catastrophic failure by duplicating your project files before opening them in DVD Studio Pro 2. If DVD Studio Pro 2 corrupts the file, you can return to the copy.

Use item descriptions as extra backups. Item descriptions provide a text-based representation of project elements. They provide another approach for archiving your work, allowing you to reconstruct your project from the description.

Creating Item Description Files

Item description files store all the properties associated with project elements in a proprietary text format that can be read by DVD Studio Pro 2. Item descriptions do more than just archive; they also let you copy elements from one project to another. DVD Studio Pro 2 can archive menus (.dspMenu), tracks (.dspTrack), slideshows (.dspSlideshow), scripts (.dspScript), and discs (.dspDisc).

To save, select the element you want to archive from the Outline tab. Choose File > Export > Item Description. Enter a filename, select the folder in which you want to save the file, and click Export. DVD Studio Pro 2 writes the item description file to disk. This file contains all the information needed to reconstruct that element. Choose File > Import > Item Description to load the saved element back into the project—or into a different project.

DVD Studio Pro 2 does not let you import .dspDisc files in the same manner as other item descriptions. As Figure 12.5 shows, the Import Item Description dialog does not recognize .dspDisc files. When you want to re-create an entire project, drag the .dspDisc file onto the DVD Studio Pro 2 application icon in the Applications folder or in the Dock. DVD Studio Pro 2 (if running) will prompt you to save any outstanding work before it loads the disc item description file.

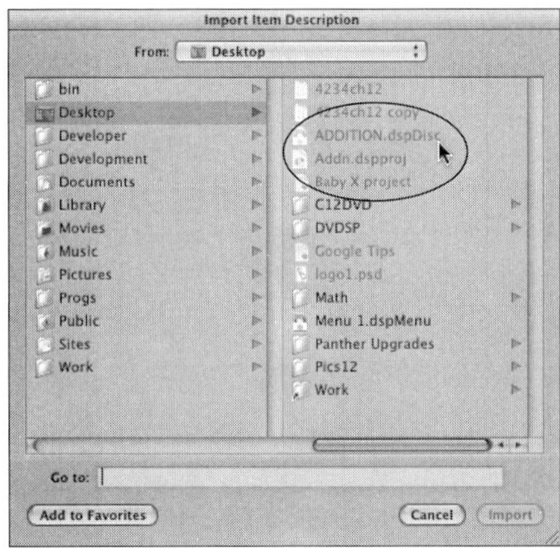

Figure 12.5 You cannot import disc item descriptions in the Import Item Description dialog. These files are grayed out. Use drag and drop instead. Drag the .dspDisc file onto the DVD Studio Pro 2 application icon to re-create the project.

Keep the following in mind when using item descriptions.

Item description files use plain text. Drag item descriptions onto the TextEdit application icon to view them. Descriptions consist of keywords and values structured as "dictionaries" enclosed by curly brackets. You can edit the description file by hand, but unless you know what you're doing, you'd be wise to edit copies of the file rather than the original.

Item description files use absolute paths. If you move your assets, the program will be unable to find and load them. DVD Studio Pro 2 opens the Missing Files dialog so that you can relink each missing item.

Missing elements create loose ends. Say, for example, you load a track whose end jump is set to a menu that does not exist in the new project. When you load an item description that references a missing element, the link reverts to not set.

Using Replicators

Most DVD service bureaus now accept submissions on recordable DVDs. These include the commercial ("General") DVD-R(/W) and DVD+R(/W) 4.7GB discs that you burn in your SuperDrive or other recording DVD drive. Replication facilities can transfer data from these to 4.7GB DVD-5 discs, which offer as much playback compatibility as the DVDs you'd find at Blockbusters. Replicators also accept DLT (needed for advanced features and dual-layer/dual-sided discs) and often accept disc images on portable hard drives.

Many service bureaus now offer in-house duplication, using special DVD burners to copy data to DVD-recordable blanks. Duplication is used if you only need a hundred or so discs and allow you to bypass the expense of creating (costly) "glass master" discs that are needed for high-end DVD manufacturing. Most replicators will need a minimum of a 1000-disc order to replicate. The in-house nature of duplication also lets you receive your discs more quickly (although project turnaround time is always a negotiable—and potentially expensive—commodity).

Replication is a cost-effective way to produce hundreds or thousands of discs. Expect to pay about a dollar per disc for a small run of about 1000 discs. Smaller runs, starting at 50 or 100 discs, may run $2 to $4 per disc. A thousand discs is generally the magic number for most replicators; at this point it becomes equally cost effective to replicate or manufacture discs.

Finding a Replicator

You can usually find a local facility by searching the Internet. Here are some key points to keep in mind when checking out a new DVD service bureau.

Replicators must be licensed. DVDs are a copyrighted technology. Replicators and manufacturers must pay a small royalty on each and every disc produced. Make sure your service bureau offers a current license.

Ask for references. Replicators should be able to furnish you with several references of *recent* projects. Do the legwork and make the calls. You may have several thousand dollars at stake. The Better Business Bureau is an excellent resource for investigating whether a replication facility has a history of complaints.

Know what you want. Specify the way you want to package and deliver your discs. Unless you stipulate such details as Thin-pak or Amray cases with silk-screened discs and cigarette-stripped shrink-wrap, you may end up with DVDs shoved into CD jewel cases. Sit down with a service bureau representative and go through the packaging options.

Know when you want it. Turnaround time is negotiable. Although the standard turnaround for most replication runs is ten business days, most service bureaus offer rush jobs.

Ask for a check disc. This needs to be part of your contract. And, when you receive the disc, test it on as many players as you possibly can. The replicator is not responsible for proofing your disc to make sure it works in players.

Ask for bids. Treat service bureaus just like you would any other business. Ask for estimates and bids, and shop your order around to find the best match for your needs and budget.

Replicators may farm out work. Some facilities offer "direct partnering" with Sony or Philips. This allows them to pass on all manufacturing to the Sony or Philips factories. Find out in advance exactly who will be doing the work on your project.

You'll pay for what you get. Replicators typically create between a 10% overrun or underrun. Your contract will specify the amount you pay per disc. If you receive 1002 discs, you will pay for 1002 discs.

Submitting Your Work

Once you've settled on a facility and a price for your replication run, you'll need to put your materials together. Always submit two copies of your disc. This adds little to the cost of your project but can save a lot of headaches, particularly if one of the discs does not play back correctly.

Conform exactly to the artwork specifications. The replicator will provide precise specs for disc and package art. Most replicators accept artwork created in Adobe and Quark products. Art approval is usually part of your contract—expect a true color proof or PDF produced from your submitted material.

You'll be asked to sign a copyright waiver. This form assures the replication facility that you are the owner of licenses for the content on your disc.

Getting Help

As a DVD Studio Pro 2 user, many helpful resources are available to you. Here are just some of these resources.

Electronic Documentation Choose Help > DVD Studio Pro 2 Help (⌘-?) to open a PDF version of the DVD Studio Pro 2 documentation in Adobe Acrobat Reader. This file replicates all the information in the DVD Studio Pro 2 User's Manual and is fully searchable. Choose Help > Late Breaking News to view a list of last-minute hints shipped with the program. Choose Help > Keyboard Shortcuts to display a list of all program shortcuts for your reference.

Apple DVD Studio Pro Support Site Choose Help > DVD Studio Pro Support, or point your browser at http://info.apple.com/usen/dvdstudiopro. Apple offers a searchable knowledge base of DVD Studio Pro 2 questions and answers.

Discussion Resources Visit the Apple DVD Studio Pro boards (http://discussions.info .apple.com/), or sign up for the e-mail DVD-Video Authoring list at http://lists.apple .com/mailman/listinfo/dvdlist. The 2-pop site (www.uemedia.com/CPC/2-pop/) also offers an excellent DVD Studio Pro forum.

The FAQ Stop by Jim Taylor's excellent DVD Demystified FAQ (www.dvddemystified .com/dvdfaq.html) and learn more about all things DVD.

On the off chance that you find a new and exciting DVD Studio Pro 2 bug, point your browser to www.apple .com/feedback/dvdstudiopro.html and give some feedback to the development team. Your information may help improve future versions of the program.

Solution: Adding DVD-ROM Data

To add DVD-ROM data to your DVD Studio Pro 2 project, follow these steps:

1. **Create a project.** Use your own project, or take advantage of the Addition materials Is in the chapter folder on the companion DVD.

2. **Open the Disc Inspector.** In the Outline tab, select your disc, and then press ⌘-⌥-I to open the Inspector. Select the General tab.

3. **Enable DVD-ROM content.** Locate the DVD-ROM section of the General pane. Check Content. Click Choose, and navigate to the folder whose data you want to include on the disc. For this project, use the ROM_Content folder, found in the chapter folder on the companion DVD. Select it and click Choose. DVD

Studio Pro 2 adds the folder to the Location field. For simplicity's sake, the sample ROM_Content folder contains a single PSD image.

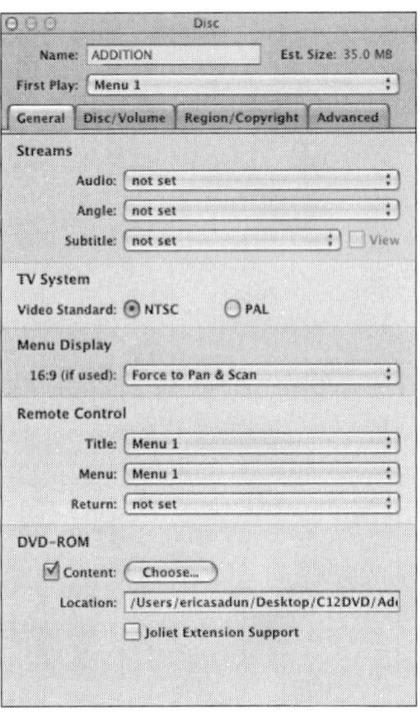

4. **Build your project.** Click the Build icon in the toolbar, navigate to the desktop, and build your Video_TS and Audio_TS files.

5. **Create a disc image.** Click Format, and choose Hard Drive as your destination output device and .img as your output format. Click Format again, enter a name, and choose where to save. DVD Studio Pro 2 creates a new disc image file on your hard drive. When the image is built, click OK.

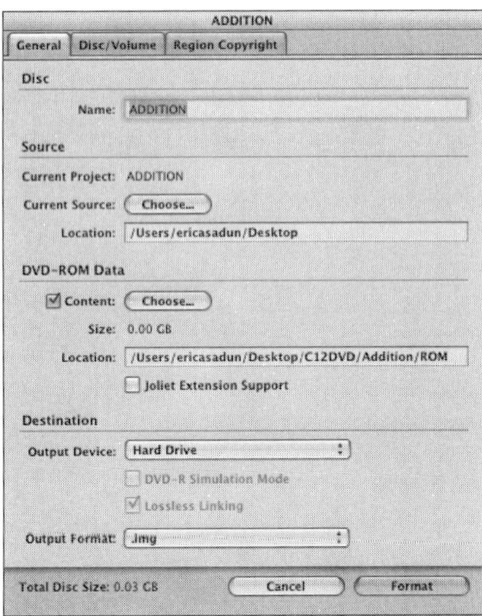

6. **Open the image.** Double-click the new .img file to open it on your desktop. A virtual drive appears. Open the drive and inspect the contents. In addition to the Video_TS and Audio_TS files, each file in the assigned ROM folder will appear. For this project, the PSD file from the ROM_Content folder shows up at the top level of your disc image.

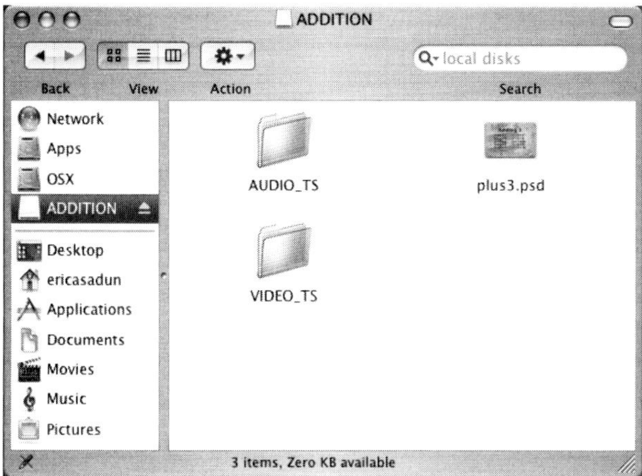

Index

T